Theater Enough

Theater Enough

American Culture

and the Metaphor of

the World Stage,

1607–1789

JEFFREY H. RICHARDS

DUKE UNIVERSITY PRESS
Durham and London, 1991

© 1991 Duke University Press
All rights reserved
Printed in the United States of America
on acid-free paper ∞
Library of Congress Cataloging-in-Publication Data
appear on the last page of this book.

For Ann Dennis
and George Ariffe

CONTENTS

PREFACE
Toward a Theatrics of Culture   xi

ACKNOWLEDGMENTS   xix

ABBREVIATIONS   xxi

PROLOGUE
Democratic Spectacles: Medium, Message,
and Metaphor   1

I
A Theater of the World, to 1630

1. Politics, History, and Theatrum Mundi:
Some Early Formulations   15

2. American Origins I:
A Theater of Theaters   38

3. American Origins II:
A Theater against Theaters   61

4. Prospero in Virginia:
The Example of Captain John Smith   85

II
The Theater of Faith, 1630–1730

5. A Theater on a Hill:
Puritans and the Rhetoric of Performance   101

6. Playing the (Trans)Script: The Antinomian Crisis   127

7. *Theatrou Mestoi*: The Example of Cotton Mather   148

III
The Theater of Action, 1676–1776

8. The Field or the Stage: Democracy, Theater, and
Anglo-American Culture   177

9. Theater of Blood:
The Rituals of Republican Revolution   201

10. Providential Actor: The Example of John Adams   230

IV
The Theater of Glory, 1776–1789

11. A Theater Just Erected: America at War   247

12. Play and Earnest on the Postwar Stage   265

13. Stage Metaphor and the New Republic   280

EPILOGUE
Instant Theater   293

WORKS CITED   299

INDEX   325

An affectation of displaying ones gifts before Throngs, is too often
an abominably proud Fishing for popular Applause; but my work
in the Pulpitt, must bee, rather to acquit myself well, in the
Discharge of the Duties incumbent on mee there, before the *All-
Seeing Eye* of that Majestie, who to mee, shall be *Theatre* enough.
—COTTON MATHER, 1685

For lo! America has become the theatre, whereon the providence
of God is now manifested.
—JAMES MADISON, 1781

Toward a Theatrics of Culture

The colonization of America by the English includes both a physical settling of the land and a rhetorical shaping of the experience of settlement. The process by which experience is re-experienced through the creation, transmission, and reading of texts is obviously a complex one. Writers respond to a variety of factors: their sense of a national identity, membership in a family or other subnational group, gender, education, religious background, economic status, individual identity, and the dominant rhetorical patterns of their perceived culture *at that time*. Add to that selective list, then, an encounter with a new land, and one has the beginnings of a reoriented discourse where experience is changed to match the old rhetoric or the rhetoric begins to change to frame the new conditions.

Theater is one of the rhetorical figures imported from England and used by colonists, and later by American-born writers, to express their version of life in the New World. What is meant by theater, however, is not always consistent from writer to writer or group to group, nor is consciousness of theater necessarily (in America) something that is universally held; but whatever social, religious, political, or even cultural differences may distinguish one American writer from another, theater grows out of the religiously dominated rhetoric of the seventeenth century into the politically dominated rhetoric of the eighteenth century as a common figure that expresses aspects of both life in general and the peculiarities of experience in what is now the United States.

Why theater? What conditions in American colonial life might induce a writer to think in terms of theatrical metaphor? Again, the reasons are various, but for the moment I will focus on two: the rhetorical traditions to which Anglo-American writers are heir and the social conditions created by the formation of towns and cities in a wilderness during the period 1607–1789. In the chapters that follow, I will look at texts as products of a rhetorical development that includes the history of theater metaphor in Western literature—and specifically, *theatrum mundi*, the world stage—as both a religious and a political trope. At the same time, I will consider the choice to use theatrical figures of speech as one made because of—or in spite of— the sociohistorical conditions that arise out of the conflicts engendered by American colonial settlement. In other words, that British Americans draw upon a tradition of stage metaphors is not in itself exceptional; however, for those writers committed to a special American status, whether as a separate polity or as the home of a transplanted European culture, the ways in which the figure of theater is applied show the differences between British and American to be more than just a matter of rhetoric.

In *A Mirror for Americanists: Reflections on the Idea of American Literature* (1989), William Spengemann has rightly challenged the bases on which scholars declare that a literary artifact or an author is American or that American politics or culture has a peculiar history, unconnected to others. Too often, commentators on the American situation have imagined a culture springing sui generis from the land. Spengemann's criticism that scholars make too much of the difference between British and American authorship does not necessarily invalidate a doctrine of American exceptionalism; it does, however, force critics and historians to rethink the criteria by which they evaluate the claims for American specialness. With that caveat in mind, I suggest that the immigrant writers from England bring with them a rhetoric that allows "American" literature to mirror "British" but that over time, that rhetoric, measured by the gauge of theatrical metaphor, is transformed to meet the needs of a New World society whose crises mark out a corollary yet distinct history from that left behind in the Old World.

In fact, theater appears frequently in American writing as a metaphor for history itself, even while such usage reflects the rhetorical history of theater as a trope. As a result, I have structured this book with both histories in mind. In the Prologue, I offer a kind of narrative in reverse, a looking backward from recent history, as a way of showing that at least one set of issues faced by early American writers remains today—in particular, how a performance medium creates its own rhetoric, how that rhetoric can be adapted to new conditions, and how it guides people to think about their experience in new ways. In part 1, chapters 1–3, I take the opposite direction, tracing through example some of the rhetorical possibilities of theatrum mundi from Classical Greece to the European and English Renaissance. I include these excursions outside the title-page chronology in order to minimize the distortion of looking at American usage in a vacuum, especially when the argument supports an exceptionalist reading of American texts. After all, most literate European colonists to the New World would have been exposed in some fashion to the image of the globe as a stage, although not necessarily to the one most of us know—Shakespeare's in *As You Like It*. Beyond that, it is helpful to remind ourselves how pervasive and how complex stage metaphors are, how the American colonist who might chance to employ one draws on a many-threaded history of usage that reflects not only the writer's own age but also earlier attempts to render the world in theatrical terms. Since America does not, as it were, enter the stage of this history immediately, I take the liberty of asking readers to include in this American story even Plato, a writer who understands earlier than most the tension that sometimes exists among theater, politics, and human relations to the divine—and who, as a consequence, anticipates the collocation of theater, revolution, and Providence that engulfs the American colonies in 1776.

Chapter 4 marks a transition from European traditions to American ones. There, I look at Captain John Smith as a writer who, when he leaves Europe for America and later when he tries to explain America to Europe, not only renders his experience in the terms of an Elizabethan convention, the figural stage, but does so in the context of seeing the real stage as a rival to the global theater on which he acts. This rivalry then becomes a theme in the remaining parts, which focus on the American story. In chapters 5–7, I examine Puritan New

England, and especially Cotton Mather, its most prolific and stage-minded minister, in order to account for the persistence of theatrical metaphors in a culture that condemns the theater but is physically removed from one. Chapters 8–10 take up the eighteenth century and the pre-Revolutionary struggle, identifying, particularly in the writings of John Adams, what seems to be a growing self-consciousness about the application of theatrical tropes to the political struggles with England. The last chapters examine the war, its aftermath, and the growth of republican rhetoric as writers turn to the theater in both trope and play to celebrate the new political order. In the Epilogue, I recapitulate some of the argument and suggest possibilities for further connection between past and present usage.

Essentially, I wish to look at a historically limited, primarily literary issue—the appearance of theatrical figures of speech in early American writing—in the context not only of Western rhetoric but also of an ongoing process in American culture, namely, how a class of metaphors both shapes and reflects the development of what might be termed a national-self identity: the nation defined in a self, as Smith, Mather, and Adams all manifest. Though what I have to say is grounded specifically in the American example and what I propose has much to do with the peculiar circumstances of American cultural development, I hope that the terms of analysis will have some application outside the borders of American literature or any of the disciplines that define themselves as having an American emphasis. Therefore, I intend this preface to an American study to serve also as a prolegomenon to some future, more fully developed theoretical statement of how it is that cultures can be scrutinized through the figure of the stage—a theatrics of culture.

Literary critics and historians have traditionally examined theater metaphor as an essentially literary choice, made in the context of other (usually belletristic) writers who decide on tropes for philological reasons. In recent years, however, the cross-fertilization between anthropology and literary study has made it possible for us to see a writer's choices in terms other than simply "literary" ones. Thus, from the work of such people as literary theorist Kenneth Burke, sociologists Erving Goffman and Kai Erikson, philosopher Bruce Wilshire, social historian Richard Sennett, and anthropologists Clifford Geertz and Victor Turner, we can begin to look at texts as reflecting the dramatic and theatrical conditions of specifically (or generally) demarcated aspects of cultural life. To some extent, then, figural theater does not depend entirely on the presence of an active institution of theater for its usage—though ultimately, of course, the reading of a particular histrionic trope depends upon the reader's understanding of basic theatrical conventions.

Where that understanding comes from, of course, is an open question. Turner, in applying the term *social drama* to crises in both preindustrial and industrial societies, sees drama as an underlying form of human response; that is, the modern stage as we understand it is a reflection of a pretheatrical need to shape mundane life in extraordinary ways. Others, like Geertz, argue for a more limited but deeper symbolic reading of anthropological evidence, choosing to see theater in certain rituals or cultural activities (as in the political spectacles of nineteenth-century Bali or Balinese cockfights). In any event, there is an extraordinary divergence among social scientists about the nature of theater and society, from the broad notion that self is found by casting off masks (Goffman) to nearly the opposite idea, that self is expressed only through playing roles (Wilshire). Society, then, can be viewed as a constant performance, a kind of ever-present aestheticized metatheater, that forces all people as role-players into the roles, ironically, of perpetual spectators, evaluating the performances of themselves and others. At some point, however, this kind of analysis, if allowed to become all-inclusive, breaks down into absurdity. On the one hand, Richard Sennett shows that the conditions of eighteenth-century urban England inspire writers to remark self-consciously about role-playing and spectating, making theater a valuable tool of cultural analysis; on the other hand, as Bruce Wilshire demonstrates in his criticism of Erving Goffman's work, theater has limits as a metaphor if it is to have any meaning at all.

Jean-Christophe Agnew, in examining the relationship of theater to changing concepts of the marketplace in Renaissance England (and later, in America), strikes, I think, the right note and one that I have followed here: "The meaning of the theatrical perspective is neither as timeless as its principal metaphor nor as timely as its current sociological embodiment in role theory" (16). That is, theater as a figure has greater relevance in certain historical periods than in others in the same way that—again, if it is to have any meaning—it accurately describes social phenomena only under certain specialized conditions; or else it may be, as Yi-Fu Tuan suggests, that theater and society change their metaphorical relationship constantly over time. By analyzing texts, one can observe when the writers themselves show cognizance of the theaterlike aspects of life—and therefore postulate how the rhetorical use of theater functions as a way of making sense in a discordant world.

To avoid the dangers of seeing theater in all things, I have for the most part restricted the perspective here to applications of theatrical language to the world at large or to America in particular. I am less concerned with the theater itself (after all, there is not much to speak of in America until the mid-eighteenth century) than with its figures of speech; even so, some plays will be looked at later. Further, I have chosen to examine theater largely as an expression of group needs (or the needs of a self who stands for a group) rather than individual or private identity, though the two often overlap; in other words, theater emerges in American usage as a metaphor largely for conveying covenantal goals (in the case of the Puritans) or political ends (in the case of the Revolutionists) rather than the boundaries of private selfhood. The sorts of endless self-mirroring or intricate relationships of self and theater that one finds in a play like *Hamlet* or in the writings of a protean Renaissance Englishman like Thomas More (as analyzed, for example, in Stephen Greenblatt's *Renaissance Self-Fashioning*) do not, as a rule, show up in early American writing.[1] This is not to say there are not subtleties and shades of meaning to be considered; but in American public language, even the private language of public persons (one inscribed by people who are more aware of themselves as

1. One possible exception might be Benjamin Franklin. As Mitchell Breitwieser points out in *Cotton Mather and Benjamin Franklin: The Price of Representative Personality* (1984), Franklin is a subtle fry when it comes to the question of selfhood. But as a writer of prose, the printer-inventor-politician-author does not use theatrical tropes very often; and while one might say, as David Leverenz and Mark Patterson do, that Franklin is a theatrical personality, self-consciously adopting roles, he does not refer to himself, in the *Autobiography* at least, in the specific language of the stage.

ministers or housewives or lawyers than as writers), theatrical figures most often appear to serve the purpose of defining life, the world, the country, or institutions.

There is a basic difference, too, between *theatricality* as a generalized critical term for modern commentators and *theater* incorporated as an explicit figure of speech. The two cannot be entirely separated; as one can observe from reading Kenneth Silverman's and Peter Shaw's studies of Revolutionary culture, the increased frequency of the use of theatrical tropes during the Revolution has something to do with the crises and theatricalized events taking place in the streets and courts and meetinghouses and even fields of eighteenth-century America.[2] Indeed, as Rhys Isaac has essentially shown in his study of colonial Virginia, the analogies to theater presented by the rituals of planter, yeoman, and slave life cannot be ignored just because the surviving texts do not always express things in ways an ethnographer two centuries later may find to be significant. Isaac admits that the particular "episodes" he examines are portrayed as if "displayed in a theater." But like Agnew he makes this qualification: "Yet it is not to be supposed that the writer mistakes the world for a stage. Limited aspects of life may be illuminated, but the whole . . . can never be summed up in any interpretative scheme" (*Transformation*, 326). The world

2. Two works that have helped me see more clearly the pervasiveness of theater during the Revolution and to which I will refer more frequently later are Silverman's *A Cultural History of the American Revolution* (1976) and Shaw's *American Patriots and the Rituals of Revolution* (1981). Silverman discusses theater as one of the arts whose importance grew during the Revolutionary period, and in that context, he sees the Stamp Act protests, for example, as opportunities for "testing out new possibilities of conduct"—in other words, for trying out new roles at a time when an "air of theatricalism" prevailed (82). For his part, Shaw sees the antimonarchical demonstrations that lead to the Revolution as forms of folk theater, enactments of mock parricide rituals designed to kill off the old father-king and allow the American son to achieve independence. I see my discussion as embracing both perspectives but putting things in a different context. Theater during the Revolution cannot be entirely divorced from plays or folk acts, but it also has a life outside both art and ritual. What I wish to assert is a more inclusive notion that sees theater as a historically derived rhetoric—one that sometimes expresses itself in written drama, at other times in popular street protests, but that *figurally taken* needs neither play nor demonstration in order to sway thought and action.

can still be called a stage, but it makes more sense to speak of it that way when conditions bring participants in a literate culture to see it as such. Thus, theater as an institution, as a literary figure, or as a tool for social or anthropological analysis has its separate spheres, but at times they must necessarily conflate.

For the point is, finally, that many early Americans use theater not simply as a rhetorical nicety but often as a trope deeply reflective of America's *place*—and the spatial meaning is intended—in history. Americans share with British writers a common language of stage, actor, play, and mask; but by the late eighteenth century, that language often separates British and American interests. For the British, as well as for their Anglicized sympathizers in the colonies, *theater* serves as a metaphor that illuminates the play sphere of life; the figure highlights a performative rhetoric that befits an urbanized, leisured class, aware of themselves and each other as sharing in a play of society—and aware of outsiders, including Yankee bumpkins, as acting in a different, lesser performance, gathered largely, like the mechanicals at court in A *Midsummer Night's Dream*, for the amusement of the British aristocracy and the bourgeoisie.

The Americans, I will argue, develop in the spaces left by a largely, though not entirely, stageless culture an ideology of theater that carries with it the weight of history and cosmology. In essence, this figural theater amounts to the continuation of conventional classical and Renaissance theatrum mundi tropes but with the qualification that America is a special case, a special stage in the theater of the world; at the same time, this idea of theater becomes an ideology when it is expressed as a theater of Providence. This theater amounts to a tacit or overt rejection of the performative rhetoric, the aesthetically self-aware playing of social roles, that characterizes urban British society. The Revolution, then, is fought on two stages or two ideas of stage: one is play, one serious; one social, one historical-political; one reductive, one amplifying. The Revolution may well have been caused as much by rhetoric as anything else; but that rhetoric, whether it uses Calvinist echoes or Whiggish buzzwords, reflects some theatrical urge that has been present in American literature since its origins. What follows is a way of accounting for those times when theater appears, or erupts, as a trope in early American writing—and why it is that victory in a revolution has been encoded in the American rhetoric of theater from the start.

ACKNOWLEDGMENTS

*M*any people have offered me encouragement and assistance. My wife, Stephanie Sugioka, and my children, Aaron and Sarah, have not only endured my retreats to the study with patience, but they have also, through their good humor and endless support, inspired me to get the job done. To them I owe a special thanks.

I am grateful to Keith Striggow for granting me a leave of absence from Lakeland College that I might begin serious research. At the same time, I wish to thank Joseph Flora for hiring me in a visiting position at the University of North Carolina at Chapel Hill and giving me a running start on the book, and John Bassett at North Carolina State University both for finding me a position and for supporting this project in many ways. To those colleagues at Lakeland, UNC-CH, and NCSU whose kind words have kept me pointed toward completion, I am pleasurably indebted.

Classes long ago with Richard Atnally and Laurence Avery have influenced my thinking on theater metaphor and American drama. Meredith Strange, Robert Bain, Richard Edens, and Harry West have mentioned sources or given me ideas that appear here. Ritchie Kendall kindly lent me galleys of his book and shared thoughts on the English dissenters. Charlene Turner at NCSU typed the manuscript with an accuracy that defies belief. Reynolds Smith at Duke University Press lent a knowledgeable and sympathetic ear to my proposal and enlisted two readers, Claudia Johnson and Daniel Shea, whose wise counsel has made this a better book. Paula Wald edited the copy text with rigor and tact. And Michael Skube, who has watched my prose with his Pulitzer Prize eye, has given the encouragement of a friend. Thank you all.

At Lakeland College, head librarians Linda Bendix and Charlotte

Wells squeezed budgets to secure materials for me. My thanks to them and to the library staffs at the University of Wisconsin-Madison, UNC-CH, and NCSU for guidance. In those libraries, I found works by some scholars to be of uncommon value; those texts are cited frequently in the notes.

Throughout this project, a few people have had special impor-tance. My longtime friend Lawrence Earley gave me both the benefit of his knowledge of colonial literature and his skill as an editor and professional writer. Robert Brinkmeyer, a classmate of yore, never let me forget that I could finish. But without two gentlemen-scholars, I might never have gotten started. For longer than he had reason to, John Seelye steadfastly put my feet to the fire at those times when they got coldest. For his part, Everett Emerson graciously took my first scratchings and found there ideas worth nurturing. Both read the manuscript in its entirety and provided insightful comments. Would that I could repay these four with a faultless text.

ABBREVIATIONS

Frequently cited works have been designated throughout by the following abbreviations (full citations can be found in Works Cited):

AC   David D. Hall, ed. *The Antinomian Controversy.*
AFC   John Adams et al. *Adams Family Correspondence.*
DA   John Adams. *Diary and Autobiography.*
MCA   Cotton Mather. *Magnalia Christi Americana.*
SL   Cotton Mather. *Selected Letters.*

Democratic Spectacles: Medium, Message, and Metaphor

*W*hen Americans watched television on July 4, 1976, they saw a spectacle: the images of tall ships and Ms. Liberty in New York harbor, local parades, perhaps, or grand fireworks displays, compressed within the space of a 26-inch—or 20- or 13-inch—glass screen. They celebrated themselves and the national polity with which they defined themselves on that Bicentennial Day; and what they assumed, in the televised pictures of self-congratulation, was that everyone else assumed that any spectacle that proclaimed the nation's greatness must be large and grand and visible for all the plugged-in world to see.

Not only was television the most compelling medium for transmitting the minor festivals and major spectacles of the nation's two hundredth birthday, but it still remains a peculiar mirror of the conception that many Americans have of themselves. Television is, at one level at least, a figure, a form of discourse that serves to describe by analogy the way in which the (Americanized) world works. Most Americans assume the importance of their country in world affairs; they measure themselves not only by the real economic or military power that the United States has compared to other countries but also by the images and the media in which largeness, greatness, and power are expressed. In 1976 the world's tall ships came calling, but they were absorbed into an image that could be appropriated for American use. It was right and proper, in American eyes, that the world's

1

stateliest vessels should gather in our harbors to recognize, as America's first true poet, Anne Bradstreet, would say somewhat ironically of men in her day, our "preheminence in each, and all" (7).

More important than the actual appearance of the ships in New York was the broadcast version and all that television as a vehicle of significance conveyed. Television is a mode of perception, a code that says without saying how people think or what they believe or how nations relate to the world at large. As Marshall McLuhan identifies in *Understanding Media* (1964), it is a medium whose "content" is determined by the rhetoric of the form: the medium is the message (8). To have watched the bicentennial celebrations was to have seen several subjects simultaneously: the spectacle, the spectacle as instant history, and the figurative view of that history, one whose method of presentation—tall ships on a small screen—was as much the point as the actual event portrayed.

Neil Postman, in his study of television discourse, *Amusing Ourselves to Death* (1985), carries McLuhan one step further. Not only is medium message, it is also metaphor; and because "metaphors create the content of our culture," he argues, television is further an epistemology, one that determines by its form what and how Americans think (15, 16). Postman laments what he sees as a decline in the ability of modern media to carry the burden of serious ideas. By contrast, he holds up to view the "typographic" culture of eighteenth- and nineteenth-century America as one where lofty, reasoned discourse held sway, where ordinary people could listen to analytical arguments in politics or religion for hours (44–63). In Postman's terms, the Age of Exposition was replaced by the Age of Show Business (63); and since "entertainment is the supra-ideology of all discourse on television," any event of importance, once televised, becomes reduced to just one more situation comedy or drama, an entertaining performance and nothing more (87).

While I would agree that television creates special problems for sustaining sophisticated analytical discourse, Postman's reading of history does not fully reflect the fusion of medium, message, and metaphor that earlier Americans encountered. Political decisions have for years been made in the context of entertainments, whether as ritual or for delight, and the discourse about political and social issues has been shaped by analogies to the performance media. Television is only the most pervasive such medium for modern political discourse. In a "dramatised" society, as Raymond Williams explains, one in which the television exposes viewers to more "drama" in a week "than most human beings would previously have seen in a lifetime," the medium that carries that drama carries the politics too (5). For pre-cinematic America, the medium that people recognized as a metaphor, that served as both a vehicle for entertainment and a metaphor for the presentation of political discourse, was the stage.

Though modern Americans recognize that one's appearance on television, for any reason, confers a kind of instant fame, their nineteenth-century counterparts found that stardom by means of a stage had its own distinctive American allure. As in our own time, actors, with the stage as a platform and print as a supporting medium, could seize the public attention and convert it to idolatry. More importantly, however, stage acting served as a rhetoric through which the desire of individuals for fame and that of the masses to confer greatness could be jointly expressed. Even literary figures could be swept up by starlike acclaim; the tours of Charles Dickens (taking into consideration his account, *American Notes*, 1842) showed that no amount of dislike for his audience could keep a British writer from traveling through America as a Great Author. Certainly, as P. T. Barnum demonstrated with his Jenny Lind tours (described self-admiringly in Barnum's *Struggles and Triumphs*, 1869), a foreign artist could be feted simply by being foreign; and the tour itself becomes the medium by which greatness is conferred by an adoring (usually) American public who appropriate the foreign as their own through popular spectacle. Though Americans have long been derided, and frequently by their own countrymen, for their boorish attitudes toward art, they nonetheless make the art and artists of the world their own by buying, exhibiting, repackaging, selling, and applauding them on their soil. P. T. Barnum may be the prototype of the ultimate lowbrow promoter, but he has a curious avatar in the film character Charles Foster Kane. Citizen Kane, in one scene, brings home "the loot of the world" from one of his European junkets; the employees of his newspaper stage a little show that appears, through the use of deep-focus cinematography, to be monumental; but at the end of the film, after his death and the conclusion-less investigation into his life by a reporter, we see that the loot stacked up like so much "junk," as one character calls it, is nothing more than an oversized monument to Kane's oversized sense of himself. He tells the public that he has always been one thing—"an American"—and his grandiosity mirrors the aspirations of the limitless American to subsume the world in his national-self identity.

If the huzzahs for candidates, actors, and literary lions all sound remarkably the same, they only demonstrate how in America the lion will lie down with the huckster and mass politics will take their shape as enlarged analogies to performing arts. In monarchies, coronations have their own theatrical splendor, but splendor is essentially a product of a rigid class structure, dependent on a wealthy elite who announce their unalterable difference from the exploited poor. In the democratic process of election—of presidents or, by acclamation, the giants of mass culture—one finds a distinct American expression in the festivals and spectacles of symbolic enlargement. Americans give to their essential rituals of nationhood a spectacular (but not splendorous) bigness because they know the form represents the propagandized inclusiveness to which politicians and others swear belief.

Of early or mid-nineteenth-century writers, Walt Whitman articulates most openly the complex relationships among Americans, severally considered, and their ideals of performative greatness. As Carroll Hollis has shown, Whitman's poetry grows out of a sense of language as speech—not talk, but speechifying, the oratory of the personality/persona who mounts the stage and delivers forth inspiring wisdom for *all* the people. Central to Hollis's thesis is a note he discovered in the Feinberg Collection of Whitmaniana detailing the poet's projected career as a public speaker. No doubt influenced by the literary figures who, in the local television talk shows of their day, toured the lyceum circuit (this is analogy, not equivalence), Whitman created on paper a scheme that far exceeded any ability he had to prosecute it.

While the project seems at odds with the retiring life of the "good gray poet" persona he adopted in his later years, the notion that Whitman would become a presence on the public stage is entirely consistent with an opera-loving poet of plenitude and raunchy excess. With some modifications to the form (I have omitted cancelled words), here is Hollis's transcribed version of Whitman's note:

Abrupt sentences—concise
Lectures (?Readings.)
Agonistic Arena

Short, Lapidary, and fit for an original and vital style of elocution

(not taking more than an hour to be delivered.)
    The whole presentation, from its directness to *you, audience—*
from *the amazing and splendid athletic magnetism of its vocalization*
—and from the charm
—of its *abandon* and *hauteur* and *imperative decision*
making merely as an entertainment—attraction, something far
beyond any of the
ordinary attractions of the theatres, the minstrels, concerts +c.   (12)

Out of Whitman's abortive experiment with public speaking—his
fantasy of peculiar stardom—came a poetry that has all the marks of
an extraordinary showmanship packaged in the rough gossamer of the
moral lecture. As Hollis remarks, "What Whitman did was to rewrite,
reshape, revamp his never-given speeches to gain and maintain the
immediacy, the urgency, the audience involvement, the excitement,
the emotional uplift of the public performance that might have been"
(18). We can infer from Hollis's observation that had Whitman been a
real performer, he would not have been a poet—or at least, not the
poet he would become. Yet even if we were to imagine a Whitman
with *"athletic magnetism"* and good poems, too, one phrase gives
away the futility of the enterprise: *"Agonistic Arena."*
    How does one reconcile the vital struggle for purity of soul—the
agon of Whitman's poetic self—with performance on the arena stage?
Will *"you, audience,"* witness the agon with the same stupefaction
reserved for a nimble hornpipe, a dog-and-pony show, an exhibition of
exotic and purposeless machines? No wonder Whitman demands of
the elocutionist *"magnetism,"* for it would take a hypnotic power to
wrench the audience from its propensity to cheer the spectacle and
miss the struggle. Nathaniel Hawthorne, another writer who once
fancied himself, or at least a persona, as an itinerant speaker, a teller of
tales, understood the near impossibility of turning literary performance into mass art. The theme appears in many stories but most
directly in "Main Street." There, a showbox operator presents the

history of Salem by relying on his narrative abilities more than the visuals provided by the wretched drawings on the showbox canvas. His performance depends on a delicate balance between his skill in creating romance and the audience's willingness to accept his language as the determinant of reality. Once denounced, as it is in "Main Street," by one unhappy patron who wants a better show for his money, the illusion is shattered and the high seriousness of the showman becomes tawdry entertainment, the stuff for gibes.

Hawthorne, of course, would never commit himself to an agon; he is too busy drawing veils over the "inmost Me," as he remarks in the "Custom-House" sketch, too keen on interposing wry or ironic narrators between himself and his audience to appeal to them in the same way as Whitman projects. By contrast, the poet's stage self is closer in conception to that dramatic, self-defeating life imagined by allegedly antitheatrical Puritans than it is to anything asserted by his theatrically self-conscious, anti-Puritanical (with qualifications), fiction-writing contemporary. For it is the Puritans and their proto-Protestant forebears who most directly conceive of life as a dynamic struggle for mastery of the soul, as something to be acted sincerely on the stage of a stageless world; but a life in which the ending must, to its worldly audience, always remain in doubt. By the nineteenth century, such fearful lack of definition can no longer be tolerated. Whitman proclaims that his agon will be concise, *"Short, Lapidary, and fit for an original and vital style of elocution* (not taking more than an hour to be delivered)."

The brevity of address conflicts with the ultimate expansiveness of "Song of Myself" and its announcement to the world that the pure American democratic self is "large" and contains "multitudes." To be American, one opens the harbors of the self to the heterogeneous many and becomes in that self an entire nation. In Whitman's poem, the more wretched and outcast people are, the more suitable they are for inclusion, though presidents and prostitutes finally occupy the same simultaneously leveled and exalted rank. The poet perfects his soul by a multivalent struggle to project the loafing, boasting barbarian belching welcome to all—and yet he remains "delicate around the bowels" and invisible, as in the parable of the lonely woman and twenty-eight male bathers, a tender, lovelorn Paul Pry.

In his poetry, Whitman proposes in essence to be an agent of a caste-shattering revolution far more comprehensive than the War of Independence ever proved to be. That in his note he hopes to frame the struggle as an agon of the arena—and not, say, as a faceless armed conflict or social upheaval—speaks deeply of American ideas about revolution in the first place. Revolution is *self*-centered, when self, both denied in its separateness and exalted for its inclusiveness, stands for all Americans; it is providentially guided, the speech act of an attentive God who has made America the arena of prophecy; and it is dramatic, even theatrical, but "beyond any of the ordinary attractions of the theatres" themselves.

From what does the notion that revolution is expressed through the medium of a histrionic national self arise? Let us back up a little further to an earlier celebration of the nation's founding, the Jubilee of July 4, 1826. As it has been since the early postwar years, the creation of the Republic is remembered in villages and cities with spectacles and speeches. As the speakers no doubt know, the sitting president, John Quincy Adams, faces the nation's fiftieth anniversary with four living former presidents—though by day's end, two of those, John Adams and Thomas Jefferson, will be dead. Those speakers will certainly address the Revolution, and their listeners will hear the word itself as a code for the ritual mastery of American history. As one speaker, Josiah Bent, Jr., of Braintree, Massachusetts, tells his patriotic audience, "Long ere our Revolution began, we trace [God's] hand in relation to our present glory. It was He that saved the New World, so long unknown to the overloaded Old world, to be the theatre of new scenery to our race" (*National Jubilee*, quoted in Bercovitch, *American Jeremiad*, 144n). And for those in the audience unoppressed or unaware of their oppression, the speaker's formulaic yoking of race, glory, New World, God's hand, Revolution, and theater will sound comforting and familiar. These words and phrases emerge out of and make up the popular discourse of the dominant culture, shaping a world view.

Of course, by 1826, there was a growing theater, no longer held in check by the laws or customs of the earlier century. Already, actors were competing with, even replacing, political figures as cultural icons. Thus any sort of metaphoric discourse in which theater dominates could draw its vitality from a lively institution. Yet in the context of Josiah Bent's remarks, among the cliché-ridden language of a Fourth of July address, the "new scenery" he evokes has only peripheral connection to the set of a real stage. More likely, Bent draws upon a preexisting stock of ready-made phrases, one of which is a variant on the theatrum mundi figure that Bent's predecessors in more contentious arenas used to great effect.

Even before the celebrants gathered in 1826, other events had been leading up to the final day of Jubilee. In 1824 and 1825, the Marquis de Lafayette had returned in triumph to the land where he first won fame. As Fred Somkin has documented in his book *Unquiet Eagle*, the ceremonies honoring Lafayette were themselves spectacles of self-congratulation, the taking in of a Frenchman and once again making him one of America's own. Only Washington could claim the more exalted attention of sacred civic memory, for Lafayette's presence in the United States, important in itself, also served to remind Americans of his commander-in-chief, their country's Father. Washington, Lafayette, Yorktown—"The play is over," Lafayette had said when Cornwallis surrendered. And though the old hero may have wondered, in all the festivities of *his* tour, whether a play were still going on, it was an appropriate remark to have made in 1781.

For if we back up even further to the era of the Revolution itself, we find a colonial culture with little actual theater but with a varied and frequently articulated theatrical discourse. Even then, of course, theatrum mundi tropes rolled trippingly off the tongues or flowed obligingly from the quills of speakers, men and women of letters, and political pamphleteers. The language of the world stage may only have been the catchwords of the day, but for a modern reader—and quite possibly for some eighteenth-century readers as well—the encounter with a slightly elaborated analogy or with an awkward or an unusually well-placed figure brings one in contact with cartloads of assumptions that illuminate the reiterated, though otherwise invisible, metaphoric clichés.

But the question then emerges whether or not a metaphor in itself constitutes a world view. How conscious are writers or cultures of their social theatricality? of theater as an epistemology? an ideology? a cosmology? The presence of a trope does not necessarily indicate full consciousness of either tenor or vehicle, but if developed at all, a figure of speech most certainly reflects a style of thinking that is derived from a literal reading of the originating metaphor. George Lakoff and Mark Johnson in *Metaphors We Live By* (1980) argue that almost all language is metaphor and that figurative expressions lead us to think of phenomena in ways peculiar to a given culture. In this scheme, even the cliché plays a significant part in shaping cultural assumptions. As their introductory example, Lakoff and Johnson cite argumentative language. English is replete with war metaphors (attack, defend, defeat) to describe argument; though we may not be conscious of the analogy, the metaphors, they assert, serve to lead us into an essentially combative form of discourse. Though the degree to which this extension of metaphor can be taken has been challenged by Samuel R. Levin in his book *Metaphoric Worlds* (1988), the central principle holds: metaphors have histories and those histories function as sub- or supratexts to the text being considered (S. R. Levin, 4–12). Because theater is such a rich and old metaphor, determining what of its history is relevant takes some sorting out.

Consider, for instance, a passage from an Election Day sermon preached by Izrahiah Wetmore in Hartford, 1773. As with many such sermons, Wetmore's subject turns to the relationship between secular and ecclesiastical authority and their mutual connection to the history of New England. Magistrates, says Wetmore, are apt to think of "civil Government" as "the grand Object of divine Providence in this lower World," in contrast to their view of Christianity as something "admitted, chiefly to enlarge, fill up, and diversify the great DRAMA." Though probably like his Congregational colleagues he has no wish to open the colonies to stage plays, Wetmore uses the dimensions of the dramatic figure to rebut the idea that the worthies of religion will, in T. S. Eliot's words, only "swell a progress, start a scene or two," then bow out for the providentially ordered show of politics. Not surprisingly, Wetmore counters that Christianity is "the special Design of Providence in all Ages; and will continue so to be, 'till the Consummation and final Close of all Things" (*A Sermon*, 11; see Heimert, 237). His use of "DRAMA" to describe secular attitudes conditions our reading of "Close" to signify last things; all is shaped anyway to providential ends, "under the Direction of a most wise and skilful

Manager—even our LORD JESUS CHRIST" (6). That is, in the spare style of the Congregationalist, Wetmore evokes the theatrical construction of history—imaged as competing dramas between rival though ultimately cooperative companies—with some of the same assumptions held by post-Revolutionary generations, who would speak of a providentially favored, theatrically conceived land turned nation.

During the Revolution, Americans exposed to the full variety of contemporary media—sermons, orations, pamphlets, poems, newspapers, cartoons, folk rituals, political demonstrations, and the stage—cannot avoid the sound or sight of theatrum mundi figures or histrionic representations of current political affairs. Whether they do so deliberately or not, many of those Americans frame their epoch-making actions (or those of people around them) as upon a world stage where individuals collectively act out roles in their rituals of independence. And everyone, it seems, is watching. A tea-dumping masque in Boston harbor plays through official communication before the London court. The mock parricide rituals of the Stamp Act crisis, crude though they be, are performed as for a larger audience than the street crowds who gather to join in or watch.

Thus, during the earliest days of the Revolution, spectacles played before the eyes of the world conjoin with statements of American distinctiveness to become the spectacles through which American eyes will look at their enterprise. The day after the signing of the Declaration of Independence on July 2, 1776, John Adams describes what should be the model for all future celebrations of "the great anniversary Festival": "It ought to be commemorated, as the Day of Deliverance by solemn Acts of Devotion to God Almighty. It ought to be solemnized with Pomp and Parade, with Shews, Games, Sports, Guns, Bells, Bonfires and Illuminations from one End of this Continent to the other from this Time forward forever more" (AFC, 2:30). For Adams, spectacle itself is a medium for expressing the message of American greatness; all Americans should have immediate contact with the unfiltered "Shews" to remind themselves of "the most memorable Epocha, in the History of America" (AFC, 2:30). At the same time, the spectacle is merely an acting out of the idealized metaphoric theater in which Whigs have expressed their politics. Where Americans in 1976 see their celebrations through the filtering rhetoric of television, those of 1776 imagine, and later create, celebrations in the shape of theatrical and amphitheatrical entertainments. For people of the television age, the sight of a spectacle on the small screen may only dimly reflect John Adams's prophetic vision of providential favoritism made manifest, but for celebrants of both eras, to recognize one's Americanness means to make a show before all the world.

Indeed, well before the Revolution or even its prefigurations in the 1760s and early 1770s, Americans aware of their peculiar status in the English-speaking world express the feeling of being curiously exposed to view. In sermons like John Winthrop's famous "A Model of Christian Charity" (1630), people are told they are like a city on a hill (Matt. 5.14) and in other religious writings reminded that they are a spectacle before angels and men (1 Cor. 4.9). At the moment of Revolution and back to the moment of founding, Americans style their discourse in terms of being observed by the eyes of the world, and the Eye above all, of having to perform in the great "DRAMA" whose "Close" is figured as both Apocalypse and climax of civilization.

And still further back: Poised in space on English soil, and in time on the cusp of the Renaissance, colonists check their baggage and their number to see what and who they will bring on their journeys. Some will hear sermons like that of William Crashaw to the Virginia Company, 1610: "This enterprize hath only three enemies, 1. The Divell, 2. The Papists, and 3. The Players" (A *Sermon*, 58, reprinted in Alexander Brown, 366). Whatever you do, keep out the players; for those who playact, who, because they only imitate, mock events of great moment, serve but to distract the world's viewers from more important sights: the metaphoric dramas enacted for the age on the theater of the world. One might keep the players out of Virginia or New England; but no one, not even the archest Puritan, can prevent a figural imagination from setting sail. In the small ships of English adventurers, the colonists bring their metaphors with them, entering unheralded—and by the Indians, unwanted—into the natural harbors of the New World. "*The worlds foure Quarters*," writes William Grent for his friend, the Virginia colonist Captain John Smith, are "*like four Theaters to set thee forth.*" What Englishman Grent says of world-actor Smith, English-speaking Americans will later say of themselves and the figural Theater-Quarter they occupy: "*The last whereof* (America) *best showes / Thy paines, and prayse*" (J. Smith, 2:52).

I

A Theater of

the World,

to 1630

Politics, History, and Theatrum Mundi: Some Early Formulations

*E*ven before the Virginia adventurers or the New England sojourners set sail, they are being shaped by another history than their exploits, a history that establishes the parameters of their soon-to-be transplanted figural imagination. The colonists create their new polities through contention and crisis and use a diction that often nurtures a personalized, dramatized view of political events. By the later eighteenth century, that language will resemble the characteristic turn of phrase that John Dickinson gives in an anti–Tea Act broadside (1773). The British East India Company, he remarks, having already ravaged Asia, "cast their Eyes on *America*, as a new Theatre, whereon to exercise their Talents of Rapine, Oppression and Cruelty" (A *Letter from the Country*; see P. Davidson, 15). Here, "Theatre" translates the whole affair into a performance; the British officials appear on stage as acting out nearly allegorical roles of villainy in a land converted for their pleasure into a playhouse. Dickinson's metaphor derives its power not only from contemporary Augustan rhetoric or even additionally from the tradition of theatrum mundi in America but also from further back, from deep sources of metaphorically theatrical thinking.

For as I have stated, the application of *theater* to political or historical issues has a long history itself; the trope of the world as a stage, theatrum mundi, is an old one, dating in the Western tradition from the ancient Greeks. Survey histories of the metaphor can be found in several sources (notably, Curtius, 134–44; Stroup, 4–11; Warnke, 68–89; and Burns, 8–21), and studies of theatrical figures of speech can be found for individual authors and periods, especially for Shakespeare and his contemporaries (for example, Anne Righter's *Shakespeare and the Idea of the Play*). For early American usage, the brief discussion by Babette Levy of theatrical metaphor in seventeenth-century preaching (127–30) and the longer analysis of Revolutionary theater and theatricality in Kenneth Silverman's *A Cultural History of the American Revolution* provide useful insights and references. However, there is neither any full-length work that looks exclusively at early American usage nor one that treats the whole Western tradition comprehensively. To understand American applications of theatrical figures, one must go beyond simply repeating the clichés of a given era; consequently, I have chosen to look at the metaphor historically, as it may have been received by English colonists heading for the New World. A writer like John Dickinson draws upon a figure that appears to have a life of its own, removed as it is in America from the institution of the theater itself.

For this chapter, I have selected authors who either represent particular cultural-historical periods or whose formulations may have been influential in the codifying of theater metaphor. Because the metaphor has political applications in American writing, I have tried especially to attend to usages which emphasize the complexion of society, social roles, and the relationships of individuals to a state, to humanity in general, or to the divine. I do not intend that this discussion be read as a direct-link chain, though in some cases, later writers comment specifically on earlier uses of theater metaphor. Instead, I wish to show that these separate formulations contribute in their variety to the intellectual and cultural heritage that is drawn upon by English-speaking writers in the New World colonies.

PLATO

Politics and the Tragicomedy of Life

Renaissance writers sometimes claim either Pythagoras or Democritus as the originator of the theatrum mundi figure; Robert Burton's adoption of "Democritus Junior" as the theater-seeing prefatory persona in

The Anatomy of Melancholy is clearly based on this tradition. But the twentieth-century scholar E. R. Curtius assigns the origins of theater metaphor to Plato, in whose writings, he remarks, "lie the seeds of the idea of the world as a stage upon which men play their parts, their motions directed by God" (138). Plato's tropes not only reflect an understanding of how the basic relationships among individuals, society, and the divine can be expressed as theater but also show how the metaphor becomes problematic once applied to the idea of humans as civic beings. In fact, his use of the metaphor at all is ironic, given his opposition to theater and art in *Republic* and *Laws* (see Barish, 5–37); but in a sense the works of Plato serve as a model for the later Puritans, whose own dual notion of theater contrasts the figural with the literal.

Plato (ca. 429–347 B.C.) writes his dialogues at a time when great drama has already become a significant element of Greek culture. As has often been observed, his dialogues frequently show a dramatic freshness, especially those on the death of Socrates—*Euthyphro, Crito,* and *Apology.* The dramatic metaphor has a certain grandness, for instance, in the dialogue *Philebus,* when Socrates, discoursing on the conflict between and the mixture of pain and pleasure, says, "In dirges, tragedies, and comedies, not only on the stage, but in the whole tragi-comedy of life, distress and pleasure are blended with each other" ([50b]50).[1] In the way that our individual lives can be seen as blends of conflicting feelings, so life in general has elements of both comedy and tragedy. This is not to say, however, that comedy and tragedy have equal weight. The well-led life will have in it more of the gravity and high seriousness of tragic poetry than it will of sense-based gaiety. In any event, Plato's idea of life as a kind of drama has other implications that he works out in the *Laws* for the relationship of human beings to God and to the state.

When he thinks about life theatrically, Plato, through the figure of the Athenian in the *Laws,* has in mind a potentially reductive vision as well, one where human beings are manipulated by puppet master gods

1. For quotations from longer classical texts, all of which appear in English translation, I have included traditional section or reference numbers in brackets as well as the page numbers of the translation. For shorter works or, in the case of Plautus, for plays without original act and scene numbering, I have only cited the page numbers of the translation listed in Works Cited.

who use them for devices beyond human understanding: "Let's consider each of us living beings to be a divine puppet, put together either for [the gods'] play or for some serious purpose—which, we don't know. What we do know is that these passions work within us like tendons or cords, drawing us and pulling against one another in opposite directions toward opposing deeds, struggling in the region where virtue and vice lie separated from one another" ([1:644d–e] 24–25). That humans, like puppets, can be jerked about by their passions between vice and virtue becomes in Plato an important element of his concept of the state, especially in its approach to art. Whereas in the *Republic* artists occupy a position of low degree—or are ideally excluded from the state—in the *Laws* they are permitted to perform their crafts, but under censorship by rulers. The theater, therefore, comes under close scrutiny. When it panders to popular taste and gives one debased pleasure (that is, does not engage the intelligence), a performance should be criticized in the interest of public good: "The true judge [at theatrical festivals]," the Athenian suggests, "will oppose himself to those who provide the spectators with pleasure in a way that is not appropriate or correct" ([2:659b–c] 39). Instead of allowing theater to be governed by democratic tastes, the state should use performances to educate and improve public morality. As the Athenian argues, "An audience should be continually hearing about characters better than their own, and hence continually experiencing better pleasure" ([2:659c] 40). Consequently, Plato suggests a hierarchy of theatrical performance, with puppet shows (and their appeal to the immature) on the bottom and with epic and tragedy (and their appeal to wiser, more mature minds) on the top ([658c–d] 38–39).

That humans are puppets of the gods (an idea repeated several times throughout the *Laws*) would seem, then, to make painfully obvious the low stature of the race, one greatly subordinate to the gods and to the state. But it is also true that if humankind is "the plaything of God," that connection, even if by a puppet's cords, "is really the best thing about it" ([7:803c] 193). In Plato's hierarchical vision, that which most imitates the good is best; and thus a state, ruled by those most capable of the knowledge of good, becomes an expression of wisdom and morality to which its citizens owe obeisance because they, too, are brought closer to the good.

Interestingly enough, Plato in the *Laws* envisions the state in metaphorically dramatic terms, the expression of a collective art as close to the ideally beautiful as possible. Were some peripatetic tragedians to enter the state, says the Athenian, and were they to ask to perform, they would have to submit their works to the rulers in order to measure them against the local art: " 'Best of strangers,' we should say, 'we ourselves are poets, who have to the best of our ability created a tragedy that is the most beautiful and the best; at any rate, our whole political regime is constructed as the imitation of the most beautiful and best way of life, which we at least assert to be really the truest tragedy' " ([7:817b–c] 208–9). The human puppet acts also in the tragedy of state, that is, in a drama that imitates the beautiful. Those who would act in the theater, Plato implies, simply imitate an imitation; those who act in the tragedy of state, however, seek to imitate "the most beautiful and best way of life," which Plato identifies in his dialogues as residing in the realm of the forms. For Plato, as for many later writers who voice objections to the theater, the drama provides a metaphor that *as figure* supersedes the acting on a material stage that inspires the metaphor in the first place. Thus, for a John Dickinson or any American author who re-creates history in theatrical terms, it is not necessary to have a stage in order to convert politics into a tragedy of state; indeed, the example of Plato suggests that the metaphor gains power when the actual theater is excluded.

Plato's metaphorical expression of life contains an "idea of a theater," to use Francis Fergusson's phrase, that reflects a concept of the human being implicit in Greek drama. In the play that Aristotle chooses as a model of the form, Sophocles' *Oedipus Tyrannos*, we can see, says Fergusson, that "in one sense Oedipus suffers forces he can neither control nor understand, the puppet of fate; yet at the same time he wills and intelligently intends his every move" (18). While the drama, as Plato does, gives voice to a dual-natured being, the puppet and the tragic striver, it should be noted that Greek tragic dramatists do not, as a rule, make self-referring observations about the world and play. This is not surprising given the reputed origins of drama in Greek religious rituals; theater from its beginnings encodes stories and rites that have already been known and gives them, through representation on stage, a new immediacy. It would be redundant to suggest to an audience who already believes it that what happens on stage is like life. Indeed, where tragedy also serves to teach, in a religious sense, nothing is gained by self-referring remarks to performance.

Nevertheless, turning myth into theater and citizens into a chorus, or in reverse, turning actors into heroes and gods, makes inevitable the likening of world to stage for audiences who, over time, become increasingly removed from the ritualistic origins of drama and respond more on an aesthetic or philosophical level. Thus Aristotle's *Poetics*, with its notion that dramatic art is an imitation of human actions, is only possible in a culture where the conditions of performance allow distance, that is, where one discriminates between real life and the quality of its representation on stage. Aristophanes' comedy *The Frogs*, with its satiric debate between Aeschylus and Euripides—and a history of dramatic competitions behind it—suggests to us that there is among the pre-Platonic Greeks at least a formal self-consciousness about theater.

Plato, then, makes overt what has been implied in the drama itself: not only is theater like life, but life is like theater, both tragic and comic. In fact, Plato seems to say that life is far more like theater than theater is similar to life (a point of view that Aristotle later contradicts). As material beings, acting within the limits of nature, humans are laughable puppets; as souls, pursuing knowledge of the good through dialectic, they achieve the sort of dignity that is represented in tragic plays. Theater may be proscribed or censored, but one may nonetheless render an elevated concept of civic duty as theater. Plato anticipates by two millennia how the figure will be applied by patriotic Americans to their own need for a dignified political identity.

PLAUTUS

Politics of Comic Reversal

Roman writers, living in a culture where playgoing is a chief diversion, find theater as a metaphor serves two primary functions: to lampoon pretension, and thus be used largely as a figure for satire, and to describe the relationship between humans and the divine. Indeed, perhaps more than the Greeks, the Romans live in a broadly theatricalized world, where plays coexist with a variety of entertainments, circuses, spectacles, mimes, puppet shows, and triumphs among them—not to mention the extensive rituals and rites associated with ancestor, god, and, later, emperor worship. Roman comic writers suggest that theatrical behavior pervades the culture; Stoic writers, however, take a more limited view, rejecting the histrionic aspects of behavior and asserting instead the need to act virtuously on a stage ordered by Providence.

As with the Greek, Roman dramaturgy implies a world view—or several such views—that ultimately inform both contemporary and modern expressions of theater metaphor. Unlike Greek tragedy, the plays of Plautus (ca. 254–184 B.C.) are comically self-aware expressions of a world used to seeing itself in theatrical terms. These comedies of manners, based on Greek New Comedy, exhibit characters from a histrionically lunatic and ludic[2] world—swaggering braggarts, scheming slaves, lusty youths, and foolish old men, caught in the shape-shifting of lies, disguise, and role reversal—a world where the established order temporarily is turned upside down. With its audience-baiting prologues and applause-begging epilogues, its frequent interruptions of the action for asides and its plots built around playacting, Plautine comedy is manifestly *play*, a self-satirizing form that makes comedy as much out of viewing a play in the theater as it does out of presenting humorous scenes on stage. When the Prologue in *The Prisoners* (*Captivi*) begins to upbraid audience members for not paying attention to his setting of the scene, spectators realize that playfulness is everything: "Do you want to make a poor actor lose his job? I'm not going to rupture myself to suit you, don't think it" (57).

This self-conscious comedic world suggests itself as a metaphor, one that describes human behavior as a series of poses, either deliberate or naive. Oftentimes, lowlife characters have the upper hand; the slave Palaestrio in *The Swaggering Soldier* (*Miles Gloriosus*) serves as the designing intelligence behind the unmasking of Pyrgopolynices for the "swaggering braggart" soldier he is. No one can take being human very seriously after watching one of Plautus's plays: "Man is a thing of

---

2. I use "ludic" throughout to suggest the qualities of a world given over to play (taken in the broadest sense), as in the Latin *ludere* (to play) and *ludus* (game). See Johan Huizinga, *Homo Ludens*, 35–36.

nought, you well may say, / As we perform, and you attend, our play" (59). If one is to ascribe any connection to the divine, then it is as part of a jest: "See how the gods make playthings of us men!" the Prologue reminds the audience in *The Prisoners* (58).

In his plays, Plautus focuses on human behavior as a series of performances that are either laughed up or down by the characters on stage; this is mirrored by the appeal of the actors at the end of the play for applause. On the one hand, Plautus leads us to a benign moralism in which the vices of the elite classes are ridiculed: "Spectators," says the Epilogue in *The Prisoners*, "you have seen today / A highly edifying play" (95). On the other hand, the embracing of comedy offers a perspective that continuously undermines—or comes close to doing so—not simply human pretensions but the structure of an ordered society. Plato in the *Laws* would prohibit any "poet of comedy, or of some iambic lampoon," from mocking a citizen ([935d] 338), for this would certainly deflect public attention away from those persons or behaviors that should be imitated. The conflict between the claim that comedy has social utility by routing vice and the counterclaim that comedy by its very nature corrupts the state plays itself out in England and to some extent in the New England colonies centuries later. For in a world conceived of in Plautine terms, a hierarch might fear more than loss of reputation. When servants become masters (*The Prisoners*) or a slave orders events (*Pseudolus*), the very structure of hierarchy is threatened. By granting slaves three days of free speech and activity per year during the December Saturnalia, the Roman elite defuse revolution; masters and slaves, as Horace suggests in the *Satires*, share the same vices.

There is still another subversive aspect to life imagined as a Plautine comedy: the request for popular approval. Epilogues ask for "loud applause," usually for the complexities of plot, clever dialogue, or bawdry just seen on stage. When the kind of applause seeking that occurs at a dramatic festival enters into the society, those who adhere to absolute truth fear that popularity itself will emerge as a counterforce to truth seeking. This fear is the basis of Plato's critique of rhetoric in *Gorgias*, but in the *Laws* he proscribes praise seeking for political reasons as well. If judicial courts, for example, do not conduct their business above mass opinion "but are full of noise just like a theater, judging each of the orators in turn with shouts of praise and blame, then the whole city is wont to undergo a harsh experience" ([876b] 272). To seek popular approval for an oration distorts the judicial (truth-seeking) process, but it also attacks the civil order. If actors seek applause for their portrayal of comic reversal, the household revolution they have depicted remains contained within the limits of theatrical performance. But if social institutions metaphorically assume the characteristics of Plautine theater, without the time and space boundaries of the stage, then social upheaval would seem to follow. One suspects that political considerations lie behind the denial to actors of Roman citizenship and thus of their right to hold political office—or even to *watch* plays (Barish, 42); the ability to wear mask and costume, to playact, and to draw popular approval for reordering society would be dangerous if the elite no longer possessed the assurance that their privileged position would be maintained after the comic reversal is exposed.

But comic reversal has social reverberations only when the view of humans it offers is something greater than "nought." In the post-Augustan court, the pursuit of taste becomes a life-or-death matter only because the arbiter is imperial whim. Petronius, Nero's "Arbiter of Elegance," still mocks social pretensions in the *Satyricon*, but the context has been reduced to people who have little other desire than to pursue their lusts—except to discourse on the appropriate ways to gratify them. Encolpius, the narrator, and his friends travel through a culture based on disguise, imposture, and performances of all kinds. Besides desire, nothing seems fixed. When the lover of Encolpius, Giton, chooses to go with the narrator's companion, Ascyltus, Encolpius laments the unsureness of friendship. In a poem inserted after that complaint, Petronius hints that in a world viewed theatrically, nothing final can be determined until the play is over:

> The mime has begun
> And the father is there,
> And here is the son
> And the millionaire.
> Then closes the page,
> When played is their part,
> On the laughter upstage
> And the masks of their art—
> Then their true faces appear.   ([80] 94)

The stage world of comic reversal or its poeticized equivalent, if not seen as belonging to the theater only, enters culture as criticism of social performance. If so, then in Roman terms everyone is reduced to the same low status; the "true faces" that appear are ironically those of actors.

THE STOICS
Act Well the Given Part

Despite some important differences, the Stoics emerge from the contending schools of Hellenistic philosophy as something like the Puritans of the time. For the Stoics, belief in Providence shapes all human behavior; the divine orders things for inscrutable reasons, leaving human beings to choose to accept providential authority or not. Much of the philosophy, then, is directed at helping people to find ways to harmonize themselves with the humanly unchangeable nature of the universe. The belief in an integrated universe may have been attractive to Renaissance thinkers; Epictetus, Seneca, and Marcus Aurelius, late Stoics for whom complete texts were still extant, were all translated and republished in sixteenth-century Europe. John Calvin thought Seneca to be "a master of ethics," and Calvin's own theatrical view of the universe may be derived in part from Stoical use of dramatic figures (Long, 238–40).

The Stoics insist that humans are directed by the divine, a belief that lends itself readily to theater metaphors. Indeed, the best one can do is follow providential guidance willingly, for resistance is futile, even embarrassing (Stough, 222–23). Cicero (106–43 B.C.), though not a dogmatic believer, borrows from Stoical attitudes when he applies the life-as-drama metaphor in his essay on old age. Speaking in the voice of Cato the Elder (the Censor), Cicero explains to the young the satisfactions possible when one grows old. Those "who have made good use" of the prerogatives of age granted to older speakers in public debates "have acted life's drama nobly to the end. Not for them is the sort of incompetent performance which breaks down in the last act!" (239). In the larger drama of life, one must remember not to exceed the amount of time one has been allotted: "An actor need not remain on stage until the very end of the play; if he wins applause in those acts in which he appears, he will have done well enough. In life, too, a man can perform his part wisely without staying on the stage until the play is finished" (241; see Curtius, 139). Restraint in acting lends dignity to one's performance; the role has been determined by forces larger than the individual's own power to change it without bringing on him or herself the opprobrium of others.

This belief in a lack of control over the larger shape of events leads other writers to denigrate human inadequacy. Horace (65–8 B.C.), for instance, though often critical of Stoic efforts to explain away evil by insisting that all is for the best, uses Stoic doctrine to satirize the illusion of power among the slaveholding classes. In satire 2.7, Horace's slave, Davus, has been given license by the Saturnalia to speak his mind. Having heard of a Stoic lecture from a hall-porter, Davus uses his freedom to ridicule Horace for his self-delusions and hypocrisy: "Here's a further point, no less cogent: a man who takes orders from a slave may be called a sub-slave, as he is in your parlance, or a fellow-slave; anyhow, isn't that what I am to you? For you, after all, though you lord it over me, cringe before another master. You are jerked like a wooden puppet by strings in someone else's hand" (108). Not to realize one's essential powerlessness is to be reduced to a puppet; the play of authority is only that—a message "Horace" in the satire does not want to hear. Like the Puritans centuries later, the Stoics find false playing undermines the moral integrity of human action. In letter 80, Seneca (ca. 4 B.C.–65 A.D.) takes aim at the wealthy, seeing the hypocrisy of their presumed happiness. For most of us, the problem may come from not recognizing the theatrical nature of life. We live out "this drama of human life, wherein we are assigned the parts we are to play so badly" (Epistulae, 217). In a world where people only play parts, without accepting them, the wise person must be able to distinguish the falsely happy from the true. Of the former, Seneca tells us that "in every case their happiness is put on like the actor's mask. Tear it off, and you will scorn them" (217). Thus in the Stoic world of assigned roles, one must not make the mistake of being an actor only, parading wealth and power as if in the end they had any meaning in the whole drama of life.

In theatrical terms, Epictetus (ca. 55–135 A.D.) expresses most succinctly the moral implications of harmonizing one's actions with the behests of the ordering agent. His *Manual*, the *Enchiridion* (in reality, a posthumous summary collected by a pupil, Flavius Arrianus), available in printed form during the Renaissance as early as 1495 (Long, 239), stresses the need to behave as if one had no choice in deciding life's course: "Remember that you are an actor in a drama of such sort as the Author chooses—if short, then in a short one; if long, then in a long one. If it be his pleasure that you should enact a poor man, or a cripple, or a ruler, or a private citizen, see that you act it well. For this is your business—to act well the given part, but to choose it belongs to another" ([17] 22–23). On the surface, the doctrine expressed above in the *Enchiridion* is a conservative one; one accepts one's lot as a role given by a director with whom there is no argument. Yet many of the Stoical virtues motivate Roman opponents of dictatorial emperors (Cato the Younger, Brutus), and, as will be explained later, those same virtues inspire the imitators of Stoic opposition to tyranny, the revolutionaries in America. For the latter, the belief that one is acting in a divinely appointed drama lends justification to reversing rather than maintaining the status quo. One only has to imagine the drama serving republican rather than imperial ends.

In the *Meditations* of Marcus Aurelius (121–80 A.D.), one finds a fully developed understanding of why theater serves as an ideal analogy for the Stoic life. Addressed essentially to himself, the emperor's thoughts on right behavior reflect his reading of Epictetus among other philosophers and his ambivalence, even distaste, for the trappings of imperial rule. As a later reader of Epictetus, John Adams, does during a period in his life of increasing public exposure, Marcus fends off the demands of fame as something ephemeral: "How empty is noisy applause" ([4.3] 26). To value applause deflects one's attention from a life of genuine value: "The praise of the multitude is only a clacking of tongues" ([6.16] 51). Therefore, all decisions come down to this: "to act or not to act in accordance with the way we were made" ([6.16] 51–52).

Like Plato in the *Laws* and Horace in the *Satires*, Marcus finds that the life of the senses is one full of "contradictions"; death, then, comes as a "rest . . . from being jerked like a puppet by the strings of desire" ([6.28] 54). Until death comes, the path is clear: "Erase imagining. Still the puppet-strings of passion. Circumscribe the present" ([7.29]

66). By nature, one harbors within the most contemptible of actors, a wooden imitation of an imitator; to overcome that deflation of dignity, one must apply reason. For Marcus, the assorted entertainments of Rome outside the narrowly defined province of the drama provide analogies for the dreariness and folly of human existence; one must distinguish with one's reason between Stoical action and acting in a theater for the masses. In a culture given to spectacle, the Stoic discovers that the spectacular enervates through repetition rather than excites through ingenuity: "As the performances in the amphitheater bore you because you are always seeing the same things and the monotony makes the spectacle tiresome, so too you feel about the whole of life: everything up and down is the same and due to the same causes. How much longer then?" ([6.46] 58). Likewise, the amphitheater provides examples of those who seek to play more than their allotted parts allow; one must be true to virtue and not grasp foolishly to life as does the beast wrestler who, torn by animals, begs to be allowed to live in order to undergo the same fate the next day ([10.8] 100). Indeed, popular entertainments for the Stoic supply not only analogies to life but also a test of character: "The empty pursuit of triumphal parades, the dramas of the stage, flocks and herds, battles with the spear, a bone thrown to puppies, scraps thrown into fish tanks, the calamities and burdens of ants, the scurryings of excited mice, puppets jerked by strings—amidst these you must stand with kindliness and without insolence, but realizing that the worth of each depends upon the worth of his pursuits" ([7.3] 61). By acting through reason, one elevates oneself from the puppetry of the sensual life while at the same time gaining sympathy for the low condition of the rest of the race.

Although Marcus includes stage drama in his list of futile activities, it does serve him as an edifying figure of speech. The very repetition that bores the spectator in the amphitheater makes plain the shape of history. For those who would govern, being prepared for the revival of old political shows in new performances provides a valuable lesson: "Bear in mind continually how all such things as are happening now have happened before; bear in mind too that they will happen again, whole performances with the same scenery, all of which you know from your own experience and from earlier history. Keep these before your eyes; the whole court of Hadrian, for example, the whole court of Antoninus, the whole court of Philip, of Alexander, of Croesus. For these were all of the same kind as now, only with different actors" ([10.27] 105). In Marcus's vision, there is nothing new under the sun or on the stage either. With his fellow Stoics, he bequeaths to posterity a trope that denies progress or essential change. For the Stoics, history is "whole performances with the same scenery"; by the time American writers make use of Stoic variations of theatrical figures, however, they will look to a "theater of new scenery" as the culmination of historical change.

Viewing life theatrically allows one to be ready for all of life's difficulties. In a particularly revealing entry, Marcus reflects on the history of Greek drama and its moral applicability in daily life. He singles out the earliest form, tragedy, for its special relevance to the Stoic: "Tragedies were first produced to remind us of what happens, to show that this is how things naturally happen, and that you should not be vexed on the larger stage of life by things which delight you in the theater; for you see that this is the course they must take, and that even those who cry 'O Cithaeron' [i.e., the king in Sophocles' *Oedipus Tyrannos*] endure them" ([11.6] 111–12). Old Comedy, too, offers lessons: "Its freedom of speech . . . and its very directness reminded the spectators of the evils of arrogance" ([11.6] 112). But afterward— and here Marcus offers an implied criticism of Plautine drama— Middle and Late Comedy "gradually slipped into mere love of the techniques of representation" ([11.6] 112). That is, a drama whose end has no other point than to portray manners does not serve an identifiable moral function. This distinction between life viewed as a tragedy and life viewed as a comedy of manners marks an essential division in world views; as will be discussed further, it underlies for eighteenth-century American writers the basic difference between a British culture based on social performance and an American one based on obedience to virtue and providential direction.

In his last entry in the *Meditations*, Marcus chooses a theatrical figure to reiterate his definition of a purposeful life. As Cicero and Epictetus have argued, Marcus here declares that one must live within the limits set by the "Author." Death brings no fear to one who recognizes when it is time to get off the stage; and in his final meditation, Marcus suggests a reason why the younger Cato, who committed suicide in a failed rebellion against Caesar, would have become a Stoic hero: he knew when the show was over. In the *Meditations*, however, the emperor has his eyes on himself:

> Mortal, you have been a citizen in this great city, what matter to you whether for five years or fifty, for what is in accord with the law is equal for all. What then is there to fear if you are sent away from the city not by a dictator or an unjust judge, but by the same nature which brought you to it, as if the magistrate who had chosen a comic actor were to dismiss him. "But I have not played the five acts, but only three." "You have played well, but in your life at any rate the three acts are the whole play." For he sets the limit who was at one time the cause of your dissolution. You have no responsibility for either. So depart graciously, for he who dismisses you is also gracious.   ([12.36] 129)

Though many of the Stoic virtues would find their way into early Christian thought, total resignation is not one of them. The church fathers also see a world in theatrical terms; but unlike that critic of early Christians, Marcus Aurelius, they imagine a different show, a single progressive drama that as a figure reshapes the theatrical conception of history.

THE CHURCH FATHERS
Pulpit versus Stage

By the fourth and fifth centuries, theater bashing by Christian writers becomes a rhetorical sport that rivals, in its own way, the plays and spectacles the church fathers so strongly condemn. From Paul's proscriptions against idol worship and the rituals associated with false gods to Augustine's attack on theater as a cause of the fall of Rome, one finds a constantly flowing stream of propaganda that reaches near flood stage by the early fifth century. It is clear, given the conditions of imperial theater and the anomalous position of actors, that Christians have strong ideological reasons for denouncing the immorality of the stage in language that will not, in its intensity, reappear in Europe until the parallel phenomenon of Puritan diatribes against the theater in sixteenth-century England. But the Christian denunciation of theatrical entertainments, though well-known, is still poorly understood,

especially by modern theatrophiles who ascribe the hyperbolic fulmi-
nations of such Puritan writers as William Prynne to mere "prejudice." The English war on the theaters will be discussed later, but the
connection of that conflict to the patristic war on Roman entertainments, with its metaphoric implications, illuminates to a large degree
the ultimate turn of affairs for the American inheritors of the antitheatrical tradition.

At one level, the early Christians react vehemently to stage performances as provocations to immorality: "Those who return from the
theater . . . who rise from their seats there are on fire, burning with
sinful desire. Indeed, when they have seen those lavishly decked out
women on the stage, and have received innumerable moral injuries
from the sight, they will be no more at peace than a billowy sea"
(Chrysostom, *Homilies* 2 [60]: 145). Simply attending the theater is
enough to corrupt. When one recalls that theater during the first
centuries of the Christian era included gladiatorials and lion feeding,
the entertainments of the amphitheater, the patristic revulsion seems
largely justified. But for these writers, as for the Elizabethan revivalists
of the antitheatrical tradition, the charge of lewdness spreads by association—and by presumed links in origin—to performances that contain any suggestion of immoral behavior. Tertullian (ca. 160–ca. 230
A.D.), for instance, extends his attack on Roman spectacles to all
secular performances, including stage drama: "If tragedies and comedies are the bloody and wanton, the impious and licentious inventers
of crimes and lusts, it is not good even that there should be any calling
to remembrance the atrocious or the vile" (*De spectaculis*, in *Writings*, 25). In this view, revived by Puritans in England, any modeling
of human behavior that does not figure virtuous action subverts morality; in proscribing stage drama, with its "bad" characters, in addition to
amphitheatrical entertainments, Tertullian acknowledges the power
of the stage to engross and influence an essentially weak and innately
corruptible human nature (see Barish, 43–65).

Although much of the antagonism to the stage among the early
Christian writers is the same, there are different points of emphasis.
For Augustine, theater is pernicious because it evokes, and is sanctioned by, the corrupt gods of Greek and Roman pantheons; that is,
the standards of behavior offered to believers by the divinities of

Roman religion amount to a moral sacking of the empire. As David Leverenz remarks, Augustine's antitheatrical rhetoric seems aimed more at the portrayal of lasciviousness among the gods than at the theater itself (27), although it would be hard for any Christian to praise an institution that considered randy deities to be entertainment. Augustine hates most the conciliation of the gods through the debauched ceremonies, passed off as theater, that weakened Rome and opened it, finally, to attack:

> This propitiation of such divinities—a propitiation so wanton, so impure, so immodest, so wicked, so filthy, whose actors the innate and praiseworthy virtue of the Romans disabled from civic honours, erased from their tribe, recognised as polluted and made infamous;—this propitiation, I say, so foul, so detestable, and alien from every religious feeling, these fabulous and ensnaring accounts of the criminal actions which they either shamefully and wickedly committed, or more shamefully and wickedly feigned, all this the whole city learned in public both by the words and gestures of the actors.   (*City of God,* [2.27] 71)

In the virulence of Augustine's blast at the theatrical conciliation of the gods, however, one can see the rhetorical strategy that would enable patristic writers to use theater metaphor for their own devices. In a universe where a person's actions are watched constantly by a divine audience, theatrical metaphor provides a compelling code for expressing the relationship between human and divine. In Augustine's view, we are, in fact, on stage all the time; even the birth of a child has radical implications for the dramatis personae on the theatrum mundi: "Boys when born speak like this to their parents: 'Now then, begin to think of removing hence, let us too play our parts on the stage.' For the whole life of temptation in the human race is a stage play; for it is said; *Every man living is altogether vanity*" ("Exposition on Psalm 128," in *Expositions,* 6:46). In the life of temptation, a person must choose a theater carefully—the lewd miming of disenfranchised actors or the saintly imitation of the life of Christ. The choice for a Christian should be obvious. In a church, like the theater, one learns things "from a raised platform in presence of all." But there is a difference: "For no filthy and wicked action is there set forth to be gazed at or to be imitated; but either the precepts of the true God are recommended,

His miracles narrated, His gifts praised, or His benefits implored" (*City of God*, [2.28] 72). The vehemence of antitheatrical rhetoric can be traced at least in part to this: the world of God and church and the world of the secular stage are very rivals for souls.

For Augustine's contemporary Chrysostom (ca. 347–407 A.D.), this rivalry guides his preaching. In his *Homilies* on the gospel writer John, Chrysostom speaks to an audience fully knowledgeable of, and susceptible to, the temptations of the stage. If people flock to see a great athlete or performer, they should be even more desirous to listen to the preacher's words about John: "He [John] is not taking part in a play, or concealing his head by a mask (for he will not discourse on topics suited to this). He is not mounting the platform, or beating time on the stage floor with his foot, nor is he decked out in golden raiment [like an empty-worded Sophist], but he enters clad in a garment of indescribable beauty" (1 [1]: 4). Chrysostom emphasizes that John is not "playing a part" (1 [1]: 5). Rather, by implication he *is* his role: "He has heaven for his stage; for theatre, the world; for audience, all the angels, and also, as many men as are already 'angels' or even desire to become so" (1 [1]: 5). The gospel writer does not need to disguise his words in glitter or exhibit himself in "the Devil's pomps" to attract followers (1 [2]: 10–11); his is a theater of openness and of teachings "clearer than sunbeams," stripped of show (1 [2]: 17–18).

By extension, then, the preacher of John's word also participates in a theater of his own. In his homily on John 1.1, Chrysostom speaks directly to his auditors, noting that in "your unwillingness to leave, though closely packed together, until this spiritual theatre is dismissed, your clamourous applause and all such things may be thought indicative of the fervor in your soul and of your earnest desire to listen" (1 [3]: 27). The competition between theater and church is keen; Chrysostom shrewdly calculates that if he acknowledges the attraction of pagan theater, he can more proudly proclaim the superiority of his theater, the theater of John and God: "Now, tell me: If it were possible for you, seated in company with rulers and kings, to watch and enjoy the spectacle, would you not think that this was a very great honor? Then, will you not hasten to such a spectacle here to watch it in company with the King of angels and see the Devil seized from behind and making every effort to escape, but not succeeding?" (1 [32]: 321).

And if it is glory one wants, attend to that "immortal glory" in John's message: "It is better with your efforts, for its theater is more brilliant and its prize, greatness" (1 [42]: 433).

This rivalry between church and theater appears as a theme in many patristic writings, but the most suggestive element of the conflict seems to be the contention between real theater and its metaphor. As Chrysostom remarks, Christianity is at heart a "spectacle," a more glorious counter to those entertainments one might see in the amphitheater. The earlier Tertullian, however, develops the spectacle metaphor more elaborately than Chrysostom does in the *Homilies*, as if at pains, like later writers, to persuade an audience used to the profanities of the imperial stage that the show put on by God has no real peer. Like Chrysostom, Tertullian recognizes that the real theater has an allure: "When a tragic actor is declaiming," he asks, "will one be giving thought to prophetic appeals?" (*De spectaculis*, in *Writings*, 31). Tertullian's attempts to convince his audience of the superiority of his theater are worth quoting at some length in order to see the intensity of his rhetoric:

> If the literature of the stage delight you, we have literature in abundance of our own—plenty of verses, sentences, songs, proverbs; and these are not fabulous, but true; not tricks of art, but plain realities. Would you have also fightings and wrestlings? Well, of these there is no lacking, and they are not of slight account. Behold unchastity overcome by chastity, perfidy slain by faithfulness, cruelty stricken by compassion, impudence thrown into the shade by modesty: these are the contests we have among us, and in these *we* win our crowns. But would you have of blood too? You have Christ's.   (34)

Tertullian proposes metaphors to replace physical activities: to imagine chastity is to figure a wrestling match with its enemy, unchastity. All pales, however, before the metaphor of spectacle for things final, the conclusion, the triumph of Christian history:

> But what a spectacle is that fast-approaching advent of our Lord, now owned by all, now highly exalted, now a triumphant One! What that exultation of the angelic hosts! what the glory of the rising saints! what the kingdom of the just thereafter! what the city New Jerusalem! Yes, and there are other sights: the last day of judgment, with its everlasting issues;

that day unlooked for by the nations, the theme of their derision, when
the world, hoary with age, and all its many products, shall be consumed
in one great flame! How vast a spectacle then bursts upon the eye!   (34)

In the struggle against sensuality and its display in the theater, patristic
writers propose a rival stage, an amphitheater of God's special effects.
As revolutionaries do in all ages, the church fathers incorporate the
rhetoric of their rivals in their own counterappeal to the people. Stay
away from the theater—but come watch our show.

Behind the uses of theater metaphor by early Christian writers lies
an agonistic vision of reality contending with disguise, truth battling
deception, the uncostumed followers of God ripping off the masks of
hypocrites and sending them to judgment, offstage. And as a historical vision, the patristic view of the Bible transforms the rhetoric
derived from pagan theater to produce a language of triumph, an
imperial-style celebration of victory over the Devil's troops—and over
time itself. When the Puritans would come in later centuries to speak
some of this same language, that rhetoric, at least in America, would
also serve as part of an emerging national enterprise, one whose
triumph in the Revolution would be figured in spectacles affirming
the right conclusion to world history—and the just stage direction of
Providence.

JOHN OF SALISBURY
Comedy or Tragedy of This World

Between the collapse of Rome and the beginnings of the Renaissance,
theater as a rhetorical figure appears seldom in European literature.
The *Policraticus* (1159), John of Salisbury's critique of court life,
provides one of the few medieval texts known to contain an extended
use of theatrical metaphor. Given its popularity through the seventeenth century both in Latin and in English translation, it may well
have had some influence on Elizabethan and Jacobean writers in their
formulations of histrionic tropes (Curtius, 139–40). The *Policraticus*,
laden as it is with references to Roman history and writings, could
serve just as well as an analysis of ancient Rome as a twelfth-century
European court, for it is clear that John (ca. 1115–1180), the friend of
Thomas Becket (to whom *Policraticus* is dedicated), sees in the halls of

power a kind of perpetual theater. In John's view, the very theatricality of life provides its own lessons, if one is willing to stand aside and recognize what it means to live as if all life were like a play. His idea of theater, if less ideologically colored than that of patristic writers, is like that of the church fathers, but his use of the metaphor, stripped of the emphasis on spectacle, reduces rather than enhances the importance of actors on the world stage.

John cannot escape the doctrine of the Church that condemns actors for following a "dishonorable" profession ([1.8] 36, 38–39), but he also argues, in his own myth of declension, that contemporary actors have fallen in stature from their classical counterparts. In the days of Plautus, Terence, and Menander, "there were once actors who by the magic of gesture, of language, and of voice reproduced vividly for the audience both fact and fiction" ([1.8] 36). "Forced into retirement," legitimate actors have given way to jesters, jugglers, mimes, and other frivolous entertainers, persons whose actions bring such harm to spectators that one would "be glad to see and laugh when a juggler is drenched with urine, his tricks disclosed" ([1.8] 38). For persons then to mimic the mime, turn flatterer, fawner, actor for personal gain or advancement, "brands with infamy those whom innate or acquired dignity seems to have delivered from the disgrace of such a mean calling" ([3.4] 160).

As in many such critiques, however, the term *actor* also has a more general, and abstract, application to humankind as a whole. In his chapter "The Comedy or Tragedy of This World," John discusses a passage from Petronius that he has quoted earlier (*Satyricon*, [80] 94). There, as has been suggested above, the Roman writer uses theater as a deflating metaphor to describe shifting fortune. John comments that if Petronius is right and "almost the entire world . . . is seen to play the part of actor to perfection," then there is a kind of universal danger for the unaware: that is, "the actors gazing as it were upon their own comedy and what is worse, [becoming] so absorbed in it that they are unable to return to reality when occasion demands" ([3.8] 172). Like the child who imitates the stutterer so often that he or she becomes one, adults too become enrapt by their own roles and fail to see the transitoriness of life, even their own lack of control over the play they enact: "So this comedy of the age affects the thought of even great men. The different periods of time take on the character of shifts of scene. The individuals become subordinate to the acts as the play of mocking fortune unfolds itself in them" ([3.8] 172). And those who would seek fame from doing anything other than those great deeds that get written about could learn something else from play metaphor, since "whatever popularity and renown" they would achieve would be no more than "the applause of the theater, no sooner begun than done" ([1.Intro.] 7).

Like Plato, John sees elements of both comedy and tragedy in life; whether it is finally one or the other, the *Policraticus* does not say. "The life of man appears to be a tragedy rather than a comedy in that the end is invariably sad" ([3.8] 173), John remarks, but it finally does not matter what one calls it as long as one recognizes that all of us play parts ([3.8] 175). Calling the world a stage, however, is not an idle figure. In perhaps the most important instance of the metaphor of theatrum mundi in the work, John presages the more commonly recognized Elizabethan view: "It is surprising how nearly coextensive with the world is the stage on which this endless, marvelous, incomparable tragedy, or if you will comedy, can be played; its area is in fact that of the whole world" ([3.8] 176). Yet even with such a vast correlation between stage and world, there is an end to the drama; and for those who have stood apart and resisted the temptation to play the role of honor-seekers, there is a happy ending, one that coincides not with the illusion of fame but with the reality of the afterlife. To be truly virtuous (and John cites biblical and classical examples) is to be "deemed mad by fools" and most probably to die without praise because such paragons "have disdained to corrupt the dignity of nature by donning the costume of the actor on the stage of the world" ([3.8] 180). Those who forsake the role of actor have another part to play when the drama has finished: "These are perhaps those who from the lofty pinnacle of virtue look down upon the stage of the world, and scorning the drama of fortune . . . view the world-comedy along with Him who towers above to watch ceaselessly over men, their deeds and their aspirations, for since all are playing parts, there must be some spectators" ([3.8] 180).

To find oneself, then, in a universe of divine spectators puts the human actor in a vulnerable and exposed position. No longer can one

simply seek the approval of peers or patrons and expect eternal rewards. As the Puritans would make manifest, John stresses the importance of being aware of one's audience; everyone, in fact, is being
watched: "God . . . his angels, and . . . a few sages . . . are themselves also spectators at these Circensian Games. Rather should one
himself blush if on such a brilliantly lighted stage his movements be
unseemly and he completely discredit himself by his farcical antics"
([3.8] 180). Since theater and actors have fallen in quality since
classical times, individuals must beware that they, too, do not follow
the same fate in their actions at court. Knowing that we act before
God, as the Stoics also state, we are more likely to be accountable for
our actions in hopes of joining the celestial spectators. John stresses the
need to resist playing for laughs here on earth in order to dignify
ourselves in the sight of the Almighty.

✑

CHAPTER TWO

American Origins I:
A Theater of Theaters

*S*eventeenth-century American colonists receive theater metaphor most probably from Renaissance writers, although certainly the more modern formulations are often based on classical models. Educated emigrants from England would have known about theater through two related yet divergent channels: writers whose use of theater as a figure presupposes the unquestioned presence of theater as an institution and writers for whom the metaphor is the only aspect of theater worth preserving. Among the former group, who will be discussed in this chapter, are the Continental humanist authors and their followers in sixteenth- and seventeenth-century England, including playwrights. Among the latter, who will be examined in the next chapter, are the early religious nonconformists and later the Protestant radicals. Though the second group has the most immediate influence on early New England writers and the first on the cavaliers of the southern colonies, both traditions ultimately contribute to a blended American usage of theatrical tropes.

ERASMUS
Bows to Folly

With the revived interest in the alleged greatness of humankind among prominent Renaissance thinkers, a shift in emphasis occurs in the application of theater metaphor. In the famous "Oration on the

Dignity of Man" (1487), Pico della Mirandola asserts that humans are great not by virtue of their fixedness in the order of being but because of their protean qualities. Pico echoes the writer who would proclaim that "on this stage of the world, as it were, . . . 'There is nothing to be seen more wonderful than man'" (223). This creature is the one who can rise to the height of the gods or sink to the level of animals simply by acts of free will and whose abilities inspire humans to admire themselves.

This position is a far cry from the Stoical idea that each person has, at birth, a predetermined role to enact. On a practical level, the person who is flexible in choice of roles stands a better chance of contributing something to the political life of a commonwealth. As "More" tells Raphael Hythloday in Thomas More's *Utopia* (1516), "Academic philosophy [i.e., scholasticism] thinks that everything is suitable to every place. But there is another philosophy, more practical for statesmen, which knows its stage, adapts itself to the play in hand, and performs its role neatly and appropriately" (49). In this new philosophy, one no longer acquiesces to a fixed role in a single lifetime play; rather, one finds that different characters suit different dramas. The skilled political philosopher, then, is one who can change voice and costume, who can distinguish what is best for either comedy or tragedy: "Whatever play is being performed, perform it as best you can, and do not upset it all simply because you think of another which has more interest" (49). In this case, the play of state gains a Platonic dignity by the right choice of attitude toward one's adopted role; at the same time, however, More cautions that human flexibility must be tempered by a more stalwart dedication to purpose (for other theatrical tropes in More's writing, see Greenblatt, 11–73).

Perhaps the most elaborate metaphorical celebration of human roleplaying is that of Juan Luis Vives in his "A Fable about Man" (1518). There, Vives imagines Jupiter creating the world as a giant amphitheater for the entertainment of Juno and the other gods: "Uppermost, to wit in the skies, were the stalls and seats of the divine spectators; nethermost—some say in the middle—the earth was placed as a stage for the appearance of the actors, along with all the animals and everything else" (387; see also van den Berg, 50–51). After the animals perform, the human actor begins to show his protean dexterity, mimicking plants and animals, social and political humanity, even the lesser gods and Jupiter himself. For Vives the theatrical setting affirms human greatness; Jupiter praises his human imitator as the best actor because he is so adroit that he can even play the god of gods. Indeed, the ability to enact the creator-god earns the human actor a place among the divine spectators at Jupiter's banquet table.

But the Renaissance perspective is multifaceted, and for all the proclamations that the species is a paragon, there are reminders throughout the period that human actors are also a "quintessence of dust." Erasmus, for instance, shares with his Spanish contemporary Vives a vision of an earth-stage watched over by gods who appraise the performances of human actors. As expressed by Erasmus's creation, Folly, however, praise often means mockery. For his friend Thomas More, whose name provides the pun in *Encomium Moriae* (*The Praise of Folly*), acting various roles in the play of state should be encouraged. By contrast, the theater metaphors in *Praise of Folly* (1509) suggest both the transience of fortune and the capacity of humankind to cling desperately to its illusions (Erasmus, 17–19). As Folly asks, "Now what else is our whole life but a kind of stage play through which men pass in various disguises, each one going on to play his part until he is led off by the director? And often the same actor is ordered back in a different costume, so that he who played the king in purple, now acts the slave in rags. Thus everything is pretense; yet this play is performed in no other way" (66). Suddenly to interrupt the play and reveal the true nature of the actors behind the characters would "destroy the illusion [and] upset the whole play" (66). As on stage, so it is in life that the one who would break us of our beliefs in things as they seem rather than things as they are would be denounced as "dangerously insane" (67). Like the alienated few in John of Salisbury's *Policraticus* who absent themselves from the play of life, the one who, in Folly's world, "demands that the play shall no longer be a play" is labeled as hopelessly "perverse" (67).

Whereas John of Salisbury never commits himself (though he leans toward tragedy), Folly does not hesitate to name the play of this life a comedy. Indeed, the "followers of Folly" themselves put on the best show: "Men put on a superb daily performance for the gods. In the morning, of course, when they are sober, the gods are busy settling quarrels and hearing prayers; but later in the day, after they have had several drinks and are tired of the office, they find a seat in the grandstand and look down at the human spectacle. It's the greatest show on earth! No theater has as many comic acts. I sometimes take a seat alongside the gods myself" (88). In much of the remainder of *Praise of Folly*, Erasmus has Folly observe the foibles of humanity as if she were comfortably viewing from her box the antics of her followers; but even for Folly, the comedy wears thin. She expresses disgust for the contemptible role-players below, for, as she says of preachers and pedants, "these play-actors and pretenders . . . are as ungrateful for my benefit as they are dishonest in their affectation of piety" (107).

Yet *Praise of Folly*, for all its wit, conceals within its irony the sort of fear that would plague Protestant writers later in the sixteenth century. Erasmus may have accepted, despite his critique, a theatrical view of life; certainly the form of his *Colloquies* would suggest at least a recognition of the potency of dramatic form. More to the point, a figural theater puts a comforting limit on human potentiality, even if, as in the case of Vives, the stage appears to be an open-ended metaphor. But the discrepancy between form and substance that Folly accepts as the way of the world is something that radical Protestants would zealously try to destroy. Their insistence that a person conform inwardly to his demeanor, that a saint be visible, would seem to be the view of the killjoy whom Folly chides, in the language of her followers, as perverse or insane. In the world of Folly, people like the Puritans play the "spoilsports," those whom Johan Huizinga identifies as the disrupters of the play world (11)—that is, the sort of fanatics who would expose the woman on stage as a man or the youth as an aging adult. Were that to happen, says Folly, not only would the revelations "spoil the whole play," but what would follow would be frightening and unknown: "For at once a new order of things would arise" (66). Few Renaissance writers follow up on the anarchic possibilities of a world completely at play; yet it is precisely that shattering of a play's power of illusion that radical Protestants will later desire. The very establishment in America of a Puritan polity is a sort of fig to Folly, an antitheatrical gesture that, ironically, declares the power of a new, idealized theater where all things should be as they seem. With the routing of illusion, "a new order of things" should arise.

SHAKESPEARE
Plays of Self and State

Though much has been written about Elizabethan contributions to the history of the theatrum mundi trope, primarily to show a harmonious correspondence between the rising stage and the new world it represents, there is another aspect to the Shakespearean use of the figure that seems less well recognized: how the metaphor subverts itself when it is delivered in the theater. By the 1560s, the decade of Shakespeare's birth, theater and play metaphors appear with increasing frequency in English literature, either in the writings of native authors or through English translations of foreign works. As a reiterated commonplace expression, the figure is largely static. In "the first play in which an attempt was made to use the image of the world as a stage in a consistent and structured fashion" (Righter, 75), *Damon and Pithias* (1564/1571), Richard Edwards writes a brief homiletic from traditional materials. Like many a good Renaissance man, Damon cites an early Greek philosopher as the source for the figure:

> Pithagoras said, that this world was like a Stage
> Whereon many play their partes: the lookers on, the sage
> Phylosophers are, saith he, whose parte is to learne
> The maners of all Nations, and the good from the bad to discerne.
> (lines 348–51)

Here, Edwards shows no particular awareness of what it means to speak the metaphor of the stage on the stage. This is an ancient use of theater as a simple, structured image, that Stoic acceptance of the nature of things wherein a profession is a part, played out fully over the whole course of adult life. If any use of theatrum mundi can be said to be orthodox, this seems to be it.

A more elaborately developed figure can be found in John Alday's translation of Pierre Boaistuau's *Theatrum Mundi* (1566). Like Edwards, Boaistuau relies on the image of a cosmic theater in which parts are apportioned and roles played out; but he depicts his theater in terms more familiar to Folly than the self-congratulation contained in Juan Luis Vives. At the end of the drama of life, we do not look about in triumph; rather, we all stand leveled before the withering scorn of the Great Spectator: "What else is this world but a Theatre? [Some play parts of low degree, some high.] And nevertheless when al these have cast of their visards and masking garments, and that death commeth and maketh an end of this bloudie tragedy, then they acknowledge themselves al to be mortal men. And then the Lord that is in heaven laugheth at their foolish enterprizes and vanities (as the Prophet David witnesseth) but with such a fearfull and terrible laughter, that hee maketh us tremble and quake for feare, and the earth also" (quoted in Stroup, 14). In Boaistuau, Edwards, and others who use the trope in the early Elizabethan period, the acting of human beings on the world stage can be measured in two ways: either the divine spectator evaluates our fulfillment of the roles we have been given and rewards accordingly, or he blasts us all for our ineptitude and inevitable foolishness on the stage.

When we consider Shakespeare, however, we have to take into account a variety of situations in which *acting* becomes a complex and intricate language that expresses as often the protean quality of humanity as the fixity of human endeavor. For many scholars, it is acting and the stage which are the point, not work and the world. In the studies of Frances Yates and Kent van den Berg, for instance, we see Shakespeare as a playwright trying to establish the primacy of the stage as a world, the theater as a globe, the playhouse as a cosmos. Other scholars, following Lionel Abel, see Shakespeare in a tradition of the artist as self-conscious formalist. Abel's Shakespeare is one of two chief Renaissance creators (the other being Calderón) of *metatheater* or self-referring drama. In this view, the world itself melts away as a referent of the stage; characters do not simply imitate human action but become playwrights themselves, as Hamlet literally does. A metaplay or meta-drama, as James L. Calderwood calls it, is a work of theater "about life seen as already theatricalized" (Abel, 60). In talking about life from a metatheatrical view, Abel leaves us with "two basic postulates: (1) The world is a stage and (2) life is a dream" (105).

This concept, which seems to appeal to those who see the world from inside a theater, has its problems as a full expression of the Elizabethan "world view." Without getting overly involved in the controversies surrounding metatheater or the existence of a one-dimensional Elizabethan point of view, I do wish to stress that the language of the period works back and forth, from stage to world and world to stage. As van den Berg observes, theater metaphor differs from other metaphors by referring not to a thing in itself but to a representation: "The theatrical metaphor reverses the mimetic relationship and gives it a reflexive structure: the stage represents a world that resembles a stage; the actor impersonates a character who plays the actor" (52). With this in mind, a playgoer or reader does not simply lose himself in the playwright's dream. As van den Berg continues, the metatheatrical view only offers part of the story: "If the world resembles a stage, then a stage can indeed represent a world. If everybody plays the actor, then the actor truly does epitomize humanity" (53). The question still remains, however: how is life "theatricalized"? Once both stage and world begin referring to themselves in terms of each other, we are faced with the dangers of holding mirrors up to mirrors, creating an infinite regression of representations that leave us wondering where reality and imitation begin or end.

Shakespeare's forest of Arden is As You Like It (1600) may not be a precise copy of nature, but its disgruntled inhabitants surely speak as much to life as to the stage. When Orlando tells his desperate story to the refugees in the forest, the banished Duke offers the sadly comforting thought that

> we are not all alone unhappy.
> This wide and universal theatre
> Presents more woeful pageants than the scene
> Wherein we play in.   (2.7.136–39)

Like Abraham Fleming's evocation of "an ample and large theatre" in The Dramant of Devotion (1586), a possible source for Shakespeare, the Duke's personal and seemingly ahistorical vision asserts an image that Harold Fisch would call Hellenic, one that "suggests the eternal sameness of things" (Stroup, 17; Fisch, 86). This Hellenic vision is reinforced by Jaques's "All the world's a stage" speech, that depiction of the seven ages of a man, expressed as seven parts performed. Following the Duke's embracing vision of universal theater, Jaques's words chill us with his cynicism and dreadful accuracy. To make the world a stage where "all the men and women [are] merely players" reduces life to a series of pathetic personal histories, each presented in many parts, but each with the same ending, the character "sans every thing." This speech is the cousin of Macbeth's last rational assessment of experience, in which he shrinks life to a "poor player / That struts and frets his hour upon the stage / And then is heard no more" (5.5.24–26). Thus while Jaques may give the most succinct English for what Damon tells us that "Pithagoras said," the world he describes bears little resemblance to the universal theater of social responsibility that Shakespeare's Duke and Edwards's Damon implicitly affirm. In the exchange between the expansive Duke and the reductive Jaques, Shakespeare shows us that to say "All the world's a stage" means nothing without further context.

In some of the comedies, several of the histories, and the tragedies, characters who are melancholy or more darkly designing than, say, a Sir Toby Belch envision theater extended beyond the momentary comedy of mistaken identity. For the melancholy character, as Robert Burton later maintains, the persistence of theatricality becomes a reason to view the world with gloom. Jaques, we presume, maintains his dour perspective even though the masquerading lovers are united and the banished Duke restored. Another melancholiac, Antonio in *The Merchant of Venice* (1596), begins the play trapped by his metaphor:

> I hold the world but as the world, Gratiano,
> A stage where every man must play a part,
> And mine a sad one.   (1.1.76–78)

Stripped of its theological context, the orthodox or conservative reading of the theatrum mundi figure reveals itself to be a restrictive, nearly tyrannical world view, especially for those discontent with the parts they play. Even with God restored, this Stoic theater has limits. Because the melancholy personality prefers retreat to rebellion, he is no threat to the social order; but implied here is a question about the nature of theatrum mundi. Shakespeare's theater may be the Globe, but the globe he sees may not be the stage envisioned by his melancholy characters.

If his plays are taken as a whole, it should be obvious that Shakespeare does not entirely support the static vision of Jaques or Antonio. To do so, he would have to deny the energizing principle of the comedies—disorder—and its intimate connection to theater. Comedy in Shakespeare often emerges from the clash of rival theaters. On the one hand are those who maintain one is one's role; on the other are those few who take advantage of that belief by playing something other than what they are presumed to be. This temporary, dynamic theater has its risks, of course, but in the comedies the suffering is usually limited, as when the Puritan Malvolio in *Twelfth Night* (1601), caught in the manic pranks of Sir Toby and Feste, begins to see himself as Olivia's lover, not her servant, and plays the fool to the "whole pack" of mocking clowns.

More disturbingly, some characters push theater beyond the desire for merriment or love to that for power or revenge or some personal indulgence that endangers the society at large. The usurper king in *Richard III* (1593) turns the kingdom into a stage upon which he acts the many roles that will gain him the crown. For Richard, the secret to good theater is to act what one is most not, "seem a saint when most I play the devil" (1.3.338). Both Richard and his cohort Buckingham immerse themselves in play. After the death of his brother, King Edward IV, Richard as the Lord Protector must name a coronation date for his nephew. By being late to a council, Richard nearly lets Hastings speak for him. Buckingham chides,

> Had not you come upon your cue, my lord,
> William, Lord Hastings had pronounc'd your part,—
> I mean, your voice,—for crowning of the King.   (3.4.27–29)

Later, however, Richard anticipates Hamlet by giving his own instructions to his player, Buckingham, who assures Richard that he can "counterfeit the deep tragedian" (3.5.5) or "play the orator" (3.5.95). In advising Richard to be coy about accepting the offer of the crown, Buckingham himself urges the murderer to "Play the maid's part; still answer nay and take it" (3.7.51). By the same token, Richard's longtime antagonist, Margaret, knows a rat and a piece of theater too. The martyrs made by Richard—Hastings, Rivers, Vaughan, and Grey— she calls "the beholders of this frantic play" (4.4.68); Elizabeth, Edward's widow, she sees as nothing more than a "poor shadow, painted queen. . . . A queen in jest, only to fill the scene" (4.4.83, 91).

For all its vitality, Richard's personal theater of mask and murder tyrannizes by its idiosyncrasy; he can advance only at the expense of those who more universally accept something like the orthodox view of the theater of the world. When Richmond kills the crookbacked king, he destroys the chief actor of the realm, at once eliminating the principle of disorder and, as Richard's successor, restoring union, "smooth-fac'd Peace, . . . smiling Plenty and fair prosperous days!" (5.5.33–34).

In a more subtle play with a related theme, *Richard II* (1595), Richard, though king by rightful succession, falls in love with the role of majesty, enjoying the crown itself as well as its prerogatives. He parades his kingship as the splendor of costume and an eagle's eye; by pressing beyond the limits of simply being king to embrace rhetorical excess, he defies the role as given and lives instead for the pleasures of the kingly conceit. "King Richard doth himself appear / As doth the blushing discontented sun," observes Bolingbroke before their confrontation (3.2.62–63).

Richard pays the price for his discontent. What looks to the Duke of York as "so fair a show" on the castle walls is reduced, when Richard is deposed, to the dusty indignity of the second-rate player. The Duke of York tells his wife how Richard rode with Bolingbroke into London:

> As in a theatre, the eyes of men,
> After a well-grac'd actor leaves the stage,
> Are idly bent on him that enters next,
> Thinking his prattle to be tedious;
> Even so, or with much more contempt, men's eyes
> Did scowl on gentle Richard.   (5.2.23–28)

Left to himself in Pomfret Castle, Richard continues to see his place in the world in theatrical terms that resemble those of Jaques:

> Thus play I in one person many people,
> And more contented. Sometimes as I a king;
> Then treasons make me wish myself a beggar;
> And so I am.   (5.5.31–34)

But for Richard the roles are fluid, not fixed in the eternal sameness of the seven ages of a man. Richard must be deposed because his playing at king and his obsession with the actorly qualities of his national self threaten the integrity of England; his downfall, then, ends the disordering theater of state and restores some measure of harmony to the kingdom. At the same time, his personal theater, the shifting inwardly between beggar and king, makes him a dynamic figure, one unwilling to accept the death plotted for him by Sir Pierce of Exton. He dies fighting and so finishes the action of the play with a flourish. Boling-broke, the antitheatrical successor king, gains from his triumph a disordered conscience and the prospect of a troubled reign. (On role-playing motifs in Shakespeare generally, see Van Laan.)

Though Bolingbroke eschews the theatrics that mark Richard's style, the Duke of York's simile leaves the impression that the usurper is the "well-grac'd actor," not the deposed monarch (Mack, 194–95). On the one hand, Bolingbroke, later Henry IV, conducts his affairs for the good of the state in full view of others; as such he has value to the state because he has replaced a destabilizing, theatrical monarch with one who performs with consistency the role of king. On the other hand, because he has violently displaced a ruling head of state without having the purity of motive that a Richmond does in killing Richard III, he has some personal sufferings to bear. In Shakespeare, kings rise and fall according to their ability to separate private theatrics from the public performance of kingship.

Though Shakespeare becomes one of the most widely read of British authors in the colonies, the doctrine of kingship that the playwright proposes does not translate readily into American terms. In England, the monarch traditionally *is* the nation, but he or she does not play in the royal person all parts. Rather, the monarch, though standing for all, ideally plays only one role in the performance of state: the person with a crown whose individual conduct declares how the rest of the state shall be. Richard II, by shifting roles, violates an implicit compact; one can sympathize with the lowly but cannot be one of them. In America, many of those who have sought to represent the nation are also writers; as such, the representative selves they project, while often expressed in theatrical terms, take on a different function from that of monarch. Captain John Smith has, as governor of Virginia, real political power; but as the self in his histories who best represents the qualities one needs for running a colony, Smith takes into his book-being the others as well—soldiers, layabouts, savage warriors and kings, even a princess. Cotton Mather, too, though he has with his father Increase some political influence, turns his often mannered struggle for the right to claim New England as himself into a book-being that absorbs all of New England's worthics— and witches also, as in the *Magnalia Christi Americana*. John Adams, great reader of Shakespeare and architect of a representative democracy (and a man accused of harboring monarchist sympathies), uses the power of both politics and pen to represent the nation in his own ambitions—as elected delegate to governing assemblies, as president, and, through the book-being of his letters, as fervid rewriter of his country's history. And in the republican era, the politically powerless poet Walt Whitman unites in the book-being of "myself" an entire nation, adopting roles as various as the people—for in a democracy, it is good to be many.

In Whitman, the process of American divergence from the Shakespearean theater of monarchy is most fully manifest. A democratic national self differs profoundly from a royal one by celebrating multiplicity and inclusiveness, therefore declaring its health to be marked by heterogeneity. A monarch by contrast ideally dissolves differences in favor of the homogeneous self and removes him or herself from an identification with the people in their separateness. In the world of Whitman's poetry, national health depends on the ability of each individual to see in the self the distinctive identity of all others; in the world of Shakespeare's plays, the country restores its health by replacing a player king with a ruler willing to conform to a single role based on the political principles of hierarchy, balance, and order.

In both the comedies and the histories, the rituals of state or society replace the temporary plays that upset order; whether it is an impending marriage or coronation, some universally recognized pageant succeeds the more intimate or perverse theatricals of transformed lovers and player kings. Depending on the situation, disorder may be necessary for order to triumph, as in *The Tempest* (1611); or, with affairs of state, disorder may undermine and sometimes nearly destroy the meaning that belonging to a polity has for individuals, as in *Richard III*. In Shakespeare's tragedies, however, the strained relationship between state and theater receives its most compelling treatment.

Ritual and ceremonial thinking dominate the Rome of *Julius Caesar* (1599); everyone, it seems, remains conscious of the symbolic nature of action. When the conspirators prepare to commit their disordering crime, they know that they must act well so as not to give away their plans. Brutus tells his associates,

> Good gentlemen, look fresh and merrily.
> Let not our looks put on our purposes,
> But bear it as our Roman actors do,
> With untir'd spirits and formal constancy.   (2.1.224–27)

To "counterfeit the deep tragedian" means in *Richard III* to steep oneself in hypocrisy; here, to play the Roman actor puts the conspirators onto a more public stage, as if to say the high political moment must take a theatrical form. Yet they must choose their moment carefully, picking their way among the dreams, auguries, and ceremonies that complicate the clash between republican principle and imperial authority.

Characters measure their success by their abilities to seize upon a prophecy or a ritual and play it for their purposes. After Caesar has been assassinated, Brutus urges a ritual washing of hands "in Caesar's blood / Up to the elbows" (3.1.106–7). Cassius follows by developing the theatrical significance of the act, in the language of providence:

> Stoop, then, and wash. How many ages hence
> Shall this our lofty scene be acted over
> In states unborn and accents yet unknown!   (3.1.111–13)

Shakespeare rarely allows such a coup de théâtre to last long. Things turn badly for the conspirators when they run afoul of a more subtle actor, Marc Antony, whose play of humility before the Roman people and manipulation of audience response assures, in the context of the drama, the defeat of Brutus and the restoration of imperial government. Even so, Brutus remains true to his own sense of theater. His ritual suicide, in grudging imitation of the Stoic hero Cato, earns for him the accolades of his theatrical rival, Antony: "This was the noblest Roman of them all" (5.5.68).

Though Brutus recognizes a metaphoric stage, it is an extratheatrical one; he fails to triumph over his enemies partly because the Stoic theater on which he acts can demand his death without guaranteeing his *personal* success. Antony, on the other hand, because he sees the

world in intratheatrical terms, recognizes that any regicide who desta-
bilizes rather than restabilizes the state must be punished in order to
preserve the dramatic principle of harmony. When the American
political conspirators of the 1760s and 1770s self-consciously re-create
their own version of the Roman republican struggle, they must be able
to override the internal requirements of British drama with an extratheatrical drama that asserts the dynamic power of history against the
short-term need for restoration of a preexisting political harmony.

No play of Shakespeare's has had its theatricality probed as much as
Hamlet (1601). For the critics, the Prince is actor, director, spectator,
and playwright and the Denmark he inhabits is a theater of plays
within plays. As Alvin Kernan suggests, "So totally does reality take on
the form of theater in *Hamlet* that the world itself becomes the outside
walls of a theater, 'this goodly frame the earth'—'frame' being the
technical term for the outer structure of the theater—and the heavens
themselves are finally no more real than the painted underside of the
cover of 'shadow' extending out over the stage, 'this majestical roof
fretted with golden fire'" (103; see also Forker). The very intricacy of
theatrical images and themes in *Hamlet* reveals that when theater as a
metaphor is contained within an actable play, it both gains dimensions—theater as self-reflexive—and loses them. The degree to which
one can view the world as a stage is limited, ironically, by one's
familiarity with the theater itself. Those who write from within the
theater understand that the stage is a world, and so, if they transpose
the formula and see the world as stage, they may find that world to be
contained within the circumscribed arena of theatrical performance.
Those who only have in mind an ideal stage, however, can project
upon the world more expansive ideologies than dramatic criticism
alone can contain. Reading Shakespeare may have made eighteenth-
century Americans more theatrically minded, but it is likely that the
theater those Americans imagined was as much, or more, a political
stage as it was a dramatic playhouse. Therefore, to read *Hamlet*
outside the internal rhetoric of the theater (as many colonial Americans did) is to see that this play, too, like the other plays discussed
above, posits a world outside the "frame" that is not distorted by the
regressive illusion upon illusion that the figurative mirrors of Elsinore
seem to reflect. While the play may make its subject a practitioner of

metatheater, as Lionel Abel holds, *Hamlet* nevertheless addresses the question of theater and state by converting private drama into public spectacle, that which is "amiss" into "the rites of war" (5.2.413, 410). There is more to play than the play within (see Nelson).

The dying Hamlet asks Horatio to convey his private story. Specifically, Horatio must tell it to Fortinbras, the Norwegian whom Hamlet has chosen as successor in a telling line: "He has my dying voice." When Fortinbras arrives, simultaneously with the English ambassador whose job it is to announce the deaths of Rosencrantz and Guildenstern, Horatio seizes the moment and redirects the bloody revenge tragedy into a suitable spectacle for an international audience:

> But since, so jump upon this bloody question,
> You from the Polack wars, and you from England,
> Are here arriv'd, give order that these bodies
> High on a stage be placed to the view;
> And let me speak to th' yet unknowing world
> How these things came about.   (5.2.386–91)

Though "stage" here means platform, we surely cannot help but see that another stage is also referred to; indeed, Horatio has dramatic matter to relate, with the bodies in view, taking upon himself to speak in Hamlet's voice (5.2.403). Fortinbras as well knows the value of ritual theater. He orders Hamlet borne "to the stage" where "The soldier's music and the rites of war / Speak loudly for him" (5.2.410–11). Whatever we might learn from the personal drama of Hamlet and the royal family, the responsible ruler must subordinate such tales to the larger needs of the state. Fortinbras appropriately orders that the disorder in the hall be cleaned up, to have its anomalous battlefield appearance removed, and that Hamlet's "passage" to death be marked by ceremonial shooting. Because Hamlet has asserted the primacy of public action over a private drama of conscience, Horatio and Fortinbras ensure that his "noble heart" will be celebrated by those who remain.

"Used in a multitude of ways," Anne Righter tells us, "the play metaphor was for Elizabethans an inescapable expression, a means for fixing the essential quality of the age" (84). Yet Shakespeare's plays may also be taken as a caution against metaphoric theater, if that metaphor is spoken from within a stage-world of disguise, deceit, and privacy. The theatrical imagination poses counterglobes to that which we inhabit. Shakespeare's most dangerous characters—Iago, Macbeth, Richard III, even Hamlet—re-create the world in their own dramaturgical images. Inevitably, however, the need for stability in a state overwhelms and defeats theatrical characters, no matter how just or noble their cause, if their theatricality threatens to turn the world upside down.

Though more baldly put than anything like it in Shakespeare, Francis Bacon's warning in *The Advancement of Learning* against falling under the sway of poetry seems to be the lesson of at least some of the plays: "It is not good to stay too long in the theatre" (247). Bacon elsewhere (*The New Organon*) accuses the error-filled philosophers of "received systems" of passing on "Idols of the Theatre," that is, "so many stage-plays, representing worlds of their own creation after an unreal and scenic fashion" (471; see also van den Berg, 58, 149). Although Bacon uses theater to express the idea that things which cannot be verified empirically cannot be asserted as true, one can see another warning in his words. If one stays "too long in the theatre," one faces endless mirrors of theatricality, as in *Hamlet*, for example, that dissolve the world outside the stage; if one remains outside the theater, or embraces an ideology that limits the place of the playhouse in culture, one may save the reality of the larger world but at the same time risk being labeled a theatrically illiterate fool. For the dynamic characters in Shakespeare's histories and tragedies, to liken the world to a stage may have its value in the short term as a means to some private end, but as a replacement for the fundamental truth of history, private and therefore unverifiable theater cannot be sustained in the public realm—unless it is converted to ritual—without presenting a danger to the social order.

BURTON

Theaters of Life and Retreat

Among Shakespeare's plays, there appear to be two different versions of theatrum mundi applicable to the public sphere: a static rendition of the world as stage where the course of life is seen as so many acts or roles and a dynamic expression in which some part of the world at some moment becomes a stage for only as long as it takes the play of state to work itself out. Shakespeare uses other forms of the theatrical topos as well; in the late comedies, especially *The Winter's Tale* (1610) and *The Tempest*, he unites dream and theater in what Frank Warnke suggests is a baroque theme of insubstantiality, the notion shared by such European writers as Calderón that life is a dream (Warnke, 88–89). But for those writers who continue to speak of the world as a public realm, not simply the fantastic emanation of the subconscious, theater in the post-Elizabethan era becomes both dynamic and all-pervasive, a figure for the worldliness as well as the melancholy and world-weariness of the age.

On the one hand, theater metaphor serves to express a *contemptus mundi* that appears in the general religious rhetoric of the Jacobean and Caroline periods. As John Donne remarks in "The Second Anniversarie of the Progres of the Soule" (1612), "What fragmentary rubbidge this world is" (*Poetry and Prose*, line 82). In such a world, one can hardly account too highly the value of performance for its own sake. Of the late Elizabeth Drury, whose death occasioned Donne's *Anniversarie* poems, the poet would have us think well because she, like the soul, kept earthly life in its place:

> Shee, to whom all this world was but a stage,
> Where all sat harkning how her youthful age
> Should be emploid, because in all, shee did,
> Some Figure of the Golden times, was hid.   (lines 67–70)

For the person facing death, pleasure comes when the drama is over. Dying may be, as in Holy Sonnet VI, "my playes last scene," but death itself brings the comfort of escaping "the world, the flesh, the devill" (*Poetry and Prose*, line 1).

On the other hand, John Donne the divine recognizes another component to the world rendered as theater: it can also be a goad to action. However much one may diminish the value of the world, one may still see life as a kind of show, an entertainment whose purport must be carefully observed and in whose acts we all must share. For Donne, the world has been shaped theatrically by the Creator in order that humankind may have something good to do: "Hath God made this World his Theatre, *ut exhibeatur ludis deorum*, that man may represent God in his conversation; and wilt thou play no part? But think that thou wast made to pass thy time merrily, and to be the only spectator upon this Theatre? Is the world a great and harmonious Organ, where all parts are play'd, and all play parts; and must thou only sit idle and hear it?" (*Sermons*, no. 3, 1:207; see Stroup, 18). In Donne's work the tensions between private and public experience have as their common field the figurative theater. For the individual soul, the stage is populated by the flesh and the devil, best exited quickly in one's last scene; but the person in the world, and of it, must play a part in order to complement the harmoniousness of creation and view the self as a stage where one might see God. In a later sermon, Donne elaborately and subtly develops the theatrum mundi trope to distinguish between ways of apprehending God. Publicly, we see what others do insofar as we are human animals: "For our sight of God, our Theatre, the place where we sit and see him, is the whole world, the whole house and frame of nature, and our *medium*, our *glasse*, is the Book of Creatures, and our light, by which we see him, is the light of Naturall Reason" (*Sermons*, no. 9, 8:220). Privately, a believer must turn to the church and the "Medium of Ordinances" to find the "light of Faith" (8:228); but unlike the Puritans, Donne celebrates both a carnal world theater *and* the church, natural reason *and* faith as complementary. In the end, it is love of self, in the sense of "seeing God in the Theatre of the World" combined with "knowing God in the Academy of the Church," that leads one "to know God himself, in himself, and by himself, as he is all in all" (8:236; see Schleiner, 146–49, and Warnke, 68).

Thomas Browne maintains the same kind of private-public dichotomy in his figures as Donne uses. The meditative writer of *Religio Medici*, who, in his short life, has seen pass many monarchs and popes, knows that death need not be feared: "I perceive I doe Anticipate the vices of age, the world to mee is but a dreame, or mockshow, and wee all therein but Pantalones and Anticks to my severer contemplations" ([1.41] 52). Yet no matter how contemptuous one might be of life as a "mockshow," there is a larger production that inevitably engages us, the show of last things and the meting out of divine justice: "This is that one day, that shall include and comprehend all that went before it, wherein, as in the last scene, all the Actors must enter to compleate and make up the Catastrophe of this great peece" ([1.47] 57). Like the nonconformist providentialists, Browne recognizes that theatrical satisfaction is a potent analogy to the just conclusion of God's creation.

Perhaps it is one of the great attributes of English Renaissance theater that the stage can be used for the enactment of the principles of justice. With religious themes all but eliminated from English drama after the mid-sixteenth century, writers show the power of universal catastrophe microcosmically. In the Jacobean period, this catastrophic justice takes the form of the revenge tragedy or theater of blood. Whereas the Shakespeare of *Hamlet* never fully allows us to forfeit a belief that the theatricality of Elsinore will be brought under control, a dramatist like John Webster turns contempt for the world and its antic shows into fear. As the Duchess of Malfi contemplates suicide, she recognizes that self-murder is the one action she can take to seize control of events:

> Who must dispatch me?
> I account this world a tedious theatre,
> For I do play a part in 't 'gainst my will.
> (*Duchess of Malfi*, 4.1.79–81)

But the Duchess has no more control over events or her life than anyone else. Even the chief murderer himself recognizes the ultimate theatricality of actions and the impossibility of identifying a guiding hand. After Bosola accidentally kills Antonio, the father of the Duchess's children, he excuses the death as having occurred

> In a mist.
> I know not how: such a mistake as I
> Have often seen in a play.   (5.5.96–98)

For Bosola, the world is "gloomy," a "shadow, or deep pit of darkness" (5.5.102–3). Though he functions as an agent of doom, Bosola implies that the real director of events—if there is one—cannot be known. On Webster's stage the justice seems right, but it is the more terrifying for occurring without the comfort of one's being sure that Fortune, Fate, or Providence has been the ordering force.

No one in the English baroque period gives better voice to the pervasiveness of theater in the world—and thus, perhaps, of neurosis—than does Robert Burton in *The Anatomy of Melancholy* (6th edition, 1641). His narrator is Democritus Junior, an "antic or personate actor" who "so insolently intrudes upon this common theatre to the world's view" (15). Not only is Democritus the laughing one of a pair of philosophers who in the baroque represent the poles of possible world views (Heraclitus is the tearful other), but he is also one of the reputed sources for theater metaphor itself. Like the other meditative writers of the seventeenth century, Burton's narrator styles himself as one withdrawn from the follies of ordinary life, "as Democritus in his garden . . . *ipse mihi theatrum*" (18). The quality of being a sufficient theater to himself, of being unbeholden to the world for entertainment, makes this second Democritus the ideal observer, "a mere spectator of other men's fortunes and adventures, and how they act their parts, which methinks are diversely presented unto me, as from a common theatre or scene" (18). Nevertheless, in a world where any public utterance occurs as on a stage, the observer must take the abuse that being an actor demands: "I have . . . put myself upon the stage; I must abide the censure, I may not escape it" (26–27).

For the first Democritus, to be judged mad by a mad world was no reproach; and for Burton, it is a mad, melancholy world we inhabit. Burton, like other writers of his time, seems to have been strongly influenced by John of Salisbury and his chapter in the *Policraticus*, "The Comedy or Tragedy of This World" (see Warnke and Curtius). John's amended quotation from Petronius, *"Totus mundus agit histrionem,"* was, of course, put above the entrance to the Globe Theatre when it was built in 1599, a fit complement to Shakespeare's "All the world's a stage." Burton has other purposes, however, more in accord with *Praise of Folly* than *As You Like It:* "For now, as Sarisburiensis said in his time, *totus mundus histrionem agit*, the whole world plays the fool; we have a new theatre, a new scene, a new Comedy of Errors, a new company of personate actors" (52). This is no temporary theater, however new the Comedy of Errors might be; over history, after all, our vices remain the same: "We keep our madness still, play the fools still, *nec dum finitus Orestes* [and the play is not yet finished]" (53).

Such a theater destroys public life because "everyone is for himself, his private ends" (64). What was praiseworthy for Pico della Miran-dola, the human ability to change, represents for Burton one of the major dangers to individual and political health. Democritus Junior asks, "What's the world itself? A vast chaos, a confusion of man-ners, . . . the theatre of hypocrisy" (64). Whereas human variability occasions Hamlet's "What a piece of work is man!" speech, it attracts the scorn of the physician from Burton's persona. A reader of T. S. Eliot's "The Love Song of J. Alfred Prufrock" would find a kindred spirit in a voice that decries the affectation of humanity; a person feels the need to change "like a chameleon, or as Proteus, . . . to act twenty parts and persons at once for his advantage, to temporize and vary like Mercury the planet, good with good, bad with bad; having a several face, garb, and character for everyone he meets" (65). Burton envisions a mad masquerade of constantly changing actors and cos-tumes, a swirling plenitude of "whifflers, Cuman asses, maskers, mummers, painted puppets, outsides, fantastic shadows, gulls, mon-sters, giddy-heads, butterflies" (52). Like his Puritan counterparts, Burton recognizes that he lives in a diseased society where "men like stage-players act variety of parts, give good precepts to others [to] soar aloft, whilst they themselves grovel on the ground" (66).

Though Burton does not directly attack the stage, he seems to say that the theatricality of life calls into question all assumptions. He wonders rhetorically how Democritus would "have been affected to see" the disordering reversals of contemporary society, a list of which it takes Burton three pages to complete. All the problems enumerated by Democritus Junior—"children rule; old men go to school; women wear the breeches"—can be summarized "in a word, the world turned upside downward! O viveret Democritus!" (68). For Burton, one re-verses the reversals, rights the topsy-turvy world, by curing the indi-vidual's melancholia. Like Donne, Browne, and other seventeenth-century meditative writers, Burton's Democritus looks to the inner self for correction and not to the energy that emanates from his "common theatre" of whifflers, maskers, and cranks.

Coincidental with Burton's observations, an uncommon theater holds sway at Whitehall—the courtly masques (see Strong, 213–43). As Stephen Orgel describes the productions of the Jacobean and Caroline regimes, these masques, written by people like Ben Jonson and Thomas Carew and designed by the incomparable Inigo Jones, seek to preserve an "illusion of power" to show to their select audience that theater and politics are one. But if the masques allegorize the king as a beneficent authoritarian, divinely ordained to rule, the play of seventeenth-century power comes to an end theatrically too. Andrew Marvell, no lover of royal prerogative, looks at the execution of Charles I as a piece of public theater, as uncommon in its way as the court masque was from the common theater of ordinary life:

> thence the *Royal Actor* born
> The *Tragick Scaffold* might adorn,
>   While round the armed Bands
>   Did clap their bloody hands.
> *He* nothing common did, or mean
> Upon the memorable Scene.
> ("An *Horatian* Ode," lines 53–58)

Despite the fact that, as Orgel remarks, "the absolute rule of the Stuart monarchy was revealed as a royal charade, a theatrical illusion" (89), what transpires historically during the years of the Commonwealth is a letting loose of a swarm of sectaries, many of whom are millenarian and militant; in other words, it is the creation in England of a world turned upside down (see Hill).

No wonder that writers like Burton look inward: without resorting to raw power, an individual could little hope to turn the chaos of an overturned order into a graspable political reality. More than one privileged person in the political arena might have concurred with the speaker in Marvell's translation, "The Second Chorus from *Seneca's* Tragedy, *Thyestes*":

> All I seek is to lye still.
>
> . . . .
> In calme Leisure let me rest;
> And far from the publick Stage
> Pass away my silent Age.   (lines 3, 5–7)

Yet as Burton holds, even Democritus in his garden is an actor. Escape from the "publick Stage" may itself be an illusion. The question then becomes whether one can be a "sufficient theater" unto oneself. The writings from early America suggest another tactic. If English baroque writers counsel escape from a world so thoroughly theatricalized that philosophers fear for their mental health, then some American authors by their personal example—Captain John Smith and Cotton Mather in particular—convert private experience into public history and their own distrust of the theater into a newly imaged figural stage, fully "publick" and for all the world to see.

CHAPTER THREE

American Origins II:
A Theater against Theaters

*L*iterate English colonists to the New World share in a literary, intellectual, and cultural tradition that finds theatrical metaphor to be a readily available figure for expressing the place of humankind in the universe. Sixteenth- and seventeenth-century readers, whatever their attitudes toward the theater itself, could be exposed to the theatrum mundi trope in a variety of ways. Some of that diversity has been illustrated in the previous chapter.

For the Puritans, however, there is another tradition that informs early American discourse, namely, the rhetoric of English nonconformism. Whether in form or as figure of speech, drama and theater shape not only the language but the world view of Protestants in general, including strict Calvinists. At one level, proto- and early Protestant writers emphasize that the spiritual life requires the kind of confrontation and dialogue reminiscent of staged drama. At another level, some Protestant writers imagine the Apocalypse as a grandly produced theatrical event. Between the two is an ongoing theater of God's providential displays, full of reproofs and wonders, which give to each generation of believers a vision of what the final triumph will be. One form of expression, then, renders personal experience as a private "drama of salvation" in the rhetoric of the public debate. Another imagines global experience as a grand show, the spectacle of last things. A third form of expression depicts God's ongoing relationship with a particular people as a multitude of shows and exhibitions, designed to influence the social and political life of a nation.

THORPE
The Agon of Debate

For early nonconformists, a dramatic conflict between the true Christian and his earthly antagonists mirrors the struggle for the soul. Ritchie Kendall, in his study of English nonconformist writing, *The Drama of Dissent*, suggests that "the debate is the natural form of Lollard discourse and of all subsequent nonconformist writing as well" (44–45; see also Hudson, 220–23). In the vision of spiritual warfare shared by the followers of John Wyclif and other ancestors of English Puritanism, the antagonism with the representatives of a corrupt Church produces a ready-made dramatic mode, found in various forms but most certainly in the prelatical examinations of heretics. As Kendall describes it, such a work as the *Examinacion* of Master William Thorpe, an autobiographical account of an appearance by the Wycliffite Thorpe before Archbishop Arundel in August 1407, is a piece of "displaced drama," a writing that uses dramatic elements without itself being overtly a play (58). Most of Thorpe's text takes dialogue form, being written in alternating sections that begin with "And the Archbishop said to me," followed by "And I said to the Archbishop." The difference between the combatants suggests a morality play; the Archbishop, hot-tempered, vicious, and threatening, seems almost comically different, in the manner of a Vice character, from the cool, deliberate Thorpe. Thus, in Kendall's assessment, the literal trial provides a form of discourse in which the writer can make manifest the figurative trial the true Christian must undergo in order to avoid the traps of this world.

Ironically, the discourse itself presents a potential trap. Were Lollard debate literature ever to become plays, it would run the risk of seducing its audience into a misplaced vision, where attention is drawn not to Christ or God but to the actor in his stead (Kendall, 54, 62). Nonconformists from the days of Wyclif forward distinguish themselves from their fellow Christians by dividing true religion from false at the juncture of Word and image. Those forms of worship that attract one's attention by sight or sound only confuse or distort the message of God's words by turning the parishioner's contemplative faculty away from the text (Barish, 66–79). Of the theater of the time,

fourteenth- and fifteenth-century nonconformists might have sub-
scribed to the condemnation of miracle plays in A *Tretise of Miraclis
Pleyinge*; the action in those plays, often humorous at the wrong
places, does not prepare one properly to hear the Word in its full
solemnity. Even those stage techniques that elicit great crying at
Christ's passion are condemned in the *Tretise* because of biblical
injunctions not to be swept away by grief (Hudson, *Selections*, 102).
Thus while the sensual image works counter to the text, one must not
at the same time divorce word from action. Another criticism of
miracle plays centers on the distinction between "signs" and "deeds";
plays are signs, not deeds, only images of, say, love, not true love; stage
representations are nothing but "gynnys," tricks of the devil (Hudson,
Selections, 100–101).

In Thorpe's text, the writer puts himself into debate in order to
show the superior reason of his position against that of the intemperate
Archbishop. Thorpe must remain true to the Word without resorting
to empty speechifying. Once his test becomes theater, he loses; but if,
as Kendall argues, the inherent drama in the confrontation with
Arundel is "displaced," that is, deflected or muted, then Thorpe can
draw attention to his position as a kind of martyr without taking away
the glory that is genuinely Christ's. In the agon of prelatical examinations or similar debates, Thorpe and other nonconformist writers tread
a narrow path between drama as an implied but necessarily suppressed
mode of discourse and drama as a dangerously alluring stage play. As
with the later authors of Puritan jeremiad, the early nonconformist
writers defer the wholeness of artistic satisfaction to somewhere beyond the purview of either reader or writer in order not to seem to force
God into following a humanly conceived script.

FOXE

Apocalyptic Comedy

Nevertheless, for a period in the mid-sixteenth century, there was a
nonconformist theater in England that required stage actors to play in
allegorical or biblical dramas. John Bale, best known for his historical
drama *King Johan* (1534–61), is also an author of religious plays that
attack church corruptions. In A *Comedy Concerning Three Laws of*

Nature, Moses, and Christ (1538), Bale marks out the lines drawn between a coarse theater of indulgence—directed by the Vice Infidelity and peopled by such Catholic arch-buffoons as Idolatry, Hypocrisy, Sodomy, and Ambition, who appear in a show of dialect-speaking, clerically costumed obfuscators of God's truth—and the more arid, asensory drama played by Christian Faith. For the nonconformist, the "drama of salvation" is an agon, a struggle against internal and external enemies that is at once comic and flat, a conflict whose best ending is the hope of victory (see Kendall, 90–131). For there cannot be countenanced the illusion that triumph is either sensory or temporal. Otherwise, Faith would be playing by the same script as the world, the flesh, and the devil. Even though the community of Christians knows for certain that there will occur a global triumph over evil, the individual can never be sure of a personal triumph over sin. In a sense, Bale's drama, like medieval morality plays, expresses the struggle for a soul in a peculiar and ultimately conservative language.

Kendall's treatment of Thorpe, Bale, and other nonconformist writers is highly suggestive and has influenced my thinking about this period; however, he does not completely address one important question: What does it mean to say that Wycliffite or early Protestant writers exploit the tension between drama as form and drama as metaphor, between their antagonism to the stage and their use of theatrical tropes? It is one thing to be able to identify the debate as a dramalike discourse; it is quite another to show that the writer's adoption of a strategy is deliberate or arises out of something more conscious than confusion. Obviously, showing intentionality is not always necessary; but in the case of Renaissance-era authors, the matter of incorporating drama into discourse can neither be explained as accidental nor simply assumed because the sixteenth-century is a "theatrical age." Protestant writers who use theatrical figures must get something from them, displaced drama or no. For Kendall, dramatic discourse has the purpose of creating "identity in a theater of the soul" (204); but as we can see from another dramatist, John Foxe, more is at stake than the spiritual identity of individual believers.

For while this theater of the particular soul is an important component in the concept of a drama of salvation, it is only one. An internalized theater limits the drama to the individual struggling with himself to achieve mastery over the main antagonist, sin. Another strategy, expanding the vision to the globally triumphant aspect of Christian faith, is made explicit in John Foxe's Latin play, *Christus Triumphans* (1556). Subtitled *Comoedia Apocalyptica*, Foxe's drama would seem to rely heavily on the patristic vision of the Second Coming as a cosmic spectacle, a divine comedy in which vice is routed and the church glorified. By making the Apocalypse a drama (one fully intended to be a stage script, most probably for university actors and audience), Foxe heightens the tension between metaphor and realized theater, a tension that requires some explanation from the author. Theater is only a device, a temporary measure, to help an audience understand ecclesiastical truths. Thus "real" theater itself is only a shadow, a "netting" that signifies another order of reality: "Would that the same Christ Triumphant come to us all, not in the theater but in the clouds" (Foxe, 207). Indeed, the Prologue speaks the nonconforming Protestant's sincerest hope: "Perhaps it will not be long before stage representations will lie neglected; then indeed we will see all with our own eyes, when God sends in actual fact what he now only promises" (Foxe, 229).

That desire for direct experience with the Almighty (quite probably Foxe's own: the future martyrologist was in exile from the Marian persecutions when the play was published) does not prevent the author, however, from writing a play that in the more contentious antitheatrical climate thirty years later would probably not have been written by a true nonconformist. For Foxe, the fact that all the material in his drama is "totally sacred and totally apocalyptic" is enough for the Prologue to command the audience not to be "ashamed" (229). Unlike the distinctly unspectacular, though sometimes humorous, *Examination* of Thorpe, with its minimalist set and restricted action (the Archbishop occasionally wanders to the window or smacks a cupboard), *Christus Triumphans* demands more in effects to be played properly. The ending is imaged as the marriage between Ecclesia and her bridegroom Christ: "*Here from the upper part of the theater, when the curtains open, are shown as if from heaven thrones with books placed upon them. At the same time garments are lowered in which Ecclesia is dressed and prepared for the wedding*" (363). But there is not much more to show. Even this play must stop short of representing final things. The "final catastrophe," that is, the dramatic ending, is the arrival of the Bridegroom: "When that will happen none will say for sure" (371).

In its certainty of the event, but not the time, and in the dramatic nonappearance of its eponymous hero, this sixteenth-century play is a forebear to its modernist rendition in Samuel Beckett's *Waiting for Godot*. It is quite true that there is little comparison to be made on the level of artistic satisfaction. Sixteenth-century Protestant drama shows a greater concern with doctrinal purity than aesthetic control. Still, that Foxe sees comedy where Beckett sees tragedy (or tragicomedy, as he calls his play) illuminates one aspect of nonconformist apocalyptic thought. If Calvinism, with its doctrine of selective salvation, intensifies the desire of the believer for his own comic ending, it also frustrates that desire by withholding knowledge of last things. Foxe's play ends with an admonition and a polite request: "Be warned, be on your guard with prudence, I pray. And do applaud" (371). Though Foxe's play may be over, the drama of which he writes, the apocalyptic comedy, still wends its way toward the conclusion. Whether patient or urgent, Christians can measure the differences among themselves by the degree to which they believe that the postponed performance of the Bridegroom's return will occur in their own time.

CALVIN

Theater of Providence

Between the agon of the individual soul and the spectacle of the Apocalypse lies a medial strategy: the image of the world as a vast, contemporary theater of God's powers, where the public exhibition of providential pleasure plays before the whole of humankind for its adoration and comment. In his recent "portrait" of John Calvin, William J. Bouwsma devotes a chapter to the place of "drama" in that author's writings, leaving little doubt of the importance of dramatic and theatrical tropes in Calvin's work. Like the Puritans who will follow him, Calvin makes distinctions, as Bouwsma notes, between theater expressed as a figure for God's universe and the vice-laden stage of his own time; but the Genevan theologian does not appear to be as rigidly antitheatrical as those in England a century after him who press for the closing of theaters altogether. It is as if he recognizes the utility of a real-life stage for his own metaphoric purposes: "Let this [church] be my theater," he writes Melancthon, "and content with its approval, though the whole world should hiss me, my courage will never fail" (Aug. 23, 1555, quoted in Bouwsma, 178). For Bouwsma, drama pervades Calvin's writing as a way of talking about the self, both about the plot lines of Christian life (pilgrimage or warfare) and about the bifurcation of the individual between an actor before God and a spectator of one's own behavior. Bouwsma remarks further that while Calvin adopts a Platonic line in his *Commentary* on Daniel 3.3–7 by condemning the false persuasions of the actual stage, his approving application of the figure for his perceptions of God's wondrous acts suggests that "he was drawn back to theatricality even by his effort to escape it" (179, 180).

In his *Commentary* on Genesis, Calvin shows the two poles of figural theater for the Protestant: as a metaphor by which to condemn the deceitful acts of the devil and his followers and one by which to glorify creation. As Thomas Hooker will do a century later, Calvin recognizes the etymological connection between the hypocrite and the actor (Sermon no. 105 on Job, cited in Bouwsma, 179), and consequently, the term *mask* appears on several occasions as an expression of the fear that certain people only ape belief: "Such persons truly, by external works, strenuously labour to deserve well at the hands of God; but, retaining a heart inwrapped in deceit, they present to him nothing but a mask; so that, in their laborious and anxious religious worship, there is nothing sincere, nothing but mere pretence" (*Genesis*, 1:197). But like his humanist contemporaries, Calvin does not stop at the expected denunciations of vanity, the "foolish delight" of overmuch sense stimulation, and hypocrisy; rather, he magnifies what God has made by using an enhancing similitude of world and stage. In the introduction to the Genesis commentary, Calvin remarks, "For this is the argument of the Book: After the world had been created, man was placed in it as in a theatre, that he, beholding above him and beneath the wonderful works of God, might reverently adore their Author" (1:64; see Cannon, 218). Though we often associate Calvinism with the diminution of human beings, there is something both moving and beautiful in this theatrical image. He is clearly at home with at least one element of Renaissance humanism: "Man . . . is deservedly called by the ancients, *microcosmos*, 'a world in miniature,'" he says, reflecting the love of correspondence that characterizes the age (*Genesis*, 1:92).

In England, the Puritans would attack the stage on several fronts, but one potent argument centers on the abuse of the Sabbath by those who indulge themselves in amusements and recreations on that holy day, to the peril of their souls. Yet in Calvin, as the letter to Melancthon cited above indicates, one senses an almost desired rivalry between stage and pulpit, as if the latter can somehow be enlarged by comparison to the former. In his commentary on Genesis 2.3, "And God blessed the seventh day," Calvin returns to the expression that characterizes his argument for the whole of Genesis, showing that the original Sabbath itself was the occasion for reverential spectating at the universal stage: "God claims for himself the meditations and employments of men on the seventh day. This is, indeed, the proper business of the whole life, in which men should daily exercise themselves, to consider the infinite goodness, justice, power, and wisdom of God, in this magnificent theatre of heaven and earth" (1:105–6). For the Calvinist Protestant, humans act to fulfill their providentially chosen roles, but not blindly. The wonder of the Sabbath is contemplation of creation, the actions of Providence, and the peculiar relationship of the playwright God to his people. There is no place for beguiling splendor; but the spectacle of the universal commands our awareness, even as we fail finally to understand God's workings. Calvin enjoins believers to consider God's hidden ways as the brilliant plottings of a writer and man of the theater: "Let pious readers carefully exercise themselves in meditation upon it, in order that they may acknowledge those things which, in appearance are fortuitous, to be directed by the hand of God" (*Genesis*, 2:337). Thus biblical history, in which Egyptians or Hebraic kings are brought before readers "as it were, in a theater" or "on the stage," offers to the faithful a playwright God as much concerned with entertaining us by a good show as terrifying us by talk of damnation (commentaries on Exodus and Jeremiah, quoted in Cannon, 220, and Bouwsma, 177).

Among English Puritans, Richard Sibbes gives voice to the light-like glory of God's absolute sovereignty in a similar way. Whereas Calvin expresses God's creation as a spectacle that dumbfounds its viewers into reverence, Sibbes, a writer also popular with American Puritans, expresses the wonder of God's majesty somewhat more ineffably. For human beings, "reason is a beam of God, . . . judgment is a spark of God, nature is but God's candle, it is a light of the same light that grace is of, but inferior. . . . Every creature has a beam of God's glory in it, the whole world is a theater of the glory of God" (*The Excellency of the Gospel above the Law* [1639], quoted in Stoever, 4; see also Solberg, 52, and Sasek, 80). It is this sort of image that suggests how closely Puritanism brushes against the overtly theatrical depictions of God's glory as rendered by such artists of the Catholic baroque as Bernini. At once rejecting orgiastic sensuality, in the picture of God's (Protestant) theater the Calvinist celebrates the grandeur of creation. It is as much a part of Calvin's legacy as the grim doctrine of predestination.

MARTIN MARPRELATE
Playing the Dunce

Calvin seizes the theatrical moment from the stage itself and expands it to include all of biblical and ecclesiastical time; he is content to have actors as occasional whipping boys but sees no essential contradiction in criticizing the institution while employing theatrical tropes in praise of God. Yet it is precisely Calvin's tolerance of the stage— indeed, he seems on more than one occasion to have defended dramatic productions against the bias of more doctrinaire colleagues (Bouwsma, 280–81 n. 14)—that mitigates in his work the revolutionary potential of theater as a political figure. In late sixteenth-century England, however, other forces are at work; with the increasing popularity of the secular stage, nonconformist writers show greater awareness of the figural potential of theater at the same time that they expand their attacks on the stage and players.

This division between figurative and literal understandings of stage is expressed more directly by William Prynne, who is discussed in a later section, but it also appears indirectly in the works of writers whose immediate objects of concern are matters other than the stage itself. In the curious antiepiscopal writings known as the *Marprelate Tracts*, the pseudonymous Martin Marprelate and his offspring imagine a world where bishops and their supporters are so many clowns or rogue actors, not only indulging in an unscriptural sensuality but also playing the fool so often as to be comical. To counter the buffoonery of his enemies, Martin in his first tract of 1588 feels obliged to match the bishops' unintentional tactics with a like, though intended, comedy. The immediate occasion of the first tract, the publication by Dean John Bridges of a long defense of Anglican orthodoxy against Puritan criticism, calls forth this apology from Martin: "To the right puissant and terrible priests . . . 'May it please you' to give me leave to play the dunce [spelled "Duns" in the original] for the nonce, as well as he [Bridges]; otherwise dealing with Master Doctor's book, I cannot keep *decorum personae*" (17). In fact, so far does Martin depart from "*decorum personae*" that even the Puritans whom he defends feel obliged to criticize the indecorousness of Martin's fooling.

Whatever the theatricality of Martin's own approach (as per Kendall, 173–212, who sees Martin as a "master of ceremonies" to the many voices he uses), he clearly senses the tension between stage and church among a corrupt episcopate. In a feigned dialogue with Thomas Cooper, bishop of Winchester, "Reverend Martin" recounts an episode in the life of one "Glibbery of Halstead," a former actor of Vice parts turned priest: "A boy in his church, hearing either the Summer Lord with his May-game, or Robin Hood with his Morris Dance, going by the church—out goes the boy. Good Glibbery, though he were in the pulpit, yet had a mind to his old companions abroad (a company of merry grigs, you must think them to be, as merry as a Vice on a stage), seeing the boy going out, finished his matter presently, with John of London's Amen, saying, 'Ha, ye faith, boy! Are they there? Then, ha' with thee.' And so, came down, and among them he goes" (226–27). The call of the stage seems as indelible in a former actor as the call of the wild in a domesticated beast; and for the Puritans, who assert that we receive a Stoiclike calling from Providence, nothing could be more inimical than a priest-player turned player-priest (another example can be found in Marprelate, 369–70).

Thus one of Martin's "sons," Martin Junior, encourages his "father" to resist the attacks on him and on the presses that print his tracts: "Wherefore, reverend Father, if you be as yet set on your seat, and have escaped out of the danger of gunshot, begin again to play the man" (328). Having played the dunce to mock the bishops, Martin must now counter his counter by being other than a playful boy; as a consequence, all those who criticize the critic are themselves culpable for being mere actors: "Fear none of these beasts, these pursuivants, these *Mar-Martins*, these stage-players, these prelates, these popes, these devils, and all they do" (328).

Ironically, the bishops use the theater to attack Martin; the writer has to confront not only pathetic doggerel (by one "Mar-Martine") but also plays (Pierce, 221). The fate of Martin will be repeated among certain early Americans and, because of that, is worth some attention here. In calling for a new order, Martin faces diminution from a church that allies itself with the mockers of the stage. Martin Junior, in trying to rouse his father to action, attempts to disenfranchise the theater as a vehicle for criticism: "There be that affirm the rimers and stage-players to have clean put you out of countenance, that you dare not again show your face. . . . I do think that aside their tyranny, all the bishops of England are too weak to deal with a scarecrow that hath but the name of reverend Martin written upon it" (328). The real enemies are not the actors themselves; though Martin's Puritan allies will find them convenient targets in the war on the stage, Martin recognizes the power behind the players:

> The stage-players, poor, silly, hunger-starved wretches, they have not so much as an honest calling to live in the commonwealth. And they, poor varlets, are so base-minded, as at the pleasure of the veriest rogue in England, for one poor penny, they will be glad on open stage to play the ignominious fools for an hour or two together. And therefore, poor rogues, they are not so much to be blamed, if, being stage players, that is, plaine rogues (save only for their liveries) they, in the action of dealing against Master Martin, have gotten them many thousand eye-witnesses of their witless and pitiful conceits.   (330)

The writer understands that the stage can promulgate and entertain but that ultimately it is impotent to effect change. In confronting a conservatizing stage, nonconformists must look for another avenue of attack. Martin's satire, while to modern eyes a welcome relief from the dreary religious tracts of the times, cannot last among proponents of a belief in the playless sincerity of the true Christian. Though Martin's perspective on the exploitation of actors is admirable, it ultimately cannot serve the need for a more powerful rhetoric in the battle against the pride of position, wealth, and indulgence among opponents of a new order. By appropriating *play* so openly, Martin faces the prospect of endless mirrors and mar-mirrors of the same thing; revolutionaries must learn a rhetoric that both absorbs the figures of their enemies and shatters the glass through which opponents stare at each other's common need for game *and* earnest.

BEARD

Theater of God's Judgments

More typical of Puritan rhetorical strategy than that of Martin Marprelate is the vision of providential theater in Thomas Beard's often-reprinted book about the downfall of sinful monarchs. In *The Theatre of Gods Judgements* (4th edition, 1648), Beard strikes a frequent nonconformist theme: the greater iniquity of the contemporary world than of times before. Lest his readers be themselves inclined toward wickedness without fear, Beard intends to show to "mens memories" that even the great ones of history do not escape the wrath of God for their crimes: "I purpose to set downe the great and fearefull judgements wherewith God hath alreadie plagued many in this world, especially them of high degree; whose example will serve for a glasse both for these that live now, or shall live hereafter" (6). Beard's God is a master of the spectacular, one whose wonders are terrors and whose stage effects are far more gruesome than the seamiest revenge tragedy. He must, after all, get our attention, and nothing works better than, for example, destroying Anabaptists "by troupes and by thousands" (100). There is, then, a purpose for divine slaughter: "By all which things God doth exhibite and set before our eyes how deere and precious in his sight the pureness of his holie word, and the union of his Church is" (100). In Beard's amphitheatrical vision, God desires by his examples to sway a mass audience to his cause.

But the Great Director, a term used by American playwright Mercy

Otis Warren, can also manage a closer stage with arch cleverness. In his chapter "Of Epicures and Atheists," Beard takes a seeming delight in recording the death of dramatist Christopher Marlowe. God has clearly planned a fitting end for this "scholler . . . Play-maker, and . . . Poet of scurrilitie" (149); he stabs himself in the head, cursing his divine enemy to the last: "It was not only a manifest signe of Gods judgement, but also an horrible and fearefull terror to all that beheld him. But herein did the justice of God most notably appeare, in that he compelled his owne hand which had written those blasphemies to be the instrument to punish him, & that in his braine, which had devised the same" (150). Such scenes in history resemble those dramatic moments of revelation or terror created by Marlowe himself, establishing God, once again, as a rival to human playwrights. By the same token, Beard's portrayal of this "Theatre of his Judgements" (188) removes itself from the tradition of nonconformist theater discussed above. As David Hall points out, Beard's book fits into a larger Puritan literature about prodigies and providences that feeds an audience fully prepared to accept wonders in the world they inhabit ("A World of Wonders"). Neither simply personal nor purely apocalyptic, Beard's metaphoric theater of the macabre shows the providential playwright to be a master entertainer, ultimately far more spectacular in effect than the shows on England's small stages.

Another example of God's deft and self-conscious theatrical art can be seen in the playing of "a tragedie of the death and passion of Christ in shew" (206). A series of grisly accidents, beginning with the fatal wounding of the actor who plays the crucified Christ, concludes the drama "with foure true, not counterfeit deaths," all arranged "by the divine providence of God, who can endure nothing lesse than such prophane and ridiculous handling of so serious & heavenly matters" (206–7). And as Beard describes other true-life catastrophes on stages around England, one gets the image of a supremely jealous God, especially one conscious of contending for audiences on the Sabbath. Beard recounts another episode in Bedfordshire "where the floor of a chamber, wherein a number were gathered together to see a Play on the Sabboth day, fell downe, by means whereof manie were sore hurt, and some killed. Surely, a friendlie warning" (212). Following Tertullian and the patristic tradition, Beard judges plays to "have no other use in the world but to deprave and corrupt good manners, and to open a dore to all uncleanesse" (436).

Such criticism of the theater only makes apparent how potent theater is for the Protestant mind. Where the little theaters of England corrupt and deprave, the larger theaters of politics and the world instruct and warn. The killers of Julius Caesar were "actors in this tragedie," and they all themselves became involved in a further series of "pitifull Tragedies" (268) marking their own downfalls. Likewise, Pontius Pilate, an alleged suicide, "became a notable spectacle of Gods justice" (311). The punishments visited upon the great and powerful, as well as upon the low and mean, all serve to show history as a vast pageant of exempla for Beard's contemporaries. The moral Beard delivers after describing the death of a vile swearer serves for his vision of history as a whole: "It is not therefore without just cause that God hath propounded and laid open in this corrupt age a Theatre of his Judgements, that everie man might be warned thereby" (188). For Beard, political history is religious history. The conflation of the two makes possible a vision of providential theater, one that teaches and terrifies—and paradoxically uses the real-life disasters of Elizabethan theatrical history for its scenes.

For Protestants generally, history reproves persons of all degree, though of course the *de casibus* formula makes the most entertainment from the fall of the mighty. The reader of literature that evokes the image of providential theater understands one lesson as a profoundly conservative appeal to the fixity of the social order, but with disquieting overtones. Non-Puritans might prefer a more personal application of theater metaphor such as that in Joseph Hall's *Meditations and Vows* (1606, 1621). Unlike the nonconformist who asserts God's awful sovereignty, Hall suggests that the theater of the world holds opportunities for individuals to share in the writing of their own plays:

> The World is a Stage: Everie man an Actor; and playes his part here, either in a Comodie or Tragedie. The good man is a Comedian; which (how ever hee begins) ends merrily: but the wicked man Acts a Tragedie; and therefore ever ends in horrour. Thou seest a wicked man vaunt himselfe on this Stage: stay till the last Act, and looke to his end (as David did) and see, whether that bee peace. Thou wouldest make Tragedies, if

thou wouldest have but one Act. . . . The best wicked man cannot be so envied in his first shewes, as he is pitiable in the conclusion.   ([2.30] 71)

For Hall, good and bad are apolitical terms; that is, they carry with them no agenda for anything other than personal reform. Hall implies that no prior act has meaning of itself; plays are written from the conclusion backward. This idea resembles in concept the noncon-formist view, except that, for the latter, the play of life can never be observed in its personal ending. With Hall, one has the comfort that simple conduct determines the nature of the play one is in.

Puritan rhetoric, however, contains within it a different conception of providential reality. The appeal to God's sovereignty may serve, on the one hand, to justify the existing order; but as with Beard, that appeal may be used, on the other hand, to warn those in power that through the agency of Providence they may be removed at any time. Expressed in the terms of theatrum mundi, Providence may an-nounce itself as revolution, speeding up the drama to the here and now and clearing the stage of actors whose time has expired. Though Beard focuses largely on monarchs, he implies through his application of theater metaphor that no one is secure. In an image that anticipates Jonathan Edwards's sermon, *Sinners in the Hands of an Angry God* (1741), Beard directs his reader to the rotten platform of a real stage whose collapse leads to the deaths of the actors thereon. In Edwards's rendition, sinners walk over the rotten flooring above Hell, kept from plummeting to their doom only by the pleasure and the hand of God. In either formulation, the insecurity posited by Calvinist doctrine carries with it revolutionary implications. If we cannot know the mind of God, we cannot logically assert that any *political* order has any guarantee of longevity beyond God's desire to keep it—that is, keep its rulers—from plunging into the pit. At the same time, God's theater is enhanced by purging the land of mere players and their stages.

PRYNNE

Histrio-Mastix

As the large body of literature on the subject indicates, the Puritan attacks on the stage spring from a variety of causes. I do not intend to replay the English battle over theater here, but I do wish to look at the close rhetorical relationship between the condemnations of the theater and theater itself. Clearly, the Elizabethan theater held a special allure for Puritans, one that provoked the inspired hostility sustained by Northbrooke, Gosson, Stubbes, Prynne, and others in their famous diatribes. So great was their anger that Puritans risked sliced-off ears (William Prynne) to condemn the stage and earned the mocking enmity of theater people ever since. Yet the opposition came from a group who, as we have already seen, wrote plays or playlike tracts— and who used theater to describe the workings of God in the world.

Perhaps one explanation is that the more intense the opposition, the greater the chance for contradiction. In the war against the stage, ironies abound. Alvin Kernan expresses one of the socioeconomic ironies: "While the theater was antithetical by its very nature to Puritan interests and ways of thinking, it was at the same time, in some of its aspects, very much a part of the new and coming world of which Puritanism was the religious manifestation. It was organized financially in an entrepreneurial and capitalistic manner, it played to a democratic audience, and it was popular in appeal" (89). The Puritans had many reasons to oppose the new public theaters that appeared in 1576 and after—some moral, some practical (fear of catching such diseases as the plague or being victimized by criminals). But as Kernan suggests, theaters as institutions must have seemed uncomfortably close to the world Puritans had begun to shape in England. Such closeness must also have instigated a sense of competition, natural, perhaps, to supporters of the new economic order but threatening too. Though representing values we would now call middle class, public theater provided a kind of recreation that to Puritans seemed of a piece with other types of sportive play: it diverted citizens from the tasks of a workaday world (Solberg, 48). In the late sixteenth-century debate over "lawfull and unlawfull recreations," the theater was considered unlawful for a variety of reasons. It was, after all, the sort of diverting amusement that made its participants, in Dudley Fenner's words, "slothfull and idle to all goode works" (quoted in Leverenz, 26). Theater was, in that sense, an opiate of the people, stupefying them to the significant labor Puritans felt was ordered by God.

Nevertheless, it is difficult to account for the intensity of reaction by nonconformists (and even some mainstream Anglicans) to the theater.

Russell Fraser puts the attack in the context of a pre-Puritan "war against poetry," an antagonism to the deceits and maskings of literary art, which the Puritans continue in the spirit of a new materialism. More specifically, Jonas Barish sees the Puritan response, and that of William Prynne in particular, as emerging from a deep-seated "anti-theatrical prejudice" whose origins may be found in Plato; but in addition, Barish considers many of the opponents of theater as essentially neurotic and their antagonism a species of pathology (87–89). Thus, while he finds there are some reasons that make sense for the time—he is correct in noting that Puritans connect plays to the playlike Roman liturgy (165)—Barish ultimately ascribes the heat in Prynne's *Histrio-Mastix* (1633) and related texts to something virtually unknowable in the antitheatrical character. This prejudice "bestrides too many centuries, it encompasses too many different climes and cultures. It wells up from deep sources; it is 'ante-predicative,' and seems to precede all attempts to explain or rationalize it. It belongs, however, to a conservative ethical emphasis in which the key terms are those of order, stability, constancy, and integrity, as against a more existentialist emphasis that prizes growth, process, exploration, flexibility, variety, and versatility of response" (117). Although Barish acknowledges a complex process at work in the attack on the theaters, with Puritan fear of protean representation as part of it, he slights other causes. In contrast, Jean-Christophe Agnew suggests that Prynne's criticism of artificiality "was something more than an envious and literal-minded reaction to the recreational pastimes of others" (100). Prynne, says Agnew, sees the problem as one of "theatricality reconceived as a dimension of secular life"—a theatricality enforced by the new conditions of a "boundless market" and the restructuring of selves and their relation to ordinary life that accompanies the Renaissance (113). Market conditions are not the whole story, either, but the coincidence of a number of socioeconomic changes with a radicalizing of Church language and polity forces us to look beyond (though not ignore) prejudice as an explanation.

Another factor for Puritan hostility, that plays were given on Sunday, points toward the complex competitive relationship between church and theater. On one level, as Winton Solberg maintains, the Puritan opposition to plays comes out of the general fear that the

Sabbath would be destroyed by the recreation fad that filled up English Sundays (47–53). The problem manifests itself in simple head counting; fewer attending parishioners means a lower take in the collection basket. Still, with the new liturgical emphasis on the sermon, more than money was being lost when the faithful went to plays. As Lawrence Sasek summarizes the Puritan position from Northbrooke on, opponents of the theater complain that "the common people often went to see plays when they might and should have gone to hear sermons" (93). For the Puritans, the medium is the message. In his *Anatomie of Abuses* (1583), Philip Stubbes remarks that a play of "divine matter," delivered at the theater, is "most intollerable" because it is performed "without any reverence, worship, or veneration" for God (pt. I, 2:140). As Lawrence Sasek summarizes Richard Baxter in his *Christian Directory*, the church and the theater are rivals, the one serving God, the other the devil (98).

But once the opposition is made between pulpit and stage, invariably the terms of one will be applied to depict the other. If the actor is a false priest, leading his flock to devilish ends, the preacher looks more and more like an actor—for one who abhors hypocrisy, a terrifying possibility. No doubt, Puritan plain style in language and preaching technique emerges out of a suspicion that some essential reality disappears when one dresses up the message—or the message-giver—in clothes more distracting than edifying. Giles Firmin, in *The Real Christian* (1670), noting that in his own style he prefers an "Apodictick Syllogism *before a* Jingling Paranomasie," puts the matter in piecegood terms to separate false from true writing: *"Silken Language sutes not those who are cloathed in Sackcloth"* (xxxi). But Firmin also recognizes that a variety of ways to preach may be appropriate if the character of the minister is sound. His own teacher, John Rogers of Dedham, used histrionics of an extreme sort, even grabbing the canopy above the pulpit and enacting the agonies of those in hell (D. Hall, *Faithful Shepherd*, 65); and while Firmin admits that Rogers preached on a "wild note," and "though such actions and speeches in other men would have been ridiculous, yet in him, being a man so holy . . . they went off with as much aw, upon a very great and reverent authority" (77).

Though Rogers may be an extreme case of the preacher crossing over into histrionic excess, the closeness to which Puritan rhetoric and style sometimes approach the theatrical suggests a deep ambivalence about the theater and about the intrusion of theatricality into daily life. However virulent the opposition to the profession of acting or the conditions at the theaters or the irreverence of the plays themselves, Puritans still find ways to grant legitimacy to the form. Stephen Gosson in *Playes Confuted in Five Actions* (1582), Philip Stubbes in *The Anatomie of Abuses*, and William Prynne in *Histrio-Mastix* (1633) all use either acts and scenes or dialogue to structure their attacks on the theater. Stubbes, in the introduction to his first edition (1583), acknowledges that drama has historical precedent for its acceptance: "For otherwise (all Abuses cut away) who seeth not that some kind of playes, tragedies and enterluds, in their own nature are not onely of great ancientie, but also very honest and very commendable exercyses, being used and practised in most Christian common weales, as which contain matter (such they may be) both of doctrine, erudition, good example, and wholsome instruction; And may be used, in tyme and place convenient, as conducible to example of life and reformation of maners" (pt. I, 1: x). The preface, far milder in tone than the main text, was not reprinted in subsequent editions, but the idea that plays can be found which elevate rather than corrupt remains with later writers. Prynne frames the question primarily as one of intent. To write for the theater—presumably, to write for applause—is not "warrantable," but one can still grant that a poem written in dramatic form "may be done without offense if it be pious, serious, good, and profitable" (835; see Sasek, 107); in fact, he exempts playwright John Foxe from his overall condemnation of the theater because of the seriousness manifest in the martyrologist's drama (834). Richard Baxter, too, allows for the possibility that a play could be "lawful, and very edifying." But all the writers seem to agree with Baxter's caveat: "I think I never knew or heard of a lawful stage-play, comedy, or tragedy in the age that I have lived in" (*Christian Directory*, quoted in Sasek, 97).

For Shakespeare and his playwriting contemporaries, the theater of the world corresponds to the theater in which their plays are acted. Thomas Heywood's famous rejoinder to the attacks on the theater, *Apology for Actors* (1612), makes overt the macrocosmic-microcosmic

relationship between world and stage. Heywood views the world stage
as a place much like Beard's theater of judgments, one

> In which Jehove doth as spectator sit
> And chiefe determiner to applaud the best,
> And their indevours crowne with more than merit,
> But by their evill actions doomes the rest,
> To end disgrac't whilst others praise inherit.
> (sig. A4v; see Allman, 3, and Bradbrook, 92)

His point, of course, is to justify the stage: "He that denyes then
Theaters should be, / He may as well deny a world to me." Yet as
Barish observes, Heywood's defense concedes so much to the opposition that it hardly constitutes an argument for the aesthetic pleasures of
the theater (117–21).

For the Puritans, however, acknowledgment that the theatrum
mundi trope can be applied to their vision of the world forces an
either-or proposition. To accept a judging God who thrusts before us
the lives of saints and sinners as somber entertainment for our souls
seems to mean that any other stage must be rejected. Stubbes describes
the end awaiting actors on profane stages, performers whose very
profession is an insult to a critical God: "Doo these Mockers and
Flowters of his Majesty, these dissembling *Hipocrites*, and flattering
Gnatoes, think to escape unpunished? beware, therefore, you masking
Players, you painted sepulchres, you doble dealing ambodexters, be
warned betimes, . . . what wil be the reward thereof in the end, least
God destroy you in his wrath: abuse God no more" (pt. I, 2:141).
Despite their obvious differences, Stubbes and Heywood share a similar vision of God as a spectator whose ire must not be provoked. As
Stubbes reminds us, one profaner of the Sabbath, a mere stick-
gatherer, "was stoned to death by the commaundement of God from
the Theator of Heaven" (pt. I, 2:138). At the same time they are being
watched by God, Puritans live constantly under the observation of fellow human beings, their roles continually judged. In *Histrio-Mastix*
Prynne renders 1 Corinthians 4.9 in such a way as to stress the
histrionic nature of daily life: "We are made a theatre or spectacle unto
the world, unto Angels, and to men" (723).

While competition may have fueled Puritan antagonisms toward the theater (or anti-Puritan prejudice on the stage), there seems to be something else at work: the assertion by nonconformists of a concept of acting that involves no masks, no illusions, no shape shifting. Instead, those elements of the microcosmic theater are to be stripped away in a rigorous process of revelation on the macrocosmic stage. In this scheme, the world is a theater, but danger arises when human stages attempt to mimic, or mock, the divinely created one upon which we all tread. Since Calvinist doctrine insists on the unknowability of heavenly intent, the playwright who rounds off his work, the director who seeks to satisfy the desire of an audience for completeness, the actors who cozen the audience into believing that people can become "whores, queanes, bawdes, scullions, knaves," and the like (Stubbes, pt. I, 2:143) by donning costumes and changing voices, all participate in a false theater. That is, even if one portrays on stage the punishment of the wicked, the fact that an actor walks away or rises from the dead to take a bow indicates what a mockery such a portrayal must be.

The best theater for Puritans is a metaphoric one, a theater conjured in nondramatic prose, a theater that frames human action within a world and historical narrative governed by Providence. Indeed, William Prynne, citing Thomas Beard's recently reprinted *Theatre of Gods Judgements* (3d edition, 1631), makes essentially this case: the theater generates iniquity, but drama that is "serious"—a play by Foxe, for instance, his own book, or by extension, the life of the true Christian—has warrant when played on a larger stage (see Lamont, 28–33). Certainty of the ultimate outcome of the drama coexists with uncertainty about the ends of individual players. But one thing remains sure: the actors who plunge through the rotten boards of the stage to their deaths do not rise again to change costumes or seek our applause.

It is easy to lampoon antitheatrical Puritans, as playgoers discovered in the seventeenth century. Ben Jonson's Zeal-of-the-Land Busy in *Bartholomew Fair* (1614) is but one of many Puritan types put upon the stage for mockery (see Holden). Even today, as Barish's book makes clear, prolix extremists like William Prynne garner little sympathy—perhaps because the Puritans were indeed successful in closing the English theaters in 1642. And while in the narrow view the closing satisfied the moralists, something far more profound occurred than the cessation of microcosmic theater. Stephen Orgel's analysis of Stuart masques shows how intimately theater serves to justify regimes; indeed, the seventeenth-century masques at court can be seen as the precursors to the twentieth-century "staged" media events in the present-day United States. Implicit in the anti-Puritan satires is not only a presumption about the value of the status quo but also a fear of the political changes occasioned by a society that denies to various segments of the population the masque, the play, the pageant, or the festival.

From the Puritan perspective, once people stopped wasting time at one or another stage, they could attend to far more important performances being mounted throughout England in the political upheaval that led to the Civil War and the establishment of the Commonwealth. For the period of the Interregnum, in fact, it appeared as if radical nonconformist theater—the world theater stripped of its "doble dealing ambodexters" and the beguiling displays of Anglican ritual—would triumph in England. As Christopher Hill points out, the era of the Puritan accession was also a period that saw the galvanizing of "masterless men" and radical groups throughout England, primarily through the agency of Oliver Cromwell's New Model Army (68–69). With the death of the "Royall Actor," Charles I, and the securing of the Commonwealth, radicals of all kinds, including millennialists like those in the Fifth Monarchy movement, began to push for satisfaction in their time (Capp). "Poor, illiterate, mechanic men," remarked William Dell, a onetime New Model Army chaplain, "turned the world upside down" (quoted in Hill, 75).

Whatever political or social reasons one might offer to explain the rise and fall of radicals in seventeenth-century England, it is not entirely accidental that the most tospy-turvy period in modern English history occurred during a time when the playhouses were closed. Into the void left by the suspension of monarchy, as well as by the overturning of the hierarchical social order, rushed Quakers and others declaring the immediacy of Christ and the prerogatives of democracy that their doctrine entailed (Hill, 78, 86). Without having to compete with the represented but illusory world of theatrical performances, antitheatrical idealists began to assert their visions of a better world in the arena of real life. In other words, the function in English society normally occupied by stage performance was being taken up by radical millennialist politics. Thus, whereas ritual or any socially symbolic performance usually keeps an idealized vision of the culture within the strict rules such performances traditionally have, the replacement of ritual with the real thing violates the safe limits imposed by the particular species of performance.

Consider, for example, this description of the difference between ritual behavior (in this case, carnival) and real life:

> In ritual . . . it would seem that we wish for the consistency that all the idealized versions of the social world reveal. For this reason rituals demand preparation—as do spectator sports, cinema, and theater. And since we want a consistent world—opposed to the automatization of the everyday—we radicalize life in rituals, making it take on again a shine, rigor, certainty, and contrast. We create, then, a special space where the routines of the daily world are broken and where it is possible to observe, discuss, or criticize the real world seen standing on its head.   (DaMatta, 236–37)

The implication is that a society devoid of opportunities to turn the world upside down in ritualized performances will be without controllable ways in which to "radicalize life." That was the situation in which England found itself after 1642.

At this time of political division, the mother country began to draw back Puritans from New England who had become disaffected with the pace at which, in Philip Gura's words, "a true revolution of the saints would occur" (143). Some of the returning New England men, notably Thomas Vennor and Sir Henry Vane, were eventually identified as plotters against the government and arrested. Though figures like Vennor and other Fifth Monarchists must have tapped into a widespread disgruntlement over social and political conditions, they found Old England no more congenial than New. Vennor, named "a principle actor" in a millennialist conspiracy against the government, made a histrionic appearance before Cromwell; and as the Protector's chaplain describes it, the accused "spoke and behaved himself with [as] great impudence, insolence, pride and railing as . . . you ever heard of" (quoted in Gura, 142). The execution of Vennor, the collapse of the Commonwealth after Cromwell's death, the Restoration, and the execution of Henry Vane for plots against Charles II effectively ended radical threats to the political order. England was not yet ready for revolution.

But by Vane's death in 1662, the theaters had reopened. Even before, during the Commonwealth, complaints arose that entertainments were not available for the masses. The London Lord Mayor's pageants, suspended in 1640, were resumed in 1655, no doubt in response to concerns such as those expressed by a preacher, Edmund Gayton: "For anniversary shows and harmless and merry recreations, without a moderate permission of them, [there is] very little to content the multitude" (quoted in Hill, 285). By denying theater to the "multitude," the nonconformist forces created the conditions for mass discontent, thereby increasing the likelihood of a revolution of more than saints. With the return of mass entertainment and then the reopening of the theaters, the potency of metaphoric theater, played out in the religious and political arenas, was gone. Any God-driven millenarian revolution would have to be deferred to some vaguely appointed time. After 1660, then, when English writers use theatrical metaphor, they most commonly speak to the social conditions of everyday life— conditions far removed from the apocalyptic and providential rhetoric of the nonconformists.

CHAPTER FOUR

Prospero in Virginia:
The Example of Captain John Smith

*D*uring the Elizabethan period, writers who accept what I have called the orthodox version of theatrum mundi seem conscious of trying to keep the correspondence between stage and world within the limits of social and political order. During the Jacobean period, however, theater as a figure appears less benign and more representative of a world moving out of kilter. Both in Burton's analysis of social theatricality and his expressed need to retreat into a personal theater of philosophy and in the Puritan desire to destroy the theater altogether, we see two different but curiously related strategies for coping with a world that has become a nearly inescapable stage and with a court for whom the masque has become an instrument of political policy. Together, these responses to an increasingly theatricalized culture presuppose the weakness of the individual to avoid being subsumed by performative chaos or to stand above the crowd of indeterminate playactors and have one's actions judged by a higher standard than that of courtly taste. For a person like Captain John Smith, who chooses a different path from the ideological narrowness of the Puritans and the effete histrionics of the Anglican elite, some other strategy is required. He escapes urban England, but not to his garden; instead, by seeking out the battlefields of continental Europe and the unconquered spaces of North America, Smith carries with him a theatrical vision that transforms those zones into stages of history—and that, in the case of Virginia, makes him the central actor in a land free of playhouses and an enervating obsession with social performance.

Smith is a problematic figure for literary history; the author of "the first account of the Jamestown colony's first year to reach London" (J. Smith, 1:5), Smith has never earned much praise as a writer nor have his writings always been thought of as literature. Reasons for his low standing are easy to find: his style is inelegant, the works themselves were badly "edited" by contemporaries, and much of what Smith printed under his name was in fact written initially by others. Even in his introduction to the modern *Complete Works*, editor Philip L. Barbour describes Smith as "autobiographer," "compiler," "geographer," "ethnographer," "soldier and governor," "sailor and admiral," and "trader"—but never "writer" or "author" per se (1:lxiv–lxix). The very problem Smith's works have today in gaining a literary reputation the captain had in his own day with getting recognition for his efforts in Virginia—a problem he thought he could solve by being both "actor" and "author" at once.

Yet his ordinariness as a writer coupled with an expansive self-image makes him just the person to start a literature; that is, his style in itself is something old, but his adventures in a strange land make his texts something new. In fact, it is significant not only that Smith is a "compiler," a writer-editor who includes the voices of many in his texts, but also that he tacitly knows the literary and cultural value of talking about oneself. "In a broad sense," as Barbour says, "everything John Smith himself wrote was autobiographical" (1:lxiv). In both the rhetorical and political histories of America, he occupies a threshold position, for as English adventurer, colonizer, and writer, Smith is bold and naive enough to imagine himself to be the representative of a new world. He projects upon his American life both the imagination he inherits and a revised one that is shaped by his encounters with a fresh, unconquered landscape—then he projects that life back onto Virginia, making its history into his story. As a writer, he has some knowledge of the stage and its metaphors, but he often lets others frame the figural theaters in his texts. At times, Smith uses play devices and language to give life to his sometimes primitive discourse, but he does not write plays in the Elizabethan sense; indeed, he protests against the treatment of his adventures on stage. As a scion of the European humanist tradition, John Smith the Renaissance man understands the conventions of theatrum mundi; as a traveler from Old World to New, he carries the metaphor with him and, through the filter of his ego, alters the trope to fit a reconsidered view of what theaters the world contains. In essence, he creates paradigmatic linkages of self, history, and metaphoric theater in order to express the significance of his American experience.

That the world is a stage John Smith seems well aware. Of his friend, Robert Norton's, book, *The Gunner* (1628), Smith remarks that it is "A Present well-befitting this our Age, / When all the World is but a Martiall Stage" (3:370). For most of his life, Smith had encountered the world in combat, using for weapons sword, tongue, and pen. As a soldier of fortune, he had fought throughout Europe, most notably against the Turks. As an adventurer and colonist in Virginia, he had battled both the Indians and the corrupt members of his own company. And as a writer, he had struggled to maintain the truth of his life's travails against mockers and doubters. Captain Smith, man of action and firsthand commentator, knew from experience the worth of standing above and fully in the sight of his contemporaries in a warlike and theatrical age.

War and stage have long had a formal connection through the word *theater*; yet in Smith's case, both theaters overlap. Elevated as one of his martial stages, Smith's Virginia emerges from the pages of his works, especially *The Generall Historie of Virginia* (1624), as a land suitable for displaying a hero of epical dimensions. Smith is conscious of the connection between history as a chronological shaper of events and the spaces on which those events take place; he makes the most of his being in a land that is not England but that can, through word as well as deed, be ordered to look like it. In the fifth book of the *Generall Historie*, Smith introduces his chapter on the Bermudas with a passage that stands for the rest of his work: "Before we present you the matters of fact, it is fit to offer to your view the Stage whereon they were acted, for as Geography without History seemeth a carkasse without motion, so History without Geography wandreth as a Vagrant without a certaine habitation" (2:338; see Barbour's note to this passage, 2:389n). In Smith's own case, the wanderer, the escapee from theatrical contentions at home, must find that "certaine habitation" that will provide the "Stage" for his actions; at the same time, America, merely a "carkasse" without him, is brought into history by the dynamic actor who suddenly gives the geographical corpse new life.

Coincidental with the actor in history, the hero's double, the writer-arranger, stands in the wings, reminding us of *his* presence. Because Smith the author knows how to dramatize events, especially those in which the captain plays a central role, he anticipates another American, Cotton Mather, who is conscious of having compiled the stories of others through the medium of his own representative life. For Smith, the figure of the forceful leader serves as an image that brings order to the chaos of his compiled texts (see Emerson, "Editor," and Barbour's notes throughout Smith's *Works*). Similarly, Smith the writer hopes that Captain Smith the hero will make it possible for the propagandist to return order to Virginia, especially after the massacre of 1622. As Cotton Mather will assert at the end of the century, Smith also believes that a significant public personality, dynamic and self-dramatizing, can bring the attention of the world to colonial outposts in the wilderness. To this end, the theatrical figures of speech in Smith's works serve to highlight his role in the English settlement of America by providing a code for the linkage of the individual to history and geography. In other words, Smith shows us how the individual can stand against the tedious, delimiting theatricality of the social elite yet for the figural theater of heroic history, thus justifying the focus on himself in his apparently egotistical relations.

For his audience of readers, the two parts played by John Smith, adventurer and author, shape and give meaning to each other. "I am no Compiler, by hearsay," he announces in the introductory letter to the *Generall Historie*, "but have been a reall Actor" (2:41). As John Seelye suggests in *Prophetic Waters*, Smith plays Miles Gloriosus on a literary stage of his own devising (61), but he earns the right to be the Plautine braggart soldier by having struggled in a genuine wilderness. As Smith says further in the introductory letter, "That which hath been indured and passed through with hardship and danger, is thereby sweetned to the Actor when he becometh the Relator" (2:41). For him, writing turns his adventures into public commodities; it doubles his value at the same time as it halves potential disapproval: "He that acteth two parts is the one more borne withall if he come short, or fayle in one of the them" (2:41). The unevenness of the *Generall Historie* may well be the result of Smith's frustrations with the Virginia Company and a bruised ego, but in turning to writing, Smith makes the best of a second-best option (Emerson, *Captain John Smith*, 77).

If Smith is actor on the martial stage of Virginia, then publication of his books is itself a theatrical event—appropriate, certainly, for a man playing multiple parts. In an intricate simile, "I. H." (John Healey?) addresses the "Courteous Reader" of Smith's first Virginia book, A *True Relation* (1608), in a way that shows both I. H.'s coyness and Smith's dual role as author-actor:

> So it is, that like to an unskilful actor, who having by misconstruction of his right Cue, over-slipt himself, in beginning of a contrary part, and fearing the hatefull hisse of the captious multitude, with a modest blush retires himselfe in private; as doubting the reprehension of his whole audience in publicke, and yet againe, upon further deliberation, thinking it better to know their censures at the first, and upon submission to reape pardon, then by seeking to smother it, to incurre the danger of a secret scandall: Inboldening himselfe upon the curteous kindnesse of the best, and not greatly respecting the worst, comes fourth againe, makes an Apology for himself, shewes the cause of his error, craves pardon for his rashnes, and in fine, receives a generall applauditie of the whole assemblie: so I [help publish this book though Smith be the author].   (1:24)

Though Smith would never use such self-amused rhetoric, the passage suggests an intense self-consciousness about the presentation of a book to the public, an attitude that seems characteristic of the seventeenth century. From the beginning of his New World adventures, Smith regards publication as central to his conception of himself. Writing with a zeal matched by few early American self-apologists as well as drawing upon the rhetorical resources of diverse hands (including I. H.), Smith emphasizes the need for both an informed commentator and an inclusive performer. Other men and women, whether writers or actors, appear in his works as serving his needs or reputation. I. H.'s simile, reminiscent of Shakespeare's figure in Sonnet 23 ("As an unperfect actor on the stage") of one who lets his writing do his speaking, encourages us to see Smith's significance in contrast to less able others. Unlike the "unskilful" player whose best hope for applause is in the theater, Smith calls himself a "true actor" (1:176), that is, one who *is* one's part and who acts, in his case, in Virginia, on the stage of the world. Therefore, as "Relator," he is that playwright-director of a literary event, the chief declaimer of the play in which Smith the adventurer-actor is the star.

Smith is no Shakespeare, but the comparison is worth making, if only to show the differences between the intra- and extratheatrical imaginations as each confronts the fact of America. Shakespeare himself draws upon the history of early Virginia, specifically the wreck of the Gates expedition in the Bermudas, and he makes of that history something both similar to and different from what his contemporary Smith makes of it. In *The Tempest* (1611), playwright and sometime player Shakespeare turns America into a fairyland, a place only possible in the mind or on stage, and the story of removal to a new world into an aesthetic fantasy of the artist and his power. In the *Generall Historie*, prose writer and true actor Smith, while showing that Virginia manifests a sometimes curious and transformative power of its own, sees the action there in the language of a well-recognized artisan skilled in realpolitik. Smith the writer creates a character something like that of a politically savvy Prospero; throughout the Virginia narratives, the adventurer appears to manipulate events, turning adversity into opportunities for displaying his prowess. If Virginia is a brave new world, then it requires new tactics from a brave man to tame it. The Captain Smith of the histories—with the "nonpareil," Pocahontas, as his savage Ariel—often finds his suggestions ignored or ridiculed (in which case, trouble soon follows) and himself more sinned against than sinning, but he never wavers or gives himself over to despair and cynicism as a more thoughtful, less active man might.

But the real power of Smith's rendering comes from author Smith who transforms raw, localized experience into tragicomic action on a grander scale. Like Prospero in his cell, he can bring forth seemingly supernatural forces—the sudden arrival of supply vessels, the interventions of Pocahontas, a timely frightening of the savages—though he is careful to attribute good fortune to "divine providence" (2:151). He can even induce that editor of travel documents and master of twisted syntax, Samuel Purchas, to provide a commendatory poem:

> Can Pilgrim *make a* Maker; *all so well*
>   *Hath taught* Smith *scoure my rustie out-worne* Muse,
> And so conjur'd her in Virginian Cell.   (2:47)

From his Virginian cell—by 1624 a space in his selective memory—Smith conjures a world both prosaic and fantastic. For the Indians, the adventurer describes lands and customs beyond their imagining; when with a bulbous, glass-covered compass, "that Globe-like Jewell," Smith explains "the roundnesse of the earth, and skies, the spheare of the Sunne, Moone, and Starres, and how the Sunne did chase the night round about the world continually; the greatnesse of the Land and Sea, the diversitie of Nations, varietie of complexions, and how we were to them Antipodes, and many other such like matters, they all stood as amazed with admiration" (2:147). Brave new world, indeed! Thus when the Indians still want to tie him up and shoot him, the compass in the raised hand of Opechancanough, king of Pamunkey, becomes transformed again, this time to a totem of Smith's survival.

For his readers, Smith re-creates the "most strange and fearefull Conjurations," the ritual dances and performances mounted by the Indians at Pamunkey (2:149). The animal costumes, the painted bodies, the orations and "antique tricks" may be frightening on the surface, but Smith renders them almost as varieties of English folk theatricals. He, after all, does not flinch. Still, the native ceremonies to which Smith is subjected move beyond the realm of simple history or protoanthropology, as might more nearly be found in A *True Relation* or *Proceedings*, into something more akin to stage romance, where one has warrant to display the products of a fertile, feverish imagination. No doubt, these theatricalized scenes appeal to later readers who themselves write for an audience comfortable with real stages. For the nineteenth century, Smith's narratives could be readily translated into drama or into theatrical metaphors, as James Nelson Barker in his play *The Indian Princess* (1808) or William Gilmore Simms in his biography of Smith (1846) show.

If Smith in the *Generall Historie* exploits a nascent gift for romantic stagecraft, the character he creates remains pragmatic and single-minded. In all his narratives, the test of character is to be "true," as the titles of his first and last important works, A *True Relation* and *True Travels*, indicate. The Machiavellians who subvert the real work of the world are like those chronic dissemblers in Shakespeare's plays for whom the only truth is falseness. Thus those who act but lack principle, like the Dutchman Valdo, a betrayer of English interests to Powhatan, are "meere Imposter[s]" (2:226). Those who do their proper work and whose word can be trusted are, on the other hand, the "true actors," whose integrity, unfortunately, makes them targets for liars and cheats. As Smith says in A *Map of Virginia*, "The wisest living is soonest abused by him that hath a faire tongue and a dissembling heart" (1:176). True actors are those who are true to their calling, who are what they seem—and thus are opposed to the hypocrites and dissemblers, who are really better *players*, because they are untrue to themselves, than those who act their characteristic parts in the world. As a writer, Smith claims to have little skill, his "rough Pen" producing only "poore ragged lines" (2:41), though he sometimes is clever, even stylish. Still, for many readers, this advertisement for himself as "true" is an honest one. Ironically, Smith's pragmatism leads the main character in the Virginia narratives into some dissembling of his own, most notably with Powhatan; but because he has a purpose, the raising of a colony, Captain Smith's most skillful masking makes that best of Virginia actors true to the nobler ends of history.

Because he takes his own place in history seriously, Smith shows contempt for those who abuse their colonial roles, who cannot both speak and act from a collective goal. Those who spend their time dreaming of gold and talking about imagined wealth Smith labels "meere Verbalists" (2:157), men as deserving of scorn as the "meere Imposter" Valdo. In another situation, recorded in both *Proceedings* and the *Generall Historie*, the writer dismisses those onetime complainers about privation turned gourmands by the autumn hunt as "Tufftaffety humorists" (1:212). This characterization of his fellow colonists prepares us for a subsequent line. The transition between the calming of the Tufftaffety humorists and the deaths of George Cassen, Jehu Robinson, and Thomas Emry on Smith's exploratory voyage up the Chickahominy River emerges in *Proceedings* as a dramatic reversal of fortune: "Our comaedies never endured long without a Tragedie" (1:212), remarks the writer, saying more than he might have intended by the lowercase *c* and uppercase *T*. When Smith then describes how he individually holds "200 Salvages" at bay, killing two and suffering little himself, we readily see the contrast between the captain and the comedic others. For though the account in *Proceedings* is less detailed than his earlier rendering of the Chickahominy episode in A *True Relation*, Smith leaves off much of the personal bristling for a more rhetorically elevated approach. Writer Smith assigns to Captain Smith, now an actor in high Tragedy, a greater role. And while he probably means by "Tragedie" something like adversity borne nobly, his dramatic trope nevertheless underscores the value to history of the true actor. When Smith tells us that by the time of the captain's release, "those Salvages admired him as a demi-God" (1:213), the point is well made: Captain Smith supersedes all ordinary mortals in Virginia.

If the true actor must assert himself in order to counter the Tufftaffety humorists, who debase the play of colonization, then he must also battle with the subtle deceptions of his Indian opponents. Unlike the layabout whites, however, Smith's "Salvages" at least recognize the elevation of experience that theatricalized ritual can bring. When Christopher Newport arrives with orders to appease Powhatan by giving him an elaborate coronation, he sends Smith ahead to tell the king of English intentions. At Werowocomoco Smith is entertained by what he calls in the *Generall Historie* "A Virginia Maske," another "entertainment" striking in its parallels to old English festal rites as well as to the masques at court:

> In a faire plaine field they made a fire, before which [Smith was] sitting uppon a mat; suddainly amongst the woods was heard such a hideous noise and shriking, that they betooke them to their armes, supposing Powhatan with all his power came to surprise them; but the beholders which were many, men, women, and children, satisfied the Captaine there was no such matter, being presently presented with this anticke, 30 young women came naked out of the woods (only covered behind and before with a few greene leaves) their bodies al painted, some white, some red, some black, some partie colour, but every one different; their leader had a faire paire of stagges hornes on her head, and an otter skinne at her girdle, another at her arme, a quiver of arrowes at her backe, and bow and arrowes in her hand, the next in her hand a sword, another a club, another a pot-stick, all hornd alike, the rest every one with their severall devises. These feindes with most hellish cries, and shouts rushing from amongst the trees, cast themselves in a ring about the fire, singing, and dauncing with excellent ill varietie, oft falling into their infernall passions, and solemnely againe to sing, and daunce. Having spent neere an houre, in this maskarado; as they entered; in like manner departed. (1:235–36)

As the masque is for the Jacobean court, the Indian masque is an instrument of state, although its allegories elude our no-nonsense observer (if not the critics, some of whom, as J. A. Leo Lemay explains, note the "sexual exoticism" of this passage; see Lemay, 123). To Smith, the show is an annoying, fiendish, yet necessary accompaniment to the state banquet at which he is an honored guest, although to later readers, the scene has a theatrical charm that belies the writer's businesslike attitude (see, for example, Simms, 232–33). Such ceremony contrasts with the degeneracy of affairs at Jamestown, where ritual seems confined to the men's loitering about the tavern. Among his own people, Smith fights for position and reputation, which are both hard-won and easily lost. Among the Indians, however, he is a dignitary, a demi-God, a byword that, according to Powhatan, causes even that great chief to fear (1:247).

With few Englishmen to praise—and few direct quotations from whites other than himself—Smith turns his literary ear to the speeches and actions of the Indians. When Smith speaks, he models himself after Powhatan, the chief whose name is also the tribe's. Implying that his voice utters the collective wisdom, Smith *is* the colony, its captain, its president, its representative man. Smith's works constitute a declaration of national selfhood as barbaric as "Song of Myself" claims to be, but unlike Walt Whitman, whose national self openly embraces all races, Smith in the self of his texts must insist on difference, an unlikeness ironically predicated on the similarity between Smith and Powhatan as wily and forceful leaders. Writer Smith structures his accounts in order to focus on verbal confrontation; in the Virginia narratives, acts of war give way in prominence to acts of speech. Oration and counteroration lead to a speechifying, declamatory rhetoric that seems both elevated and eloquent, sometimes awkward but often passionate. One might argue that Smith assigns to his adversary Powhatan a more poetic utterance than he does to anyone else, including himself, as if Caliban were suddenly to speak in the language of Milton's Satan. But even Powhatan's remarks serve to raise Smith above the rest, for both *Proceedings* and the *Generall Historie* make clear that only the captain among the English can inspire such language from a foe.

This oblique elevation of Smith—and, consequently, of Vir-

ginia—can be seen in "Powhatans discourse of peace and warre" in
Proceedings (1:247). Smith and his men in early 1609 seek food from
the Indians, who counter that the captain's intentions are more martial than peaceful:

> What can you get by war, when we can hide our provision and flie to the
> woodes, whereby you must famish by wronging us your friends; and whie
> are you thus jealous of our loves, seeing us unarmed, and both doe, and
> are willing still to feed you with that you cannot get but by our labours?
> think you I am so simple not to knowe, it is better to eate good meate, lie
> well, and sleepe quietly with my women and children, laugh and be
> merrie with you, have copper, hatchets, or what I want, being your
> friend; then been forced to flie from al, to lie cold in the woods, feed
> upon acorns, roots, and such trash, and be so hunted by you, that I can
> neither rest, eat, nor sleepe; but my tired men must watch, and if a twig
> but breake, everie one crie there comes Captaine Smith, then must I flie
> I knowe not whether, and thus with miserable feare end my miserable
> life.   (1:247)

This skillfully crafted lament with its rhetorical and real questions, its
series and deliberate repetitions, its proverbs and biblical cadences,
Smith calls a "subtil discourse" (248), meaning of course that its
matter is not to be trusted. But its manner, full of high sentence in the
tragic mode, tells all. Machiavellian though he may be, Powhatan acts
the noble villain in Smith's political play. In that "subtil discourse"
one can see the essence of the tragic vision. Though Smith the
colonist fully aims to thwart any of his rival's plans to disrupt or destroy
the Jamestown settlement, Smith the writer needs Powhatan, the true
actor of a false part, in order to claim a space for Virginia on the world
geopolitical stage. In the circumscribed arena of Werowocomoco, the
seat of Indian power, Smith and Powhatan trade declamations in a
Senecan rhetoric that ennobles the event, even while each seeks to
undermine the other. Still, from Smith's point of view, the outcome is
not to be tragic. Rather, as the colony embodied, as a figure of the
imperial impulse, Smith the adventurer and true actor in history
becomes a personal England in America, a character in his and
history's coproduced masque.

Smith and his allies justify continuing support for Virginia by
reminding readers of the global and historical consequences of their

actions. Like the Puritans, Smith sees the American wilderness as a grand field of action, but he finds Julius Caesar (2:41), his predecessor conqueror-author, a more fitting model than Jesus Christ. As a consolidator of power and as the living image of the state, Caesar would seem to be appropriate as Smith's political ancestor. Since Smith is also a product of his time, there is another reason to connect himself to the Roman: the desire for immortality achieved through writing. In a short commendatory poem in the *Generall Historie*, Edward Worseley explains that "Like Caesar now thou writ'st what thou hast done, / These acts, this Booke will live while ther's a Sunne" (2:50). That is, as Shakespeare suggests frequently in the sonnets, the subject in a piece of writing (even more than the author) is the person best able to live on in the hearts and minds of humanity. Smith as author gives life to Smith as actor, ensuring in the *Generall Historie* that he has two parts to play, in case "he come short, or fayle in one of them."

Smith is no Caesar, except by conceit. Yet perhaps it is the other sort of conceit that turns Smith from a mere adventurer, a yeoman soldier of fortune, into one of history's true actors. That double sense of actor is reinforced by a passage from William Grent's poem for the *Generall Historie*, "Noble Captaine Smith, my worthy Friend":

> Not like the Age wherein thou liv'st, to lie
> Buried in baseness, sloth, or Ribaldrie
> (For most doe thus) hast thou thy selfe applide;
> But, in faire Actions, Merits height descride:
> Which (like foure Theaters to set thee forth)
> The worlds foure Quarters testifie thy worth.
> The last whereof (America) best showes
> Thy paines, and prayse.   (2:52)

Smith claims, of course, to have been on four continents, as he tells the Earl of Hertford in his dedicatory letter to *A Map of Virginia* (1:134) and as he announces to the world in *True Travels*. And though the general idea will be expressed more forcefully a century later, the notion that the American theater will show Smith to best advantage illustrates the wider view that America is the stage on which Western civilization will have its last, best performance. In Smith's case, as Grent continues in his poem, the fame he gathers from that American theater will be awarded for his two roles: "There *by thy* Worke, Heere *by thy* Workes," the Virginia conqueror and the English author, the living Caesar as "President" and historian (2:52).

While Smith no doubt approves of Grent's figural theaters as ones that enhance his reputation, he recoils at the playing of his history upon the English boards. In an introductory letter to *True Travels*, Smith complains of an undescribed "they" who "have acted my fatall Tragedies upon the Stage, and racked my Relations at their pleasure" (3:141). Sympathetically, a commendatory poem to the same work alludes to some performance on the stage at Richard Gunnell's Fortune theater, possibly *The Hungarian Lion*, now lost, presumably having to do in part with Smith's Eastern European adventures (Barbour, "Captain John Smith"):

> *Can it be*
> *That Men alone in* Gonnels *fortune see*
> *thy worth advanc'd? no wonder since our age*
> *Is now at large a Bedlam or a Stage.* (3:147)

Gunnell's production, perhaps other topical plays no longer extant, and Ben Jonson's *The Staple of News* (1625) with its mention of Pocahontas all serve, in Smith's mind, to reduce his "fatall Tragedies" to mere jesting and therefore deflate his heroic enterprise. He loses authorial control over the material when others "rack" his works and present their amended versions before an unprepared public; to regain it, he turns to friendly pens. The commendatory poet here, Richard James, sees the age as *"a Bedlam or a Stage,"* suggesting not only that the madhouse and the playhouse are analogous institutions but that the intrusion of stage theater into the world distorts both the truth and the sanity of the truth seekers—a lesson that also appears in Burton's *Anatomy of Melancholy*. In addition, playlike entertainments also belong to the Indians; as such, they may dazzle for the moment, but they are only conjurations, diversions from the real political work of negotiation and settlement. Given Smith's own reaction to having his life exploited in the theater, it is small wonder that he announces the colony's "not having any use of . . . Plaies" (2:158). On the quadrated world stage, "Plaies" do nothing to show Captain Smith's "paines, and prayse."

In his relations and the attendant commendatory padding, Smith divides the world into a shrunken stage where comic deflation is the rule and a vast stage on which tread the superhuman heroes of history. In the macrocosmic trope, America is a stage where history, geography, and the true actor come together; in the microcosmic theater, the new American fears to lose his greatness by being ridiculed. The lesson for Smith is that metaphoric theaters can lend dignity while playhouses only scorn. Like Prospero, who abjures his "rough magic" (*The Tempest*, 5.1.50) and gives over the island to Caliban and the fools, Smith, too, must leave Virginia and hand over his power to lesser men. Yet the lament recorded at the captain's leaving illuminates what it means to be a man transformed into an entire enterprise. As the *Generall Historie* says, Smith "loved action more then words, and hated falsehood and covetousnesse worse than death; whose adventures were our lives, and whose losse our deaths" (2:225). On the stage of the world, an individual can escape the claustrophobia of urban social performance by acting in history, in a space of his or her own choosing, as the representative of an entire people. Smith's dual conceit, his hubristic role-playing, places him above all others, while his compiled and inclusive texts dignify the rude settlements in Virginia. For Americans, not only is John Smith "the Father of us all," as John Seelye puts it (57), but he is all of "us"; his "adventures" are "our lives," and his texts are an announcement to the world that when true actors seize the American Theater, no "Plaies" are needed.

II

The Theater

of Faith,

1630–1730

CHAPTER FIVE

A Theater on a Hill:
Puritans and the Rhetoric of Performance

*N*onconformist writing includes various denunciations of the theater, some selective, some inclusive, some more virulent than others; yet as I have tried to demonstrate, that same literature employs dramatic and theatrical language and devices—actual plays, dialogues, agonistic confrontations, and tropes among them. For that reason alone, one might expect in the rhetorical baggage of Puritan migrants to the New World some of the same images and metaphors of theater used by Calvin and his English followers. In England, however, except for the period of the Interregnum, there is an active theater against which the metaphor often plays. In New England, the demands of establishing a colony in the wilderness as well as a desire to proscribe theatrical entertainments make theater an impossible luxury. Still, the almost complete absence of anything resembling traditional stage amusements does not preclude early New England writers from framing their ideas and experiences in the terms of an institution left behind at migration. In fact, except for the participants in major political revolutions, it would be hard to find in the post medieval West a more self-dramatizing people than the early American nonconformists. As Kai Erikson argues in *Wayward Puritans*, each major crisis in New England, like that involving Anne Hutchinson or the witch trials, calls for a ritual response, a "tribal ceremony" that shapes the event in theatrical ways (101); but beyond their social needs for ritual, the Puritans also make rhetorical connections to theatrum mundi that suggest a greater awareness of theater than religious beliefs and conditions of settlement alone might indicate.

John Winthrop's familiar exposition of Matthew 5.14 in "A Model of Christian Charity" makes clear how the nonconformist awareness of being observed and judged can be redirected and given dramatic heightening. In the text Winthrop chooses, the Sermon on the Mount, Jesus says, "You are the light of the world. A city set on a hill cannot be hid. Nor do men light a lamp and put it under a bushel, but on a stand, and it gives light to all in the house. Let your light so shine before man, that they may see your good works and give glory to your Father who is in heaven" (Matt. 5.14–16). Characteristically, Winthrop looks for darkness in the light, seeing not only a great opportunity for gain but a terrible possibility for ultimate loss: "The Lord make it like that of New England: for wee must Consider that wee shall be as a Citty upon a Hill, the eies of all people are uppon us; so that if we shall deal falsely with our god in this worke wee have undertaken and soe cause him to withdrawe his present help from us, wee shall be made a story and a by-word through the world, wee shall open the mouthes of enemies to speake evill of the ways of god and all professours for Gods sake" (Winthrop et al., *Papers*, 295). To be "professours for Gods sake" requires elevation to view, not only to shine light but to be seen. Winthrop's rhetoric turns a sermon about corporate responsibility into a lesson on public humiliation in which the colonists are performers in an international, even cosmic, show, one frightening in its inescapability.

Yet given the regnant metaphor of the age, Winthrop refrains from turning the "city on a hill" into a more theatrical image than it already is. The phrase is biblical and therefore has warrant in itself; but in the context, as explained below, of a rhetoric of observation, the city on a hill trope resonates with echoes of the theatrum mundi figure. Jean-Christophe Agnew sees Winthrop's decision to use the hill metaphor—and not theatrum mundi—as reflecting the socioeconomic conditions of colonization (149–51); but we also need to realize that the figure exists outside the world of Elizabethan-Jacobean drama. There certainly is little room in early New England for the dream-work," as Agnew calls it, of English dramatists; nevertheless, by the conventions of nonconformist rhetoric, theatrical thinking has already been encoded into the language of errand and covenant.

Other Puritan writers stress the same need for, yet fear of, exposure. In *Wonder-Working Providence* (1653), Edward Johnson reminds the faithful that they "are to be set as lights upon a Hill more obvious than the highest Mountaine in the World" (29), while Gershom Bulkeley in *The People's Right to Election* (1689) uses the city-on-a-hill metaphor to urge citizens to wait for a new royal charter, lest they be seen to act illegally. More fully than most, Bulkeley's father, Peter, develops the Matthew text in *The Gospel-Covenant* (2d edition, 1651) to suggest the unique position of the New England Puritans in the sight of God. In the context of a covenant theology, through which, as Thomas Shepard in his introduction explains to Bulkeley's readers, "all the evils" encountered by God's people "upon narrow search will be found to arise from breach of Covenant more or less" (*Gospel-Covenant*, sig. B2r), Bulkeley insists that the very presence of a divine audience signifies New England's particular status: "The Lord looks for more from thee, then from other people; more zeale for God, more love to his truth, more justice and equity in thy wayes; Thou shouldst be a speciall people, an onely people, none like thee in all the earth: oh be so, in loving the Gospel and Ministers of it. . . . Take heed lest for neglect of either, God *remove thy Candlesticke* out of the midst of thee; lest being now as a *Citie upon an hill*, which many seek unto, thou be left like a *Beacon upon the top of a mountaine*, desolate and forsaken" (16). The Puritan writers create out of the clarity of the Christian admonition a more complex, dramatic situation, where viewers of the light become critics of the light-bearers and the professors of Christ's word grow collectively self-conscious about the quality of their performance (see Stout, 26). As a governing metaphor for religious mission, the city on a hill becomes in essence a substitute theatrum mundi, more limited in space and action than the broadly interpreted figure from English drama; yet, because biblically derived, it gives legitimacy to an image of actor, platform, and spectator that commands behavior rather than simply expresses it.

John Bunyan in *Advice to Sufferers* (1684) makes overt what has always been implied by the Puritan reading of the passage from Matthew and in essence provides a gloss for the writings of his American colleagues: "A man, when he suffereth for Christ, is set upon a hill, upon a stage, as in a theatre, to play a part for God in the world. And you know when men are to play their parts upon a stage, they count themselves, if possible, more bound to circumspection. . . . For them the eyes of every body are fixed; they gape and stare upon them. . . . Also now God himself looks on; yea, he laugheth, as being pleased to see a good behavior attending the trial of the innocent" (296–97). Whereas the English Bunyan, in his theatrical reading of the text, imagines a laughing God in the audience, happy to see success, the Anglo-American writers are more likely to see mockers and scoffers, critics who in fact may be justified in their scorn if Christ's professors should fail. The focus in Bunyan, too, is on the individual believer; for the New England writers, it is on the company of the faithful. More to the point, a writer like Winthrop demonstrates the degree to which the Massachusetts Bay literati saw their enterprise as one in full view of angels and men, remote though the Puritans were from the devils they knew in England. Winthrop, Bulkeley, and others develop a natural Puritan need to feel themselves under obser-vation into an intensified demand for great exertion on the part of the believers as a collective entity, as if to be removed from the Old World makes them, ironically, more visible to those they have left behind. From the outset, the New Englanders look at themselves not simply as beacons of righteousness but as actors illuminated on the highest of hills by the lights of the world stage.

A corollary text in the New Testament that is often cited by Puritans is 1 Corinthians 4.9, Paul's ironical gibe at the slack believers of Corinth. In that passage, Paul portrays Christians as displayed cap-tives: "For I think that God has exhibited us apostles as last of all, like men sentenced to death; because we have become a spectacle to the world, to angels and to men." William Prynne in *Histrio-Mastix* glosses that last clause to read, "We are made a theatre or spectacle" (723), while John Cotton in *The Powring out of the Seven Vials* (1642) quotes Paul thus: "*God hath set us* (saith the Apostle) *upon a Theatre* (as the word is in the originall I Cor. 4.9) *unto the world, and unto Angels, and unto men*" (6.3.9, quoted in Kibbey, 194). In both Prynne and Cotton is the idea that exposure on the metaphoric stage glorifies the believer, a figure of speech that coexists with the analogy that will be discussed below of the hypocrite to the actor: "He was only a stage-player, a stage professor" (Hooker, *Carnal Hypocrite*, 93).

At the same time, however, Puritans recognize the seductiveness of spectacle, even one biblically derived. In his well-known election sermon, *Errand into the Wilderness* (1671), Samuel Danforth pursues Jesus's question to the disciples of what it was they *saw* in the wilderness when they encountered John the Baptist. The Greek word for the infinitive in Matthew 11.7, "What went ye out to see?" says Danforth, "agrees to shows and stage plays, plainly arguing that many of those who seemed well affected to John and flock'd after him were theatrical hearers, spectators rather than auditors [who] went to gaze upon a new and strange spectacle" (58). The same superficial response, Danforth continues, also occurred among those who heard Christ's new message. They became exhilarated "and pressed into the kingdom of God as men rush into a theater to see a pleasant sight . . . but their hot fit is soon over" (62). The very purpose of the Puritan migration is to give God's anointed a *place*—a hill-stage—on which to stand in order to be seen as a kind of universal spectacle; yet threatening to undermine this display is a simultaneous fear that all spectacles, once the "hot fit" of the audience has passed, will fade from view. As Bulkeley, echoing Winthrop and repeating himself, warns at the conclusion of *The Gospel-Covenant*,

> And for our selves here, the people of *New-England*, we should in a speciall manner labour to shine forth in holinesse above other people; we have that plenty and abundance of ordinances and meanes of grace, as few people enjoy the like; wee are as a City set upon an hill, in the open view of all the earth, the eyes of the world are upon us, because we professe our selves to be a people in Covenant with God, and therefore not onely the Lord our God, with whom we have made Covenant, but heaven and earth, Angels and men, that are witnesses of our profession, will cry shame upon us, if wee walke contrary to the Covenant. (431)

Unless it leads to madness or despair, the continual awareness of being watched and evaluated can be an extraordinary stimulus to activity. In his own way, John Smith performs before a public, though by his record, he seems to have been one of the few early Virginians to be moved to productive labor. For the New England religious nonconformists, it is a different story. Distant from all that they knew, yet fully exposed to the judgment of celestial and earthly beings, the Puritans imported with them a theatrical sense of life that lent significance to the smallest action. Not only did they require of life that it be public and performative, but they carried with them a rhetorical tradition of confrontation, dialogue, and dramatic narrative that could at once elucidate and elevate or denounce and deflate. But to say this raises a question: How aware are the Puritans of the subtleties—and irony— in their use of theatrical language?

One answer is that they were no less, and possibly more, aware than modern historians and critics of American Puritanism. Perry Miller, for instance, in his own rhetorically suggestive comment on the Puritans' "errand into the wilderness," thinks that the New Englanders lost their audience during the English Civil War, making moot their obsession with being observed: "If an actor, playing the leading role in the greatest dramatic spectacle of the century, were to attire himself and put on his make-up, rehearse his lines, take a deep breath, and stride onto the stage, only to find the theater dark and empty, no spotlight working, and himself entirely alone, he would feel as did New England around 1650 and 1660" (*Errand*, 12–13). Even if the statement is accurate for the time, it does not apply for very long; we might do better to ask the significance of Miller's critical trope. In his writings on the Puritans, Miller finds theatrical images to be convenient ways of talking about their intellectual achievements—played out, of course, in an "intellectual amphitheatre," to use but one phrase from *The New England Mind: From Colony to Province* (14). In the commentaries of other scholars, one finds frequently enough an unqualified phrase such as "the drama of salvation" to describe the phenomena of Puritan life. What does it mean, in another instance, when Kenneth Murdock in his *Literature and Theology in Colonial New England* says of Johnson's *Wonder-Working Providence* that the author "saw history in terms of God's providence and found its meaning through his firm assurance that he and his compatriots were simply actors in a drama divinely written and staged" (86)? Or what is the warrant for a statement like that of Michael Walzer on preaching as conceived of by William Perkins: "The preacher dramatized his theology by setting men on God's stage as travelers or soldiers, there to fight off the attacks of Satan or to journey, never without difficulty and hardship, toward salvation" (145)? The point is this: without always recognizing the source for their metaphors, scholars seem to be aware at some level of the theatricality of this announcedly antitheatrical people.

In one sense, the Puritan notion of Providence encourages commentators to use stage figures in order to describe the Stoiclike insistence that God directs all events and humans can do little but follow his instructions. In reading through John Winthrop's *Journal* or Thomas Shepard's *Autobiography* and *Journal*, one cannot escape noticing, as the writers themselves could not, the daily intrusions of God's omnipresent hand in the public affairs of New England. But one also sees those private moments, those tinglings of the soul that a Shepard or a Wigglesworth records in secret that also make the psychic space within the individual a platform for contending passions. In the Puritan mind, say the critics, both public and private conflicts conflate to a single view. It is a commonplace in the commentary on the American Puritans to draw analogies between the life of a believer and the performance of an actor in God's theater, or between the history of the theocratic colonies and a divinely constructed drama. In the case of Thomas Shepard's *Autobiography*, to take only one example, editor Michael McGiffert describes the theologian's reading of God's intrusiveness in the world as his seeing "a piece of divine stagecraft" (6). More revealingly, Jesper Rosenmeier delineates Shepard's sense of his life's purpose in terms that might apply to almost any minister or literate believer of the seventeenth century: "Once more on the little stage of the individual soul, the cosmic drama of redemption has been reenacted" (442). In other words, commentators on the Puritans have seen in the overall predilection for private, self-exclamatory "ejaculations" and public, communitywide displays of mission an inherent theatrical sensibility, the complexities and ironies of which have not always been fully explained. The fact remains that the Puritans themselves use theatrical figures, but not always as the critics do.

For New Englanders the question of how one viewed oneself theatrically could matter a great deal. Shepard, for instance, enjoins his congregants to honor God's grace by showing their faith; otherwise, "You have not Christian hearts in you, that will now have no care to do this work there before you are turned off the stage" (*Works*, 2:110). But one problem for Puritans that prevents a full acknowledgment of the similitude between world and stage is worry over role-playing. The pastoral warrants urge upon the faithful an absolute conformity between being and seeming, but to participate in a divine drama requires that one play a part. To "play" anything makes the Puritan uncomfortable, at the least. Play is acceptable in children, says John Cotton, "for their bodies are too weak to labour, and their minds to study are too shallow" (*Practical Commentary* [1656], 124–25, quoted in Beales, 31). For adults, however, the seriousness of life requires an earnestness in personality and a rightness in conduct that make play an absurdity. After all, the arch-dissembler is Satan, as Thomas Hooker makes clear in *Poore Doubting Christian* (1629). William Bradford, in answering charges by renegade preacher John Lyford that he criticized Lyford for "preaching to all in general," dismisses this notion as beyond logic: "Now, to procure all to come to hear, and then to blame him for preaching to all, were to play the mad men" (180). Bradford, who elsewhere refers to Lyford and John Oldham as having "played the villains" with the Pilgrims (183), makes apparent the general usage that to *play* at something leads to mischief. Shall a man, asks Hooker, told to be meek, "play the Beare amongst the Beares" (*Soules Humiliation*, 213)? No, because he must be what he is; meekness is to "the humble Soul . . . his part and position" (213).

Even worse, perhaps, playing, in the sense of playacting, can turn to something more severely disquieting than petty villainy. David Leverenz, in his post-Freudian analysis of Puritan culture, especially Puritan antagonism to the stage, sees theatrical performance as undermining the most fundamental aspects of the patriarchal order: "Men wearing women's clothes on stage horrified the Puritans," he remarks, "for whom the affront to biblical and patriarchal self-definition was a symbol of more profound fears" (103), that is, of uncertain gender identification. Whether the gender question represents the most "profound" of Puritan anxieties is an arguable point—Agnew, for example, sees the problem more as a distaste for travesty than a particular phobia about stage transvestism (131)—but it does seem as if role-playing, or role reversal, threatens the social structure of an oligarchy. If one is to take a role, it is better to be it than play it.

For if adults listen carefully to God's commands and purge themselves of self, then role-playing becomes an affirmation of Christian identity. Jonathan Edwards speaks to this in the autobiographical sketch (the so-called "Personal Narrative") that Samuel Hopkins includes in *The Life and Character of the Late Reverend Mr. Jonathan Edwards* (1765). There, Edwards proclaims his joy at being "nothing" before God so that the deity might be "all" (D. Levin, 31). Likewise, Edward Taylor's meditations are full not only of a desire for purging the self of the self, and thus letting God enter unobtruded, but also of a playing, in the sense of playfully conceived being, before God: "Make me, O Lord, Thy Spinning Wheele compleate," he urges in "Huswifery," an advancement on his proclamation in the prologue to *Preparatory Meditations*: "I am this Crumb of Dust" (467, 1). These conceits remain safe because Taylor usually adopts the nonhuman as a metaphoric identity, not the human as a temporary guise. Of course, from the pen of Michael Wigglesworth, even this strategy becomes a weapon with which to abuse oneself, as when the diarist cries, "I am vile. . . . I deserve to be the stepping-stone of thy wrath" (*Diary*, 53). But his usage is really a claim that the self, uncorrected, unpurged, plays roles despised in God's sight; in order to play the proper role, the self must be abused that God may put the shell that remains to some good purpose.

This matter of what role one plays takes genuinely dramatic shape in Wigglesworth's *Day of Doom* (1662). In an introductory poem, "To the Christian Reader," the author declares,

> Reader, I am a fool,
> And have adventuréd
> To play the fool this once for Christ,
> The more his fame to spread.   (13)

Wigglesworth writes at a time when his ill health prevents him from fully engaging his ministerial duties; unable to preach and thus deprived of his usual role, he plays the fool and takes to print, giving voice to his "prison'd thoughts" while urging his fellow Christians to "get a part in Christ" (14, 17). *The Day of Doom* itself has many elements of stage drama: it opens in medias res ("Still was the night"), it assembles a cast (Christ, train, "goats," "sheep"), it uses dialogue (sinners pleading, Christ judging), it circumscribes activity (courtroom motif), and it provides stage directions in the margins ("The wicked brought to the Bar"). No doubt this sort of dramatizing has contributed to the modern critical trope, "the drama of salvation," to describe the process of justification; but for the faithful, dramatizing life in a detheatricalized society creates its own problems.

English Puritans deride the stage because it shows evil characters and activities; the very representation of evil, they argue, will itself encourage vice, not prohibit it, even when vice is routed. But in some sermons and certainly in Wigglesworth's poem, sin is given a multitude of voices with which to justify itself. Indeed, *The Day of Doom* stands out in the literature of the period for Wigglesworth's ability to re-create so convincingly the argument of reprobates who protest against Christ's condemnation of their souls: "Can God delight in such a sight as sinners' misery?" the sinners, not without reason, ask (stanza 132). But for Wigglesworth, it is the special providence of text that makes his own voice giving acceptable. Given the rigid ideological boundaries to which he adheres, Wigglesworth imagines the whole of humankind, including, through the medium of personal dream-vision turned poetic drama, a rich variety of sinners and apostates. They play before their audience by means of re-creative sight: printed word to reader's eye to believer's heart and mind—with no distracting physical enactments to obscure the message. One group of sinners plead their case by arguing that "their betters" provided misleading "examples": " 'When men of Parts, Learning, and Arts, professing Piety, / Did thus and thus, it seem'd to us we might take liberty' " (stanza 115). Christ repudiates this logic, asserting that, because "My Word is pure, the Rule was sure," there is no excuse to follow the example of living beings, no matter how godly, when through imitation one only picks up "Good men's defects" (stanzas 116, 119).

All self-justification is defeated by the rule of justification in Christ, and those who took on unscriptural roles are condemned to hell. For showmanship, Wigglesworth's conception of the end rivals that in John Foxe's play, *Christus Triumphans*. "With Iron bands," the saints bind the hands and feet of sinners; once cast into the pit, "without respite," the doomed "wail, and cry and howl" (stanza 201). The chorus of saints, meanwhile, bursts into song, and in Wigglesworth's implied stagecraft, "ascend" (stanza 220). Those who play at life, who conceal "filthy facts and secret acts," find themselves exposed in the glaring light of Christ's coming, then pitched into darkness, out of the reader-viewer's sight. Those who lead the antitheatrical life, one in which humans resist imitation of each other and seek instead conformity with scriptural dictates, are promised through the medium of "God's bright countenance" a clean, well-lighted, theatrical end.

With a fear of overstepping the roles one can play, Puritan writers often save some of their most inflammatory rhetoric for hypocrisy. They detail any number of categories and shades of meaning and frequently show awareness of the etymological relationship of *hypocrite* to *actor* (see Harris, 1–14). Wigglesworth devotes stanzas 68–80 of *Day of Doom* to hypocrites, taking pains to illustrate their corrupting influence on church sacraments: "How durst you venture, bold guests, to enter in such a sordid hue, / Amongst my guests, unto those Feasts that were not made for you?" (stanza 78). Hypocrisy, then, and not simply its subset, sexual misidentification, seems to be the American Puritan's greatest fear, especially in the land envisioned by Winthrop, where both the opportunity for glory and the chance to be scorned are great. On the one hand, even a youthful Wigglesworth can urge the minister to act in order to enliven an oration: "Doth he take upon him to personate others in word or deedes? why he presents his hearers not with a lifeless picture, but with the living persons of those concerning whom he speaks" ("Prayse of Eloquence" [1650], 8). On the other hand, with the imagined furtiveness of the Indian as an example, and the constant pressure of being observed, Puritans plumb their hearts and look intently at each other with the purpose of exposing the role-playing that masks secret sin.

It seems natural, then, that the language of the stage would be used to describe the dangers of hypocrisy to individuals and to the commonwealth. Hypocrites threaten the elemental hierarchies fixed by magistrates and ministers. Shepard notes that "a stage player, that acts the part of a king, wants the glory of a king" (*Works*, 2:438); that is, the hypocrite is one who wishes to transcend his station by false means and thus violate the fixity of order so succinctly expressed by Winthrop in the first section of "A Model of Christian Charity." For ministers, challenges to hierarchy undermine most those who preach the Word, and since actors also live by oral delivery, the parallel is uncomfortably close, as patristic writers are well aware. Thomas Cobbett, in *A*

Practical Discourse of Prayer (1654), reserves a special vehemence for preacherly hypocrites who exhibit a want of learning: "In hypocrisie there is affectation, hypocrites are stage-players, which albeit they are illiterate dunces many of them, yet will be highflown sometimes in their expressions, their mouth speaketh great swelling words when they speak to me or God, or else they faile of their use and aime" (315, quoted in Levy, 129). While Cobbett's remarks support the contention that the Puritans abjured rhetorical fluff, they also indicate how uncertain the world is, as if the struggle to discern the real from the illusory is continual. In the New World, where preternatural occurrences present themselves with astonishing frequency, the battle has special significance. Edward Johnson finds that those who would align with Satan (like the Antinomians) and block the "Restauration of the purity of Christs Ordinances in his Churches in all places" (121) are enemies "well educated in the Masking schoole of Hippocrisy" (121–22). The task of the Christian, then, is to remove masks and expose to the world those who wear them. In his final poem in *Wonder-Working Providence*, Johnson imagines a dynamic Christ as a magician, the thaumaturge or wonder-worker who smashes the performances of his foes; the Christian could do no better than to follow Jesus and "unmaske those men that lye in corners lurking, / Whose damned doctrines dayly seates advance" (274). Yet once the public obsession with preternatural enemies recedes after 1692, the language of mask takes on a reduced potency. When Benjamin Colman in 1708 enjoins the magistrates to beware of wearing "a meer *Mask* of Religion," he is offering counsel, not, as Johnson does, a war cry for attack (*Piety*, 423).

Among the Puritans who come to America, the most eloquent writer on hypocrisy is Thomas Hooker (though Kenneth Marc Harris, on the basis largely of Hooker's categories in *The Soules Vocation*, calls that writer's targets "cartoon hypocrites" [9]). Reading through his works, one sees the attack on hypocrisy as something like Hooker's special mission (Shuffelton, 169–70). In our own time, it is hard to comprehend the horror with which the Puritans viewed the hypocrite. From the pulpits of mainline American churches today, ministers intone against famine, homelessness, and nuclear war, conditions whose magnitude or destructive capacity seems concretely apparent. For Hooker and his contemporaries, war, poverty, and sickness are simply facts of life, part of the landscape. Neither war nor hunger are as destabilizing to the Puritan as the *perception* that things are not as they seem; after all, what could be more threatening than to believe one is in the company of the faithful and find out otherwise? Hooker, in an early sermon, *The Carnal Hypocrite* (ca. 1626/1638), speaks to this fear by noting that "carnal hypocrites may have the guise and portraiture or the outward profession of a child of God" (93). In all these concrete particulars, they are the same, but in the heart, how different!

When Hooker renders his obsession with the hypocrite in theatrical terms, he speaks out of a deep sense of the reality of the stage; and while what he says about it could be known from writings and commonplace information, the lengths to which he goes in drawing an analogy between actor and believer bespeak a fascination—the reverse side of horror—for the profession that violates by its very nature the purity of motive in professing Christ:

> Look as it is among stage-players. The stage-player puts on brave apparel and comes on to the stage, and resembles the person of a king and acts the part of a monarch; but if you pull him off the stage and pluck his robes from his back, he appears in his own likeness. So it is here. A carnal hypocrite, a cursed dissembler, is like a stage-player. He takes upon him the person and profession of a godly, humble, lowly man, and he acts the part marvelous curiously, and he speaks big words against his corruptions and he humbles himself before God, and he hears and prays and reads; but when God plucks him off the stage of the world and his body drops into the grave, and his soul goes to hell, then it appears that he had not the power of godliness; he was only a stage-player, a stage professor. (93)

Puritanism abounds in, revels in, paradox. As for Hooker, no man is higher than the lowly Christian, no life's work more glorious than simple faith; thus he sets up the analogy, player-monarch-offstage, hypocrite-Christian-hell not only to emphasize the nature of the hypocrite but also to parallel kingly station and humble demeanor. In this inverse world, Hooker suggests the existence of a suppressed radicalism with Puritan orthodoxy, predicated no doubt on the biblical prophecies that the mighty shall fall and the meek inherit the earth. It seems only a short rhetorical step between plucking the robes off a player-king on a local (English) stage and plucking the robes (or lopping the head) off a real king on the world stage. Hooker's more parochial interest shows us that he reviles the hypocrite, that "stage professor," as much as a Winthrop would object to a rebellion in which "the poore and dispised rise upp against theire superiours and shake off theire yoake" ("Model," *Papers*, 283). To be sure, Hooker wants nothing of inversion; once the true believer is affirmed as the standard by which reality is measured, he demands that profession and professor be identical. But he shows that to counter the hypocrite, one must have a theatrical imagination; thus stage remains alive as a trope by which to snare the player-saint.

If the concrete reality of professing cannot be maintained in the literal body and physical actions of the believer, the world of faith dissolves into the transitory illusions typical of stage entertainments. In *The Soules Humiliation* (1640), Hooker separates hypocrites and Christians into the dead and the quick, the latter eating the bread of Christ, the former with only "the ayre of hearing, and the picture, and shadow of praying" to "feed upon" (67). Such depictions of hypocrisy put the worry about witchcraft into perspective. Though Puritans believe in the palpability of evil, the devil practices his art in a shadow world; the Prince of the Air, after all, is skilled in spectral shows, those mere pictures of godliness that dissolve with exposure or death. How Hooker would abominate film! But even that medium could not threaten so immediately as the stage, with, paradoxically, its living actors masked by dead identities and its point-for-point parallels made between the despised players and the glorified saints.

Hooker singles out for separate treatment the "vain-glorious hypo-crite," one who is "marvellous zealous for God and his truth in outward appearance" (*Soules Implantation*, 263); in his enthusiasm, in his desire to be seen, this faith-faker mocks the nearly fanatical awareness of being watched that the good Christian perched on a hill maintains: "Even as the Stage-player that sets up a great stage that he may be above the people; so it is with a vain-glorious wretch; prayer is a good stage, and fasting, and hearing, and preaching are very fine stages for him, upon which he acts his part that others may see him, that glory may come to him, and not that the glory and grace of Christ may bee extolled: hee would lift himselfe to heaven, and cast downe Christ to hell" (264). Thus, the presence of the deceiving believer makes the threat of inversion complete: where the ideal believer purges himself of self in order to glorify God and justify the cosmic order, the vainglorious hypocrite fills heaven with himself, puffs out and swells and so pushes Christ to hell. In Hooker's writing is contained the essential expression of the stage as a realm that turns the Christian world upside down—yet in it, too, is found a troubling characterization predictive of Puritans to come.

One other concern Hooker shares with other Puritans extends to ministers themselves. The act of preaching, from Puritan eyes, often seems laden with paradox, as if, like the faith they practice, it were a task nearly impossible to fulfill. On the one hand, ministers need to give life to the lessons they preach, though always remaining aware of the need to stop short of excess. As A. W. Plumstead describes the delivery of election sermons, "The preacher transcends his role as a teacher of law, and law, and becomes an actor. . . . He is to do for New England what Shakespeare did for his audience—bring the dead pages of history alive, with their shame and their glory, into significance and meaning" (35–36). On the other hand, there are always limits, and no Puritan of scruple would accept Plumstead's analogy openly, even as praise. In *The Application of Redemption* (1657), Hooker enjoins ministers to speak plainly, to say "a Spade is a Spade," and avoid "those secret wipes, and witty jerks" in the pulpit: "What! A Minister a Jester! O fearful! to make the Pulpit a Stage, to play with sin; where he should terrifie the Conscience for it? The Lord abominates the practice, he that knows and fears the Lord should abhor it with detestation" (211; see Bush, *Writings*, 14). Yet as Sargent Bush affirms, Hooker's own rhetorical style allows him to play a role, that of "incipient dramatist," by the richness of his characterizations of sinners and biblical figures (*Writings*, 182). These conflicts can be reconciled largely by placing more faith in language than in delivery; the minister in the pulpit must consciously prevent himself from turning that platform into a stage and himself into a "stage-player, a stage professor." At the same time, as Solomon Stoddard urges in *The Defects of Preachers Reproved* (1724), a minister must, through ex tempore preaching, reach for "Drowsy" congregants; he must enliven his text, within the limits of plain style, in such a way as to re-create within the minds of his auditors a living theater of God's judgments.

For the earlier generations, given the insistence on stage-acting as an analogy for hypocrisy, one can understand the objections to performance and the fear on the part of New England ministers of being thought anything like those actors they denounced metaphorically and literally from their pulpits. In old England, the presence of a vigorous theater posed a number of perceived threats. The production of plays on Sunday violated the Sabbath; the plays themselves mocked religious tenets and personages (especially Puritans); and the institution of the theater supported a world that negated all that the Puritans stood for, one, in David Leverenz's words, that was "idle, lower class, spendthrift, disorderly, womanizing" (24). In New England, however, removed from direct contact with the stage, ministers fear the abstraction more than the concrete fact. There, the threats are essentially that the theater would compete with the church; that the stage would provide a living example of hypocrisy; and that time devoted to the stage would be time diverted from the essential pursuits of a godly, industrious commonwealth (see Tichi, "Thespis").

Though the focus here has been on ministerial rhetoric, it is important to remember that not all first-generation writers use theatrical figures only to describe hypocrisy. In her quaternion poems, Anne Bradstreet uses stage metaphors in familiar Elizabethan ways. Following "The Foure Elements" and "Of the foure humours in Mans constitution" in *The Tenth Muse*, she introduces "The Foure Ages of Man" thus: "Loe now! four other acts upon the stage, / Childhood, and Youth, the Manly, and Old-age" (35). Several things can be seen in this passage. For one thing, the context suggests Bradstreet's awareness of her text as performance; in trying to find a persona that somehow links her reading in nonreligious literature with her role as daughter and wife of Puritan magistrates, she reminds us throughout the poems of a voice, aware of itself as poet, speaking before an audience whose membership may be various. This awareness of her self as writer and of text as performance is not unique to her; this issue will be explored more fully later in the chapter on Cotton Mather. Nevertheless, it suggests a dimension to Puritan writing that seems unavoidable even within the limits of nonconformist rhetoric: an awareness that every action before God, including—or especially— writing, is watched and judged.

But this secular-seeming usage in the "Foure Ages" has prompted scholars to look to Jaques's speech in *As You Like It* as a possible source, even though no printed editions are known to have existed in the American colonies before the end of the century. While she may have known Shakespeare's play, Shakespeare himself may have gotten the image from other texts; it is not necessary to show that Bradstreet knew Shakespeare in order to recognize that the Puritan rhetorical world included the theatrum mundi trope (but see Piercy, 59–60; Stanford, 141–43; and White, 64–66, 351–52). As Josephine K. Piercy notes, Bradstreet's acknowledged favorite poet, Guillaume de Salluste, Seigneur du Bartas, uses an orthodox theatrum mundi figure in his writing (Piercy, 59); and another of Bradstreet's quaternions, "The Foure Monarchics," is based largely on Sir Walter Raleigh's *History of the World* (1614), a text that also includes theatrical metaphors (White, 62; Fisch, 85). Indeed, as I have tried to show, any Puritan writer might have confronted theatrical figures from a variety of sources.

Sources aside, Bradstreet's use of stage metaphors in the quaternions, while not doctrinaire, is little different from other Puritan writers of her time. In the "Foure Ages," Youth comes "prauncing on the Stage" and certainly, finds theater an entertainment appropriate to his hot blood: "Cards, Dice, and Oaths, concomitant, I love; / To Masques, to Playes, to Taverns stil I move" (40). But even the presence of a bewitching stage does not negate the existence of a larger, cosmic one. Old Age, who has seen the innocence, folly, and confusion of the first three ages, "on the Stage am come to act my last" (44).

Another use of theatrum mundi, in her poem, "In honour of that High and Mighty Princess, Queen ELIZABETH, of most happy memory," has prompted Ivy Schweitzer to see Bradstreet's figure as part of a feminist challenge to the limitations placed on women. "The World's the Theater where she did act," says Bradstreet of the late queen; "She hath wip'd off th' aspersion of her Sex, / That women wisdome lack to play the Rex" (155, 156). Schweitzer comments that "Bradstreet's allusions to Elizabeth's public persona as a theatrical representation are curiously heretical, since the Puritans were particularly strident in their opposition to playgoing. They suggest Bradstreet's desire to flout those restrictions (as with her reading and defense of Sidney's *Arcadia*) and her awareness that Elizabeth did indeed 'play' a part which was not 'natural' for women" (304). While Bradstreet clearly intends to claim a portion for women (though as Schweitzer insightfully points out, within limits), the theatrical figure itself does not add to the flouting. It may be said that her use of the figure is more typical of the secularized version of theatrum mundi employed by non-Puritans, but her Puritan readers would have recognized the trope as well within their own tradition. As her eulogist, Rev. John Norton (nephew to the elder John Norton), writes, the passing of the Tenth Muse herself calls forth an image of a theater and a divine show of grief:

> Did not the language of the stars foretel
> A mournefull Scoene when they with tears did swell?
>
> . . . .
>
> Behold how tears flow from the learned hill,
> How the bereaved Nine do daily fill
> The bosome of the fleeting Air with groans,
> And wofull Accents, which witness their moanes.
> (Bradstreet, 534)

Indeed, her death requires a show from the other muses (itself an unexceptional pagan allusion in Puritan writing), who are character- ized by Norton as actresses:

> Farewell my Muse, since thou has left thy shrine,
> I am unblest in one, but blest in nine.
> Fair *Thespian* Ladyes, light your torches all,
> To court her ashes with a learned tear,
> A briny sacrifice, let not a smile appear.   (535)

Norton brings Bradstreet's own tropes into line with his focus on the worldwide importance of her American life. Though he stresses her belletristic contributions, he also acknowledges that she, like Eliza- beth, has performed before a watching and adoring public; the mourn- ing of her death becomes a global spectacle, right in its way for "that Pattern and Patron of Virtue, . . . Mirror of her Age, Glory of her Sex," Anne Bradstreet (533).

Whether or not Bradstreet knew Shakespeare, we do know that other Puritans thought plays to be appropriate reading. In *The Simple*

Cobler of Aggawam (1647), for instance, Nathaniel Ward quotes approvingly from Plautus's *Miles Gloriosus*—and for that matter, from Petronius (76). By the 1670s, Harvard freshmen read Sophocles, Euripides, and Aristophanes; Increase Mather has in his library the works of Plautus, Seneca, and Sophocles; and Samuel Sewall records in his diary the reading of plays by Dryden (1686) and Jonson (1706) (Meserve, 17; Sewall, *Diary*, 1:136, 551). The fact of the stage seems necessary, like the devil, perhaps, to illuminate the insidiousness of hypocrisy—but the physical theater must seem remote to New Englanders by the second generation. Nevertheless, anything outside the realm of approved ritual that resembles stage entertainment is squelched quickly. Sewall notes in his various writings a number of attempts to establish performance in New England, all without success. In 1685 dancing master Francis Stepney tries to inaugurate a dancing and possibly a drama school, claiming, says Sewall, "that by one Play he could teach more Divinity than Mr. Willard or the New Testament." The ministerial rejoinder is clear enough: "Mr. Moodey said twas not a time for N.E. to dance" (*Diary*, 1:83). For Sewall, that seems to be enough (for the time being), but the reasoning of the ministers themselves involves a number of calculations that serve to protect local interests, including ministerial hegemony: "No doubt but that if a Stage play were set up, many Children would be as much pleased with it, as now they are with the Dance. If a Blasphemer shall tell them, There's as good Divinity to be learned by a Play as by the Scripture itself, perhaps they may be debauched into the belief of it, if ever they should see Scripture stories acted in a Play, which indeed is a profane Practice common amongst the Papists, but prohibited in Reformed Churches under pain of highest censure" (I. Mather, *Arrow*, 25). The threat expressed here is not drama per se nor the playhouses of London; it is rather the intrusion of Catholic liturgical theater into reformed Protestant New England.

In 1687 costumed sword displays are tried, at the apparent instigation of a tavern keeper, Captain Wing, but he is persuaded by Sewall and others that " 'tis offensive" (1:137–38; Rankin, 3). Most horrific to Sewall is a later incident, in 1714, in which "there is a Rumor, as if some design'd to have a Play acted in the Council-Chamber, next Monday; which much surprises me; and as much as in me lyes, I do forbid it" (letter to Isaac Addington, Mar. 2, 1714, *Letter-Book*, 2:29–30). As with ministerial objections to confusing theater and church, Sewall wishes to keep the purity of the magistrates' house: "The Romans were very fond of their Plays: but I never heard they were so far set upon them, as to turn their Senat-House into a Play-House. Our Town-House was built at great Cost and Charge, for the sake of very serious and important Business. . . . Let it not be abused with Dances, or other scenical divertisements" (30).

Of course, Sewall misses a key point. The reason the Romans never confuse senate with theater is that they have stages already. For the Americans, without a theater (at least in New England), the theatrical impulse must find its space where space is available—and none is better, none closer in function, than the "Town-House" of which Sewall is so proud. Yet Sewall, as a reader of plays, may also recognize that the madcap, ludic world of a Plautus or his English imitators threatens the purpose of the meetinghouse—because it is so similar—and undermines the covenantal authority of ministers and magistrates. Though this play was never staged (Meserve, 28), it remains that among the populace is a desire for the very thing that is a sermonic byword for the worst of offenses to a Christian commonwealth. Increase Mather, ever on the alert for wrongful encouragements to lewd behavior, remarks that "there is much discourse of beginning Stage-Plays in New England" (*Testimony* [1688], quoted in Meserve, 20). But New England's place in world history must remain intact: as Sewall concludes of the 1714 episode, "Let not Christian Boston goe beyond Heathen Rome in the practice of shamefull Vanities" (*Letter-Book*, 2:30).

The example of Rome presents itself on several occasions to Increase Mather who, perhaps because he spent considerable time in Britain, seems far more worried than many of his contemporaries about the dangers of the stage. Following the deaths of two promising Harvard students by drowning, Mather in December 1696 preached his A *Discourse Concerning the Uncertainty of the Times of Men* (1697) to warn the surviving students to be aware always of their actions: "*Tertullian* speaks of a Christian Woman, that going to a *Stage Play*, an *Evil Spirit* there took possession of her, who when it was wondered at, that he should get possession of one that was a Christian, said, *I found her in my own ground*, and therefore might well take possession of her" (393). The reference to Tertullian suggests how beholden the Puritans are to that most theatrophobic of church fathers, and consequently, how they view the stage as a place where people are prey both to temptation and judgment; but it also indicates how potent theater appears as an antiecclesiastical institution. In his apocalyptical text, *A Discourse Concerning Faith and Fervency in Prayer* (1710), Mather again brings forth the theaters of antiquity as an image of the ever-waiting traps in which Christians, unaware of the impression they make on others, may be caught: "One of the most woful things that ever was in the World has been the Scandalous contentions which have been among Christians. They were for this derided by the Heathen, who would on that account expose them on their Publick Theaters, and Ridicule them in their impious Stage Plays. And has it been better in these Latter Ages?" (55–56). The answer is no, as if to say the stage still waits outside the church to convert high seriousness into buffoonery or theological knots into clownish bows. Like Chrysostom, whom he frequently cites in his sermons as the "golden-tongued orator," Mather recognizes the stage as the church's alter altar, an antiplatform where the platforms and synodical codes are rendered absurd by their theatrical confinement and perverse conversion into play.

Nevertheless, while the stage represents a variety of evils, the image of a theater provides at the same time a frame for the picture of exposed believers standing before a spectating God, a scene so apparent in the city on a hill and related metaphors. The very same Increase Mather who cites Thomas Beard and William Prynne in writing against "profane" amusements (as in *Arrow*, 15–16, 22–23)—and who keeps Greek plays in his library—also finds the stage a convenient metaphor for the passage of the generations. Invoking in one of his jeremiads a common theme of the 1670s, Mather rebukes the "present Generation in New England" as being "lamentably degenerate": "So we may say, the first Generation of Christians in New-England, is in a manner gone off the stage, and there is another and more sinful Generation risen up in their stead" (*Call from Heaven*, 61). But as Sacvan Bercovitch makes clear with the jeremiad formula, there is always hope, even expectation, that things will get better (*American Jeremiad*).

Despite his misgivings about their degeneration, Mather prays that "they who shall stand upon the Stage of the world as soon as we are gone, may be and doe better then their Predecessors" (*Call from Heaven*, sig. A2v).

In another generational jeremiad, *David Serving His Generation* (1698), Mather borrows the Pauline trope in a call to New Englanders to dedicate themselves to facing trouble in their own time: "Let us always remember what Eyes are upon us. There are glorious Eyes, which though we see not them, they are observing us in all our motions. The Eyes of holy Angels are upon us. 1 Cor. 4.9 *We are made a Spectacle to Angels.* They observe how we acquit our selves, and if we Serve God and our Generation as we ought to do, they will come in as witnesses of our Fidelity at the last day. And the Eyes of Jesus Christ the Son of God behold us. . . . And the eyes of God are upon us" (26). Uncharitably, we could dismiss this and similar Puritan texts as the rantings of paranoiacs; but even in the most sympathetic reading, we can hardly overlook the linking of mission to a kind of constant performance. Such a use of stage deflects into the future the culmination and completion of the American errand; it requires further acting before the all-seeing God before one can say that the errand is finished. It is amazing, after all, "that when *new-Jerusalem* should come down from Heaven *America* would be the Seat of it," Increase Mather tells us, that land being "so dark a corner of the world" (*Call from Heaven*, 56). But it is that spatialization of metaphor that gives the American concept of New Jerusalem its special intensity. In his study of New England millennialism, Philip Gura notes the need to keep completion of the Puritan mission open as a future, not a currently realizable goal: "Rather than viewing their errand into America's wilderness as almost accomplished and the New Jerusalem virtually built, the colonists redefined it *geographically* and deferred it forward into *historical* time" (182). Paradoxically, then, stage becomes the ideal metaphor to express the millennialist mission. New England is that space, identified in particular geographical terms, where a truly historical event will occur. As a circumscribed space, New Jerusalem surrounded by the wilds of forest and sea, New England is that stage where the generations enter and exit, playing their manifest parts in history.

While the stage makes a convenient negative analogy to aid ministers in the war against hypocrisy, on the corporate level the figural stage embodies more completely than other metaphors of mission—the vine, for instance—the Puritan emphasis on action, plot, character, being watched, and deferral of satisfaction into future time (with proper attention to signs, portents, and foreshadowing), which are all parts of the nonconformist conception of life. If in the background of American Puritan rhetoric lies the apocalyptical stage of John Foxe, in the foreground and nearer to New England are the heavens above for the display of God's messages to his people. Those potent signs of destruction to come, comets, are, as John Sherman describes in his introduction to Increase Mather's *Kometographia* (1683), "Periwigged Heraulds" who appear, almost as Restoration actors, on the "aethereal stage" (sig. A4r).

Below the heavens are other theatricalized signs of God's presence. As David Williams has suggested, executions and execution sermons make ready-made scenes for purified dramas on the world stage. With the collapse of witchcraft prosecutions after Salem, the effort to convert common criminals seems as fully ceremonial as the rituals of confession and execution used in this century by the Communist regime in China. In his account of Esther Rogers, a woman declared guilty of infanticide, John Rogers (no relation) describes her conversion just before execution as one of those expected wonders in a godly commonwealth: "Thou mayst behold a Tragick Scene, strangely changed into a Theater of Mercy" (*Death the Certain Wages of Sin* [1701], 118, quoted in D. E. Williams, "'Behold,'" 828). Even without theater, even among those with a decidedly antitheatrical ideology, New Englanders see themselves as treated frequently to shows on a grand scale, in the thaumaturgical theater of God's thrilling displays of condemnation and mercy.

By 1710, the date of Ebenezer Pemberton's election sermon, *The Divine Original Dignity of Government Asserted*, ministers so inclined feel little hesitation about including a developed stage metaphor that does not simply attack hypocrisy. Pemberton's thesis has two essential parts: civic leaders must recognize that, like other men, they are mortal and therefore ought not to hold themselves too far above the people; and yet, as "gods," that is, as people acting in God's stead and by his commands, they must not be falsely attacked or over-thrown. With the first argument, Pemberton soaks the Christian message in Stoic broth, giving the whole sermon an Epictetian flavor. Leaders must learn above all the lessons of prudence, says Pemberton: "These will prompt them so to act the part assigned them on the Stage of Life, that their External condition may be found in conjunction with the more valuable inherent Dignity of a vertuous Mind; that when Death shall shut up the present scene, a brighter scene of Glory may open upon them; and they appear with Superiour characters on the Stage of true Glory and Immortality" (3). But the cautionary note is that death levels all; and whatever "visible Ensigns of distinguishing Greatness" may mark an individual, all men of power shall "retire off the Stage of this World in a stage of Equality with the meanest" (9). For Pemberton, the world *is* a theater, life is a stage. It simply must be put into perspective. Thus the bogey stage of Hooker gives way to a milder trope that has shown up from time to time since Shepard. Indeed, Pemberton returns to the metaphor one last time to clinch the point: "After all their Pomp and Parade on the stage of Life," he says to his audience of magistrates, "they drop into their Graves, and nothing of all their *Glory descends after them*" (63; see Plumstead, 23–24).

What precisely does it mean for a Puritan to suggest that the earth or life is a stage? For the use of this world makes all the difference, even if one must come to despise the "shows" of temporal life. Jonathan Mitchell (d. 1668) gives what may be construed as a typical vision in his sermon, A *Discourse of the Glory* (2d edition, 1721): "This lower World was made but to be a Stage for men to act their parts for a few ages, and then taken down: Hence it stands but on Crazy shows, it may and will e're long fall on heaps: It is like a Tent or Tabernacle that stands on stakes thrust into the ground. But the third Heaven stands on strong unmoved foundations, Heb. 11.10" (73). Mitchell urges several things by this metaphor: this world is *lower*, and therefore "but" a stage, suggesting impermanence, reduced importance, transition, in-deed, the transitoriness of the earth itself (see also Levy, 129–30). Life is confined to "Crazy shows," and the stage will soon be "taken down." One cannot overvalue one's acting, even though conversion depends on the quality of one's actions (in the heart and thus outwardly as well in this illusionless theater) before God. Later ministers, however, by implication, take the metaphor almost for granted. Whether in John James's elegy for John Haynes, "Who made his Exit off the Stage of this world: Nov.—1713," or in Joseph Baxter's phrase, "the Stage of Being," to signify the troubled space occupied by Adam's progeny, eighteenth-century preachers assume that such tropes rest easy on readers' eyes or in congregants' ears (Meserole, 426; Baxter, "Sermon on Isaiah 57.1," Dec. 24, 1727, quoted in Stout, 154).

But when the corporate mission of New England gets invoked specifically, as opposed to generalized reiterations of theatrum mundi, the metaphor deepens. As Increase Mather uses stage to signify the passing of generations, so too does Thomas Shepard, Jr., in his election sermon, *Eye-Salve or a Watch-Word for Our Lord Jesus Christ unto His Churches in New England* (1673), turn to the stage to illustrate this change. Unlike Mitchell, however, the younger Shepard sees something substantial in the world, something fixed. While part of his theme is that responsibility lies with the current backsliding generation to mend its ways, Shepard first must establish the principle by which the passage of generations may be judged. The earth, he says, is "the stage of Action, Eccles. 1.4, *One Generation passeth away and another Generation cometh*, but the Earth (the great stage of Action, upon which all Generations are to act their part), abideth forever" (2). What Shepard suggests is that it is not only the earth that lasts but potentially, by extension, the theogeographic entity of New England as well. People have a commitment to combating turmoil and division among magistrates and ministers, which is implied by the longevity of enterprise; that is, while the millennialist strain in New England preaching keeps before the people the immediacy of the Second Coming, the jeremiad forces the opposite conclusion, that one must remember the distance yet to be covered before community unity can be achieved. In this sense, the governing mode is history, and the primary need is for New Englanders to keep their peculiar history before them at all times: "[The first generation] should leave behind them *Registers of Gods mighty acts*. . . . And let those of the second generation, that are entred, or upon the point of entring upon the stage of action in the service of their generation, *see the Word of the Lord also*" (35). Though some scholars such as Jonas Barish have come to see the Puritan distaste for theater as part of an antimimetic prejudice (as one might see in *The Day of Doom*), the parade of saints on the stage of action becomes, in essence, a drama of mimesis; progress is measured by generations, but action is determined by the closeness to which the present actors follow the example of the fathers. Of course, each generation must achieve its own genuine relationship with God and renew the covenant. Still, the reiterated connection between generation, mission, and stage suggests not only a consciousness about performance (in already scripted roles) but also a need to convert those feelings through metaphor into a manageable code.

Each generation, then, has an injunction to perform deeds, record them, and pass them on before retiring from the stage. For individuals within a generation, however, there are competing demands. Separately, the state of one's soul is always in doubt; seen outside the purview of a culturewide errand, the individual in New England often appears lost, confused, flushed with skepticism, uncertain, or pathologically anxious—the message one gets from reading ministerial diaries or the confessions recorded by Shepard's father in his Cambridge church (see also Caldwell, *Puritan Conversion Narrative*). For the collective saints, however, the younger Shepard delivers a different message: the stage persists and one's actions make sense, have a purpose and plot, when performed before greater audiences watching the theater upon the hill. In other words, New England Puritans resolve the purposely self-destructive doubts to which they are prey by an appeal to a socially fulfilling goal. To act by oneself is a lonely, and quite possibly unforgiveable, task. To act with others as a larger body before angels and humankind, however, promises resolution of doubt into the certainty of glory in the climax of history. More than a real stage can, stage metaphor, in this context, serves the corporate ends of the jeremiad by providing the hope of satisfaction for individuals otherwise uncertain about their salvation. In a sense, theater metaphor replaces the playhouse in Puritan culture—at least for ministers; after all, as Cotton Mather announces confidently in his diary, "the *All-Seeing Eye*" of God "shall be *Theatre* enough" (*Diary*, 1:93).

CHAPTER SIX

∽

Playing the (Trans)Script:
The Antinomian Crisis

*T*he Antinomian crisis, that antilegalist rebellion against covenant theology, has attracted scholarly attention for a variety of reasons. One can look at the episode as a theological test between doctrines of grace and of works that New England successfully passed; as the creation of a feminist victim-heroine in Anne Hutchinson; as the triumph of John Winthrop; as the quashing—or originating—of democracy in the New World; as the near undoing of John Cotton; or as the culmination of events, including the Pequot War, that marked the Puritans as a group dedicated to an oppressive political policy of "might makes right." It also forms a pattern for future social conflict in New England, and it provides future generations with the rhetorical strategies needed to assert control over threats to the governance of a God-favored state. In essence, the Antinomian controversy, as a narrow theological debate, provokes from the combined pens of its scribes nonconformist America's first play of culture, a self-generated drama that fixes in the minds of the oligarchs a pattern for Providence as that force guides the destiny of New England.

The chief events essentially are these: John Cotton arrives in September 1633 with a reputation as a brilliant Calvinist and a theology to match, one stressing the helplessness of individuals to work toward their own salvation. Anne Hutchinson, a onetime listener to Cotton's sermons in England, arrives a year later and finds a climate ripe for objection to a covenant of works. Complaints from Hutchinson and others lead to accusations against John Wilson for being a "legalist" preacher, one to be disposed of in favor of John Wheelwright, who the Antinomians think is the only true preacher, with Cotton, of the Gospel. For his alleged role in inciting the challenge to ministerial authority, John Cotton appears before his colleagues to answer queries about his teachings; a Fast Day is called to settle the dispute; but ultimately, when the antagonism between popular and ministerial forces does not subside, a series of formalized special events forces the confrontation into the arenas of power, specifically the General Court and the Church. Cotton lines up with oligarchic authority by retracting some controversial views; Anne Hutchinson, who, because she is an assertive woman, makes a convenient target, is trapped into claiming that she receives direct revelations; and Hutchinson, Wheelwright, and a few others are expelled from Massachusetts, the former bearing with her an order of excommunication. The controversy, over by 1638, dies down quickly, but ministers long after make oblique references to this period in a series of sermons designed to bring the colony into a doctrine that recognizes both the unpredictability of grace and, if New England is not to be made a byword, the necessity for effort among believers (Battis; AC, 3–23; Lang, *Prophetic Woman*, 15–71; Solberg, 146–51, see also C. F. Adams, *Three Episodes*, 2:559–78; Hutchinson, 486–87; Johnson, 124–39, 170–76, 185–87; Shuffelton, 238–52; and the documents in N. Shurtleff, 174–227).

Because transcripts of Anne Hutchinson's inquisitions survive, along with other contemporary documents, we can look at the Antinomian crisis as something like the Ur-crisis for Massachusetts. Not only do the Antinomians mount the first serious challenge to ministerial authority, but they do so in a way that requires public display of persons and events. Certainly in form, with its court stages and dramatis personae, the crisis on paper resembles the high drama of the playhouse. To say so, however, is not simply to use a language of convenience. Kenneth Burke, in *The Philosophy of Literary Form*, identifies drama, specifically "ritual drama," as the "Ur-form," the "hub" of all human action, with subsidiary action spreading out from ritual drama as spokes; in other words, to talk about human affairs at all is to use something like dramatic criticism (103). Since Burke developed this idea, with its corollary rhetorical categories, the so-called dramatistic pentad, outlined in *A Grammar of Motives*, a number of social scientists, notably Erving Goffman, Kai Erikson, Clifford Geertz, and Victor Turner, have begun examining not only customs but also historical moments in terms suggested by the phrase "ritual drama." Kai Erikson, in fact, sees the Antinomian crisis as one of three major events in seventeenth-century New England (the Quaker persecutions and the witch trials in Salem are the others) that deserve scrutiny as signal experiences, whereby the citizens of Massachusetts Bay could "clarify their position in the world as a whole [and] redefine the boundaries which set New England apart as a new experiment in living" (67). Erikson suggests that ritual drama is a social necessity that dictates the action of participants regardless of their awareness of its significance: "The confrontation between Anne Hutchinson and the magistrates of Massachusetts was a tribal ceremony, a morality play, a ritual encounter between two traditional adversaries. . . . Like dancers tracing the steps of a familiar ceremony, all the participants in the drama must have known what its eventual outcome would be; but the form of the ritual had to be observed if that outcome were to have any lasting meaning" (101).

The matter of determining social necessity from literary strategy is not an easy one. From a literary perspective, the major characters in the crisis show themselves to have drama at least partly in mind as events unfold; at the same time, the historical crisis with its literary artifacts shapes itself as a drama by the colony's need for redefinition. Anthropologist Victor Turner provides a means of analysis, through his theory of fields, paradigms, arenas, and social dramas, that applies to conflicts like the Antinomian crisis, particularly those that confront the issue of exclusion. After summarizing Turner's terms of analysis, I wish to examine the Antinomian controversy first as a social-historical phenomenon and then as a literary one.

Fields, explains Turner, are "the abstract cultural domains where paradigms are formulated, established, and come into conflict"; *paradigms* are "sets of 'rules' for which many kinds of sequences of social action may be generated but which further specify what sequences must be excluded"; *arenas* are "the concrete setting in which paradigms become transformed into metaphors and symbols with reference to which political power is mobilized and in which there is a trial of strength between influential paradigm-bearers"; and *social dramas* "represent the phased process of their contestation" (*Dramas*, 17). Turner's methodology for social analysis applies directly to the Antinomian crisis. The controversy is a paradigmatic situation, one in which a social drama, in Turner's language, is used to resolve the conflict caused by the Hutchinsonian rebellion against political authority. At the same time, the participants and observers themselves turn this social drama into the rhetoric of theater, providing not only a paradigm for conflict resolution in the social arena but also a literary pattern in which control over experience is generated by the emergent yet preexisting metaphor of theater.

For the first five years, the Massachusetts Bay colony might be said to represent a harmonious society in which clear norms emerge out of a common theological and ecclesiastical tradition. Now practiced in the relatively open environment of the New World, Massachusetts Calvinism is, in a sense, decontextualized, removed from the conflict-laden world of Laudian England; because of a relative uniformity of belief and a universally perceived, practical need for governance, it finds itself in a new context, one that is essentially conflict-free. Until that society is tested, however, until its rules over who is included and who excluded are made manifest, it lacks some fundamental structure for continuance. The dissatisfaction that Anne Hutchinson discovers—and exacerbates—on her arrival in Massachusetts waits as a force to be harnessed, one that will test the polity as a fully defined social domain (see Gura, 274–75).

In Turner's terms, then, the field is the peculiar oligarchy of New England, where the shapers of a new way rely on *Sola Scriptura*, the Bible alone, as a governing tool (Stout). Several tests arise: Roger Williams and his assertion of individual interpretation; the Pequot Indians and their rejection of English hegemony; and the Antinomians, Anne Hutchinson and her supporters, who seek to strip the ministers of their newly privileged powers. Only the conflict instigated by the latter, however, qualifies as a social drama. In the case of Williams, the challenge is not from a representative of a large group but essentially from a "lone hand" whose exclusion has few immediate repercussions for the shape of society as a whole. The Pequots, though a group and summarily excluded by the militarily and rhetorically

satisfying means of massacre, lie outside the "system of social relations" required of both parties in a paradigmatic contention (Turner,
Dramas, 38). The Indians are strictly other, a fact that allows the
generally humane William Bradford in *Of Plymouth Plantation* to
gloat grotesquely over the bloody business of exterminating them
(331).

That leaves the Antinomian crisis as the first major rift which
qualifies as a fully fledged social drama. Considered as such, it must
satisfy four essential "phases of public action" (Turner, *Dramas*, 37–
38): a *breach* among members of a uniform "system of social relations"
in which some norm is flouted, though not necessarily in a criminal
act, and in which the instigator represents some group, as Anne
Hutchinson clearly does; an increased *crisis* where social "cleavage"
occurs, spreading itself to "the widest set of relevant social relations to
which the conflicting or antagonistic parties belong"; a *redressive
action* whereby members of the power structure act through some
correcting "mechanism" to heal the breach; and "*reintegration* of the
disturbed social group or of the social recognition and legitimization
of irreparable schism between the contesting parties" (38–41).

As many commentators have noted, the breach incited by the
Hutchinsonian forces has major consequences for Massachusetts Bay.
Anne Hutchinson herself, as a female contending with patriarchs,
obviously risks censure; that the ministers and magistrates make her
out to be a monster may say more about them than about her. In a
world where control over the pulpit rests in the hands of men, and
where those men maintain the power of the pulpit by distinguishing it
from the stage, the presence of a woman who mimicks their sermons
and establishes a rival arena of discourse would be sufficiently threatening to create a breach. When she later appears in the confined space
of the court, Hutchinson seems to her male judges as a woman who
would be a man, the mirror of a man who would act a woman on the
playhouse stage. Her sex incites in male authorities a desperate search-
ing for the mechanism by which the doctrinal "errors" she commits,
ones that tap into deeper fears of sexual anarchy, can be isolated and
redressed. She "is but a Woman," say her ministerial inquisitors, who
continues "still in seducinge to seduce and in deceavinge to deceave,"
and whose religious conviction that "*the Resurrection be past*" leads

inevitably to "that filthy Sinne of the Communitie of Woemen and all promiscuous and filthie cominge togeather of men and Woemen without Distinction or Relation of Marriage" ("Report," 370, 385, 371, 372). Her social role as inverse minister would seem to be enough to provoke in a patriarchy a social crisis.

In addition, she threatens the status quo by the popularity of her cause, as demonstrated by the extraordinary attendance at her weekly meetings and by the demands of a majority in John Wilson's church that their pastor must go. By rejecting the call to public obedience from the ministers and magistrates as a grace-denying "works righteousness," she brings genuine cleavage. As Harry Stout describes, "Her words threatened to undermine all faith in the New England Way, which depended on a bridge of trust and mutual commitment linking minister, congregation, and Word into one united organism. Without that trust, social and spiritual order would collapse; there were no other external institutions to rely upon" (25). The crisis she inspires has the widest possible social ramifications. Though from the surviving documents one might get the impression that at first the ministers who listen to her queer opinions are perplexed yet forbearing, failing to see—or not wanting to see—that this woman could be anything except an inspired eccentric (Battis), by 1636 they seem fully cognizant that the breach has widened to crisis. It is a time, as Turner explains for the general case of societies in crisis, "when it is least easy to don masks or pretend that there is nothing rotten in the village" (Dramas, 39).

After the failure of the Fast Day in January 1637 to produce a full reconciliation between Winthrop, Wilson, and the ministerial majority on the one hand and the Antinomian governor Henry Vane, John Cotton, John Wheelwright, Anne Hutchinson, and the Boston popular majority on the other, various formalized events are initiated as a redressive action. These events include the March General Court that sentences one Antinomian for his condemnation of ministers as preaching a covenant of works only; the May election of Winthrop to replace Vane; the Cambridge Synod which condemns eighty-two Antinomian errors then circulating; the November General Court that banishes Anne Hutchinson and John Wheelwright; and the March 1638 excommunication of Anne Hutchinson. In describing the usual case for an incipient social drama, Victor Turner outlines precisely the responses of the Massachusetts power structure to their female antagonist. The reactions of the authorities to crisis "may range from personal advice and informal mediation or arbitration to formal juridical and legal machinery, and, to resolve certain kinds of crisis or legitimate other modes of resolution, to the performance of public ritual" (38). A society in crisis becomes highly self-conscious about its unity, and unless it regresses to phase two (as Massachusetts does not), there is a push toward exclusion and consequent reintegration (39). In the Antinomian crisis, efforts are made up to and into the excommunication trial of Anne Hutchinson to keep her within the greater society of church affiliation and the New England Way, even in banishment. Because she resists, she is expelled from church and society. Most of her associates, however, reintegrate; and like Hutchinson's inspiration, the side-shifting John Cotton, they find the psychological, philosophical, and social means to rejoin the field, understanding as they must what the paradigmatic rules for inclusion or exclusion will be (on Cotton's attempt to reintegrate Wheelwright, see Bush, "'Revising'").

Because New England lacks a set of release rituals, the festivals or carnivals left behind in Europe, its ritual or social dramas are normally acted out within the framework of official or quasi-official ceremonies for which the meetinghouse or public square served as arenas. In the terminology of social drama, "The arena is a scene for the making of a decision," that is, the stage on which everything is made explicit (Turner, *Dramas*, 134–35). In the Antinomian crisis, the significant arenas are the meetinghouse on Spring Street in Newtown and Boston's First Church (Battis, 180). As we have seen from Samuel Sewall's fear that a meetinghouse would become a playhouse, the tension between a public need to heal a breach and another need, to view life in terms of entertainment, renders the experience in that arena ambiguous. As a circumscribed space, the meetinghouse must hold within its frame the fully manifest contentions between the Winthrop and Hutchinson forces and bring them to resolution. The results in Newtown and Boston are indeed dramatic, but that drama most especially persists as *metaphor*, in a literary (or subliterary) rendering of a paradigmatic contest. In Newtown at the civil trial, then in Boston at the ecclesiastical examination of Anne Hutchinson, the meetinghouses provide the arenas where Puritan life becomes, in Roberto DaMatta's term, radicalized, where "the routines of the daily world are broken," where the colony risks a complete reversal of the status quo (237). It is as if, in trying to undo this woman who would rather be "a Magistrate than a Subject," the oligarchs confront a world like that posited by Plautine comedy, one of mayhem and inversion; but the form of the episode, drawn from the language of the participants themselves, is ultimately perceived as tragic ("Report," 383). By containing the threatened low comedy within the bounds of the meetinghouse arenas, the authorities ensure that the completed crisis be exhibited on the elevated stage of the federal covenant—what Thomas Beard calls the theater of God's judgments.

There is more to the theatrical nature of this controversy than a contemporary application of social theory might suggest. The Puritan participants themselves, through tradition and expression, help shape our modern response to the events of 1636–38. Anne Hutchinson, for one, enters the arena with secondhand experience, at least, in "displaced drama" (Kendall). Her father was Francis Marbury, a preacher sufficiently nonconformist to have earned himself a "conference" in November 1578 with the bishop of London, Aylmer, over his religious views. Like many disputatious Protestants of the sixteenth century, Marbury was able to fulfill his own sense of mission by both confronting the oppressive ecclesiastical authorities and leaving a written record of the inquiry, a document that allowed the disputant to claim at least a rhetorical victory over his opponent. Like the *Examinacion* of William Thorpe, Marbury's conference text shows a testy bishop easily bested in debate by a younger, more clever preacher (F. Gay). In the headnote to his transcript, Marbury notes that there were "many people standing by," an audience in the "Consistorie in Paules" who must have appreciated his wit and skill in debate (F. Gay, 283). Whether or not Marbury was a Puritan is unclear; later, after being stripped of his parish, he was rehabilitated at a time when other nonconforming Protestants were losing pulpits in large numbers (Battis, 9, 11). Nevertheless, like those Calvinists who rejected episcopal or presbyterian control over their ministry, Marbury appears at one stage of his life to have accepted the belief that combat in a dualistic, antagonistic world, such as one finds throughout the "pseudodramatic

or debate literature" of proto- and early Protestantism, was a require-
ment of the faith (Bush, *Writings*, 132). As one popular biographer of
Marbury's daughter puts it (though unfortunately without the appropriate context), Marbury's sense of drama and conflict makes him a
"proper playwright" (S. Williams, 16).

How ironic it is, then, that Anne Hutchinson should appear before
an ecclesiastical tribunal composed of men who, like her father, have
had their faith tested by rhetorical combat or who at least are conversant with the tradition. But for the social drama to work, for the events
to play themselves out in a way satisfying to all, the colony requires an
antagonist skilled in debate, one who can make the authorities feel
sufficiently challenged that their own faith in a contentious universe
remains fixed. That role might have been played by John Cotton
except for two factors: Cotton is too much like the prosecuting oligarchs for them to feel justification, to borrow a theological word, in
their debate with him, for his defeat would also be their loss; and, until
he changes his mind, he seems oblivious to the implications of his
works-denying doctrines. Thus Anne Hutchinson makes the perfect
player for the part: a person of the faith, but female; clever, but
unnaturally so; mistaken in views, but darkly cognizant of what her
positions mean for the status quo—in other words, the image created
of her is like enough to the ideal Christian congregant that her
otherness marks her with the stain of the grossest hypocrisy.

All that the colony requires of Hutchinson is that she play out her
part; the rest, the implications and interpretations, the ministers will
appoint to themselves. The threats she represents, however, all have to
do with reversal, with forcing people to encounter the possibility of
otherness in themselves. She becomes responsible, passively, for the
institutionalization of dread in which those within frighten themselves
with the prospect of being like those who will soon be without. By
ensuring a vigilance against reversal of the social order, the voices of
orthodoxy acknowledge the theatricality of Puritan faith. What happens most profoundly is that, in her and in the resolution of her case,
two images of theater, one as a figure for hypocrisy and the other as a
trope for the macrocosm of God's stagecraft, conflate into a dynamic,
ambidextrous rhetoric of social cohesion and political tension.

The term *antinomian* means to oppose the moral law; it is a word

whose specificity, in meaning a rejection of a strictly "legal" interpretation of scripture, masks a variety of anxieties for the Puritan
polity. To be Antinomian suggests that one is enthusiastic, a state of
being that fosters anarchy; in the case of Anne Hutchinson, Winthrop
thinks that she evidences "the most desperate enthusiasm in the
world" ("Examination," 342). Another term often used to describe the
Hutchinson faction is Familist, denoting the so-called Family of
Love, a sect thought to promote sexual license and freedom from sin;
in other words, by their reliance on spirit and feeling rather than study
and premeditation, the American Antinomians could threaten the
order of a society where the rules are rational and obedience to them
deliberate and necessary (see Lovejoy, New World, 33–43). A related
concern is that Hutchinson might be engaged in prophesying, using
"divine prompting" to see into the heart of scripture rather than
relying on the studied interpretation by those trained to preach from
the Bible. Politically, then, Hutchinson and the Antinomians, like
other religious dissidents within radical Protestantism, propose to
replace conservative notions of order with a potentially revolutionary
democracy (Lovejoy, New World, 53).

This fear of the commons usurping the role of the governors
emerges as a direct challenge more to the understanding ministers
have of their roles than to the structure of the oligarchy. John Wilson,
the much-harassed establishmentarian, complains that Hutchinson's
chief fault is "the slightinge of Gods faythfull Ministers and contem-
ninge and cryinge downe them as Nobodies" ("Report," 380). Not only
Hutchinson but other radical spiritists, like those discussed by Philip
Gura and David Lovejoy, undermine the very identity of ministry by
rhetorical wizardry, converting the clergy by simple "cryinge downe"
into nonentities. Ironically, the radical Samuel Gorton thinks that the
remnants of Anglo-Catholic ritual in the purified churches justify
his calling the preachers "Necromancers" (quoted in Lovejoy, New
World, 95). But Gorton's challenge is mere name-calling compared to
what Wilson (who also charges that Hutchinson will turn them all into
"Epicures") remarks, for what he fears is more terrifying than any
misnomer. To be called Nobody is to be labeled with an antinomer or
really no name at all; and the loss is not only individual but corporate.
To deny the ministers identification means to deny the rhetorical

elevation of the city on a hill; it converts the individual's wrestling with faith into an isolated, monadic, ahistorical struggle. If Christ comes a second time only in the souls of separate believers, then Revelation loses its historicity and New England loses its potential as New Jerusalem (Rosenmeier, 442; Gura, 91–92). No wonder Wilson and his colleagues respond as they do.

Another fear held by the ministers, one suggested by Patricia Caldwell in her article, "The Antinomian Language Controversy," comes from Hutchinson's frequent retractions or denials that things she has said have any more meaning than as mere expression. In Caldwell's reading of the trial transcripts, the magistrates and churchmen become alarmed at the way Hutchinson disconnects words from things, at her rhetorical conversion of real "error" into simply a "mistake" or, in Caldwell's term, a "misspeaking," as if she and they operate with separate language systems. As one more element of the social drama, language must be preserved as a shared experience for the drama to have meaning across the field as a whole. What Gura and Lovejoy see in the Antinomian crisis, the challenge of a radical individualism against a hierarchical polity, is only part of the threat. The loss of ministerial identity, the discontinuity of language, along with the harboring within the borders of their society the principle of its destruction set into motion psychosocial forces that require, for the survival of the colony, a textlike plot in which identity is restored, control over language asserted, and the dramatic object of tension expelled from the arena.

In a text central to understanding the conflict, John Winthrop attempts to provide a plot that will satisfy the needs of the colony for a dramatically conclusive experience. His appropriately named *A Short Story of the Rise, reign, and ruine of the Antinomians, Familists, & Libertines* (1644), in conjunction with the two lengthy transcripts of proceedings against Anne Hutchinson, remains the principal document of the Antinomian crisis (for a brief history of editions, see AC, 200). Winthrop is Hutchinson's chief magisterial opponent (and her neighbor from across the street), an active participant in the examination that leads to her order of banishment, and, in the *Short Story*, the dramaturge of an establishment view that justifies the actions of power. This book gives the illusion of thoroughness and justice so effectively that a fourth edition is printed in 1692—in time to give advice for another theatrical crisis, the Salem witchcraft trials. Winthrop devotes much of the book to a rehearsal of errors held by the radicals, but once "Mistris Hutchinson" enters the narrative, his prose quickens and his overall design displays itself. At one point he likens the travail New England faces to "the Tragedy of *Munster*," using an often-evoked reference to the violent takeover of Münster in Germany in 1534 by radical Anabaptists and the consequent, violent retaking of the city in 1535 by "orthodox Protestant forces" (*Short Story*, 275; Battis, 41–42; Horst, 66–73; AC, 275n). Münster represents the rift within Protestantism from the very beginning, that between anticlerical spiritists and the more conservative, church-centered hierarchies of minister and Word. That Münster is a tragedy, however, also fixes for Winthrop the shape of his narrative a century later. Indeed, he goes so far as to say that the Devil at Münster is much more "simple a Devill" than the one afflicting New England in the 1630s: "Satan seemed to have commission now to use his utmost cunning to undermine the Kingdome of Christ here . . . so as the like hath not beene knowne in former ages, that ever so many wise, sober, and well grounded Christians, should so suddenly be seduced by the meanes of a woman" (*Short Story*, 275–76). By likening the Antinomian crisis to a recognized tragedy, Winthrop elevates the events he has witnessed to the grand scheme of world history; using the special agency of a woman, a Satan more "cunning" than heretofore known threatens the very "Kingdome of Christ."

Essentially, Winthrop converts a dirty little local dispute, social drama or no, into something larger and, he hopes, more to the credit of New England in the eyes of the world. In the structuring of the crisis by the rituals of synod, examination, and trial, tragedy makes an appropriate form. As Kenneth Burke states of ritual drama, "Tragedy uses the stylization of ennoblement, making the calamity bearable by making the calamitous situation dignified" (*Philosophy*, 129). Our contemporary reading of this episode often makes the individual, Anne Hutchinson, the victim and the "calamitous situation" a case of Puritan bullying; but for Winthrop, calling the crisis a tragedy ennobles, justifies, and makes plausible the casting of corporate New England as victim, a godly commonwealth under siege by the devilry of an individual woman.

When Winthrop explains Hutchinson's actions, he structures them thus:

1. Her entrance
2. Her progresse
3. Her downfall.   (308)

These terms, all familiar ones to literary drama, allow Winthrop to arrange evidence carefully. In "her entrance" to New England, she appears godly and righteous; among six items he lists to her seeming credit, one is that the "Rule she pretended to walke by, was onely the Scripture." Her walking by that rule justifies the actions of a trusting, covenanted people in taking her in. "Thus she entred and made up the first act of her course" (308). In "her progresse," however, she becomes an enlarged and necessarily formidable opponent; many people into whose hearts she had "insinuated her selfe" began to grow "into so reverent an esteem of her godlinesse, and spirituall gifts, as they looked at her as a Prophetesse, raised up of God for some great worke now at hand, as the calling of the Jewes, &c." Like all truly tragic figures, she overreaches herself, for she seizes ministerial prerogatives so effectively that more people "resort to her for counsell about matter of conscience, and clearing up mens spirituall estates, then any Minister (I might say all the Elders) in the Country" (308). "Her downfall," therefore, plays out as an exposure of her "delusion"; "now in this last act," intones Winthrop, the "*American Jesabel*" finds that her attempts to redeem her reputation are brought to light as a "subtilty of Satan," a discovery that leads "to her utter shame and confusion" (309–10). In an extraordinary way, Winthrop envisions the conclusion as a spectacle of joy, where there is a "setting at liberty of many godly hearts, that have been captivated by her to that day" and where the Church, once "neere to dissolution," is "hereby sweetly repaired" (310). But in his last words, devoted to the fallen antiheroine, Winthrop also gives a prefiguration of Milton's Satan, fierce, powerful, unrepentant:

> She is not affected with an remorse, but glories in it, and feares not the vengeance of God, which she lyes under, as if God did work contrary to his own word, and loosed from heaven, while his Church had bound upon earth.
>
> FINIS.   (310)

Winthrop, it seems, tries to have it both ways. The story of New England is a near tragedy, almost overthrown, but the tale of Anne Hutchinson is also tragic, the defiant "imposter," a female Prometheus, doomed by God. Providentially, all works for the best. Like her sympathizer Mary Dyer, Anne Hutchinson afterward gives birth to a "monster," an act signifying her "monstrous" opinions. Even better, she is killed in her exile by Indians. Although the latter event is outside the purview of Winthrop's *Short Story*, it is discussed by the writer of the preface to the second edition, Thomas Weld, who fixes the seal of drama upon it: "(And now I am come to the last act of her Tragedy, a most heavie stroake upon her selfe and hers, as I received it very lately from a godly hand in New-England)" (218). Throughout the course of events, but especially afterward, Winthrop has acted as something like a dark playwright, orchestrating the attacks on the Antinomians, effectively seizing the governorship from the mystically minded Henry Vane, shaping the crisis as a coherent dramatic narrative, and finally exulting in the downfall of villains and the triumph of the orthodox order.

Yet it would be fallacious (*tu quoque*) to insist that Winthrop is everything he has accused Hutchinson of being while she is only a passive victim of patriarchal fury. More likely, both Winthrop and Hutchinson need each other in some magnetic way; indeed, they find themselves impelled by social dynamics toward a theatrical resolution of their conflict. In the transcripts entitled, "The Examination of Mrs. Anne Hutchinson at the Court at Newtown" and "A Report of the Trial of Mrs. Anne Hutchinson before the Church in Boston," documents which give more detailed and "objective" accounts than does Winthrop's *Short Story*, separate dramas emerge which both complement and run counter to the governor's arrangement of events. As transcripts, the documents read like plays and give us a vivid sense of Anne Hutchinson's "nimble wit and active spirit" (*Short Story*, 263). Though the often testy, even sardonic, remarks by people like Thomas Dudley, the deputy governor, make clear that Hutchinson is deemed a public nuisance, to be gotten rid of at all costs, the "Examination" shows men of power in a desperate struggle to claim dramatic control over contending concepts of Providence. The theological issue of grace versus works melts away in Hutchinson's insistence that her accusers, "six undeniable ministers," all take oaths ("Examination,"

324). What Winthrop obviously expects will be *quod erat demonstrandum* turns surprisingly into a contention over satisfaction. As deputies, ministers, witnesses, and accusers all query each other or demand to be satisfied in the legal sense, the transcript records another satisfaction in the Newtown arena, the social necessity that conflict be resolved through exclusion. Thus more than Winthrop's story, the transcripts reflect directly the historical social drama of a culture correcting itself.

In the first part of the "Examination," the ministerial witnesses trot forth their memories of events, without further evidence than their own word for what they allege Hutchinson has said; but she denies the purport of their remarks. Winthrop, seeing that the hour grows late, must adjorn the court; before he does that, however, he makes clear to the accused that the purpose of the proceeding is "to bring you to acknowledge the error of your way that so you might be reduced" (326). Having said that, Winthrop locks himself and the court into a predetermined judgment that must be realized at all costs.

As if to underscore the foreshadowing in Winthrop's line, the text resumes with the direction, "*the next morning.*" A comically tedious debate then follows over the taking of oaths and the court's need "to be satisfied." The legal wrangling incited by the antilegalist defendant comes to an abrupt close when Anne Hutchinson details how she came to her understanding of scripture. Put simply, she tells the court that the Lord "hath let me see which was the clear ministry and which was wrong."

> *Mr. Nowell.* How do you know that that was the spirit?
> *Mrs. H.* How did Abraham know that it was God that bid him offer his son, being a breach of the sixth commandment?
> *Dep. Gov.* By an immediate voice.
> *Mrs. H.* So to me by an immediate revelation.
> *Dep. Gov.* How! an immediate revelation.
> *Mrs. H.* By the voice of his own spirit to my soul. (337)

Nothing could destroy her own case as effectively as an open acknowledgment that she has received a special message from God. In the terms of the drama, nothing could better provoke the trial toward a swift, and from the orthodox view, satisfying, conclusion.

Following the climax, the other principal, John Cotton, comes forward to distinguish for the court among possible revelations. Though the ending is now known to all in the meetinghouse, Cotton strings out the tension, remaining the last prominent minister to defend her position, or at least to delay the rush to judgment: "That she may have some special providence of God to help her is a thing that I cannot bear witness against" (341). Though he acknowledges the limitations of language to speak of such things, Cotton suggests a dramatically plausible reasoning that could lead to Hutchinson's exoneration. He distinguishes between two primary types of revelation: one in which the Bible or a minister may be an agent, that is, where "the revelation be in a word or according to a word," and therefore possible; and another which may "be in a way of miracle or revelation without the word," and therefore, because outside nature, only a "delusion" and not to be accepted (342). Cotton's distinctions, however, fall on hostile ears. "Sir, you weary me and do not satisfy me," says Dudley. "It overthrows all," says Winthrop. All that remains in the plot is for the rituals to be completed and the lessons made manifest. Dudley mentions Münster in open court as a fearful precedent; Winthrop proclaims Anne Hutchinson's revelation to be a "delusion"; and the trial recorder adds, *"All the court but some two or three ministers cry out, we all believe it—we all believe it"* (343). Though some further discussion follows, the tone is one of petulant weariness. A last piece of interest is generated when the recorder comments, *"Here now was a great whispering among the ministers, some drew back others were animated on"* (346), but there is little else to say. After the decisive vote against her is taken, Hutchinson demands of Winthrop why she is banished. "Say no more," he closes, "the court knows wherefore and is satisfied" (348).

The transcript illustrates Winthrop's insistence on getting a particular conclusion; indeed, one of the few deputies who sympathize with Hutchinson, William Coddington, chides Winthrop for trying "to force things along" (345). Yet the transcript also raises a dramatic question not addressed in the governor's *Short Story:* why does Anne Hutchinson allow herself to be exposed on grounds she very well knows will ensure her banishment? Kai Erikson speculates that "perhaps her high sense of theater got the better of her" (97), that is to say, she could not help it. To say that Hutchinson is moved by a "high sense of theater" requires some qualification. With Turner we might say that such a sense comes from the sociological situation itself; the drama naturally asserts itself as a model for confrontations, as if the conclusion is already contained in the inciting action of the crisis. For New England Puritans, however, there are other considerations besides the laws of "tribal ceremony." Anne Hutchinson, through the experience of her father, and the university-educated oligarchs, through their reading or personal understanding, know the confrontational heritage of nonconforming Protestantism and the "pseudodramatic" form of debate literature that comes out of it. In addition, the peculiar sensibility of New Englanders, who see their colonies in grandiose terms and who see their adopted land as no less than the hill-stage for the kingdom of Christ on earth, ensures that conflict over elemental doctrinal issues will burst forth in a public arena.

Further, as the "Report" shows, the churchmen are obsessed with roles, role-playing, and hypocrisy to the point where even private acts in the home become matters of public performance. Cotton admonishes Anne Hutchinson's sons, for example, for encouraging their mother and "applaudinge of her in her Opinion"; better they should correct her, Cotton continues, for "than shall you performe the parts of faythfull Children indeed" ("Report," 370). Hugh Peter, whose own ruthless Puritanism eventually carries him to Cromwell, sees that her lack of repentance comes from a skewed sense of her domestic role: "You have stept out of your place, *you have rather bine a Husband than a Wife and a preacher than a Hearer*" (382–83). Thomas Shepard especially rankles at her lack of sincerity, calling her a "Notorious Imposter," one who has not "altered her Judgment, but only her Expression" (383). And John Wilson accuses her of being "A *dayngerous Instrument of the Divell*," a person who "sayth one thinge to day and another thinge to morrow" (384).

New England's success as a colony might very well be attributed to this intense awareness of role-playing and the need for public, ritual exposure of threats to the social order. Without theaters, without some sanctioned space for playacting, American Puritans require of themselves what revolutionary regimes almost always demand of their cause: purity of motive and fixity of form. Thus any challenge to roles becomes by implication a challenge to polity. Even to allow the possibility that one might distinguish between warranted and unwarranted revelations renders nearly meaningless a person's ability to tell of his neighbor whether he be pure or polluted or whether she be a conduit for Christ's word or an instrument of the Devil. In times of crisis—and in New England crisis is chronic—a theaterless society becomes radically theatricalized; every act becomes a test of one's ability to differentiate mask from face, friend from foe, orthodox revolutionary from counterrevolutionary. Winthrop recognizes not only the threat of Anne Hutchinson but even John Cotton's subtle distinctions: "It overthrows all." Because tragedy as a form has a strong conservative thrust in the eventual defeat of the tragic rebel, Winthrop stamps the social drama with a literary seal. For future generations, the language of theater and tragedy provides for Americans in times of crisis an instrument by which disorder can be ordered, the purity of mission enhanced, individuals praised or condemned, and the workings of Providence made manifest before a spectating world.

Yet it must be said that in one case, at least, transcripted theater becomes tragedy for reasons having more to do with failure than success. The analogy of the witchcraft trials of 1692 to drama has been made before. Certainly, Arthur Miller in his play *The Crucible* makes manifest on stage what seems obvious from the sensational material he had to work with: the whole episode is intensely theatrical. Once set in motion, as Kai Erikson maintains, the trials have to play themselves out before the voices of reason can be heard, key participants like Samuel Sewall can admit their errors, and the courts can begin processing claims for restitution as well as restoration of innocence and good name to those once prosecuted and declared guilty of witchcraft.

For the first-generation prosecutors of Anne Hutchinson, the distinction between appearance and reality is clearly made; with Hooker, they know the actorlike quality of the hypocrite. For later generations of Puritans, however, the issue grows more complex the further removed people are from the theater itself. Having declared the saints free from false presentation, ministers are then saddled with a logic that turns appearance into reality—or thoroughly confuses the two. In an early tract, *Memorable Providences* (1689), Cotton Mather sets out to show to the world that there is a witchcraft. He explains that the bizarre behavior of John Goodman's children can have no other cause, since the parents have kept an unquestionably upright household: "In a word, Such was the whole Temper and Carriage of the Children, that there cannot easily be any thing more unreasonable, than to imagine that a Design to Dissemble could cause them to fall into any of their odd Fits; . . . it was perfectly impossible for any Dissimulation of theirs to produce what scores of spectators were amazed at" (100). If godly people, by definition, cannot dissemble, then all noncharacteristic behavior in such persons must be assigned an external cause; and further, if unusual behavior is not of God, then that cause must be the devil or his agents, the witches.

Thus the spectacular descriptions—the controversial "spectral evidence"—of likenesses and hallucinatory images that emerge in the witch trial testimony of 1692 can only be countenanced as serious in a society for whom dissembling of any kind is anathema and dreams are despised. When Anne Hutchinson's private "revelations" become public, they lead to her immediate condemnation because she has misled the court; when prosecution witnesses in 1692 make public their private experience, they speak to a culture that denies that such individualized "entertainments" of intangible phenomena (the specters) can exist at all *except* as the products of devilish causation. If by ministerial proscription you cannot be an actor, then you must be a witch or the victim of one. The most boundless fantasy, the most histrionic behavior (as that of the "victims" who scream or have fits at the mere nod of an accused witch on the stand), can never, in this scheme, be self-generated once it is denied to the godly to have a self in the first place.

Not even the Puritans could sustain the ruthlessness of this logic, and within a few years petitions are made and granted to disregard spectral evidence and to compensate families of prosecuted witches (see posttrial documents reproduced in Boyer and Nissenbaum, 3:963–1046). More important, however, the retractions by Sewall and others remove the summary judgment of the events from the pens of unrepentant prosecutors. The high tragedy of the Antinomian crisis, as conveyed by the transcripts and Winthrop's *Short Story*, has been displaced (almost literally) by dog-and-pony shows: talking dogs, witches who suckle birds or pigs or cats, the strange hybrid monkey with cock's feet and man's head that John Louder believes is sent to him by Bridget Bishop (Boyer and Nissenbaum, 3:750, 1:105, 106, 320, 100). But no one laughs, except demonically. The examinations of Bishop and many of the others cannot by themselves stand up as tragic literature in the way the interrogations of Anne Hutchinson can; the responses of the accused often are laconic or reflect their low social standing, while the questions of the judges are blunt and bludgeoning, without the search for subtleties one sees in the Antinomian trials. As a consequence, the fits and sensational accounts as expressed in courtroom behavior or in depositions provide both for the Puritans and for modern commentators what the structure of the witchcraft proceedings lacks: the means by which the culture gets the social drama its continuance requires—and the devices through which historians can shape their own narratives in dramatic terms. But for the Puritans, the witch trials are finally more distraction than justification of a regime. The trials are showy, far more so than the crisis in Newtown; yet the judges' admission of spectacle to the proceedings is a clue that they lack the firm sense of authorial and histrionic control that John Winthrop and Anne Hutchinson, whether by design or not, maintained over the Antinomian conflict two generations before.

The failure of the trials to produce a consensual expulsion of evil (with a suitably providential end for the perpetrators, as for Anne Hutchinson, thrown in) makes them into a figural drama of a different sort. The events of 1692 are "Tragedies," but the word is that of Robert Calef, an opponent of the methods of the trials and of one of their principal ministerial supporters, Cotton Mather. Now it is the worldly merchant, not the godly ministers and magistrates, who accuses people of dissembling; indeed, as Calef makes clear in More Wonders of the Invisible World (1700), it is the accusers of the witches who wear a "Mask of Zeal for God" (299). The logic of the trials is absurd, he explains; if we accord such powers to the devil as have been alleged, what does that say about the power of God? Indeed, not much—and if there is a lesson to be drawn, it should be one of admitted error and miscalculation. Those who have not condemned the trials outright (he has in mind Cotton Mather) should state the case plainly for future generations: "And as to most of the Actors in these Tragedies, tho they are so far from defending their Actions that they will Readily own, that undue steps have been taken, etc., Yet it seems they choose that the same should be Acted over again inforced by their Example, rather than that it should Remain as a Warning to Posterity, wherein they have mist it" (305). The witchcraft trials stand as a caution: if a covenanted enterprise is to have rights to figure an event as tragedy for the purpose of elevation, it must be careful it does not stoop to follies to earn the name. As Americans prepare to enter the eighteenth century, they must, if they are to preserve a sense of mission, keep alive the theatrum mundi without allowing the dramas enacted thereon to be scorned, especially by themselves. The reality of witches notwithstanding, Calef in essence calls on the powerful to realign themselves with God's ordinances; indeed, the ex post facto statements of judges and jurors account their erroneous participation in the trials a "Delusion" (Calef, 388). Thus the Salem trials are converted into another of New England's trials whereby God shows his displeasure with his people, and the events of 1692 are styled "the late Tragedy" (1696) by an apologetic General Court or "that sad Catastrophe" (1697) by a chastened John Hale (Calef, 386; Hale, A Modest Inquiry [1702], in Burr, 404). By restoring the small stage tragedies of the courtroom to the world stage tragedies of a covenanted people, New Englanders preserve the energy of a suppressed theatrical impulse for another day.

CHAPTER SEVEN

Theatrou Mestoi:
The Example of Cotton Mather

If the Antinomian crisis serves as an example of a public event in New England that displays a latent, ever-present theatricality, then Cotton Mather may be viewed, in Mitchell Breitwieser's term, as a "representative personality," an individual who shows the same thing. No Puritan before or during Mather's lifetime seems as obsessed with life played out in the agonistic arena of strenuous faith, nor does any New Englander of his time stud his writing with as frequent references to acting and the stage as does Mather. He renders his entire life as performance, a mode of being that, like election or damnation, is inescapable. As one reads through his letters, for instance, and sees the florid and obsequious openings and closings, the exclamatory enlargement of the least details of life, the continual punning and wordplay, one finds the self-portrait of a man compulsively attentive to making an impression, someone constantly performing, continually on cue, whether he be manipulating the receiver for political gain, preaching, or just doing good. Even in his private writings—if Mather may be said to have any—he directs the unnamed reader back and forth, penning prophecies and noting their fulfillment, making cross-references to other diary entries, speaking in a voice as boisterously performative as that of his public proclamations. Like his father, Mather calls his contemporaries to reform in order to preserve the covenant ideal of New England; but, paradoxically, this man, this self-acknowledged prodigy, by localizing the history of his country and struggles of the church within himself, ultimately subverts the covenant he strives so mightily to protect. The same Mather who, in the *Magnalia Christi Americana,* proclaims to all the world that New England is the stage and its greatest citizens actors in a drama of epical fame and epochal proportions also takes into himself and the ever-expanding corpus of his writing the theatricalized history of America and makes it his story—he makes his orthodox life an evangelical supersession of orthodoxy itself.

Mather's writing raises a number of problems for scholars on the issue of self. For the most part, the whole question of being a self is anathema to the Puritans. As Philip Greven generalizes, "The temperaments of evangelicals"—and this includes Mather—"were dominated by a persistent and virtually inescapable hostility to the self and all of its manifestations" (12). In looking at Mather specifically, Mitchell Breitwieser contrasts the Puritan pattern of restraint, submission, and denial with what Stephen Greenblatt calls "Renaissance self-fashioning"; he finds in the first generation the expression of a radical "self-obliteration that amounts to a disguised self-fashioning—a creative act that in later generations is lost in the need to submit to the example of the fathers. Thus, for Cotton Mather, "*self* and *sin* were practically synonymous," and life itself was defined, through the continuousness of conversion, as a chronic "annihilation of self." To remain true to the faith, Mather must purge the very real attractions of self and self-fashioning or "self-fathering" from his being in such a way that the defeat of self enhances the glory of God. In Breitwieser's construction, Mather's desire to achieve "personalized universality"—an essential quality of the representative personality—"could come to man only after the agony and from the wreckage of the gratefully crucified self" (27, 28, 45).

Although there is much in Mather's work that supports this contention, Mather also asserts an image of self that derives its energy from a theatrical conception of the place of individuals in the world. To a degree unmatched by Puritans of earlier generations, Cotton Mather imagines himself—and the worthies of New England—as actors trooping across the platform of ecclesiastical history. This need for exposure to the public view can be seen quite early in Mather's life. In a youthful letter to his uncle, the younger John Cotton, he explains the uncharacteristic shortness of his missive, saying, "I who once used to send by every opportunity a whole cartload of news, etc.—and spin out [like Translissus?] now to furl my sails, and come just like Cato on the stage, [ere?] only to go off again" (SL, 6). This is a remarkable passage, at least given the tenor of Puritan self-denial. In fact, not only does he show no shame at his simile or concern that his acting will be anything but well received, but, as Kenneth Silverman observes of his early correspondence in general, Mather's "learned, multilingual prose is a performance, an effort to strike the right pose by a brilliant youth for whom much is expected and who demands much of himself" (SL, 4; Silverman's *Life and Times of Cotton Mather*, a work to which I am indebted, notes the Cato letter and other passages in Mather's writing where theatrical expressions occur [36, 38]). Of course, the reference to Cato (whether Elder or Younger) is just right. If he means the Elder, the Censor, then one has the image of Rome's moral authority seizing the stage for a moment to redirect some bawdy play toward ends that serve the state. If he means the Younger, a man self-denying, showing through sacrifice the ideals of the nation, then Mather conjures a Cato who embraces the Stoic obsession with role and the paradox that a person is most himself when he submits to the part God has cast for him. This Cato also commits suicide, self-slaughter, for national ends. For young Cotton Mather, the same terms apply: by indulging his own obsession with performance and self-display, but in a rhetoric of self-abasement that is generated from the collective ideal of the covenant, he fashions himself as the nation—and then submits to the demand that the self be submerged in national identity (see Zuckerman, 212–13).

As with his forebears, Mather remains hostile to hypocrisy, whether in others or himself. He displays the evangelical need for unity of inner and outer beings and opposes any suggestion that only appearance matters. Even magistrates must be subject to the ideal of the unified person: "'Twere to be wished that there might never by any English translation of that wicked position in Machiavel, *Non requiri in Principe veram pietatem, sed sufficere illius quandam umbram, et simultationem Externam*" (MCA, 1:107). For Mather, no rule of governance could be more abhorrent than this: "True pietry is superfluous in a prince: it is enough if he assume its semblance and outward show." In the aggregate, New England magistrates show themselves to be examples of true piety; the individual believer, then, must chide himself when in the practice of piety his heart is "unaffected" by faith. In a typical self-critical diary entry, Mather exclaims, "Methinks, I am but a very *Parrot* in Religion" (*Diary*, 1:22), a voice in gaudy feathers, reporting pieties without feeling them.

Yet show has its undeniable attractions for Mather, who seems at times ambivalent toward the display of fashion. In his life of John Eliot, Mather notes the missionary's peculiar crankiness about matters hirsute: "*Long hair* was always very loathesome to him," he remarks, not only because it violates the practice of simplicity, but it confuses the sexes (*MCA*, 1:539–40). Nevertheless, Mather himself wore a periwig, as his portrait shows, and according to Samuel Sewall, he once preached on the line (from John of Salisbury via the London stage), *"Totus mundus agit histrionem"*:

> Said one sign of a hypocrit was for a man to strain at a Gnat and swallow a Camel. Sign in 's Throat discovered him; To be zealous against an innocent fashion, taken up and used by the best of men; and yet make no Conscience of being guilty of great Immoralities. Tis supposed means wearing of Perriwigs: said would deny themselves in any thing but parting with an opportunity to do God service; that so might not offend good Christians. Meaning, I suppose, was fain to wear a Perriwig for his health. I expected not to hear a vindication of Perriwigs in Boston Pulpit by Mr. Mather.   (Mar. 19, 1691, Sewall, *Diary*, 1:276)

Mather uses theater metaphor to reverse the expectations of the congregation. The hypocrite is not the actor, as Hooker has it. Now, everyone is an actor on the stage of the world, and the hypocrite is the one who would make much ado about an "innocent fashion" once thought to be a foppish, histrionic excess. While Sewall resisted wearing a wig, even when requested to do so by one of the women he courted late in life, Mather awakens his age to a justifiable worldliness. His sophistic argument signals an important shift in Puritan self-conception toward the idea that expression of faith is tied to the fashion of the times.

To be an actor requires that there be a spectator, and as with his father, Cotton Mather acknowledges the constant viewing of his divine sovereign: "My Mind, with all the Dispositions, and all the Operations of it, is continually under the Eye of the omnipresent God. Not only my Wayes, and my Words, but also the Thoughts and Frames of my Mind, come under the observation of the glorious One" (*Diary*, 2:155; see Breitwieser, 28). Though nonconformists from the earliest days recognize this spectating as a necessary part of being a true Christian, Mather presents it with a self-aware completeness not always seen in other writers. No one, he says in characteristic formula, has the potential for such baseness as he, but if he acts to please the Almighty—and he indicates that God often shows pleasure with his "remembrancer"—then he need not worry about other eyes. In a letter from 1724 to the lieutenant governor, William Dummer, Mather stresses that, in the matter of "gospellizing the aboriginal natives," it is more important to impress "Greater Eyes than those of the Governor and Company on the other side of the water" (*SL*, 381). But even *his* making such an announcement suggests that Mather is aware of eyes all the time, whether God's, the governor's, or the world's.

The process by which Mather converts concern over human eyes to those of the divine can be seen in an episode he records in his diary on April 5, 1685. That particular Sunday, a day he is scheduled to preach, Mather notices a smaller than usual congregation in church. As a young and as yet unordained minister, he understandably would be self-conscious about low attendance and his own responsibility in the people's "withdrawal." But it is clear from his comments on the matter that Mather has in mind an unchurchly need for public recognition of his talents as a preacher. He must, he reminds himself,

especially bee careful to apprehend, that an affectation of displaying ones gifts before Throngs, is too often an abominably proud Fishing for popular Applause; but my Work in the Pulpitt, must bee, rather to acquit myself well, in the Discharge of the Duties incumbent on mee there, before the *All-Seeing Eye* of that Majestie, who, to mee, shall be *Theatre* enough.

Satis mihi pauci Auditores, satis unus, satis nullus.   (Diary, 1:93)

Mather's insistence that he should be satisfied with only a few, one, or even no listeners strikes one not as a private reflection of genuine disappointment but as a public posture, a seeking of approval for not seeking approval. For many Puritans, the differences between public and private nearly disappear; but in this case, the private life gets publicized, made to seem exposed while remaining in its privacy, quite unlike our contemporary ideal of making public figures "human" by actually exposing to the world their private lives. For Mather, life in the sight of God alone is a theater, one exclusive of the world; necessarily, however, that theatrical relationship with the "*All-Seeing Eye*" must contend with another, that between a pastor and his flock—or that between a providentially favored nation and an expectant world.

In *Magnalia Christi Americana,* Mather insists on the primacy of private playing before God as an ideal of piety. Thomas Shepard—like Mather, an intense, passionate diarist—draws the historian's praise for his ability to limit his role as actor to performing before that same Eye who observes his biographer. Shepard is known for his godly habits, especially those of conversation: "Now, to take true measures of his conversation, one of the best *glasses* that can be used is the *diary,* wherein he did himself keep the remembrances of many remarkables that passed betwixt his *God* and *himself;* who were indeed *a sufficient theatre to one another*" (MCA, 1:390). Though *glass* here suggests a measuring device, a barometer, the word retains its connotation as something with which to see, a window or mirror on the "remarkables" moving between God and Shepard. In any event, his comments on Shepard provide a gloss on—or a glass into—Mather's own diary. Theater is really a conceit, a figural conversion of inaction into action and contemplation into show.

He gives yet another example of "sufficient" theater in the biography of his late younger brother, Nathaniel Mather. Though Nathaniel died at age nineteen, Cotton presents him as a model of intense and prodigious piety, one who in *his* diary tries to reach "as high a pitch in Christianity as any that I have known." As with his biography of Shepard, Mather shows his brother as a person whose private testimonials are the sort of strenuous strivings for which other more public figures receive acclaim: "He then, in the strength and through the love of God, set himself into a way of strict, secret, laborious devotion; whereby, tho' none but *God* and he fill'd the Theatre which he acted upon, he would be 'in the fear of the Lord all the day long' " (MCA,

2:164). Despite the relative insignificance of Nathaniel's public life, Mather uses this variant of the theatrum mundi figure to turn adolescent devotionals into a model of mature Christianity. In essence, by the power of rhetoric, Mather reverses our expectations and converts Nathaniel's youthful, private theater into an accomplished public exhibition.

To some extent, the enlargement of microscopic events with a macroscopic lens comes with hagiography, the saint's-life formula used by Mather throughout *Magnalia*. Beyond that, however, the ever-curious Mather adds to the form his own special interest in unusual phenomena of all kinds. Besides his well-known attention to science and the natural history of his native land, he seems obsessed with anything large or grandiose, including stage spectacles. His reverence for the spectacular both counters and complements the theater of the solitary believer found in Puritan diaries. He seems especially interested in the ways in which spectacle can be used figurally to describe political events. In a curiously oblique application of spectacle, Mather uses his life of Simon Bradstreet to depict the state of New England before the Glorious Revolution. He does not want to say anything directly about the politics of that time, he says:

> Only I have sometimes, not without amazement, thought of the representation which a celebrated *magician* made unto Catherine de Medicis, the French Queen, whose impious curiosity led her to desire of him a *magical exhibition* of all the Kings that had hitherto reigned in France, and yet were to reign. The shapes of all the Kings, even unto the husband of that Queen, successively showed themselves, in the *enchanted circle*, in which the conjurer had made his invocations, and they took as many *turns* as there had been years in their government. The Kings that were to come, did then in like manner successively come upon the stage, namely, Francis II., Charles IX., Henry III., Henry IV., which being done, then two cardinals, Richlieu and Mazarine, in red hats, became visible in the spectacle: but after those cardinals, there entred wolves, bears, tygers and lions, to consummate the entertainment.   (MCA, 1:139)

Mather follows this long passage with a comment linking "*rapacious animals*" in government to the onset of changes in 1689, but at the same time he reveals his fascination with spectacle as a type of prophetic or allegorical entertainment. Unlike the Puritan opponents of the theater decades before, writers such as Thomas Beard or William Prynne, Mather's attraction to theater seems untinged by a concomitant horror. Because he also lacks the limiting demand for simplicity found in a Bradford or an Eliot, Mather frees himself to indulge his passion for the large, the elaborate, or the grotesque.

Sometimes Mather's almost childlike amazement at spectacle leads him into unintended comedy. In another image for the era of the Glorious Revolution, this one from "Decennium Luctuosum," Mather uses a different spectacle to allude to the way in which the governor, Andros, frightens the Indians with his army: "When the keeper of wild beasts at Florence has entertained the spectators with their encounters on the stage, he has this device to make 'em retire into the several dens of their seraglio. He has a fearful *machin* of Wood, made like a great *green dragon*, which a man within it rouls upon wheels, and holding out a couple of lighted torches at the eyes of it, frights the fiercest beast of them all into the cell that belongs unto him" (*MCA*, 2:588). By such an allusion to a decadent entertainment, Mather may well be trying to appeal to a worldly European audience. He implies, of course, that real life in New England is replete with spectacles as amazing in their way as animal or dumb shows are in theirs. Yet to make the comparison at all, he must overcome Puritan ambivalence toward—or willful ignorance of—matters of the stage and immerse himself in the arcana of the theater. In fact, what Mather does is expose the ambivalence for what it is: a profound yearning for a theatrical life grander in scope than the illusionary life of European playhouses.

Whether through the image of a masque or a machine, Mather expands all aspects of the New World experience into awe-inducing stage wonders, regardless of the ironies or tortured exaggerations involved. Though he has owned a slave himself and imprecated Samuel Sewall with the term "Negar," he can still call "the *slave-trade . . .* a spectacle that shocks *humanity*" (*Bonifacius* [1710], 54). Likewise, a fire in Boston betokens God's wrath: "Our Eyes, which ought to Affect our Hearts, have newly been entertained with a very *dismal Spectacle*" (*Advice from Taberah* [1711], 1). Even phenomena as diverse as the birth of Siamese twins, "a shocking spectacle, whereof I was myself one of the spectators," and the ordination of a minister as it appears to a foreign visitor, *"a spectacle* [that] *was a solemn, serious, affecting transaction,"* reflect Mather's constant elevation of the unusual or the ritual into events of global or cosmic importance (*SL*, 132, 133). Mather's world is one where reality not only is stranger than fiction but, because it is so incredible, also demands of its spectators the same responses usually reserved for wonder-working entertainments. To Mather's credit, he recognizes that his reading audience may find his histories beyond ordinary belief. In an account of King Philip's War, Mather details the adventures of Captain Church, whose exploits bring the war to its conclusion: "And some of his achievements were truly so magnanimous and extraordinary, that my reader will suspect me to be transcribing the silly old romances, when the knights do conquer so many giants, if I should proceed unto the particular commemoration of them" (*MCA*, 2:576). Though romances, along with plays, belong in the "Devil's library," Mather recognizes that as a cultural currency, romantic inflation, like the rhetoric of spectacle, illuminates for the widest possible readership the significance of American citizens and events (*Bonifacius*, 46).

Indeed, Mather fills his writing with references to wonders and wonder-making, continuing and augmenting a tradition seen from the earliest days of Puritan settlement. One book of *Magnalia*, for instance, he entitles "Thaumaturgus," which Mather Englishes as "The Wonder-Worker; or, Book of Memorable Events," and he asserts that it contains "Illustrious Discoveries and Demonstrations of the Divine Providence." One such demonstration occurs in "The Wonderful Story of Major Gibbons." The hero of this adventure is on board a ship in distress, and his company feels a lottery must be conducted to see who must die and be eaten in order to save the rest. "It is a death now to think who shall act this bloody part in the tragedy," Mather writes, but they pray once more, and "behold!" a fish jumps in the boat, saving the company from their gruesome task (*MCA*, 1:346). In this episode, Providence works the wonder that saves a saint, while Mather frames the scene as theater to give it its dramatic due.

In another context, essay 23 of *The Christian Philosopher* (1721), Mather calls his readers to consider signs from the earth as evidence of God's word: *"The Lord by Wisdom has founded the Earth,"* he begins;

"A poor Sojourner on the *Earth* now thinks it his Duty to behold and admire the *Wisdom* of his glorious Maker there." In the admiring catalog that follows, Mather sees nothing *but* wisdom, especially in such violent phenomena as earthquakes and volcanoes. What are the tremblings of the earth but instructions to God's people? "Indeed," Mather concludes, "what is the Earth but a *Theatre*, as has been long since observed? In which," to translate his Latin, "are to be contemplated infinite and glorious spectacles of the Divine providence, goodness, power, and wisdom" (*Selections*, 293, 301, 301n). If the earth is a theater, and God the director, then it follows that not only natural phenomena but also the performances of God's people can be adjudged spectacles worthy of our contemplation. In fact, *Magnalia* records Mather's preoccupation with exhibitions of all sorts; it is extraordinary in its scope, perhaps, but not unusual in kind among a people already predisposed to see spectacles in the earth and to be seen themselves on God's global stage.

Given his proclivity to see wonders everywhere, it is no wonder that Mather so graphically records those of the "invisible world" during the Salem witchcraft craze. Affected people are "entertained" with ghosts, and the *"chief evidence"* raised against the accused comes from *"spectral exhibitions"* (MCA, 1:209). For his readers, Mather enhances the spectacular nature of these exhibitions by claiming, in *The Wonders of the Invisible World*, that he records events "not as an advocate, but as a historian," one who, because "not present" at any of the trials, has no "personal prejudice at the persons thus brought upon the stage" (54, 55). He creates in his writing a world of special effects like those found in the stage spectacles he uses figurally; Mather's New England is a land where the unbelievable is irrefutable and the fantastic is concrete. This wonder-working enhancement occurs not only in his self-proclaimed objective histories of spectral phenomena but also in his "reserved memorialls." There in his diary he records the incursions of the spirit world on his private sense of himself with the same abhorrence that he tells us the colony feels when "an army of devils is horribly broke in upon" New England ("Enchantments Encounter'd," *Wonders*, 7). As historian, he shapes and directs events; as victim, however, he loses control and appears to become but a puppet of malign agency: "A young Woman being arrested, possessed, afflicted by *evil Angels*, her Tormentors made *my* Image or Picture to appear before her, and then made themselves Masters of her Tongue so far, that shee began in her Fits to complain that I threatened her and molested her, tho' when shee came out of them, she own'd, that *they* could not so much as make my *dead Shape* do her any Harm" (*Diary*, 1:178). The devil is a necromancer, giving false life to images, erecting dead shapes, seizing others' tongues, creating the illusion that the most vigorously pious of the Lord's servants haunts young women. With some reason, Mather worries about his precious reputation, one later sullied by Robert Calef, and the danger that would be caused if people hear "that the Divels in *my Shape* tormented the Neighbourhood" (1:178). For Mather the actor, nothing threatens more than having a demonic double acting *him* and thus comically deflating the stern spectacles he has so resolutely inscribed for America.

It is important, then, to assert one's ability to read the thaumatographs that are placed in front of us—before someone less qualified, or more malicious, provides a false interpretation. Deciphering the world of wonders has its other rewards, too: first, in the thrill of amazement, and second, in the service one can render to a people. In *Thaumatographia Christiana* (1701), Mather comments on the life of Christ as a series of wonders, at which one stands amazed rather than in which one analyzes or probes. A particular wonder is the image of Jesus with his bright face being spat upon by scoffers: "Behold, the *Lord of Hosts*, yet made a *Mock King* in a play, and mock'd, and jeer'd, and scoff'd until the Mockers were weary of the Sport" (25). The bondage of Christ becomes a piece of theater, at once made repellent, by its analogy to secular plays, yet wondrous, a spectacle of forbearance—perhaps how Mather felt about himself after Calef's published attack. With the bondage of a nation, wonder-reading becomes more complicated. In his jeremiad *The Short History of New England* (1694), Mather alludes to the period of witchcraft, noting how little New England would listen to its prophets: "While a People are thus under *Enchantment*, it is a Vain thing, to Advise them, to Exhort them, to Warn them" (62). To combat enchantment requires a different kind of wonder-working, a special ability based on knowledge of the necromantic enemy: "Now if a man have, *The Right Skill of Encountring Enchantments*, he may do great things for the People of

God; he may be a Glorious Instrument of bringing things to rights" (62). Mather justifies his ambiguous role as a theatrically minded minister by showing himself to be both a martyr to mockers in externally contrived plays and one, by virtue of his special knowledge in determining illusion from reality, capable of *"Encountring"* the spells that lead an unwitting people to deviltry.

Like other Puritans, Mather knows that the literature of entertainment competes with the literature of instruction. Not surprisingly, in his instructions to parents in *Bonifacius*, he advises that they select their children's reading materials: "Keep a strict eye upon them, that they don't stumble on *the Devil's library*, and poison themselves with foolish *romances*, or *novels*, or *plays*, or *songs*, or *jests* that are not convenient" (46). That last clause leaves a lot unsaid, and the word "foolish" makes an ambiguous qualifier, but along with the other genres, plays are for Mather a potential source of distortion of the Christian message. Like Captain John Smith, Mather fears what happens to exemplars when their weighty acts become the targets of comic actors; indeed, he speculates that the stage and stage plays (not, one presumes, the works of the classical dramatists he quotes in *Magnalia*—Plautus, Seneca, and Terence) have become in his time a more effective form of scourging and martyr-making than the violence suffered by nonconformists in earlier times.

The person who would essay to do good, he explains in *Bonifacius*, must be prepared to endure all manner of ills, including *"DERISION"*: "It is a thing of late started, that the way of *banter*, and *scoffery*, and *ridicule*, or the *Bart'lemew-Fair* method, as they please to call it, is a more effectual way to discourage all *goodness*, and put it out of countenance, than *fire* and *faggot*" (11). In the possible allusion to Jonson's play, *Bartholomew Fair* (1614), and its scornful portrayal of the Puritan Zeal-of-the-Land Busy, Mather underscores the power of the theater in passing false judgment on God's people. Mather even suggests that the Devil chooses theatrical persecution because he is "somewhat *chained* up in several places" from tormenting believers in the more violent ways of the past. His prophecy for those who elect to do good focuses on the future derision suffered by Christians on stage: "Exquisite *profaneness* and *buffoonery* shall try their skill to laugh people out of [essays to do good]. The men who abound in them shall be exposed on the *stage*; *libels*, and *lampoons*, and *satires*, the most poignant that ever were invented, shall be darted at them; and *pamphlets* full of lying stories, be scattered, with a design to make them *ridiculous*" (11–12). If hypocrites are the bugbear of the first generation, then professional actors are the same for the third-generation Mather. He reveals in this and other passages how absorbed he is in the role of language-user, for no one is as vulnerable to verbal ridicule as one who makes his career by the word. The enemies of Matherian man forge their weapons from the genres of jest, and in the context of a stage, persecute the essayists of good with their linguistic barbs. He warns his readers again in *Bonifacius* that one ought not account it "*strange*" to hear defamations of strenuous pietists or think it unusual "if ever so many *Aristophaneses* fall upon you; if *javelins* are thrown at you with a rage reaching to Heaven; and if *pamphlets* are stuffed with vile figments and slanders upon you" (148). It is as if Mather acknowledges here that the world and its wars are all constructed out of language—and that the literal stage, with its corps of modern-day "*Aristophaneses*" waiting with sharpened wits to pounce upon unarmored good-doers, can make martyrs merely by the sleight, or slight, of mouth.

Mather reveals in *Bonifacius* a thirst for martyrdom, but of a particular kind; that the stage itself should become the stage whereupon martyrs will be made seems appropriate to one whose every action is a performance. Still, Mather's peculiar prophecy is the more peculiar when we remember that he writes in a land where the theater is proscribed. For someone like the professional Virginian John Smith living in London, worry about the shows of the London stage is quite natural. Yet Mather, living his whole life in New England, displays a more than casual interest in the goings-on of English theater that belies his warnings not to heed the lampoons heard there. In his sole surviving letter to Michael Wigglesworth, Mather recounts a theatrical example of the "impenitency" of England. It seems that a terrible storm struck that country, a literal catastrophe, the sort of event that in New England would bring forth sermons and fast days. But there, "on the very day of the storm, as soon as it was over, it, and the thunder and lightning and falling of houses that accompanied it, was acted on the public stages and made a ridicule" (Apr. 17, 1704, *SL*, 69). No doubt, then, that Mather took particular delight in copying down Jonathan Swift's "Esquire Bickerstaff's Praedictions for 1708," which includes for May 23 the entry, "A famous Buffoon of a Play-house will dy of a ridiculous Death, suitable to his vocation" (the title and rendering are Mather's, *Diary*, 1:600). Nevertheless, even until his old age, Mather would be dogged by a mocking English stage. After his break with Governor Joseph Dudley, Mather became the subject of widespread abuse. Through a letter from John Winthrop (1681–1747), Mather hears of a "sort of farce or comedy" about both himself and his father that was "pretended to have been acted at the play-house in London" (ca. 1725; Winthrop, "Correspondence," 428; see Silverman, *Life*, 221–22). It seems that the fate of those men who personally embody the American mission is to suffer, as John Smith says, the indignity of having their "fatall Tragedies upon the Stage." Mather, lacking the humor of an earlier object of theatrical ridicule, Martin Marprelate, and ideologically constrained from replying in kind, must somehow learn to suffer it away. With its potential for comic reversal, the stage can show a world flipped on its back or ridicule even the realm of the divine. Therefore, better to be a martyred victim of ridicule than to be ridiculous on stage yourself. In a letter to Dr. James Woodward, Mather begs his correspondent to excuse the writer's shifting topics, hoping that he "will not charge my friendship with the solecism of that actor, who when he cried *O Terra!* pointed up to the heavens" (Nov. 19, 1712, *SL*, 113). For Cotton Mather, ridicule ennobles the sufferer and mocks the mocker, a position that comes from an implicit belief that the stage itself is a comically deflated version of the theatrum mundi; only a stage as large as the world is "sufficient" to hold both Mather and his God.

If the real stage undermines the solemnity of history, then the historian by a greater art can appropriate and solemnize the stages; and so it appears that in the greatest work of seventeenth-century America, *Magnalia Christi Americana*, Cotton Mather does precisely that. Readers of Mather have long recognized that his hyperbolic, periodic, exclamatory prose deviates sharply from the plain style of his forefathers, but his contemporaries must also have seen something other than baroque excess in the achievement of *Magnalia*. In "A Prefatory Poem" to the "Church-History," as Mather called his book, Nicholas

Noyes praises the author as a *"well-instructed Scribe"*: "He's all *design*, and by his *craftier wiles* / Locks fast his reader, and the time beguiles" (*MCA*, 1:19). This vision of writer as basilisk asserts the potency of the word, but the emphasis on design and craftiness makes clear that others perceive Mather's reiterated signs of a plan to link the disparate texts of New England's ecclesiastical history. The elevated praise for his art creates a paradox, for as earlier Puritans perceived, a super-subtle style deceives and generates illusions that, like the dreams attacked by Thomas Shepard, run counter to the truth. Mather himself disclaims the presence of any romanticizing or authorial interven-tion. To be fair, we can say that Mather believes his work is all to the greater glory of God, but even with that premise, we stretch our own credulity if we accept at face value his cries of artlessness. In the introduction to book 3, he asks us to envision a literary procession of "the *fathers* of *New-England* [introduced] without the least fiction or figure of rhetorick" (1:234). To acknowledge fictional enhancement, rhetorical flourish, or authorial design would be to violate the de-mands on a servant of God to render his plan accurately—indeed, it would make him an "idler," as that self-aware descendant of Puritans, Nathaniel Hawthorne, fears *he* will be called by his other ancestors (*Scarlet Letter*, 11).

In a metaphor that reflects the Puritan fascination with wonders, another prefatory poet, Benjamin Thompson, describes Mather's method as coming from the dark arts:

> Is the bless'd MATHER *necromancer* turn'd
> To raise his country's fathers? ashes urn'd?
> *Elisha's* dust, life to the dead imparts;
> This prophet, by his more *familiar arts*,
> *Unseals* our *heroes'* tombs, and gives them air:
> They rise, they walk, they talk, look wondrous fair.   (*MCA*, 1:20)

Like a thaumaturge, Mather resurrects the corpses of the fathers of New England and gives them breath: "They rise, they walk, they talk"! With a literature conceived thus, what culture would need a stage? Mather's own fascination with spectacle merges with the needs of propaganda to image America as a land where the ordinary is fraught with miracles, where, as the title of a later section in *Magnalia* indicates, "Dead Abels [Are] Yet Speaking." Though Mather fears that his own necromantically driven "dead shape" will be thought the bane of the neighborhood, he enthusiastically embraces a literary necromancy, as if his book is a gigantic showbox history of New England, and he turns lifeless materials into a masquerade of history. His claim for rhetorical plainness notwithstanding, he tells his readers that he is well aware Thompson's metaphors apply to his design. His life of Samuel Whiting, for example, is notable more for Mather's figures than for the events in the life of that "Man of God and an Honourable Man." With his usual revisionist typology, Mather turns Whiting into an avatar of the biblical Samuel, a likeness that sends Mather to the dispute over whether or not, in the witch of Endor episode, Samuel appears as himself or as a specter: "Let the disputants upon this question wrangle on: while we by a very lawful and laudable *art* will fetch another Samuel from the dead: and by the happy *magick* of our pen, reader, we will bring into the view of the world a venerable old man—a Samuel who shall entertain us with none but comfortable and profitable tidings" (1:502). The magic of the historian's pen raises the dead, countering the magic of the invisible-world wizards who populate New England with evil specters (see D. Hall, "World").

But Mather suborns his rhetorical necromancy to his governing metaphor of *Magnalia*, the world stage. Mather the historian is *histor histrionicus*, the learned, theatrical shaper of his country's past. Like the thaumaturgical Providence of which he writes, he appropriates profane entertainment to send a sacred message. His desire to write "THE CHURCH-HISTORY OF THIS COUNTREY" bubbles out of the cauldron of social ferment in the period immediately after the witchcraft trials (July 1693, *Diary*, 1:166). Perhaps Mather felt that the latent suspicions about the veracity of the trials needed to be disarmed by something else, equally miraculous but more spectacular—and it is a mark of Mather's genius that he recognized how to submerge the furor over witchcraft into the larger context of history. Whatever the impulse, Mather stamps his works with the unmistakable cadence of epic, underscoring them with references to Homer and Virgil, but he needs another form, a platform perhaps, in and on which those dead Abels can speak. First, he will tell us of the original settlements, created out of the translation (*translatio*) of "the WONDERS of the

CHRISTIAN RELIGION" from Europe to New England; "and a *Field* being thus prepared, I proceed unto relation of the *Considerable Matters* which have been acted thereupon." *Field* in this context denotes something like stage, a space for display; it does, additionally, mean something similar to what Victor Turner suggests when he uses the term to denote a cultural environment before a social drama takes place. In other words, as God has exhibited on earth, so Mather will in his book.

Mather continues in this vein, referring to the field as if it were the theatrum mundi: "I first introduce the *Actors*, that have in a more exemplary manner served those Colonies; and give remarkable Occurrences, in the exemplary LIVES of many Magistrates, and of more Ministers, who so lived as to leave unto Posterity *examples* worthy of everlasting remembrance" (1:25). If this passage, by means of its comparison of history and biography to drama, is for Mather "a means of fusing the two genres," as Sacvan Bercovitch asserts, creating the image of "players on the stage of the New World theater," then it also intensifies for the historian-biographer his role as dramatist and consequently as scapegoat, subject to worldwide derision if the drama fails (*Puritan Origins*, 230n, 129; see also Schneider, 32, 34).

To overcome or circumvent derision, Mather, as with Winthrop in his *Short Story*, patterns much of *Magnalia* as tragedy. His own history of the Antinomian crisis also refers to the threat of the Hutchinsonians as being another "Munster tragedy"; but since the conclusion of that episode, most of the generation of heretics sent to Rhode Island are "now generally gone off the stage" (*MCA*, 2:52). Of the Quaker trespasses in the 1650s, Mather gives the only possible defense for the "*mad* subjects of these tragedies," a line from Seneca's play *Hercules Furens*: "Madness alone can prove thee guiltless" (2:527). King Philip's War also has its share of tragedies, but the conclusion follows a script crafted by the divine playwright. During the last battles, "whereof Plymouth was now the stage," Captain Church is made the instrument of history, "employ'd by the providence of Heaven at the time and place of the *catastrophe*, now waiting for a generation ripe for desolation" (2:514). Even the death of Philip has a Macbethlike quality about it. The king consults prophetic magicians who tell him he shall never die by an English hand; so when he, like Macbeth, is surprised by the manner of his mortality—in Philip's case, by the hand of a disaffected Indian—he follows his Shakespearean counterpart in leaving the scene to a chastened generation to assert their rightful power (2:576). And Mather's long section on the "mournful decade," "Decennium Luctuosum," is filled with references to "dismal tragedies" and the like (2:635).

While Mather labels crises as tragedies, he also imagines ritual events in playlike terms. In an early funeral sermon, *Elegy on . . . Nathanael Collins* (1685), Mather creates the image of family members lamenting the *"Tragedy"* of Collins's death while they are perched on a *"Stage"* (20, 15; see Silverman, *Life*, 38). Out of an experience from a year later, when Mather gained fame from the first of his execution sermons, the author creates in *Magnalia* a playlike account of his role in the conversion of the condemned James Morgan. Mather renders Morgan's death march as a dramatic dialogue between the criminal and an unnamed minister (obviously Mather) that concludes with Morgan's exclamatory "O Lord—I come, I come, I come" (Silverman, *Life*, 47–48; MCA, 2:413; see also Meserve, 21). Another such dialogue in the "Pillars of Salt" section occurs with the wife-murderer Hugh Stone. Despite the utter sophistry of the "Minister" who tries to persuade Stone of having more sins than he can recall or ever imagine, the dialogue moves briskly toward a dramatically satisfying conclusion. In effect, Mather realizes in these and other episodes that the usual anticlimactic literature of nonconformism can be enlived by a vigorous dose of pagan theatricality.

Even that, however, does not fully explain the theatrical touches Mather customarily bestows on the lives of the worthies. The biographer projects upon his subjects an image of self that grows naturally from an obsession with being watched, but one in which the deleterious effects—potential madness or, at the least, destructive neuroses—can be overcome by acting in a regulated environment. By structuring the self rhetorically in theatrical terms, Mather elevates his subjects at the same time that he tries to guard against diverting excess.

One model for his biographies is a work entitled, *Theatrum virorum eruditione clarorum . . .* (1688), which Mather translates as, "The Theater of Men of Learning down to the Present Time," by Paulus Freher (MCA, 1:246). Theater makes a convenient mode of presentation when one wants to highlight individuals in the context of some larger frame, and Mather has adopted this motif in *Magnalia*. All lives, then, become "representative" in some fashion, and in Mather's thaumaturgical method, each dead worthy comes alive by the agency of the author's "magick" pen to act his characteristic part in the covenantal drama of New England. In some cases, the histrionic historian must employ all the machinery of his craft in order to elevate his subjects.

The most famous of Mather's aggressive revisions of history is his biography of the governor and Mather political ally, William Phips. Breitwieser contends that Phips, as an "independent, self-fathered character," that is, as Mather himself says, one who is "a son to his own labours," contrasts greatly with the self-denying model his biographer has absorbed, and thus the biography is "a vicarious wish-fulfilling" on Mather's part (Breitwieser, 165; MCA, 1:167). But in the writing, Mather does the shaping of this life, making the text a form of "*resurrection*"—really, a re-creation. In this case, the biography becomes a chemist's show, where "by the like method from the *essential salts* of *humane dust*, a philosopher may, without any criminal *necromancy*, call up the *shape* of any *dead* ancestor from the dust whereinto his body has been incinerated" (1:165). Thus Mather will attempt, using the "*chymistry* of an impartial historian, to *raise* my friend so far out of his ashes, as to show him again unto the world" (1:166). If not criminal, then the method certainly smacks of spectacle, where the historian is not only showman but also quondam God to a demi-Christ.

As with many of his biographies, Mather's presentation of Phips has more interest as a piece of writing than as an "impartial" account. Mather seems determined to have Phips be a paragon, regardless of his desultory American career. When his hero considers his life's work in England in 1688, Mather makes the decision seem momentous: "He thought the best stage of *action* for him would now be New-England it self" (1:178). Phips finds action, much of it military against the French, but his best role comes later. New England, overrun with specters and apparitions, needs someone who can bring order to chaos—and so it is to Phips that Mather gives the credit for restoring the commonwealth to itself in 1692: "But the worst part of this astonishing tragedy is yet behind; wherein Sir William Phips, at last being dropt, as it were from the *machin of heaven*, was an instrument of easing the distresses of the land, now 'so darkened by the wrath of the Lord of Hosts'" (1:207). Providence directs as well as corrects, ordering its drama with an eye toward the spectacular event; thus Phips, the man sui generis, enters the scene by no other agency than of the Director himself, using the machinery of the heavenly theater. Mather uses the image of the deus ex machina elsewhere too. In a letter to Robert Millar, the Scottish theologian, he urges continued religious struggle, regardless of the chiliastic conflagration soon to come: "And if we do not gain our point, our God from the Machine of Heaven will shortly do more than we have looked for" (May 28, 1725, SL, 406). For Mather, New England history is a Theater of Worthies whose lives, like that of the incomparable Phips, are episodes in the all-embracing Theater of God's Judgments. Whether standing upon the stage or entering from heavenly winches, these figures foreshadow in the spectacle of their lives the spectacular conclusion to history itself.

Though Mather employs all the machinery of metaphor to enhance the life of Phips, his political subject lends himself readily to theatrical metaphor. The lives of church leaders, however, by their more pious, reflective ways, make more difficult subjects for figural enhancement. As Mather must have sensed about his own life, the careers of great ministers often hang between the contending tugs of antitheatrical plain speaking and the allure of stage oratory. John Cotton, Mather records, disappointed his listeners in an early sermon because he chose to speak plainly rather than for show: "He considered that it was his duty to preach with such a plainness, as became the *oracles* of God, which are intended for the conduct of men in the paths of life, and not for *theatrical* ostentations and entertainments, and the Lord needed not any *sin* of ours to maintain his own glory" (MCA, 1:256). This focus on Cotton's deliberate fig to histrionics follows mainstream doctrine. As Mather remarks elsewhere about churches, "The setting of these places, with a theatrical gaudiness, does not savour of the spirit of a true Christian society" (2:264). But in the biography of Cotton, another figure appears, one who when he admonishes English noblemen for violating the Sabbath with recreations, stands in his pulpit and receives the accolades accorded to a player. Naturally, Cotton never loses his humility: "None of the *roses* cast on this applauded *actor*, *smothered* that humble, that loving, that gracious disposition, which was his perpetual *ornament*" (1:261; for another instance of the same figure, see *SL*, 10). The point seems to be that plainness itself, worn as an "ornament" by a minister of Cotton's stature, earns applause as surely as ostentation. Nevertheless, the metaphor of actor indicates Mather's own ambivalence about the need for humility—and the equivalent need for display and applause for that humility.

In contrast to the plain-preaching Cotton, Thomas Hooker speaks in a fluent, fiery style, one whose analogy to theatrical presentation might cause some purists discomfort. Mather, however, explains that Hooker's preaching avoids the errors of the stage by being sincere: "Though the *ready* and *noisy* performances of many preachers, when they are, as Plato speaks, THEATROU MESTOI, or *full of the theatre*, acting to the height in the publick for their applause, may be ascribed unto very *mechanical principles*," Hooker, in contrast, delivers his sermons with the spirit of God behind them (MCA, 1:337). Thus even if the ministers shun theatrical excess or the mere mechanics of stage delivery, they are actors nonetheless. Bercovitch says of *Magnalia*, "The series of biographies, and biographical groupings, demarcate the successive acts in the drama of the corporate American pilgrim," and so, from Mather's theatrical language, it would seem. But there is a problem, too, with the idea of representation, where "every one of the 'principal actors' stands for the venture at large" (*Puritan Origins*, 129). Mather alludes to an impossible stagecraft. His New England worthies remain on guard against the dangerous attractions of the earthly stage, yet they are thrust by the contentious history of nonconformism into being actors on stage. They wrestle with specters but are forced by the "lawful" necromancy of the historian into being resurrected shapes in the spectacle of ecclesiastical revision. In his life of Hooker, Mather raises the question we might ask of all ministers: How can one be full of the theater without being dragged into one? Mather suggests that the benchmark is sincerity, that is, the degree to which one is enlivened by the purity of the Holy Spirit. As he notes in *Manuductio ad Ministerium* (1726), Freher's

Theatrum gives great pleasure to one who would read of saints; nevertheless, he says, "I can tell you of *Theatres* much less worthy to be gone into" (68). The need for a playhouse is subsumed by making all New England a stage and the text of *Magnalia* a dramatic processional of saints dedicated to a single end.

Mather's own life, told by himself, tells another story. *Magnalia* documents a corporate design for the lives of each of the individuals in the episodes contained therein; yet the overtly theatrical elements, especially the highlighting of saints' lives, redirect the design from separate stories of the self denied to a history of selves fulfilled on the geographically defined stage of America. As a history, Mather's book gives public voice to an exalted view of the American colonial enterprise. It serves its Christian readership as propaganda for the ultimate land speculation, the location of the Second Coming. Mather makes it quite clear that the locus of revelation is New England, not simply the earth, and thus the lives of those who prepare the place take on special significance. Further, it would seem possible that among the worthies there be one who supersedes the rest, one whose unflagging faith, ceaseless essays to do good, and prodigious recording of wonders not only *represents* the federal mission but also *embodies* it. To that end, *Magnalia* is also about someone else whose biography is missing but whose traces are everywhere. It has as its subject the one person who could both absorb and express the totality of New England church history and at the same time stand before the world to take its spite: "*Me, me adsum qui scripsi; in me convertite ferrum*"—"'tis COTTON MATHER that has written all these things" (MCA, 1:34).

Throughout his biography Kenneth Silverman describes Mather's obsession with bigness; indeed, Mather's literary development of his life expresses a social, even cosmic, in-corporation, a taking into himself of the language of federality. It is not simply that he subjugates himself for the sake of the New England imperative; rather, he internalizes the social and political conflicts of his native land and subjugates *them* to his will. Therefore, when he *acts*—ministers or preaches or writes—he *is* New England. *Magnalia*, then, shows the wonderful work of Cotton Mather in writing and compiling the materials of New England's church history; even if he gives the glory to Christ, he gives it back to himself by the attempt in his diary to design a life undiminished by any man or thing. He never denies that he is an actor, albeit one with special challenges and gifts; but he does fear that in the theater of God and himself only Cotton Mather will do the clapping.

Mather's youthful writings are often his most revealing, not only because some of his diary entries are so ingenuous but also because he draws so heavily on earlier passages for later ones. He follows the orthodox path in lamenting his tendencies toward pride, but he specifically pronounces himself guilty of "*Applauding* of myself in any Thoughts, when I have done any Thing at all significant, pray'd or preach'd with enlargements, answered a Quaestion readily, presently, suitably, and the like. *Proud Thoughts* fly-blow my best Performances!" (*Diary*, 1:16). Pride works invidiously to taint his performances, depriving him of the applause he would otherwise receive from his fellows or his God; in other words, Mather never really repudiates applause—the danger comes from self-congratulation. It is this expressed concern of Mather's that leads Breitwieser to call much of his writing a "holy war on self" (44). But the object is more than the suppression; it is a purifying of an internal space in order that external performance be rendered unassailable.

One fascinating episode in Mather's mastery of self is his attempt to overcome a childhood stammer. As Carol Gay observes, Mather probably did not *cure* it, but he did control it successfully and brought himself a reputation as an effective preacher thereby. In his diary he recounts a number of thoughts about and programs for dealing with the stammer, which can be summed up in one of his "Rules of Speech": "*The Tongue of the Stammerer shall speak plainly*" (1:55). Mather must utter every word, every sound, mindful of its articulation; he must, in reality, resort to those same "*mechanical principles*" of speech that he claims Thomas Hooker happily lacked. If he succeeds in conquering the stammer, he must then bridge the means and end with something other than his own endeavors. To circumvent pride of performance, he resorts to a thanksgiving litany in which he credits his achievements to the interventions of divine agency.

When he eventually does overcome the defect in his young manhood, Mather adds his improved speech to the list of Heaven's "favors." He accounts it wondrous "that I should bee a great *Stammerer*, and yett bee made not only a Preacher of the Gospel, but also my

Utterance in my preaching bee not the least *ornament* of it, and I bee used in speaking more than any man of my Age in the Land, on the most important Occasions" (1:311). No wonder that Mather takes such pains in *Magnalia* and elsewhere to establish himself as an "impartial historian"; to avoid the corruption, the fly-blow, of pride, he must deflect his praise of himself to an utterer of fact—in this case, Cotton Mather the writer. The process works something like this: Mather purges himself of pride and ill appearance (his stammer) in order to purify himself for the purpose of incorporating the covenantal mission within the prepared space. Thus, when the stammer turns into ornament; when God uses him "in so eminent a Place; the most considerable Town, in all *New England*"; when he wonders, "Who am I, that God should thus use and read my poor Thoughts, for the Good of my whole Generation?" he expresses the power of his performances in "secret THANKSGIVING" and anoints himself as the one person capable of recognizing the full extent of his genius and scope (1:227).

Ironically, Mather measures his abilities in appearances; while he acknowledges to himself having "greatly miscarried in Secret," he celebrates the spotlessness of his reputation in public. Though tested by Satan, "yett my Adversary has not prevailed so far, as to make me a public Exemple of Scandal and Hissing and Horror, and the Astonishment and Execration of all the Churches" (1:578). Whatever he may do, he does not make himself look ridiculous. On the contrary, he pleases the multitude. Throughout his diary there are references to the size of crowds or the importance of his sermons. In the town of Reading he is "entertained with a very extraordinary *Attention* and *Affection* in the Auditory" when he preaches for the "rising Generation" (1:166). After another period of travel, he is struck by "the *Curiousity* and *Vanity* of the people . . . in their *great Flocking* to hear mee" (1:272). Some time thereafter, on the occasion of an execution day lecture, Mather speaks to "the greatest Assembly, ever in this Country preach'd unto. . . . It may bee four or five thousand Souls. I could not gett unto the *Pulpit*, but by climbing over *Pues* and Heads" (1:278). His popularity introduces new temptations, which he successfully weathers by resisting "the foolish *Taste* of *popular applause*"; yet he expresses an obvious satisfaction to feel that it is "the

Lord using *mee*, the vilest in all that great Assembly, to glorify Him"
(1:279).

Most of all, Mather prizes his global significance, especially as it is
spread by his written "composures." Under "the Eye, which His
Churches have upon mee," Mather finds his publications circulating
throughout Europe and the colonies. In one of his frequent prostra-
tions in the dust of his study floor (an act rescued from Perry Miller's
scorn by Charles Hambrick-Stowe, 34–36), he prophesies his the-
ogeographical importance after a visit from the "Spirit of the Lord": "I
was wondrously Irradiated. My Lord Jesus Christ, shall yett bee more
known, in the vast Regions of *America*; and by the means of poor vile
sinful *mee*, Hee shall be so" (1:234). It is precisely this kind of irradia-
tion that Anne Hutchinson described two generations before—a sense
of certainty that has the force of revelation. In a series of predictions
which he later affirms as having come to pass, Heaven, he says, tells
him what his role shall be in coming political and ecclesiastical
events. Mather, however, appropriates the Antinomian prerogative to
entertain the Holy Spirit immediately and converts it to a social, not
merely individual, imperative. In the same way that he is "irradiated"
by the spirit, America will also be irradiated by essayers of good
(*Bonifacius*, 133; see Breitwieser, 55). The Anne Hutchinson who
appears in the "Hydra Decapita" section of *Magnalia* may be in all
conventional ways Mather's opposite or "dark double"; but her claim
to be touched by the spirit, unmediated by any other agent, only
precedes Mather's even more astonishing assertions (see Breitwieser,
73, and Lang, *Prophetic Woman*, 66–70).

By absorbing the nation within himself then acting before the eyes
of church and God, Mather risks both the scoffery of his adversaries
and the ridicule of those he would please. But by limiting the theater
in which he acts to God and himself, he sits alone upon the famous
American hill—the city is simply understood. He is the antitype of
Walt Whitman—large, containing multitudes, turning his private
wrestlings into the struggles of the agonistic arena. Mather shifts
radically from nonconformist tradition by making faith not only a
dialogic combat but also a spectacle; he celebrates a self large enough
to be a nation. He asks us to assume what he assumes, but he assumes
all of us, as the scope of *Magnalia* and the even larger, unpublished

"Biblia Americana" would indicate. In his execution sermons and writings, he shows us he is with the criminal as well as the saint, if not as fully sympathetic as Whitman creates himself to be. With the largest library, the largest number of publications, the largest audiences, the largest range of interests of any colonial, Mather supersedes all previous representative lives. His theatrical rhetoric, read by his critics as bombast and bloat, in reality defines the individual as an actor, playing the nation before an international audience. What remains ahead for America, then, is the national drama universalized, where the multitudes no longer remain contained in the swollen corpus of a necromantic hierarch but burst forth, as actors on a public stage, confident of Providence, self-interested and defiant, risking derision only from corrupt men. Cotton Mather, unwittingly, has prepared the field for democratic revolution by bequeathing to subsequent generations a theatrical conception of self. It remains for the more secularized Americans of the 1760s and 1770s to turn their world upside down.

III

The Theater

of Action,

1676–1776

The Field or the Stage: Democracy, Theater, and Anglo-American Culture

*O*f all centuries in British cultural history, the eighteenth may be the most easily defined as the age of theatricality. The urban life of London, in company with that of other great European capitals of the time, notably Paris, appears to have been saturated not only with a vigorous and topical drama but also with a social obsession with appearance. In the public life of politics and the arts, masks become de rigueur, as if to be at all in the public eye requires a deliberate adoption of a role to take the place of the authentic self. Ironically, in the openly histrionic behavior of men and women in eighteenth-century society, the metaphor of theater breaks down; as Richard Sennett argues in *The Fall of Public Man*, metaphor and reality merge so thoroughly that there is no essential difference between public life on the streets of London and the exhibitions of the theatrical stage.

Henry Fielding, in his interludic essay from *Tom Jones* (1749), "A Comparison between the World and the Stage," remarks of midcentury life that the commonplace theatrum mundi trope "hath been carried so far, and become so general, that some words proper to the theatre, and which were, at first, metaphorically applied to the world, are now indiscriminately and literally spoken of both: thus stage and scene are by common use grown as familiar to us, when we speak of life in general, as when we confine ourselves to dramatic performances; and when we mention transactions behind the curtain, St. James's is more likely to occur to our thoughts than Drury-Lane" (299;

see also Sennett, 64). In Fielding's time, of course, the stage was a source of controversy; the onetime satirical playwright was driven from the theater by the Licensing Act of 1737, a law which regulated plays, put limits on theaters, and in essence proscribed material harmful to government interests. But restricting the stage does little to restrict the metaphor. Not only is stage metaphor applied to the court, but St. James's is viewed *in the terms of* Drury Lane. This notion suggests that the strategy ascribed to the court by Lord Chesterfield—that it makes use of licenses to convert the theater into an instrument of state policy—backfires when the court becomes the object of metaphoric reference and is made indistinguishable from the stage (Chesterfield, speech to the House of Lords, 1737, cited in Weinbrot, 203n).

But the fact remains that eighteenth-century English writing is filled with theatrical figures of speech, many of them directed, as Fielding says, at "life in general." Given the importance of the stage to London society, the controversies surrounding the Licensing Act, the frequent references to the Roman stage in political, historical, and neoclassical literary writing, the public-figure status of such theatrical personalities as Colley Cibber and David Garrick, the "theatricality" of scenes in contemporary oil painting, the extremes of taste in fashion that turn clothing openly into costume, the popularity among the elite of the masked ball, and the persistence of satire as a literary form (where theater makes a convenient reductive trope), not only do British writers have frequent occasion to use theater metaphors, but they also see those tropes renewed repeatedly in the mutual interaction between London stage and London life (on painting, see Fried). Theater may be a common metaphor, but it seems to me no less a lively one; even as a cliché, in the theatrically self-referring climate of eighteenth-century London, the socialized metaphor of the world as a stage speaks to British cultural assumptions as surely as the comparisons made between England and Rome.

From the theatricalized London of the 1700s, one might well expect exports to the American colonies. And indeed, by the late eighteenth century, theatrical rhetoric has entered fully into the secular life of the new nation. But the relationship between British culture and the American, though in many ways traceable, remains ambiguous at the level of metaphor. For one thing, theater is not nearly as common a trope in Boston as it is in London; for another, the meta-phor of social theater gets little help from stage-poor American cul-ture. What I wish to suggest here is that despite the intellectual and cultural dependence of the colonies on Britain, the conceptions of figural theater differ significantly between the two societies—and those differences ultimately reflect the political and ideological rifts that lead to revolution.

For Cotton Mather and American Puritans, as we have seen, one measures a life in the eyes of God first—the "sufficient theater" between the self and the Creator. Among English writers, however, especially in the turning away from the vociferations of seventeenth-century religious discourse, the only eyes that seem to matter are those of other human beings. God retreats from discourse and the world; people become absorbed in themselves as actors of shifting roles. Indeed, the emphasis on masking in ballroom culture as well as in political rhetoric (with its consequent negative, "throw off the mask" for *expose*) and in the plots of novels, suggests a world where one no longer feels obligated to live a role in the static mode (see Bailyn, *Origins*, 118n). Thus the old notions of theatrum mundi, as in the figurations of Vives and other Renaissance writers, no longer applies, or at least not with the same force. The world is a stage to be viewed by human audiences; God at his remove has little interest in the shape-shifting, in the literary masking of pseudonymous authors, or in the protean politics paradoxically played out in an age of labels.

In America, however, even among the most resolute secularists, one gets a sense that God cares. The diaristic litanies of a William Byrd, for instance, a man at ease with playgoing and acting, suggest that his own lewd and frequently masked behavior in the performative world of Virginia and London society matters to a watching, if always forgiving, God. In Congregational New England especially, but even in the Anglican South, the theological debates between Old and New Lights, Arminians and strict Calvinists, enthusiasts and rationalists tell of a strong native dissent from the rigidity of seventeenth-century religious discipline; nonetheless, the obsession with the particular plan for America in theological history persists fully into the politi-cized world of the pre-Revolutionary colonies. Millennialist rhetoric, spread into popular culture by the agency of such revivalists as Jonathan Edwards, George Whitefield, and Gilbert Tennent, becomes the vehicle for geohistorical speculation: people ask not only when the prophecies of Revelation will be enacted but also where. That many think America will be the place—the "scene" in contemporary diction—where theological history reaches its culmination runs counter to the more generalized notion among British evangelists that no *place* can be appointed by men with limited knowledge of God's workings. The world may be a stage in both Great Britain and America, but the stages and actors offer vastly different fare.

The word *theater* has many uses, and in the seventeenth and eighteenth centuries it makes a convenient book title. From *The Theatre of Gods Judgements* (1597) to *The Theater of Love* (1759), *theater* adorns religious, geographical, historical, political, literary, and scientific works in England; indeed, the whole process of book making, as we saw earlier with John Smith, becomes a self-consciously theatrical act. As David Marshall observes of the third earl of Shaftesbury's writing, the very nature of an author's published presentation as *performance* threatens to violate the integrity of meaningful discourse. For Shaftesbury himself, that means writing in diverting strategies, deflecting readers from their assumed roles as spectators and rendering ambiguous the author's place as performer (*Figure*, 36). The elaborate games of Shaftesbury offer an insight into the function of theatrical metaphor in British culture generally. As a book title, as a literary-philosophical strategy, as a commonplace of coffeehouse rhetoric, theater turns human experience into a series of aesthetic events. Cosmology and geography join political, social, and artistic criticism as kindred rhetorical situations, where the observer traps complexity and ambiguity within the known limits of theatrical response. *Theater* and *stage* function for the early eighteenth century as the qualifiers *sublime* and *picturesque* would at century's end: as conditional terms defining the limits of what one actually sees and feels.

Early in the century, when Joseph Addison and Richard Steele address their audience in the *Spectator*, number 10, as a "Fraternity of Spectators"—that is, that class "that considers the World as a Theatre"—they define for the reading public both the nature of their texts and the limits within which the readers may safely respond to the exhibitions mounted for their perusal (Addison, Steele, et al., 1:32;

Marshall, *Figure*, 9). Political argument, then, even the extraordinary writings for a semipopular press that characterize the age, becomes oddly detached from the very history it depicts. The classical masks— Publius, Brutus, Cato—worn by writers turn Roman or Greek or even modern European history into immediate scenes judged by the sort of unleashed voices that make up the eighteenth-century theatrical audience. The aestheticizing of British culture results in a concomitant dehistoricizing as well. Despite all the deliberate attempts to look at the growing British empire in Augustan (or anti-Augustan) terms and see another Golden Age at work in modern British culture, some English writers sense the deflation of a world view even as Britain expands its influence (on the competing claims of Augustanism in England, see Erskine-Hill and Weinbrot). As Horace Walpole in 1774 surveys the authorial wasteland in England, he remarks, "The next Augustan age will dawn on the other side of the Atlantic," complete with "a Thucydides at Boston, a Xenophon at New York"; but what he does not say is that "the rebellion of the Province of Massachusetts" to which he alludes later in his letter will be equipped with a different theatrical vision from that of his home country (Nov. 24, 1774, quoted in Erskine-Hill, 352). In the way that Neil Postman has criticized television in world-power America as a dangerously limiting epistemology, so one might say something similar about the theatrically minded imperial power of 1750 or 1775: the omnipresence of the figure of theater in a country where the theater is the center of fashionable activity leads to a restricting of the metaphor's political-historical significance. Removed from the purview of a providential God, Britons focus inward on themselves as actors on the small stage; each performing self asserts his or her role as an achievement of cultural history, not as a necessary element in a divinely conceived play. History might still be made, even in the transplantation of culture, but formed outside the Theater of God's Judgments to which Massachusetts is heir, it stands to lose much of its plot.

For ideological discourse, Americans borrow heavily from the tracts and treatises that inform British political debate. After the Stamp Act especially, Whig political principles foster the anti-Parliamentary tag lines of American protesters. In figurative terms, however, American adoption of Whig ideals is often attacked by Tories as the act of the rebellious child disavowing the loving parent. Such familial language serves to force recognition of similarities between the two countries, even when the borrowed rhetoric is turned against the lender. What Tories or those who would see America entirely through urban British eyes miss, though, is the translation of ideology into a distinctly American grammar. To see this change, we have to look beyond politics to some particular rhetorical exports in order to understand why the appeal to family is insufficient to deter revolt.

The big news of the London theater world in 1713 was the production of Addison's long-awaited play *Cato*. Begun in 1704, the play languished until Addison, at the urging of friends, completed the script during a time of Tory ascendancy. Through its message of noble patriotism and its rhetoric of liberty and *country* (not *monarch*), *Cato* seems to be created out of the whole cloth of Whig principles; yet the applause that greeted the play was bipartisan, with Whigs and Tories competing with each other in the audience to demonstrate who could approve it more. That such competition would occur at all tells us a great deal about the interfusion between politics and drama in Augustan England, for certainly drama becomes a chief vehicle for ideology and propaganda (Loftis, esp. 1-2, 44, 57-60). In such a world, one that has been fully theatricalized, political philosophy is offered to the public as performance and measured in essentially aesthetic terms. This phenomenon explains Shaftesbury's withdrawal of rhetoric from the conditions of theater, for as Marshall indicates, Shaftesbury thought that the stage could not support philosophical debates. Far from ennobling or elevating political discourse, the stage reduces it to the utterances of actors and the catcalls of the beau monde.

Perhaps because its career in England was so famous—it went through six editions that first year—*Cato* became a staple of American reading (and later acting) by midcentury (Colbourn, 24). Washington knew it and had his men act it before the 1778 ban on theatrical performances by the Continental Congress (Ford; Colbourn, 153; Litto, 447). Others quote liberally or refer to it as a symbol of liberty; indeed, in eighteenth-century southern libraries, it is the most popular single play (Davis, 96). Bernard Bailyn sees the coalescing of Addison's play and the topical essays by John Trenchard and Thomas Gordon, *Cato's Letters*, as a single "Catonic image" of liberty in

American political thought (*Origins*, 44). But as an English play, *Cato* neutralizes reformist sentiment. It uses a Senecan declamatory style to make its point; and even though *Cato* stops well short of bathos, the point remains that classicized diction converts the social pressures of political contention to aesthetic moments. Thus, the theater in England, even as a vehicle for propaganda, serves as an antirevolutionary institution, piquing those who last revolted, the theatrophobic Puritans, while providing an apolitical outlet for genuinely political feeling.

But the play in an American context is not the same one viewed at Drury Lane in 1713; at least one can say that in America its role is largely as a text to be read in a land without a formal theater. Addison himself suggests one approach, through his conception of the first Marcus Porcius Cato. In the *Spectator*, number 446 (Aug. 1, 1712), Addison recounts an episode in which the elder Cato, whose censoriousness matched his official position, "dropped into the *Roman* Theatre, when the *Floralia* were to be represented; and as in that Performance, which was a kind of Religious Ceremony, there were several indecent Parts to be acted, the People refus'd to see them whilst *Cato* was present" (Addison, Steele, et al., 3:376). On the basis of this episode, Martial wrote an epigram that captures the character of Cato and his relationship to the masses; in Addison's translation, the epigram not only supports Addison's demand for a more vigorous "*Stage Morality*" but also offers an insight into the American response to theater:

> Why does thou come, great Censor of thy Age,
> To see the loose Diversions of the Stage?
> With awful Countenance and Brow severe,
> What in the Name of Goodness does thou here?
> See the mixt Crowd! how Giddy, Lewd and Vain!
> Didst thou come in but to go out again?   (3:376)

Cato appeals to those who advocate the need for an uncompromising morality in political affairs; thus in New England, at least, someone who could turn the people's attention from the profane and trivial pursuits symbolized by Roman theater would earn the praise of a censorious community.

That Addison finally allowed *Cato* to be staged made it possible for the play to gain its celebrity status. As a decidedly antitheatrical character, the great grandson of the Censor appears on stage as much to serve as Addison's counterexample to "the Lewdness of our Theatre" as to play an opponent of Caesar (3:376). The younger Cato derives his high moral stance from the metaphorical relationship implicit in Stoicism between God and his human actors, as one finds described in the *Spectator*, number 219 (see Agnew, 170–71). To like-minded Americans, Addison's hero symbolizes the honor of republican Rome standing fast against the imperial dictator; thus, in the emphasis on virtue, the necessity to hold fast against the tyrant, and the injunctions against treachery for personal gain, the play would have an obvious appeal to Americans who feared imperial destruction of their liberties. At the same time, however, without a stage (until the 1730s) on which to mount the play, Americans absorb a Cato who requires a theater for his declamatory, humorless speeches. Therefore in England, where theater concentrates political turmoil and ultimately neutralizes its revolutionary impact, *Cato* may inspire political debate, but its ideological message can never fully escape its medium of presentation, that of a commercial stage production. In America, however, without a theatrical tradition to hold them, the issues raised by *Cato* are played out on a political stage that includes the streets and fields and waterfronts of the colonial landscape. The play sustains itself by becoming an inspiration to activists, who can, like Patrick Henry, declaim its noble sentiments in the public arena (Colbourn, 153). By rejecting the aesthetic imperative—at least until another time—eighteenth-century Americans fashion themselves as a society with strong antibourgeois tendencies. Theater leaps from metaphor to political act and thus retains its metaphoric quality (on the political importance of *Cato* during the Revolutionary period, see Colbourn, 24, 153; Litto; and Wills, 134–38).

The basis for this political claim to the vitality of metaphor can also be seen in another export, Bishop George Berkeley's famous prophetic poem, "On the Prospect of Planting Arts and Learning in America" (1726). Berkeley himself spent much time in the New World, imagining that he would establish an ideal society based on learning and a tolerant faith, but the details of his career in this context are less important than the act of removing himself from Britain to America.

Berkeley, like a handful of visionaries, romantics, and other disaffected Europeans, saw his age as one of decay, an idea that led to
seeing empire being celebrated not in the Old World but in the New.
The Muse, he says, seeks those "happy climes," new lands, "where
nature guides and virtue rules," free from "the pedantry of courts and
schools." But *translatio studii* is also *translatio imperii*, and with the
arts and empire comes history too. Berkeley's concluding stanza, a
favorite for American historians, reiterates what has been implied or
stated since the beginning of settlement, but at the same time it makes
manifest the rhetorical dynamics present in the translation motif:

> Westward the course of empire takes its way;
>   The four first acts already past,
> A fifth shall close the drama with the day:
>   Time's noblest offspring is the last.   (Fussell, 277)

Eighteenth-century British drama, often ironic and self-critical at the
same time that it legitimizes the bourgeois world of, in Berkeley's
phrase, "fancied beauties," depends for its success on having an
audience conscious of acting, conscious of itself acting, but uncon-
scious of locating itself within a larger context than the boundaries of
the beau monde. Berkeley, however, links American life—openly
idealized as a potential golden age—to the ancient notion of cosmic
drama, as if the show will no longer play in Paris or London. When
eighteenth-century English writers use theatrical metaphor, they are
often "bent on domesticating the somber legacy of its meaning"
(Agnew, 161); when American writers adopt the trope, they make
themselves inheritors of an older history. The drama of civilization
passing from Europe leaves behind imitators of imitations, people
aping each other and themselves in endless mirrors of fashion, in an
empty aesthetic of taste. Remounted in a new place with new scenery
and new actors, the theater of the world is restored to its former glory.
Taking up Berkeley's translatio theme, Thomas Prince in the *A Chronological History of New-England* (1736) credits Columbus with turning the attention of the audience to America: "The united Continents
of Asia, Africa and Europe, have been the only Stage of History from
the CREATION to the YC 1492. We are now to turn our Eyes to the
West, and see a NEW WORLD appearing in the Atlantick Ocean to

the great Surprize and Entertainment of the other" (78). Not only does New England take its place on the stage of history with the rest of civilization's great nations, but American history by implication will soon take the place of that in the Old World.

Though Berkeley's metaphor fits a progressive view of history (one, of course, that the American radicals would easily adopt), his age, like that of Emerson a century later, is retrospective and British political history is often perceived to be merely a reenactment of Rome. Present decay, say Trenchard and Gordon in *Cato's Letters*, number 18, parallels the "publick Corruption" of the tottering Roman Empire, but its downfall ought to make everyone especially wary: "Thus ended the greatest, the noblest State that ever adorned the worldly Theatre, that ever the Sun saw: It fell a Victim to Ambition and Faction, to base and unworthy Men, to Parricide and Traytors; and every Nation must run the same Fortune, expect the same fatal Catastrophe, who suffer themselves to be debauched with the same Vices, and are activated by the same Principles and Passions" (1:121). Though the sentiments in *Cato's Letters* feed directly into the mainstream of American Whig ideology, the authors' admonitions reflect a self-limiting world view that grants every nation its wink in the theatrum mundi though beneath the shadow of Rome. In America, writers engraft this Romanized political theory onto Berkeley's progressive metaphor; enlivened by Addison's play, this hybrid perspective points to a new vision, one that resurrects the "worldly Theatre" but suggests that the fifth act will somehow be triumphantly different from those that have gone before.

The religious revivals of the 1730s attracted another British export, George Whitefield. Already well-known in his home country as a field preacher, Whitefield arrived in America at a time when many ministers lamented the sorry state of piety in the land. Others, however, were encouraged by the weakening of Calvinist orthodoxy and its virulent anti-Arminianism. Since the divisions in American Protestantism were either already present or latent, Whitefield can have done no more than exacerbate them or make them obvious; but he forced Americans to reconsider their modes of perception of religious experience and to accept or reject the power of enthusiasm. Ultimately, by accepting enthusiasm, many Americans turned away from the aestheticizing tendencies of the age toward a theater grounded in the primitive needs of ritual and the religious impulse behind specta- cle. Whitefield himself inspired not only mass conversions of souls but also a new rhetoric of feeling that, once tapped, surged up again and again until the country was convulsed by revolt.

"Whitefield was a born actor," say his biographers, a man who by his own description read plays in his youth, acted in them, and even used one in courting (Henry, 18; Whitefield, 29, 32, 36). Not surpris- ingly, at his conversion in 1735, he renounced the theater, placing extracts from an antitheatrical treatise in the local newspaper in order to discourage a traveling troupe of players and attempting to convert the woman to whom he "'had formerly read Plays'" (Henry, 24–25; Whitefield, 54). But by many accounts, Whitefield only enlarged the theater of his actions; for much of his career, he would be followed by remarks that likened his preaching style to that of an actor. He had, as James Downey says, a "remarkable voice" as well as "a protean face, a penchant for histrionics, and an almost perfect sense of timing in both word and gesture" (168). By relying on ex tempore preaching, he could proclaim to be speaking from the heart where the "Word of God" is alive and to be reaching his listeners in the same place (Whitefield, 268). So accomplished were Whitefield's performances that legend has it he was the envy of the greatest actor of his age. His assistant late in his career, Cornelius Winter, records that "Garrick once said, 'I would give a hundred guineas if I could only say "O!" like Mr. Whitefield'" (quoted in Henry, 168; see also Downey, 168). Such oratorical skill would lead both to his extraordinary success as a revivalist and to the charge against him of fraud. His enthusiastic reception in the New World suggests a hunger among the populace for someone like him, some engaging, histrionic, and inspiring figure who would offer an electric alternative to a mechanical faith. Yet perhaps the onetime actor on the microcosmic stage needed the colonies as much as they needed him: "All Things concur to convince me," he wrote after his 1740 campaign in New England, "that Amer- ica is to be my chief Scene for Action" (quoted in Henry, 68).

In her biography of Jonathan Edwards, Ola Winslow speculates that Whitefield drew large crowds because he brought America its first piece of theater (18). Stuart Henry, Whitefield's modern biographer, takes issue with Winslow, saying that her theory "leaves unexplained the man's popularity in the old world" (177). Perhaps, though, the one also explains the other. We have already noted the pervasiveness of theatricality in England; a Whitefield could be admired for those skills by which men and women measure each other in general. In America, there may well have been an unexpressed longing for theater; but the enthusiasm generated by Whitefield's preaching supersedes even the wild expressions of approval or disapproval that greeted British actors in midcentury English playhouses. Whitefield filled a need, but for a different kind of theater: the macrocosmic stage of Providence.

We get some indication of the tension between rival theaters from a letter by Sarah Pierrepont Edwards, the wife of Jonathan, describing for her brother the preaching of Whitefield:

> He is a born orator. You have already heard of his deep-toned, yet clear and melodious, voice. It is perfect music. It is wonderful to see what a spell he casts over an audience by proclaiming the simplest truths of the Bible. I have seen upwards of a thousand people hang on his words with breathless silence, broken only by an occasional half-suppressed sob. He impresses the ignorant, and not less the educated and refined. It is reported that while the miners of England listened to him, the tears made white furrows down their smutty cheeks. So here, our mechanics shut up their shops, and the day-labourers throw down their tools, to go and hear him preach, and few return unaffected. A prejudiced person, I know, might say that this is all theatrical artifice and display; but not so will any one think who has seen and known him. . . . He speaks from a heart all aglow with love, and pours out a torrent of eloquence which is almost irresistible.   (Lovejoy, *Great Awakening*, 33–34)

This carefully written letter extends in many directions. Sarah Edwards describes Whitefield in terms of performance—orator, melodious voice, perfect music, theatrical artifice and display (though she rejects the latter, the point is still made)—to which list we might add the casting of a spell. To a sophisticated and sympathetic observer, Whitefield presents a pleasing combination of oratorical skill and simple truth telling that engages both the aesthetic imagination and the needs of faith. The letter writer notes particularly Whitefield's ability to unite people of many stations with his "torrent of eloquence." But Edwards's letter also makes clear that the evangelist's greatest appeal is to working-class people, mechanics, day laborers, the ignorant, whose unaffected response comes less from aesthetic satisfaction than some more elemental desire to make public—or share in public—those emotions tapped by the language of salvation. For them, medium and message are one; to indulge in the kind of performance criticism present in the letter of Sarah Edwards means to disengage rhetoric and gesture from word and thus delimit the power of the speaker to that of an affecting performer.

Latent in Sarah Edwards's praise is the source of detraction: that public displays of emotion which pretend to be sincere only confound the social order. If the stage is taken for the world, then the rules which apply to the viewing of performances are overthrown, and the power granted to the stage by virtue of its being contained in time and space rushes out to where it cannot be controlled. Naturally, then, the conservators of political and religious order would be most threatened by Whitefield when enthusiasm breaks class barriers or creates in the people new expectations of ruling elites. When Whitefield reached Charleston, South Carolina, during his 1740 tour, he encountered an opponent of substance, the commissary of the Episcopal church. Alexander Garden, described by Alan Heimert as "the leading Anglican minister of the southernmost colonies" (Heimert and Miller, xxv), forcefully rejected Whitefield's style for precisely the reasons enumerated in approval by Sarah Edwards. While Whitefield stayed in Charleston, Garden preached against him, publishing his sermons with a prefatory letter the following year. Addressing his readers, Garden maintains that he is printing the sermons "to guard you against the Puzzle and Perplexity of some crude *Enthusiastick* Notions, which so much prevailed about the *same Period* of the last *Century,* and are now revived and propagated by Mr. *Whitefield* and his Brethren *Methodists*" (47). That Garden should warn against repeating what he obviously believes were the mistakes of the radical dissenters—he may even have in mind the Fifth Monarchists—turns his disquisition on religion and the philosophy of taste into a political message as well, a fact that may be more important for the anti–enthusiasts than the religious issues of the Great Awakening.

Garden focuses directly on the medium of Whitefield's message. His own sermon, he says, "were preached midst the *Sound* of that

Gentleman's Voice in your Ears;—that *Enchanting* Sound! The *natural* and *alone* Cause, which produced all the *Passion* and *Prejudice*, that prevailed 'mong *Some* (the weaker *some* indeed) of you, in his Favour, against them and every thing else that opposed him; and which would equally have produced the *same* Effects, whether he had *acted* his Part in the *Pulpit* or on the *Stage*." The problem with Whitefield has little to do with substance. For Garden, too, the medium is the message, and it is the medium that is at fault, "not the *Matter* but the Manner, not the *Doctrines* he delivered, but the *Agreeableness* of the Delivery" (47). By this light, theatricality has no place in church; the effectiveness of affective preaching (Whitefield was a great weeper) undermines the stability of religious institutions, blurring their identity and threatening the political order that ensures their continuance.

When attacked frontally by clerical opponents, Whitefield could always turn to the people for justification. Other attacks, however, were problematic. Like John Smith and Cotton Mather before, Whitefield, too, felt the lash of stage mockery at the same time as he exploited its techniques. In sermons and letters, Whitefield regales against theaters as "nurseries of debauchery" and takes the usual Calvinist line against all frivolous entertainments (Henry, 128–29). He uses antithesis to make the point that the theater opposes right and righteous activity: "Which will stand you best at the day of judgment, so much money expended at a horse-race, at a cockpit, at a play or masquerade, or so much given for the relief of your fellow-creatures?" (quoted in Henry, 128). Better to have a situation where "while [sinners] are at a playhouse, you are hearing a sermon" (quoted in Downey, 175). Thus when Samuel Foote's play *The Minor* appeared on the London stage in July 1760, Whitefield was suitably upset by the parody of his preaching in the figure of Mr. Squintum: "Satan is angry," writes Whitefield; "I am now mimicked and burlesqued upon the public stage" (quoted in Henry, 159; see also Downey, 184). The preacher's complaint echoes an old theme: theater may be exploited by rhetoric or gesture for godly ends, but the stage itself is the Devil's platform, where tragedies are turned into comedies, and where plays from the Devil's library take living shape. To absorb into oneself the ideals of an enterprise, as Smith, Mather, and Whitefield all do, and to play before God and man on the providentially appointed American stage leads almost inevitably to comic deflation on the British boards. Real theater threatens always to undermine metaphor even while invigorating it. The theatrical Whitefield, inspiring as he did even such worldly listeners as Benjamin Franklin, carried to America both the possibility of great theater and its antithesis. It seems to have been historically necessary for an itinerant evangelist to come first and, by appealing to the authenticity of his auditors' emotions, prepare the way for itinerant players—Lewis Hallam, David Douglass, and their companies—to give midcentury Americans their first taste of professional theater.

Scholars have yet to determine the significance of the Great Awakening revivals. Alan Heimert's contention that they lead directly to the Revolution through the agency of New Light ministers has been widely criticized; yet recent students of the period, such as Harry Stout and Donald Weber, have identified a number of rhetorical connections between the sermonic motifs of the 1740s and those of the politically charged 1770s. One can hardly ignore the social dimensions of the revivals; the disruptions to the orderly flow of life brought about by fiery evangelists find their parallels thirty years later in more overtly political language. Beyond the debate over the social importance of religion or politics, however, the Great Awakening serves to highlight certain elements of a national imagination that have appeared all along and would continue into the Revolutionary era.

One of the frequent complaints among ministers in the 1730s and even later is the pervasiveness of spiritual deadness among the Protestant faithful. As the prorevivalist William Shurtleff looks back to the time before Whitefield appears, he laments to recall "that solid and substantial Piety for which our Ancestors were so justly renowned, having long languish'd under some Decays, brought so very low, and seemingly just ready to expire and give up the Ghost" (357). Yet even that desperate condition, looked at through the new language of enthusiasm, strikes Shurtleff as an "affecting Spectacle," a sight "no serious Christian could behold in the Time of it, without a heavy Heart, and scarce without a weeping Eye" (357). Ironically, what the English Whitefield brought with him was a weapon for battling the incursions of urban British culture on American society. Shurtleff describes what happened in churches during this period of creeping fashionability as another kind of exhibition. On pleasant Sundays, he says, "there would be a Number of Persons of both Sexes, especially in some Congregations, richly and curiously dress'd, and making as fine and glittering a Shew as if this was the Thing they chiefly aim'd at; which, with some might possibly be what they had principally in View" (357). Were American churchgoers to follow fashion and turn to each other in admiration of "Shew," they would lose more than their individual spiritual estates—they would allow the sacred mission of the fathers to "give up the Ghost."

As Jonathan Edwards had already discovered in Northampton, the spiritually dead require a considerable shock to come alive; and had someone continued Mather's *Magnalia* into the eighteenth century, that author would no doubt find many worthy successors to the thaumaturges who people Mather's history. A number of American preachers adopted Whitefield's histrionic style or at least used his success to justify their own emotive oratory. Most notable among those is Gilbert Tennent, the dynamic Pennsylvania Presbyterian who followed Whitefield into New England in 1741. Yet even a lesser light, like Jonathan Parsons, could have extraordinary success on a local level. Following Tennent's swing through Connecticut, Parsons preached an election sermon at Lyme in 1741. He has already observed that this once solemn occasion has been given over to "Feasting, Musick, Dancing, Gaming, and the like" in short, those ludic vices which religiously minded colonists have been trying to repulse from their shores since the first days of settlement. With the people suddenly made tractable by Tennent's preaching, Parsons speaks to an audience otherwise secure in its carnality, a situation that lets the preacher create a show worthy of Wigglesworth's dramatized Day of Doom:

> Under this Sermon many had their *Countenances changed*; their *tho'ts* seemed to *trouble* them *so that the Joynts of* their *Loyns were loosed, and* their *Knees smote one against another*. Great Numbers cried out aloud in the Anguish of their Souls: several stout Men fell as tho' a Cannon had been discharg'd, and a Ball had made its Way thro' their Hearts. Some young Women were thrown into Hysterick Fits. The Sight and Noise of Lamentation, seem'd a little Resemblance of what we may imagine will be when the great Judge pronounces the tremendous Sentence of, *Go ye*

cursed into everlasting Fire. There were so many in Distress that I could not get a particular Knowledge of the special Reasons at that Time, only as I hcard them crying, *Wo is me! What must I do?* And such sort of short Sentences with bitter Accents.   (200)

But if the effect of evangelical preaching is the sort of exaggerated quaking that would later find its way into American acting, the language of the sermons also shapes those responses into a predetermined rhetoric of last things. Tennent, in the first flush of the Awakening, shatters the contemplative—and thus aesthetic—moment by portraying sin or the bleeding Christ in the immediate terms of deepest feeling. In *The Unsearchable Riches of Christ* (1739) he uses the apostrophic style to snap listeners from their absorption in "terrene Pleasures" (16) and to confront images at which they have no chance to pause or turn away: "O unhappy Sinners! It would not be hard to persuade you, I suppose, to accept of worldly Riches, and why then will ye not be induc'd to accept of Riches worth Millions of Worlds? . . . O cruel Murder! O vile Ingratitude! O detestable Madness! Be astonished and horribly afraid ye Heavens and Earth at this! Ah ye blessed Angels; ye cannot but wonder to see this terrible Tragedy acted! O ye Saints of GOD! look how the adorable dying SAVIOUR, and Rich Purchase of his Blood, is slighted, by indigent, ungrateful, and degenerous Rebels!" (18). This is Greek tragedy, calling forth a cathartic response, like the knocking knees recorded by Parsons, to a scene beyond the retarding ability of intellect to grasp.

Ironically, Tennent turns the tables on the antienthusiasts by making them the actor-hypocrites, not those who stir the passions. In his most notorious address, *The Danger of an Unconverted Ministry* (2nd edition, 1741), Tennent attacks ministers who preach without showing to their parishioners evidence of their own conversions—in other words, without visible or audible enthusiasm. He implies that those who demonstrate conversion "are sincere Servants of God" while those who cannot convey such an experience are "Servants of Satan, under a religious Mask" (93). Those who rely on rhetorical eloquence to carry the burden of faith without the warmth generated by the catharsis of conversion cannot expect their measured oratory to defeat the efforts of *living* ministers: "Let *Tertullus* ascend the The-

atre, and gild the Objection with most mellifluous Ciceronian Eloquence; it will [not] perswade them, that what they have felt is but a
Fancy" (96). Tennent thus consigns ministers who resist enthusiasm
to the realm of "Pharisee-Teachers," hypocrites who refuse to be
examined fully for true faith but instead cover up their deceit in the
cadences of order and reason, mimicking the piety they preach: "And
with what Art, Rhetorick, and Appearances of Piety, will they varnish
their Opposition of Christ's Kingdom? As the Magicians imitated the
Works of *Moses*, so do false Apostles, and deceitful workers, the
Apostles of Christ" (98–99).

Though Tennent did much to polarize Protestants on the matter of
expressive conversions, he later adopted a somewhat more restrained
style. Still, he never leaves off his concern over false appearances. The
Moravians, for instance, Tennent calls those "schismatical, enthusi-
astical and deceitful *Babelbuilders*," a people whose *"sorry Shews* of
Zeal, Piety and Meekness" are practiced under "the mask of Humility" (*Necessity*, 496). In Tennent's eyes, the true Christian leaves off
one theater and takes up another. Both Moravians and antirevivalist
preachers dissemble their piety, though in different ways; their concern over appearances limits them to acting in earthbound "shews"
and prevents them from considering the larger spectacle that awaits
them. Like most evangelists, Tennent keeps his eyes on last things;
after all, in Christian cosmology, it is the conclusion that writes the
middle. Rather than be misled by pious appearances, we must be
mindful of that *"glorious State"* where all conflicts are resolved. God
obscures his design and sometimes "we cannot sound the Depths of
his providential Actings by the Line of our shallow Reason: but the
End will crown the Scene, beautify the whole Piece, and magnify the
Glory of it's Author" (*Necessity*, 503). If our reason cannot penetrate
God's design, perhaps it fails because God bypasses reason altogether.
God's chiliastic theater overwhelms its audience by its power and
spectacle; and while the imminence of the final scene becomes a
staple of millennialist rhetoric in general, Tennent has insisted that
the drama in which Americans play is the one spoken of by writers like
Tertullian and John Foxe and that the stage on which they act is in the
theater of sincerity.

Tennent's contemporary, Jonathan Edwards, asserts that part of the millennial design would be known and for a time contends that one can designate the place as well as time of the new Christian golden age. In contrast to Tennent, Edwards suggests that reason can provide some understanding of God's plan. The Awakening, then, is simply visible proof of the acting out of this design in providential history:

> God doubtless is pursuing some design, and carrying on some scheme, in the various changes and revolutions which from age to age come to pass in the world. It is most reasonable to suppose, that there is some certain great design to which Providence subordinates all the great successive changes in the affairs of the world which God has made. It is reasonable to suppose that all revolutions, from the beginning of the world to the end of it, are but the various parts of the same scheme, all conspiring to bring to pass that great event which the great Creator and Governor of the world has ultimately in view; and that the scheme will not be finished nor the design fully accomplished, and the great and ultimate event fully brought to pass till the end of the world and the last revolution is brought about. (*Redemption*, 32)

But the success and pitch of the revivals may have caused Edwards to move a step from his usual universality toward considering the American situation in particular. Indeed, Edwards's use of the word "revolution" above, though possibly alluding to the turning of Ezekiel's visionary wheel as much as to any major social or political change, has from our position of hindsight a prophetic power that links future overturnings with this same divine plan. In *Some Thoughts concerning the Present Revival of Religion in New England* (1742), Edwards cites Isaiah 60:9 to justify "a prophecy of the prosperity of the church, in its most glorious state on earth, in the latter days; and I cannot think that anything else can here be intended but America" (*Great Awakening*, 353). His logic is that of balance and paradox: Christ died in the Old World so he will come again in the New, and because God favors the lowly, "It is probable he will begin [to renew the earth] in this utmost, meanest, youngest and weakest part of it, where the church of God has been planted last of all" (354, 356).

Certainly Edwards was not alone in this concept of the "redeemer nation"; but his words carried great weight because he was not purely of the radical enthusiast crowd (see *Great Awakening*, 71–72). For staunch antirevivalist Charles Chauncy, this assertion of America as the particular place for the millennium was too much. In his rejoinder to *Some Thoughts*, Chauncy decries the specificity of Edwards's millennialism as sheer conjecture and asks rhetorically the point of such a speculation in the first place: "And can any good End be answered in endeavouring, upon Evidence absolutely precarious, to instill into the Minds of People a Notion of the *millenium* State, as what is NOW going to be introduced; yea, and of AMERICA, as that Part of the World, which is pointed out in the *Revelations* of GOD for the Place, where this glorious Scene of Things, 'will, probably, first begin'?" (*Seasonable Thoughts*, 302–3). The answer, of course, is no—and one only has to think of the tragedy of Münster, to which Chauncy alludes, to see the reason why. "It can answer no good End to lead People into the Belief of any *particular* Time" for the millennium, says Chauncy, because we as ministers only stir up desires for things that we cannot deliver or satisfy: "When they [congregants] have imbib'd from us the Thought, as if the *glorious Things*, spoken of in Scripture, were to come forward in their Day, they will be apt (as has often been the Case) to be impatient, and from their *Officiousness* in tendring their Help where it is not needed, to disserve the Interest of the Redeemer" (304). By focusing the millennium not only in time but also in space, Edwards threatens the role of a clerical hierarchy in maintaining social order; viewing America as the "scene" can only expose the impotence of the clergy and its inability to provide a spectacle grand enough to match the aroused passions of the people.

Chauncy's criticism of Edwards's prophecy (from which Edwards would later retreat when it became a point of contention for Scottish Calvinists) raises several issues, not the least of which is the revivalist's apparent inability to understand the movement which he in large measure instigated. His early proclamation of success for the revivals in Northampton can perhaps be traced to his own self-conception. In the "Personal Narrative," Edwards recounts his childhood passion for playing church in a "booth" built in a "swamp" and the ultimate conversion of that passion into his sense of the "sweetness" of God's overwhelming majesty (D. Levin, 24, 27). Indeed, in a passage that reminds one uncomfortably of Cotton Mather's private writings, he describes his desire to be more humble than anyone, abusing himself before God's "all" as if he were "nothing" (30–31). And while Edwards was no democrat, he must have seen that in others were passions like his (though he had them in stronger measure)—and that perhaps the new converts had simply turned their own play of conversion into a similar thirst for the awful sweetness of God.

Yet it seems that in some contemporary accounts the desires of ordinary people were for something immediate, palpable, sensory— and that the conversion of old habits to new was a more radical process than for the spiritually predisposed Edwards. We can see the differences between the intellectual apologist and the secularized young folk of Norwich, Connecticut, in the account of Isaac Backus. The 1741 revival "was so remarkable that the Children & yong People were broke off from Their Plays & frolicks (which they were much ingaged in before) So that if one Went from one end of the Town Street to the Other they would scarcely see a Child at Play:—& the yong People left off their Frolicks for Several years" (Lovejoy, *Great Awakening*, 43). For most young people, plays and frolics mark a kind of ritual diversion to which they wholly commit themselves, knowing all the while that play is separate from the serious work of the world (Huizinga, 18). Their leaving those amusements for the "work" of the Awakening can suggest two possibilities: either they recognize the fantastic nature of their activities, knowing that the world calls them to more serious affairs, or they convert one form of play into another—that is, excessive, obsessive sobriety becomes itself an elaborate performance. Only in this case, the new religious fervor differs from the frolics of before in that a return to true play is, in fact, the interruption of reality that performance demands. In any event, the ludic impulse must assert itself in some fashion, and if the people are not satisfied by the undelivered promises of revival, then they will find something else: rituals that grow (in part) out of thwarted idealism and that take shape as affronts to sobriety and order.

But it can also be seen that even before the emergence of the political protest rituals of the 1760s and 1770s—effigy-burnings, tea-dumping masquerades, and the like—the forces of disorder were already set in motion by antibourgeois unions. Some clerics, like Thomas Prince in Boston, approved of the new alliances generated among people by the Awakening. The revivals mark a political reordering of society along the lines promised by the coming of God's kingdom: "The day of the Power of Christ comes at once upon us, and they are almost altogether, both Whites and Blacks, both Old and Young, both Prophane and Moral, awakened, and made alive to God" (Lovejoy, *Great Awakening*, 39). Yet as often as it is extolled, this democracy of the faithful is portrayed by others as destroying the justifiable order already in place. Chauncy, for instance, finds appalling the emergence of women as prominent figures in the revivals and demands that "FEMALE EXHORTERS," including "GIRLS," "*keep silence in the churches*" (*Enthusiasm*, 241; see Lang, "'A Flood,'" and *Prophetic Woman*, 102–4). Another antirevivalist, Isaac Stiles, decries the practice of inverting ministerial reputations (perhaps referring to denunciations like those of Gilbert Tennent against an "unconverted ministry") and people's listening to itinerants who, "for ought they knew may be *Missionaries from the Pontificate of Rome (For these that have turned the World upside down, are come hither also*, whom some have receiv'd—)" (309).

More revealing than either of these two complaints, a letter from the Anglican Charles Brockwell to the secretary of the Society for the Propagation of the Gospel describes with sneering distaste the sort of enthusiasm he has witnessed. Brockwell gives us the view of the urbanized Englishman, someone who measures human actions by aesthetic standards. Through his eyes, the revivals appear ludicrous, that is, both ludic and ridiculous, because they arouse the mass populace to perform in ways that are not only unbecoming to station but also essentially amateurish. In the first place, the revivals provoke a base theatricality among a markedly antibourgeois cross section of society: "It is impossible to relate the convulsions into which the whole Country is thrown by a set of Enthusiasts that strole about harangueing the admiring Vulgar in extempore nonsense, nor is it confined to these only, for Men, Women, Children, Servants, & Nigros are now become (as they phrase it) Exhorters" (Lovejoy, *Great Awakening*, 65). Dripping from this diction is a panful of preconceptions that underlie the differences between America and Britain, at least as they were perceived by those who would contend for power some thirty years later. The people are the "Vulgar," a crowd of common boors who in their (aesthetic) ignorance admire extemporaneous "nonsense" as if it passes for (artistic) truth. For Brockwell—and for the Anglophile critics and reviewers of American culture who continue his tradition into the nineteenth century—no arts have been transplanted at all; the revivals tap into fonts of enthusiasm, a state that Chauncy calls "properly a disease" and that Brockwell says leads to "convulsions" (Chauncy, *Enthusiasm*, 231). Such a view, while attentive to the potential for social disruption those convulsions can cause, also ignores, by its very premises, the significance of mass, playlike rituals in the psycho-cultural life of the people. In other words, Brockwell's aestheticized view of culture fails to take into account that the theater and drama are themselves only imitations of more fundamental, ludic forces which cannot be judged by taste alone.

Brockwell continues in this vein by evaluating in more detail the peculiarities of performance among the faithful: "Their behaviour is indeed as shocking, as uncomon, their groans, cries, screams, & agonies must affect the Spectators were they never so obdurate & draw tears even from the most resolute whilst the ridiculous & frantic gestures of others cannot but excite both laughter and contempt, some leaping, some laughing, some singing, some clapping one another upon the back, &c." (Lovejoy, *Great Awakening*, 65–66). Within the span of a sentence, Brockwell converts his amazement ("shocking," "uncomon") at the spectacle before him to distanced mockery, re-establishing the class and aesthetic distinctions which enthusiasm threatens to break down or reverse. He does this by insisting that his perceptions be guided by the implicit dramatic criticism that passes for eighteenth-century evaluations of behavior. Nevertheless, that form of evaluation reveals as well as obscures. What finally strikes Brockwell as remarkable—though it is to be thoroughly condemned—is the playing out before him of "every dream" suddenly turned, in the minds of the vulgar, into a "Divine Vision." Properly, this acting out of the stuff of the imagination *is* theater, a fact which Brockwell perceives: "The tragic scene is performed by such as are entering into the pangs of the New Birth; the comic by those who are got thro' and those are so truly enthusiastic, that they tell you they saw the Joys of Heaven, can describe its situation, inhabitants, employments, & have seen their names entered into the Book of Life & can point out the writer, character & pen" (66). These Americans, Brockwell in essence maintains, have no more skill at acting or insight into the nature of

performance itself than Shakespeare's rude mechanicals; his metaphors only highlight class divisions between those willing to suborn
taste to cause and those for whom taste is the arbiter of behavior.

Inevitably, these plays of conversion, with their tragic and comic
scenes, cease to occupy the public stage; yet the forms somehow
remain. The Arminian and future Tory, Thomas Darling, for instance, denounces the infection of politics by New Light principles, a
process that leads to a new union of orthodox Calvinists in the years
following the Awakening. In a reply to onetime antirevivalist Thomas
Clap, who in 1755 was calling for a renewed orthodoxy, Darling
rightly predicts that a new play under old principles will threaten the
presumed stability of a reasonable society: "The Truth I fear is, that all
the Pranks that have been play'd in the Government, and through the
Country, by the scheming and political *New-lights* . . . are now a
going to be acted over again (and possibly with this Difference only,
that there are some new Actors) under the more sacred Name Orthodoxy, which probably will produce ten Times the Disorder, the Confusion, that the First has done" (589). Perhaps trying to avoid the
divisive language of a Darling, Ezra Stiles returns Congregational
rhetoric to the tradition of the grand drama. The real differences
between Calvinists and Arminians are slight, he says in 1761; so slight
that both ought to be working for a united church. Rather than act in
the low theater of the street, let us sustain our mission on the macrocosmic stage: "God has betrusted us with a part to act for posterity
and the public; let us not supinely desert it, but act it well, consecrate
and transmit the purity of religion to generations yet unborn" (*Discourse*, 605). But both theaters—an increasingly ritualized theater of
the masses in the streets and the exalted theater of God's Providence—
would have to come together in order to bring the colonies to the
convulsions necessary for revolution.

CHAPTER NINE

Theater of Blood:
The Rituals of Republican Revolution

𝒯or the ancient Greeks, theater appears to have served as a means of social and political control, offering an outlet for passions and providing rules of observation that contain any potential challenge to authority within the theater itself. For the Americans of the eighteenth century, the reverse occurs; that is, the failure of the prewar theater to gain widespread acceptance is tied to the theatricalized but uncontained protests that stir passions and lead to outright rebellion. Though the demand for theater in the colonies increases to the point that, by midcentury, people are willing to risk censure, scorn, or legal harassment to mount plays, the number of theaters and certainly the number of people supporting theater remain relatively small. Nevertheless, the widespread dissatisfaction with particular elements of British policy—the costs which the colonies had to bear for the French and Indian War, the Stamp Act, the Townshend duties, the Boston Massacre—leads to a need to dramatize the challenges to authority that arise from protest of restrictive measures. With the available theater being of limited political use, at least until the 1770s, street protests and demonstrations take on a formalized character something like that of the stage play, but with far different implications. Because the rituals and theatricalized challenges take place in public streets and squares, spaces where people expect theatrical behavior only as part of a politically neutral social aesthetic, protest takes on symbolic meaning by converting the world into stage and the actors into world-players.

Given the inability of the British authorities to contain anti-Parliamentary actions—in essence, a failure to prevent theater metaphor from becoming the reality of the theatrum mundi—these street challenges lead ultimately to a theater larger than that of the playhouse, to a self-proclaimed play of revolution with serious, real-world consequences.

With the cooling of evangelical ardor in the years following the Great Awakening and the shift in public concern to war against the Catholic French, ministers who resort to theatrical language often do so to underscore a fundamental stasis in American political and religious culture (see Hatch, 42, 51). Talk of an American millennium drops away and, with it, the overt expression of a dynamic nationalist history (Hatch, 33; Stout, 306). Even before the Great Awakening, liberal preaching reduces the immediacy of the eschatological moment and replaces it with a generalized, ahistorical vision more like that held by British evangelicals. Benjamin Colman, whose softened Calvinism anticipates the general tenor of the pre-Revolutionary period, conceives of the coming of the bridegroom Christ in terms which at first glance appear baroque but which in fact strip the event of any radical purpose: "He will come *enthroned*. Suppose on a radiant Cloud, fashion'd and blazon'd with all the Skill of Heaven into a *great white Throne*: as if a thousand Suns were made into one vast Globe, and on it *One* out-shining what he treads on, as *Solomon's Chariot* of State did the Dust it pass'd over. . . . So on a burning refulgent Cloud shall the King of Glory come: the most pompous Show the World can ever see or Heaven afford" (*Practical Discourses*, 11; see Heimert, 145). Unlike Continental baroque, these seated theatrics reflect finally a static image of religion, whereby the end is no more than a wonderful picture, a "pompous" tableau whose value is more display than movement in history (Toulouse, 66–67). This picture of an ideologically neutral stage show persists past the revivals. Taking up the more secularized rhetoric of his age, Mather Byles, in *The Flourish of the Annual Spring* (1741), uses the analogy to drama and opera to describe the Song of Songs (7). Jonathan Edwards's protégé Joseph Bellamy, in *True Religion Delineated* (1750), remarks that "the whole World was created for a *Stage*, on which a variety of Scenes were to be opened; in and by all which, God designed to exhibit a most exact

Image of himself" (20). Though Bellamy's image of the theatrum mundi is little more than that of a pleasant playhouse where God "acts out his Heart" and the "Saints here below, while they behold as in a Glas the Glory of the Lord, are ravished," the continuance of a theatrical image for cosmic intent makes it possible for other, more radical visions to be asserted (20, 8; see Heimert, 343). By the time of the Revolution, the boundaries of the figural stage fall away, and those "variety of Scenes" appear as counterplays or as antidramas to the pompous show of authority.

Some glimpse of the subsequent political challenge to the status quo can be seen in the uncharacteristic occasional sermons by Jonathan Mayhew. As Harry Stout notes, there are many attendant ironies when an Arminian like Mayhew takes to task the "tyranny" of vested authority or an otherwise mild-tongued latitudinarian adopts the strident rhetoric he displays in 1749 and again in 1754 (240). In his 1754 election sermon, Mayhew recovers himself from the vagaries of eschatology to focus more specifically on "the great *drama* of [this] world" (A *Sermon*, 294). Expressed in historical terms, Mayhew's hyperbolic rhetoric looks forward to a Protestant triumph in the New World: "And how different a scene is now opening upon me with clearer indications of truth and reality! There, insolence and injustice punished! Here, 'the meek inheriting the earth' [Matt. 5.5; Ps. 37.11]! Liberty victorious! Slavery biting her own chain! Pride brought down! Virtue exalted! Christianity triumphing over imposture! And another Great Britain arising in America!" (311–12). Whether the millennium arrives now or later, in America or elsewhere or everywhere at once, millennialist rhetoric when combined with an overtly political theme produces a more dynamic dramaturgy of history than does talk of a second coming alone. But there is a problem with the kind of exclamatory stage manager's role that Mayhew has adopted in his sermon. Excitement often begets further excitement, or in this case, overheated language in one may heat up the words of another, creating a cloying sermonic style when the marvels run out. The Virginia preacher Samuel Davies adopts this style in a sermon delivered in 1756, after news of General Braddock's defeat became known: "See the wounded writhing with Pain, surrounded with all the Terrors of Death, and groaning out their Life, in Amazement and Consternation; . . . Who can realize such a Scene, without sharing in the Sufferings of these unhappy Men" (8). After the French and Indian War is over, however, a Mather Byles can turn the same formula into a paean to victory: "What a Scene of Wonders appears to our View! Good God! what an astonishing Scene of Wonders! Methinks, a universal Transport animates every Countenance, and sparkles in every Eye" (A *Sermon*, 13; Hatch, 43). Such language of triumph, if not matched *in fact* by (or, really, by *people's perceptions* of) so-ciopolitical realities, can serve to drive a people toward some equally hyperbolic, though more socially threatening, rhetoric. This, it seems to me, is what happens after 1760 when the thrill of Protestant victory and the prospect of translatio imperii, a new Britain in America, turn to anger at the threatened loss of liberties and a revised view that another, newer triumph would be required for the course of empire to be safely removed to the American strand.

Ever since Alan Heimert's *Religion and the American Mind* ap-peared in 1966, scholars have argued about the lines of influence and the degree to which American religious rhetoric and energies infuse the political language and events of the time. Such terms as "civil millennialism" or "civil religion" describe a hybrid discourse that combines elements of both codes into a radical synthesis. Nathan O. Hatch, Catherine Albanese, Harry Stout, Donald Weber, and others make a convincing case for the rhetorical and thematic interplay between sermonic language and political debate. As Hatch delineates his term,

> The civil millennialism of the Revolutionary era, expressed by rationalists as well as pietists, grew directly out of the politicizing of Puritan millen-nial history in the two decades before the Stamp Act crisis. In marked contrast to the apolitical millennial hopes of Jonathan Edwards, which had been based on the success of the revival, civil millennialism advanced freedom as the cause of God, defined the primary enemy as the Antichrist of civil oppression rather than that of formal religion, traced the myths of its past through political developments rather than through the vital religion of the forefathers, and turned its vision toward the privileges of Britons rather than to a heritage exclusive to New England.   (53)

Republican ideology, in this view, grows out of a mixture of Whig political beliefs and apocalyptic fears and hopes; and while the propor-tions of each may be in dispute—Stout, for instance, stresses how much ministers saw the Revolution as "America's sermon to the world"—the prevailing historical view suggests an essentially dialectic synthesis between two competing elements of culture (Stout, 311).

Still, there are other energies at work in fueling a revolution, and many of these seem bound up with modes of expression outside the usual channels of law, governance, worship, or economic exchange. The theatrical language of the time suggests that there are many dimensions to the language of revolt. Even theater itself, when applied metaphorically to revolution, can have several possible components. One component, for example, is aesthetic, the ways in which an urban culture turns human events into performances and measures them by a kind of performance criticism. Another component is more directly social, that is, when theater expresses fundamental human relationships. A third is historical, where stage represents a means of speaking about providential history in nationalistic terms. And a fourth is psychological, the need of a people in crisis to express conflict in symbol, mask, and ritual. From the American perspective, the last two are the most important.

Rhetoric often reflects, and indeed it becomes itself, a claim to power arising from one or another sphere. In the case of the clergy, the old forms and modes can no longer accommodate the dynamic events of the revivals. As Donald Weber suggests, the Great Awakening forces many ministers into a change of preaching style that gives better expression to the prized values of evangelism—sincerity and enthusiasm; otherwise, ministers risk loss of power in a profession already under the burden of widespread secularity. Thus the shift which Weber describes from a narrative to an extemporaneous or fragmentary style (with its consequent thrust of the speaker into a different realm of performance) "betrays the *social marginality* of the evangelical actors/agents themselves" (151). The Calvinist ministers' "challenge to normative discourse is the linguistic sign of their outsider status" (151) and an attempt to shatter the limitations of the social, religious, historical, and rhetorical ideas that are upheld by the anti-revivalist clergy. The growth of the new extemporaneous style favored by New Light preachers reflects an overall taste for the histrionic in culture, paralleling the emergence of professional theater in America and the release of heretofore more rigidly controlled psychological energies into public discourse. "Rhetorically speaking," concludes

Weber, "the revolutionary era was 'an instant of pure potentiality,' one of those liminal moments when the multivocal dimensions of ritual discourse incorporate both old and new meanings, a linguistically creative juncture witness to the creation of new cultural myths" (154). In other words, as I hope to show below, the figure of theater, as one key element in the "ritual discourse" of the time, expresses both a traditional rejection of the stage in America and the anticipation of its eventual cultural triumph.

For ministers, an expansion of repertoire into new preaching styles and new language (political) suffices to enable clergy to keep both identity and mission relatively intact during the Revolutionary period. For others, however, the seeming lack of outlets for the "play element" in culture creates a more serious problem of expression. As republicanism takes hold, the difficulty arises of framing entertainments suitable to such a society. Despite the foothold gained by traveling companies, Americans continue to reject the traditional theater; indeed, that rejection becomes part of the whole anti-British, antiaristocratic movement toward independence. Religious revivals can contain some of this energy by providing meaningful performances but only for short periods; we can imagine that the sudden abandonment of frivolity by the young people of Lyme, Connecticut, during the Awakening cannot have lasted past the first wave of enthusiasm (Parsons).

Interestingly, it is Jean-Jacques Rousseau, writing from Calvinist Geneva, who unintentionally predicts the course of entertainment in America. In his *Letter to M. D'Alembert* (1758), Rousseau follows an attack on comedy with an insight into the social disruption that would arise should theater come to a stageless community. Theater, he tells his correspondent, ought not to be allowed in a republic even for a trial run. Should the actors then leave, "idleness, become a necessity, the emptiness of our time, that we will no longer be able to fill up, will make us a burden to ourselves; the actors in parting will leave us boredom as earnest for their return; it will force us to recall them soon or to do worse. We will have done wrong in establishing the drama, we will do wrong in letting it subsist, we will do wrong in destroying it; after the first fault, we will have the choice only for our ills" (125). But unlike the seventeenth-century American Puritans, Rousseau recognizes the need for something which expresses the nature of (a free) society beyond the strict rituals of institutions. His prescription is worth quoting at length because so much of it applies to the American scene:

> What! Ought there to be no entertainments in a republic? On the contrary, there ought to be many. It is in republics that they were born, it is in their bosom that they are seen to flourish with a truly festive air. To what peoples is it more fitting to assemble often and form among themselves sweet bonds of pleasure and joy than to those who have so many reasons to like one another and remain forever united? We already have many of these public festivals; let us have even more. I will be only the more charmed for it. But let us not adopt these exclusive entertainments which close up a small number of people in melancholy fashion in a gloomy cavern, which keep them fearful and immobile in silence and inaction, which give them only prisons, lances, soldiers, and afflicting images of servitude and inequality to see. No, happy peoples, these are not your festivals. It is in the open air, under the sky, that you ought to gather and give yourselves to the sweet sentiment of your happiness. Let your pleasures not be effeminate or mercenary; let nothing that has an odor of constraint and selfishness poison them; let them be free and generous like you are, let the sun illuminate your innocent entertainments; you will constitute one yourselves, the worthiest it can illuminate. (125–26)

Rousseau voices an idea at the end of the passage that harkens back to Plato's *Laws:* a civic polity, a bonded people, are themselves a play. There is one essential difference, however, between Rousseau's formulation and Plato's. The play of state for the Athenians is a tragedy; for the Genevans, it is a comic festival.

For Rousseau, the great appeal of the festival is its open air quality, against the enclosed, stifling, privileged spaces of the theater; outdoors, no one puts on a role. Instead, as Jonas Barish remarks, "The spectacle will constitute an expression of the general will, pouring itself out in a communal joy in which all artificial distinctions between persons will disappear" (291). The great attraction of George Whitefield might very well have been the outdoor meetings where he could, in Franklin's famous calculation, preach to crowds as large as thirty thousand (*Autobiography*, 107). Unlike the closed spaces of churches and meetinghouses, the public squares and fields could draw believers and witnesses on the run, without regard for membership requirements or pewbox status. But as with any revolution, enthusiasm inevitably wanes without constant attention; and without the immediate presence of Whitefield or the other itinerants, Americans may have felt the sort of grumbling displacement Rousseau describes as the outcome of a trial period of the theater. The warnings delivered by Charles Chauncy and other antirevivalists that the people would be stirred by millenarian promises and have their expectations raised beyond all *reasonable* levels, when seen in the light of Rousseau's remarks, are in fact correct.

If Rousseau is right, then Americans need to do two things in order to reach the Genevan ideal: first, recognize themselves as a republic, purged of the evils rampant in a class-bound monarchy; then, organize the kinds of festivals that celebrate the "new cultural myths" which emerge from a free, healthy society. In fact, both things do occur but not, at first, in that order.

As a result of a series of perceived affronts, New Englanders in 1765 took to the streets in sometimes violent, sometimes restrained mass protest. The immediate cause was the imposition of the Stamp Act and the immediate objects of the attacks were those who stood for Parliamentary authority in Massachusetts—Chief Justice Peter Oliver and Lieutenant Governor Thomas Hutchinson. But it also seems clear that a variety of needs were asserting themselves in that time, not all of them political or economic. Peter Shaw, in *American Patriots and the Rituals of Revolution*, observes that the Revolution follows a series of ritual acts that not only respond to political events but also express more primitive folk needs for symbolic parricide and psychosocial independence. For instance, in a prelude to the Stamp Act crisis, the Writs of Assistance case of 1761, Shaw describes the multitude of father-son tensions when young James Otis, Jr., stands against his old teacher, Jeremiah Gridley, lawyer for the Crown. John Adams, Otis's admirer and friend, writes years later that the courtroom battle between Otis and Gridley proved to be "a moral spectacle, more affecting to me than any I have since seen upon the stage" (letter to William Tudor, July 9, 1818, *Works*, 10:327; see also an earlier letter on the same subject, *Works*, 10:244–49, and Shaw, *American Patriots*, 110). Not only does the episode provide fodder for a psychoanalytic reading of what Shaw calls a "familial drama," but Adams's recollection suggests the degree to which the episode impressed him theatrically. The rituals of daily life take on the qualities of moral dramas—the very appeal made by Lewis Hallam and David Douglass when they tried to counter local opposition to the production of their plays.

Despite what is apparent in Adams's early writing—that theater metaphor shapes pre-Revolutionary rhetoric—it also seems that perceiving ordinary events extraordinarily does not suffice for a rising, if not fully conscious, republic. "The American colonists," Shaw suggests, "suffered from festival deprivation" (199); few of the festivals that were popular for centuries in Britain had made their way fully formed—or at all—to North America. The attempt to develop or resurrect rituals in the outdoors mirrors Rousseau's model republic, but in this case, the festivals themselves lead to the declaration of a republic. It is doubtful that Rousseau would find in the riots, effigy-burnings, and other scapegoat rituals (where Hutchinson or Oliver or someone like the king's advisor, Lord Bute, substitute for reprisal against the monarch) his precise formula for exhibiting "the sweet sentiment of your happiness"; but in psychosocial terms, a place like Boston in the 1760s, faced, as Shaw reminds us, with fire, higher taxes, smallpox, and the return of Whitefield for yet another revival, finds itself to be like the Thebes of Sophocles' play "in which the disturbed citizens of a plague-infested city feel that they must find a scapegoat to release them from their cursed situation" (31; see also Zobel, 26, 68–72, 100).

The Greek city restores its health by finally expelling the king; but that is a drama. Unable and unwilling to expel a king so soon, colonists find their own situation more complex than that of Sophocles' Thebes. For one thing, the old religious rhetoric has not lost its grip. An anonymous essayist in the *Boston Gazette* criticizes young people for misdirecting their energy by flouting the Sabbath: "A good deal depends upon the youth of a country being train'd up to virtue and good manners: *They* are to act upon the stage of life, when the *present* generation is gone" (Sept. 17, 1764; reprinted in Hyneman and Lutz, 1:39). Once the Stamp Act crisis hits, the youth do mount that stage, with virtue in mind, perhaps, but not always good manners. Suddenly, it seems, the impulse to assemble in playlike gatherings seizes the American popular imagination. Without a space in which to view an Oedipus play, Bostonians and others experiment with house-sackings, solemn consecrations of Liberty Trees, ritual processions, ceremonial toasts, bonfires, masquerades, Saturnalian mockery, numerological celebrations (45 for John Wilkes's infamous *North Briton*, number 45, or 92 for the "Glorious" members of the Massachusetts House who refused to rescind the anti-Parliament Circular Letter), and even in 1766 the pulling down, by the New York Sons of Liberty, of a "play house [at] the beginning of the 2nd act" accompanied by looting, smashing, and "crying out Liberty, Liberty" (Silverman, *Cultural History*, 97; Shaw, *American Patriots*, 21, 49, 63–67; Middlekauff, 160, 169, 171). Many of these ludic exercises are accompanied by transparencies or lantern shows, multimedia presentations that serve to engage that same working class who ran from their shops a generation earlier to hear the itinerants of the Great Awakening (see P. Davidson, 175, 188, 208). These new rituals vent the passions in an attempt to restore the colonies to health and thus affirm the Rousseauvian principle of freedom from destructive social restraint. In fact, groups like the Sons of Liberty are conscious of the need both for release and for some control over ritual protest; by standing "on a Scaffold" and enlisting citizens, the Sons literally and figuratively elevate the enterprise from mere mob action to a socially productive act (Morgan and Morgan, 251). But as American rioters and ritual makers find two hundred years later in the protests against the Vietnam War, political life does not, *without cataclysm*, sort itself out as tidily as a two-and-a-half-hour play.

There are plays, however, being performed and written during the eighteenth century in America. The early repertoire includes such Restoration favorites as Thomas Otway's *The Orphan* and *Venice Preserv'd*, George Farquhar's *The Beaux' Stratagem* and *The Recruiting Officer*, and George Lillo's *George Barnwell (The London Merchant)*; Addison's *Cato* (known to have been played by students at the College of William and Mary as early as 1736); and of course Shakespeare, the single most popular playwright on the American colonial stage (Wilson, 8 ff.; Dunn, 29–127; Carson, 223–38, 244–45; Rankin, 130, 191). Though limited largely to Charleston, Williamsburg, New York, and eventually Philadelphia, theater in the eighteenth century makes its way to other northern cities, if only for limited periods. Professional popularizers have to resort to any number of public relations ploys in order to justify to hostile communities the value of the stage. One strategy is an old one: assert the stage as a school where one goes to learn about human nature. At a performance of *The Merchant of Venice* in Williamsburg in September 1752 (which young George Washington may have seen), the prologue appeals both to cultural history and civic pride as it justifies for the audience the institution of theater. For the instruction that the stage offers,

> the Bard, on Athen's Infant Stage,
> At first produc'd the *Drama's* artful Page;
> At once to please and satyrize he knew,
> And all his Characters from Nature drew,
> Without restriction then, as Nature taught,
> The Player acted, and the Poet wrote;
> The Tragic Muse did Honour to the State,
> And in a Mirrour taught them to be great.
> (*Virginia Gazette*, Sept. 22, 1752; quoted in Ford, 13)

How much honor the American colonial stage did to the state is not immediately apparent; but certainly a Washington, whose favorite play was *Cato*, must have believed that tragic drama could teach one about the ideals of honor and duty to one's country.

The most amusing strategy to us, perhaps, is the claims for moral instruction made in playbills or in prologues, as in this advertisement for a performance of *Othello* by David Douglass in 1761:

> King's Arms Tavern, Newport, Rhode Island
> On Monday, June 10, at the Public Room
> of the Above Inn, will be delivered a Series of
> MORAL DIALOGUES
> in five parts
> Depicting the evil effects of Jealousy and
> other Bad Passions and Proving that
> Happiness can only Spring from
> the Pursuit of Virtue.
> (Wilson, 16; see also Clapp, 8–10, and Wood, *Rising Glory*, 281)

More directly, Francis Hopkinson in his prologue for Douglass's production of *George Barnwell* calls on Philadelphians to be tolerant of the theater though they see exhibited immoral acts:

Vice to expose in each assum'd disguise,
And bid the mist to vanish from your eyes,
With keener passions, that you may detest
Her hellish form, howe'er like virtue drest:
The muse to cherish, genius to inspire,
Bid fancy stretch the wing, and wit take fire—
For these we come—for these we erect our Stage.
(quoted in Rankin, 130)

Though theater in the nineteenth century becomes a genuine mass entertainment for the new Republic, the colonial audience for stage plays seems to have been limited to secular-minded or Anglican urbanites (Rankin). Nevertheless, the presence of theater in the colonies seems to lend some energy to those seeking performative outlets for desires other than simply those for entertainment or moral enlightenment alone. Kenneth Silverman, in his comprehensive *Cultural History of the American Revolution*, documents the variety of cultural expression during the years immediately before, during, and after the war and comments on the pervasiveness of histrionic forms in all realms of public life: "The prevalence of metaphor, the air of theatricalism throughout the Stamp Act protests, suggests a tentative state of mind, emotion raised rather to the point of intimidation than of retaliation, a state of becoming. Posturing and attitudinizing as angry swains, bereaved lovers, disinherited children, Sons and Daughters of Liberty, the colonists were testing out new possibilities of conduct, acting toward an ideal of behavior as yet diffuse" (86–87). As in early Augustan England, the theater in America remains in a state of tension with political upheaval. When it spills off the stage and into posters, cartoons, poems, and mock funerals, the theatrical impulse assumes an exaggerated style of discourse, "a pervasive idiom of groaning, mutilation, and rape that might be called Whig Sentimentalism" (Silverman, *Cultural History*, 82). But unlike the English taste for heightened rhetoric, which limits Whiggish cries for liberty to the safety of the theater, written discourse, or an occasional Parliamentary outcry, the American indulgence of hyperbole tends to reshape the very reality it exaggerates. This may come from the tentativeness of things that Silverman observes, but it also seems as if Americans have always worried about *becoming*. Ultimately, through prologues and eventually in the plays themselves, the American theater also provides a place where political matter can be contained; but by the 1770s, it can only serve to express a theatricality already become reality. It is, as we will see in one case, a mirror of a world turned stage. *Hamlet* aside, when the stage can only reflect the life around it—and that reflected life is already theatricalized—then theater loses its potency as a medium. To a society as self-aware as the American colonies of the 1770s, however, theater lives on, indeed, becomes exalted, as metaphor.

Given the conservative appeal made by theater promoters in the eighteenth century, it is not surprising to find that seditious or subversive plays of any kind are rare. In 1767, for instance, the "first American comic opera," the pseudonymous Andrew Barton's *The Disappointment*, was withdrawn from Philadelphia's Southwark Theater at the behest of local merchants who felt they would be satirized by the play. It also seems that its Plautine theme of class reversal, the world turned upside down, may have been too threatening for establishment sensibilities. Interestingly, the play would have featured a black lead character, one Raccoon. Instead of *The Disappointment*, the managers produced an imperial domestic tragedy, *The Prince of Parthia*, written eight years before by a young American, Thomas Godfrey, Jr. Perhaps the love intrigues, fratricide, and suicide that mark the first American tragedy are, ironically, more suited to an audience anxious to avoid controversy or morally reprehensible plays (Rankin, 117–18; see Silverman, *Cultural History*, 104–5).

Though with the building of the Southwark Theater in 1766 and the John Street Theater in 1767, David Douglass must have foreseen the rising fortunes of theater in America, he found events soon worked against him. On the night of March 5, 1770, five Bostonians were killed and many more wounded when British soldiers of the Twenty-ninth Regiment opened fire on a crowd. We know the event now by the hyperbolic title it soon acquired, the Boston Massacre. In reading accounts of and reactions to the shootings, one can readily see how it becomes so quickly codified as a piece of extraordinary theater, unwanted, certainly, except by the most radical factions but made use of with rhetorical brilliance by the new patriots. For David Douglass and other managers, the political theater would nearly sink the fortunes of the rising aesthetic one (Silverman, *Cultural History*, 250).

The massacre seems almost ready-made for theatrical metaphor. For one thing, the confined space of the shooting heightens the intensity of the event. Bostonians, long resentful of limitations put upon their early charters, had been living with what was no longer a protective force of fellow Englishmen but in essence a foreign expeditionary force. With mobs taunting the soldiers as "bloody back dogs"—that is to say, as intrusive *others*—and with the Stamp Act and Townshend duties still fresh in memory, the citizenry must have found themselves nearly strangled from expression for want of a common ritual purging (Zobel, 139). Contemporary visual depictions of the event—Paul Revere's picture of a line of nearly faceless soldiers shooting their guns at helpless citizens huddled in a claustrophobic public space, for instance—provide immediate clarity to what seems now to have been a confusing event for the participants (for full details of the event, see Zobel).

The rhetorical analogue to Revere's picture is the account published shortly after the killings, *A Short Narrative of the Horrid Massacre in Boston* (1770), by James Bowdoin, Dr. Joseph Warren, and Samuel Pemberton. Drawing on eyewitness accounts, the authors use "massacre" and "tragedy" to shape the event for the public mind, as if these were objective terms for readily identifiable actions. Early in the narrative, after giving a list of killed and wounded almost as a kind of dramatis personae, the authors state that "the actors in this dreadful tragedy were a party of soldiers commanded by Capt. Preston of the 29th regiment" (214). As for the set, the centerpiece is the Custom House from which "several guns were fired at the same time" and "before which the shocking scene was exhibited" (217). When the authors then draw from the depositions a distinction between "street-actors and house-actors," we see more meaning in the word *actors* than simply *those who do*; the rhetorical context of their remarks turns *actor* essentially into *villain*—the soldiers on the street and those stationed in the Custom House (217). The writers insist that Joseph Hooton, Jr., a deponent, "was present at the tragical scene exhibited near the Custom-house" (220) and that the appearance of an angry group of soldiers, as observed by Samuel Drowne, "was immediately introductory to the grand catastrophe" (224). The threatening band of soldiers moves on, past the sentry post at the Custom House, and in describing that action, the authors drive home the connection between Custom House set and dramatically conceived action: "This is needful to be mentioned, as near that spot and in that street the bloody tragedy was acted, and the street actors in it were stationed: their station being but a few feet from the front side of the said Customhouse" (224).

For several years afterward, the "bloody tragedy" would be nominally reenacted through the rhetoric of anniversary writers and speakers. At the first anniversary, a poet writing for the *Boston Gazette* describes the event as a "Theatre of Blood" (quoted in Silverman, *Cultural History*, 211), a phrase that would grow in popularity as hostilities worsened. At the second commemoration, Joseph Warren, one of the authors of the *Short Narrative*, gives an address that stresses the "tragical effects" of the killings. In order to re-create the *feelings* aroused by the massacre, Warren indulges in what amounts to an antilanguage of supercilious rhetoric that would later, in the works of Thomas Paine, make the case for independence. "The horrors of that dreadful night," he says, "are but too deeply impressed on our hearts"—a place in the human being beyond words where wounds give rise to extraordinary speaking. "Language is too feeble to paint the emotion of our souls," Warren continues,

> when our streets were stained with the blood of our brethren—when our ears were wounded by the groans of the dying, and our eyes were tormented with the sight of the mangled bodies of the dead.—When our alarmed imagination presented to our view our houses wrapt in flames, our children subjected to the barbarous caprice of the raging soldiery,— our beauteous virgins exposed to all the insolence of unbridled passion,—our virtuous wives, endeared to us by every tender tie, falling a sacrifice to worse than brutal violence, and perhaps like the famed Lucretia, distracted with anguish and despair, ending their wretched lives by their own fair hands. (Vaughan, 36–37)

"Feeble" though his language may be, Warren's recital has an incantatory effect, propelling his listeners out of mundane reality into a highly charged, theatrical realm of pitch, stagger, and fall.

In another instance, John Hancock's address at the fourth anniversary of the massacre directly confronts the perpetrators of the infamous deed. By calling out to those responsible for the deaths as if they were present, Hancock not only recalls the event but also re-creates it, as a gothic shadow play whose ritual revival demands bloody expiation:

> Tell me, ye bloody butchers! ye villains high and low! ye wretches who contrived, as well as you who executed the inhuman deed! do you not feel the goads and stings of conscious guilt pierce through your savage bosoms? though some of you may think yourselves exalted to a height that bids defiance to human justice, and others shroud yourselves beneath the mask of hypocrisy, and build your hopes of safety on the low arts of cunning, chicanery and falsehood; yet do you not sometimes feel the gnawings of that worm which never dies? do not the injured shades of Maverick, Gray, Caldwell, Attucks and Carr attend you in your solitary walks, arrest you even in the midst of your debaucheries, and fill even your dreams with terror?   (Vaughan, 78)

By using heightened rhetoric, Warren, Hancock, and the "black regiment" of ministers who seize upon the massacre as they do no other topical event (Stout, 272) convert their feelings of outrage into exhibitions of universal morality, suitable for a theater of God's judgments. Indeed, by the time of Hancock's speech, March 5, 1774, some Bostonians must have felt that they had already been visited by terrors or seen themselves dragged upon a stage of judgments; with the imposition of the Coercive Acts, ritual and rhetoric would no longer suffice as responses to what many were calling tyranny.

In 1775, when the presence of an augmented British force makes the anniversary speaker choose his words more expediently, Warren converts the language of "bloody massacre" into that of "sanguinary theater," wearing also a toga as a visual gesture toward the hyperreality he projects (Fritz, 128). In this address, Warren deliberately invokes theatrical figures as a way of ordering what might otherwise be perceived as wild ranting. Watched by a crowd at Old South Church that includes forty soldiers, Warren begins by tracing the early and pleasant relations between Britain and its American colonies: "But, unhappily for Britain, the madness of an avaricious minister of state has drawn a sable curtain over the charming scene, and in its stead has brought upon the stage discord, envy, hatred and revenge, with civil war close in their rear" (Pickering, 73). Warren does not linger on the solemnity of a stage draped in mourning; this arch-sentimentalist prefers to reset the scene in order to summon the "sad remembrance" of five years before:

The sanguinary theater again opens itself to view. The baleful images of terror crowd around me—and disconnected ghosts, with hollow groans, appear to solemnize the anniversary of the fifth of March.

Approach we then the melancholy walk of death. Hither let me call the gay companion; here let him drop a farewell tear upon that body which so late he saw vigorous and warm with social mirth—hither let me lead the tender mother to weep over her beloved son—come widowed mourner, here satiate thy grief; behold they murdered husband gasping on the ground, and to complete the pompous show of wretchedness bring in each hand thy infant children to bewail their father's fate—take heed, ye orphan babes, lest while your streaming eyes are fixed upon the ghastly corpse *your feet slide on the stones bespattered with your father's brains.* Enough! this tragedy need not be heightened by an infant weltering in the blood of him that gave it birth. (73)

Enough indeed, though Warren is hardly finished. The point, he says, is that Bostonians did not then sink to revenge; the soldiers left, they thought, for good: "Thus closes the important drama" (74). So what are the soldiers doing back in Boston? It appears that whatever desire the colonists have to maintain relations with Britain, another drama yet awaits them. To those patriots "who generously have sacrificed wealth and ease—who have despised the pomp and show of tinseled greatness— . . . you then will reap that harvest of renown which you so justly have deserved. Your country shall pay her grateful tribute of applause" (77). Warren's speech anticipates one of the themes of Royall Tyler's postwar play, *The Contrast*: eschew the splendor, the "pomp and show" of a culture whose corruptions lead to murder, and instead participate in the spectacle of sacrifice for one's country and earn, at play's end, its rightful response.

While Warren is not the only patriot to fill the air with inflated political rhetoric, he certainly makes the most theatrical exit. Painted by John Trumbull and dramatized by Hugh Henry Brackenridge, the martyr of Bunker Hill becomes a symbol of the Stoic actor shedding his hot blood on the glorious world stage. One wonders, in fact, if Warren is not killed by his language; that is, once having expressed the conflict with Britain in the elevated and exaggerated terms of the stage, he is almost obliged to fight with histrionic fervor. Thomas Paine's *Common Sense*, appearing as it does in January 1776, often gets credit as an instigating force toward rebellion, but from Warren's example it is clear that Paine's effort is only the (un)crowning achievement in a long line of sometimes cautious, often insistent, and at times hysterical tracts and orations whose effect, if not design, is to reconstitute reality.

The histrionic style, by the 1770s fully absorbed into Whiggish rhetoric, provokes loyalists into denouncing the form as well as the content of the antiadministration attacks. Jonathan Boucher, Anglican rector of Annapolis, represents the other side of the theatrical paradox one encounters in the Revolutionary debate. As both Anglican and urban southerner, Boucher is much more comfortable with the playhouse than his New England ministerial contemporaries. After seeing David Douglass's company perform, Boucher writes appreciatively of having good theater in America; at one point, in the early 1770s, he even writes a poem, "Church and Theatre," showing the combined value of the two institutions (Winton, 89; Silverman, *Cultural History*, 239). But when it comes to theatrical rhetoric, Boucher adopts the standard loyalist line: arguments over governance can responsibly take place only in a restrained manner. As Charles Brockwell responds to the Great Awakening, so Boucher does to the new calls for democracy. In a 1773 sermon (though probably revised after Boucher fled to England), he reduces those who "call themselves *the people*" to nothing more than "tumultuous crowds of the most disorderly persons in the community" whose attacks on the foundation of a state are conducted "in some giddy moments of overheated ardour" (*A View*, 313; Zimmer, 340). The source of those passions can be directly traced to the rise of a "flimsy oratory" that uses the catch phrases of liberty, governmental abuse, and the like in a "swoln and turgid elocution" destined to lead, as Tacitus saw in Rome, "to the decline of their empire" (Boucher, *A View*, 320). But, Boucher continues,

> This is not all: as though there were some irresistible charm in all extemporaneous speaking, however rude, the orators of our committees and sub-committees, like those in higher spheres, *prevail with their tongues*. To public speakers alone is the government of our country now completely committed: it is cantoned out into new districts, and subjected to the jurisdiction of these committees. . . . An empire is thus completely established within an empire; and a new system of govern-

ment of great power erected, even before the old one is formally abol-
ished.   (321; see Stout, 283)

If by 1773 speech threatens the integrity of empire, by 1774–75,
the dates of an exchange of essays by Daniel Leonard and John Adams
on the developing conflict, that sentimentalist oratory has become, in
Tory eyes, inflammatory and conspiratorial. Writing as "Massachusettensis," Leonard accuses the Whigs of doing anything to "inflame the
passions," including the giving of commemoration speeches on the
Boston Massacre. Images of Britain's imminent collapse and America's eminent ascent pour out of Whig orations; consequently, "When
we consider what effect a well written tragedy or novel has on the
human passions, though we know it to be all fictitious, what effect
must all this be supposed to have had upon those, that believed these
high wrought images to be realities?" (Leonard and Adams, 284–85).
It is method, almost more than message, that galls Leonard; so disturbed is he by Adams's ("Novanglus") accusations of Oliver, Hutchinson, and other officials of engaging in "a conspiracy to enslave their
country" that Massachusettensis cannot refrain from seeing Whig
oratory as a part of an elaborate revenge tragedy. If his opponent's
charges are false, then "Novanglus has acted the part of an assassin"
(342): "At first they wore the garb of hypocrisy, they professed to be
friends to the British constitution in general, but claimed some ex-
emptions from their local circumstances; at length threw off their
disguise, and now stand confessed to the world in their true characters,
American republicans" (348). But as the crisis becomes more acute,
the Tories tear a page from the Whig oratorical handbook. Joseph
Galloway, himself a onetime opponent of British policy, raises the
specter of class conflict with some inflammatory rhetoric of his own.
Those who call for independence are an "unthinking, ignorant multitude . . . armed, but undisciplined men," capable of "seizing your
property, . . . ravishing your wives and daughters, and afterwards
plunging the dagger into their tender bosoms, while you are obliged to
stand the speechless, the helpless spectators" (375–76). The danger for
loyalists is not only that they will lose the ideological struggle but also
that they will capitulate to a rhetoric they have marked out as inimical
to civilized discourse.

If the Boston Massacre itself had no immediate political consequences, radical rhetoric would force the next issue. With an added
duty on tea, the North ministry played directly into the patriots'
waiting hands, giving them the opportunity for yet another galvinizing
incident with symbolic value. When in December 1773 a band of
men dressed as Indians enacted their political dumb show by shattering casks and scattering tea in Boston harbor, observers recognized the
vitality of the performance and the degree to which it would transform
the sociopolitical picture. Though no doubt more prescient than
most, John Adams records in his diary for December 17, 1773, feelings that must have been shared soon enough by his fellow patriots:

> Last Night 3 Cargoes of Bohea Tea were emptied into the Sea. . . .
> This is the most magnificent Movement of all. There is a Dignity, a
> Majesty, a Sublimity, in this last Effort of the Patriots, that I greatly
> admire. The People should never rise, without doing something to be
> remembered—something notable And striking. This Destruction of the
> Tea is so bold, so daring, so firm, intrepid and inflexible, and it must
> have so important Consequences, and so lasting, that I cant but consider
> it as an Epocha in History.   (DA, 2:85–86)

One might argue that Adams responds as he does because of the
performative elements of the political act. The analogies between the
costumed and disciplined behavior of the "Mohawks" and a masque or
other theatrical show seem obvious enough and have certainly led
succeeding students of the Revolution to seize upon the episode as of
particular significance. The popular historian Page Smith, for instance, says, "The Boston Tea Party was what we today would call
guerrilla theater, a striking and dramatic enactment of an ideological
position," as if its inherent theatricality gave it contemporary reso-
nance (1:384). With the Revolution in general, it is difficult for
modern commentators to distinguish between their own need to frame
history dramatically and the use of dramatic or stage metaphor among
contemporary participants and observers. For example, Wesley S.
Griswold's re-creation of a scene that occurs a month prior to the Tea
Party suggests how much a modern reader can be affected by pre-
Revolutionary rhetoric. In November 1773, those who were to receive
the shipments of dutied tea were ordered by the Sons of Liberty to

meet at the Liberty Tree. As Griswold describes the episode for one consignee, we can see the problem of sorting out overlapping rhetorics of theater: "The imperious knocks on Richard Clarke's front door in Boston early that November morning in 1773 signaled the beginning of a historic drama, in much the way that the eighteenth-century stage director's raps on the floor with his ceremonial staff traditionally heralded the commencement of plays" (27). A drama for whom? Drama has long been a favorite metaphor for history (though often unwittingly applied); the word provides an instantly recognized form in which one can distinguish the relative importance of historical details. But most often, drama is a word of convenience for the writer rather than a precise term. Griswold complicates his description by adding a piece of eighteenth-century theatrical practice to his image. This modern analogy in itself, of course, does not mean necessarily that *drama* was in anyone's mind while standing at Clarke's door. Yet the rhetorical packaging of the Tea Party, even beyond its obvious masquelike character, might well lead a historian into adopting dramatic language. Since Boston in 1773 had no public theatrical tradition, the analogy to contemporary theater practice is not wholly appropriate; nonetheless, on a macrocosmic level, the patriots may well have had a figural stage in view to give force and meaning to their actions.

After other American ports became the scenes of further tea parties, a satirical piece appeared in a New York newspaper that suggested an enlarged theatrical context. In asking who was "the author of the curious East Indian farce, lately prepared in England to be played in America for the entertainment of the British Colonies," the writer provides an answer: "It is generally ascribed to Lord North; at least the finishing and preparing of it for exhibition on the American stage. It was intended only as a kind of an overture, prelude or introduction to a grand performance (I don't know whether to call it Comedy or Tragedy) in which the whole British nation were intended to be actors" (quoted in Silverman, *Cultural History*, 249). To the philosophically minded, the question posed by the writer echoes that asked by John of Salisbury of life itself—and throughout the period, the labels *comedy* (or *farce*) and *tragedy* carry great weight. To those familiar with beau monde entertainments, however, the theatrical references resonate with urban humor. On the one hand, the formal tone gives the writing a prophetic quality, which modern observers, knowing what they do about events two years later, can easily see; yet the catalog of stage language appeals most immediately to theatergoers, people who, as I have suggested earlier, are as likely to see themselves in the role of actors as the figures the audience watches on stage. To imagine "the whole British nation" as actors would, for the urban sophisticate familiar with the small world of the real theater, involve only a minor, comedic leap of thought. The fashionable set described by the Connecticut Wit, John Trumbull, in *The Progress of Dulness* (1773) would recognize the humor as of a piece with the theatricality of their own lives. Whether it is the fop, Dick Hairbrain, who shows "The pert, vivacious, play-house style / That makes the gay assembly's smile" (pt. 2, lines 225–26), or the belle, Harriet Simper, who, "rising on the stage, / Learns all the arts that please the age" (pt. 3, lines 225–26), Trumbull's characters reflect the presence in America of an audience, skilled in the falseness of social performance, that would find the "American stage" but an extension of the British.

In contrast to this urban, aestheticized response, other colonials see events following a different stagelike form. The actions in December lead to the passage in 1774 of the Boston Port Act, which closed the harbor to commercial shipping. Residents of other colonies join with Massachusetts in urging the city's resistance to the closing of her harbors. In Virginia, a colony that, as Rhys Isaac has shown, had developed a number of ritual activities that centered on music, dance, churchgoing, and courthouse attendance, support for the Bostonians takes a characteristic turn. The election of Richard Bland and Peter Poythress to the House of Burgesses is conducted as a referendum on imperial control; the unanimous choice for the anti-imperialists, complete with a courthouse spectacle of announcement, becomes, in Isaac's term, a communal *tableau vivant*, "dramatizing to freeholders the awful menace of British power and the noble solidarity of Americans" (*Transformation*, 253; see also Isaac, "Dramatizing").

Elsewhere, too, colonists rely upon regional heritage to show their unity with Boston on the theatrum mundi. In a letter from Brooklyn, Connecticut, the writer portrays Bostonians in terms familiar to Puritans from a century before. His fellow townspeople are "ready to march in the van and to sprinkle the American altars with our hearts blood, if the occasion should be. . . . You are held up as a spectacle to the whole world. All Christendom are longing to see the event of the American contest. And do, most noble citizens, play your part manfully" (quoted in P. Smith, 1:391). This echo of 1 Corinthians 4.9 reminds us of the curious interfusion in Puritan rhetoric of biblical images and theatrical language; for the Connecticut writer (possibly Israel Putnam), the Romanized command to the "noble citizens" to act their parts "manfully" coexists with the dissenting Protestant stress on *spectacle* as being a show (of faith) for God's eyes. Against the theater of appearances, the high-minded New Englanders propose alternative stages that maintain the link of American rhetoric to a pre-Augustan vision of the theatrum mundi. In his valedictory address at Rhode Island College (later Brown University) in September 1774, Barnabas Binney seizes on the post–Tea Party revival of liberty language to imagine for his listeners the metaphoric future: "AMERICA, hitherto the infant state of glorious freedom, on which surrounding nations, while still enslaved, gaze with envy, love, and wonder; *America*, no doubt the future, spacious Theatre for actions yet unthought of with the ancient worthies . . . has already illustriously exalted her fame and greatness, and increased the esteem and veneration of her friends to no common pitch" (52). This rhetoric of spectacle, infused with Whiggish sentiment, proposes a peculiarly American theater, one contradistinct to that inhabited by fops and belles, where the language of liberty and greatness can be heard most clearly.

One person's spectacle, however, is another's fraud. As Benjamin Labaree describes, the anticolonial rhetoric in England grows sharper once news of the Tea Party arrives there. "Here we see the colony patriot without his mask [of loyalty]," writes one correspondent to the London *Morning Chronicle* (Jan. 1, 1774, quoted in Labaree, 171–72). Given the view that the colonists only act out their false roles as the king's loyal subjects, other responses follow suit. As a writer in the London *Gazeteer* reports, the force of the Boston Port Act will change the "Boston Rioters" to complacent shopkeepers who, once "behind their counter," will "then assume an affecting hypocritical air, clasp their hands, cast up their eyes to heaven, [and] wonder if the King knows their oppressed condition" (Mar. 12, 1774, quoted in Labaree, 209).

But if the English look at events as leading to a comedic resolution (at the Americans' expense), many Americans imagine otherwise. In the South, where theater has been a less controversial part of colonial society than it has been in New England, something must be done by patriots to distinguish their performances from those countenanced by the British. To support the Bostonians, some South Carolinians send rice collected at a "benefit performance of 'Busiris, King of Egypt,' a play described as representing 'an injured gallant people struggling against oppression . . . wading through a dangerous bloody field in search of freedom'" (Timothy's *South Carolina Gazette*, July 4, 1774, cited in Labaree, 248). Thus, for Charleston, a play itself becomes the vehicle by which the struggles of Boston are conceived, a drama whose very performance leads to the material welfare (rice collected as admission) of an "'injured gallant people'" during their fight against tyranny. Nevertheless, even in the South, it is not theater so much as it is analogous experiences that provide the impetus to revolt. Patrick Henry's famous "give me liberty, or give me death" speech in Richmond, March 23, 1775, does far more to galvanize the people than any play. To be sure, no actor could compete with the "orator of nature," described by his contemporaries as a "SHAKESPEARE and GARRICK COMBINED!" What Americans praised in Henry's delivery, they would prize in themselves: "various, bold and original . . . never . . . studied, affected, or theatrical, or [overstepping] 'the modesty of nature'" (Wirt, 137–41, 50, 443, 431). In other words, patriots prefer to be "true actors" on the world stage to powdered players on the boards.

While some performances of older plays could serve as political commentaries on the present (as *Cato* does throughout the period), new closet dramas carry the burden of satire more entertainingly than the usual political tract. The best-known political dramatist of the prewar years, Mercy Otis Warren, wrote at least three: *The Adulateur* (1772), *The Defeat* (1773), and *The Group* (1775). Two others for which she is given credit, *The Blockheads* (1776), a crude-tongued farce that mocks John Burgoyne's anti-Yankee *The Blockade of Boston* (1776), and a midwar play, *The Motley Assembly* (1779), seem stylistically unsuitable for the often lofty and severe Mercy Warren (see Meserve, 71–72, and Laska, 49–50); nonetheless, she illustrates the trend toward written theatrical responses to political events.

The use of plays and dialogues by Whigs like Mercy Warren and Tories, too, no doubt stems from several factors, but one certainly is the heightened awareness among the politically (and literarily) astute that theater is an inescapable figure for the British-American conflict. Mercy Warren, reader of Molière and Shakespeare, sister of the inflammatory patriot James Otis, wife of the Whig politician James Warren, and friend of the witty and prophetic Adamses, immersed herself as much as anyone in the theatrical rhetoric of her time. Like many a descendant of Puritans, she voices ambivalent feelings about the drama; although she may never have seen a staged play, she expresses the necessity for both form and trope in guiding her response to the upheavals of the 1770s (see Meserve, 65–67).

More than her plays, however, Mercy Warren's letters and later her controversial history of the American Revolution show the ways in which theater frames not only the actions of street actors in the various prewar crises but also the perceptions of those for whom morality always begins with a capital *M*. In a letter to Abigail Adams, January 19, 1774, she suggests how it is that she might be drawn to drama in the first place: "The solemn strains of the tragic Muse have been generally more to my taste than the lighter Representations of the Drama. Yet I think that the Follies and Absurdities of Human Nature Exposed to Ridicule in the Masterly Manner it is done by Moliere may often have a greater tendency to reform Mankind than some graver Lessons of Morality" (*AFC*, 1:92–93; see Alice Brown, 237, and Meserve, 73). Drama, as Warren conceives it, gives "lighter Representations" than the vaguely suggested "tragic Muse"; but it seems clear enough from other writings that her vision of life cannot be accommodated by the limitations of anything intended for stage production. She uses "tragic" much as Plato does in the *Laws*: as a term that connotes the seriousness of a nearly religious ritual. In another letter to Abigail, January 28, 1775, she writes of the necessity to give oneself to duty and, interestingly, of the role of women in fighting for a cause. The brave women of the past, like Aria and Portia, she explains, have often chosen suicide when faced with defeat; she does not "think it would have been the Case with Either of those Celebrated Ladies had they Lived in the Days of Christianity, for I think it is a much Greater proof of an Heroic Soul to struggle with the Calamities of Life, and patiently Resign ourselves to the Evils we Cannot Avoid than Cow-

ardly to shrink from the post Alloted us by the Great Director of the
Theatre of the Universe, Before we have finished our part in the
Drama of Life" (AFC, 1:182). This Epictetian Stoicism—the willing
acceptance of one's chosen role in life's great drama—underlies a
pervasive rhetorical stance in Whig literature. Where Tories see hypocrisy and farce, Whigs see providential tragedies and a "theater of
blood." On the other hand, where Whigs see pernicious theater—
Faneuil Hall turned into a playhouse—and British contempt for
morality, Tories view a necessary amusement. For British sympathizers, the idea that "the world's a stage" (the title of a 1778 theatrical
prologue by loyalist poet Jonathan Odell) implies the aestheticized
domain of mask and mockery, petty elevations and petit bourgeois
lampoons (see Edelberg, 82–83). For the American patriots, however,
no such stage presents itself, except as an evil. Never having lost sight
of the cosmic stage, perhaps through the efforts of the evangelical
"black regiment," patriots like Mercy Warren or her friend John
Adams imagine a larger stage, a hill stage upon which they play out
God-given roles in a universal show, one stripped of splendor, but a
spectacle still.

For Mercy Warren, there is no confusion between the stage of the
world and its degraded microcosmic form. For the British, however,
matters are not as clear. Among the British expeditionary force were
many renowned amateurs and literary dilettantes. Occupied Boston
was to be the scene of an active theatrical life, as New York would be
throughout the war. Francis, Lord Rawdon, a captain of the Sixty-
third Regiment, writes to his uncle with delight in late 1775 when he
is transferred the short distance from listless Charlestown to Boston:
"We are to have plays this winter. . . . I am enrolled as an actor. . . .
General Burgoyne is our Garrick" (quoted in Scheer and Rankin, 97).
Garrick or not, John Burgoyne perceived the world through British
theatrical glasses. As both an actor and playwright, Gentleman Johnny
enlivens the cultural landscape of the old Puritan city; but he also
expresses the limits of the British vision of the war. A week after the
Battle of Bunker Hill, for instance, Burgoyne writes to a "Noble Lord"
of the action, as he observed it from the city looking across the Charles
River. Burgoyne's prose, crisp at times but always stylish, turns slaughter into a splendid entertainment; this was a serious affair, he claims,

but never in his account does he stray into the bloody realm of bad taste:

> And now ensued one of the greatest scenes of war that can be conceived. If we look to the height, Howe's corps ascending. The hill in the face of the entrenchments and in a very disadvantageous ground was much engaged. To the left the enemy pouring in fresh troops by thousands over the land, and in the arm of the sea our ships and floating batteries cannonading them. Straight before us, a large and noble town in one great blaze. The church steeples being of timber were great pyramids of fire above the rest. Behind us, the church steeples and heights of our own camp, covered with spectators of the rest of our army which was engaged. The hills round the country covered with spectators. The enemy all in anxious suspense. The roar of cannon, mortars, and musketry, the crash of churches, ships upon the stocks, and whole streets falling together in ruins to fill the ear; the storm of the redoubts with the objects above described to fill the eye, and the reflection that perhaps a defeat was a final loss to the British Empire in America to fill the mind, made the whole a picture and a complication of horror and importance beyond anything that ever came to my lot to be witness to. (June 25, 1775, quoted in Scheer and Rankin, 59)

Aesthetic considerations govern the whole piece; Burgoyne depicts a landscape on which war is represented, a kind of grand diorama. His perspective is behind the crowd, watching the spectators watch the battle-show.

In the aftermath, Bunker Hill would become a potent symbol for both sides of bravery and the difficulties of the ensuing war. At the same time, however, this one battle and the theatrical responses to it illustrate as clearly as any episode the powerful collusion, conflation, and confusion between a theater of buckram and a theater of blood. The patriot writer Hugh Henry Brackenridge would turn the battle into blank verse tragedy, a play to be read or declaimed for its heroic sentiments, not produced for any value it might have as entertainment. Burgoyne, on the other hand, would set his literary sights on pleasanter ends and write a farce, *The Blockade of Boston*, to mock the Americans surrounding the city. The performance of this play in early January 1776 in Faneuil Hall (turning a meetinghouse into a theater was considered but finally rejected, even by the worldly redcoats) has become legendary (Meserve, 71; Clapp, 3–4; see Scheer and Rankin, 97, and Silverman, *Cultural History*, 293). As was customary for the time, the main play of the evening was to be followed by something light—in this case, Burgoyne's farce. Martin Hunter, a British lieutenant, describes what happened:

> The play was just ended, and the curtain going to be drawn up for the farce, when the actors heard from without that an attack was made on the heights of Charlestown, upon which one of them came in, dressed in the character of a Yankee serjeant (which character he was to play), desired silence, and then informed the audience that the alarm guns were fired; that the rebels had attacked the town; and that they were at it tooth and nail over at Charlestown. The audience thinking this was the opening of the new piece, clapped prodigiously; but soon finding their mistake, a general scene ensued, they immediately hurried out of the house to their alarm posts; some skipping over the orchestra, trampling on the fiddles, and, in short, everyone making his most speedy retreat, the actors (who were all officers) calling out for water to get the paint and smut off their faces; women fainting, etc. . . . . We expected a general attack that night but the rebels knew better, and in a few hours everything was quiet. (Wright, 51–52)

To an audience so used to playacting that they can see little else, the intrusion of reality violates the epistemology of performance and for a time cannot be admitted. When it is, panic breaks out. Though nothing serious came of this event—the British would not be forced from Boston until March 17—the confusion between stage farce and real battle marks the difference between American and British expressions of theatrical rhetoric. The British elite, used to seeing the world in terms of their own stages, project upon the war the figure of farce, and thus reduce it in scope to the constricted and ordered world of manners, Europeanized military "theaters," and low comedy. As one character in *The Blockheads* puts it, his side (the British) has fallen into ignominy: "Yet, with all this force, our generals dare not peep over the entrenchments—are confin'd within three miles of garrison, writing and acting comedies" (Philbrick, 166). In the theater of war, the author tells us, arts undertaken for their own sake appear frivolous; it is no wonder, then, that serious artists like Benjamin West and Patience Wright flee to London to find, as one letter writer puts it, "the proper theatre" for their activities (Purdie's *Virginia Gazette*, May 3, 1776, quoted in Wood, *Creation*, 104).

For the American patriots, however, another theater prevails. By denying the playhouse, the Americans seize the ideological high ground; whereas Burgoyne responds to battle by shrinking war on the hill to farce in the hall, the patriots hold the hill in view and see it through greater eyes than those of British officers and their ladies. In his painting *The Battle of Bunker's Hill* (1786), John Trumbull centers the dying Warren in a compact tableau on a stagelike field, his body bathed in light from above. Projecting upon the war a figural tragedy—and indeed, in the frequent allusions to the "sanguinary theater," one might say a revenge tragedy—the rebels take a broader view than the redcoats, converting even defeat into a necessary twist of plot and ascribing it all to the Great Director. Once elevated to the tragic, the grim details of battle become the exalted actions of a justifiable sacrifice.

CHAPTER TEN

Providential Actor:
The Example of John Adams

*C*harles Francis Adams, grandson of Abigail and John Adams and editor of their writings, notes that American knowledge of the Revolutionary generation is limited to a public view of their acts, without much insight into their personal characters: "Our history is for the most part wrapped up in the forms of office. The great men of the Revolution, in the eyes of posterity, are many of them like heroes of a mythological age. They are seen, for the most part, when conscious that they are upon a theatre, where individual sentiment must be sometimes disguised, and often sacrificed, for the public good" (*Familiar Letters*, v–vi). To remedy that limitation, Adams presents the private letters of his grandmother in order to display the "individual sentiment" previously hidden from the public eye. Yet when we read the private writings of the Adams family, we can see even there a consciousness about public appearance, about roles played in a figural theater, that undermines the sharp contrast between public and private that Charles Francis suggests. John Adams, Abigail Smith Adams, and their mutual correspondent Mercy Otis Warren all share an idealized devotion to the public sphere that well into the Revolution finds expression frequently as theater. Mercy Warren never really relinquishes her fierce hold on theatrical rhetoric, as her history of the war (published in 1805) demonstrates; nor does she ever show herself in her letters to John or Abigail to be anything more informal than a lady of high purpose. Abigail, though more personable than her friend, also writes letters that are fully conscious of the theatricalized era in which she lives. And while John Adams, whose experience in France brings him to despise the well-masked Benjamin Franklin and who later feels abused by Mercy Warren in her history of the war—they even argue about the details of figural stages—bares his soul in his late-life writing, he as well continues to use the metaphor, decrying his treatment on the public stage.

But that later development runs past my present purpose, which is to trace, through the private writings of John Adams, how it is that theatrical figures come to shape the thinking of the Revolutionary generation. John Adams, like John Smith or Cotton Mather, is not entirely typical of his or any other time; yet in his extraordinariness, we can read a number of cultural assumptions writ large. Born in 1735, Adams grew up in a time of shifting sensibilities—though toward the stage, his native New England would lag behind the rest of the country, keeping essentially the same public policy it had since the earliest days of settlement. Literary drama was another matter, of course, as editions of Shakespeare and other English and Continental playwrights became more readily available and quoting from Shakespeare became the common practice of educated, culturally aware Americans. Adams may have been in the van, but he was not alone.

Though actual performances at Harvard were discouraged or certainly by 1767 officially proscribed (Tanselle, 5) during his undergraduate years Adams belonged to a literary society that gave dramatic readings. A surge of interest in oratory occurred in some schools after midcentury, and it seems that Adams found his own calling through dramatic speaking (see Meserve, 46). At his society, Adams recalls in his autobiography, "I was as often requested to read as any other, especially Tragedies, and it was whispered to me and circulated among others that I had some faculty for divine Speaking and that I should make a better Lawyer than Divine" (DA, 3:263; see Shaw, John Adams, 8). Given the fierce anger he would show toward his enemies in his later career, Adams, in selecting the law, may have made the best choice.

In his diary and letters, Adams displays a self-consciousness about his own role-playing that suggests not only a healthy ego but a wholesale adoption of a changing attitude toward one's public presence. To his future wife Abigail Smith, the young lawyer writes, "I mount this moment for that noisy, dirty town of Boston, where Parade, Pomp, Nonsense, Frippery, Folly, Foppery, Luxury, Politicks, and the soul-Confounding Wrangles of the Law will give me the Higher Relish for Spirit, Taste and Sense" (Feb. 14, 1763, AFC, 1:3). To this world of outward show, one identified with urban life, the country lawyer commits himself, hoping to enjoy the benefit of its energy and, by implication, to avoid its excesses. At the same time, however, he openly seeks the "Higher Relish" that he thinks theatricalized urban life can bring.

But if Adams's description of post-Awakening Boston sounds like the usual Englishman's description of any large city, he displays elsewhere a cognizance of other theatrical realms than the procession through city streets of human folly. "Do you ever read Epictetus?" he asks Abigail. "He was a sensible Man, I advise you to read him" (Apr. 20, 1763, AFC, 1:5). For Adams, there could be no better corrective to the sense-deceiving theater of pomp than the Stoic's advice "to act well the given part" in the divinely appointed drama; and in his library, Adams could remind himself of the wisdom of the *Enchiridion* in English, Latin, and Greek editions (AFC, 1:5n).

This dichotomy between higher and lower theaters appears a year later in further letters to Abigail. While at an inn in Plymouth that apparently housed a number of persons who had been inoculated against smallpox, Adams writes a sportive, rhetorical letter, asking what sort of letters he should pen. To be among medical patients suggests another self-conscious turn of phrase: "I am about to make my Appearance on a new Theatre, new to me. I have never been much conversant in scenes, where Drs., Nurses, Watchers, &c. make the Principal Actors" (Apr. 12, 1764, AFC, 1:24). He enters new arenas of experience with all the enunciated confidence of the star actor; yet by implication, if life itself is the proper theater, then, paradoxically, acting to entertain is no sort of acting at all. On his way to Plymouth once again, September 30, 1764, Adams complains of an unnamed "Gentleman" who excels "in the nobler Arts of smutt, Double Entendre, and Mimickry of Dutchmen and Negroes. . . . I have heard that Imitators, tho they imitate well, Master Pieces in elegant and valuable Arts, are a servile Cattle. And that Mimicks are the lowest

Species of Imitators, and I should think that Mimicks of Dutchmen and Negroes were the most sordid of Mimicks" (AFC, 1:49). Whether Adams's last remark reflects high-mindedness on his part or his own racism is not immediately apparent, but the rest of the passage takes Plato's line against actors and all forms of imitation in the arts. To speak in public requires, then, a Platonic commitment to truth and justice, rather than mere expression (rhetoric); an Epictetian awareness of which stage one is on; and a Puritan economy of language and gesture (no useless frivolity). Imitation of people as they are he rejects; as Plato might say, no one learns anything by simply copying a world that is itself an imitation. Certainly a theater that is composed of nothing more than imitations of manners would have no place in a world of John Adamses.

On a personal level, the matter of public oratory must have perplexed the future revolutionary a great deal. Lofty as his standards are, he expresses himself as one who is as subject to the winds of vanity as anyone else, especially when, as a speaker for the cause of truth, he earns applause. By the 1770s, Adams is well fixed in his opposition to British policy in Massachusetts, but he would demonstrate an exceptional integrity by serving as defense attorney for the British soldiers accused of murder in the Boston Massacre trials. While his efforts there seem to have been motivated by a keen commitment to justice over politics—or perhaps that phrase might be rendered, in the rhetorical atmosphere surrounding the massacre, as truth seeking over showmanship—another court case a year later redefines for Adams the problems of action in a public arena. After winning the case of *Freeman* v. *Child*, Adams records in his diary the complimentary remarks of an acquaintance, Cadwallader Ford, and the report of another piece of flattery,

> "That Mr. Adams has been making the finest Speech I ever heard in my Life. He's equall to the greatest orator that ever spoke in Greece or Rome"—What an advantage it is to have the Passions, Prejudices, and Interests of the whole Audience, in a Mans Favour. These will convert plain, common Sense, into profound Wisdom, nay wretched Doggerell into sublime Heroics. This Cause was really, and in truth and without Partiality, or Affectation of Modesty, very indifferently argued by me. But I have often been surprized with Claps and Plauditts, and Hosannas,

when I have spoke but indifferently, and as often met with Inattention and neglect when I have thought I spoke very well.—How vain, and empty is Breath! (July 5, 1771, DA, 2:45)

Whatever moral lesson Adams might draw from his experience, he suggests one of the most compelling reasons for recourse to theater tropes: to phrase things in terms of actor and audience and to presume that the audience works in one's favor can "convert plain, common Sense, into profound Wisdom"; in a larger arena than a courtroom, one might go further and turn an internecine squabble over taxes and representation into a revolution of universal significance. The danger exists when no favorable audience can be found and an idea or cause is met with indifference or "pretty generally exploded and hissed off the stage" (Otis, 419).

Whether Americans turn to literary drama because they increasingly speak of the world as a stage or whether their reading of Shakespeare heightens their awareness of the figural importance of theater may be a chicken-and-egg question; but it is clear that in English American culture, the figure has prominence early and has a warrant for use that theater itself will not get until after the war, no matter how popular the Bard may become. The duality that Adams feels toward public speaking is reflected likewise in the drama versus theater tension of colonial New England. Whereas a young George Washington goes early and often to the theater in Williamsburg but almost never cites a play in his writing (Ford; Dunn, 104), John Adams and his northern contemporaries refer frequently to dramas without ever—or rarely—seeing a performance. In his diary and letters, Adams alludes to or draws lessons from such Shakespearean plays as *Richard III*, *Timon of Athens*, *The Taming of the Shrew*, *Henry VIII*, *Othello*, *King Lear*, and *Hamlet* (see Schlochauer, 160). In her letters to John and others, Abigail Adams cites *Othello*, *Macbeth*, *King Lear*, *Hamlet*, and *Julius Caesar*. With these and other allusions, the Adamses show a distinct preference for historical and tragic dramas. To her friend Mercy Warren, a great reader of Molière, Abigail thus criticizes the French playwright's comedy *Le Bourgeois Gentilhomme* as not entirely seemly—and thus speaks eloquently of New England attitudes in general: "Moliere is said to have been an Honest Man, but sure he has not coppied from his own Heart—tho he has drawn many pictures of real Life, yet all pictures of life are not fit to be exhibited upon the Stage. I fear I shall incur the charge of vanity by thus criticizing upon an Author who has met with so much applause" (Dec. 11, 1773, AFC, 1:89). One can apply drama to life only by a rigid principle of selection; neither a playwright's reputed honesty nor the exactness with which he or she may copy from life is a sufficient criterion of worth. Adherence to truth of the heart may simply mean to an ideal; but it also may be, again paradoxically, that the very staginess of comic drama undermines its own effectiveness as a moral guide for a people in travail.

Thus when northerners confront the actual stage, they display a variety of attitudes, but uneasiness is surely the most prominent. On a visit to London in 1768, the Philadelphia physician Benjamin Rush, later a leading patriot as well as friend and correspondent of John Adams, describes attending the theater "three or four evenings" where he saw, among other actors, the great David Garrick. Though he is much impressed with the actor, thinking Garrick "to be equal in every respect to his fame," Rush feels obligated to remark, "I never had much taste for public amusements," and in the remainder of his autobiography he says almost nothing more about them (Rush, 64). A cousin of Abigail Adams, Isaac Smith, Jr., writes to her from London that "the beauty of the Theatre consists in the scenery and in the representation" (Feb. 21, 1771, AFC, 1:70–71), while others make a point not to be so seduced by sensuality. Another Adams relative, Josiah Quincy, states quite flatly during his 1774 trip to England that the theater is a "nursery of vice" (Shaw, *American Patriots*, 157). And in 1778, traveling with his father in France, young John Quincy Adams writes to his sister Abigail that, of the many amusements available to him, "there is however but one sort of them that I care for and that is calld by the general name of Spectacles. these I like very well but Pappa wont let me go to them so often as I wish[.] he lets me go now and then especially if there happens to be a tragedy of Corneille Racine or Voltaire" (Sept. 27, 1778, AFC, 3:93–94). In other words, unless the theater dignifies itself by asserting the noblest sentiments as tragedy, it is best avoided; as John Quincy would often be told, the "stage of action" is of greater importance than the stage of actors.

For his father John, as for many of his generation, the stage of action first presents itself during the Stamp Act crisis. The literary response to the events of 1765 sets in motion a pattern of discourse that, while already latent, intensifies up to the Revolution, during and after which it continues. Adams, in the midst of writing a series of rhetorical letters that describe the colonies from the point of view of a British observer, comes across a passage in *Henry VIII* where the Queen pleads for removal of burdensome taxes. Shortly thereafter, in a passage never published in the Clarendon-Pym series, Adams allows Clarendon to voice what he sees as the American perspective, a vision reminiscent of the jeremiads. The colonials "are extreamly proud of their Country, . . . and they have a pious Horror, of consenting to any Thing, which may intail slavery on their Posterity. They think that the Liberties of Mankind and the Glory of human Nature is in their Keeping. They know that Liberty has been skulking about in Corners from the Creation, and has been hunted and persecuted, in all Countries, by cruel Power. But they flatter them selves that America was designed by Providence for the Theatre, on which science, Virtue, Liberty, Happiness and Glory were to exist in Peace" (DA, 1:281–82). Adams's expression of providential theater comes at a critical juncture in American popular rhetoric. Immediately behind this vision are the translatio studii, translatio imperii motifs in Bishop Berkeley's poem, "On the Prospect of Planting Arts and Learning in America." Ahead of it is the literature of Rising Glory and the belief that culturally, politically, and economically America will conclude the progressive drama of history (see Silverman, *Cultural History*, 232). The energy that inspires this vision, however, is much older than Berkeley's poem and comes out of the Puritan obsession with being observed, that sense of one's being an example—a spectacle—before God and humanity. At the other end, however, one cannot see past the arrival of Liberty and her sisters what precisely that prophesied "true figure" will be.

People of Adams's era conceive of Providence variously; as Mason Lowance reminds us, Calvinists observe two basic species of providences: the *general*, those established by the Creator at the beginning, and the *special*, "those miraculous intrusions into the natural order, explicable only through reference to God's election of His saints and concern for their welfare" (63–64). For the Puritans, special providences serve as instruments to remind a backsliding people of God's constant attentiveness; for Adams and his contemporaries, however, Providence often has a vaguer aspect, as if it means progress and therefore resembles the general providences of Puritans. What God has put into motion, no man or woman may deflect or stop; and by the same token, if Providence orders human action by a play, then no actor may change the outcome or, in the Stoic vein, rewrite the script.

Nevertheless, the course of Providence, even in an age of Reason, does not necessarily conform to human expectation. A few days after writing the Clarendon passage quoted above, Adams notes in his diary that "somebody has published the very scene in Shakespears H[enry] 8, which I have put into Ld. Clarendons Letter to Pym. This brings to my Mind again Ld. Bacons Doctrine of secret, invisible Connections and communications, and unknown undiscovered Laws of Nature" (Jan. 4, 1766, DA, 1:286). Adams seems to find in the publication of Shakespeare's passage a kind of natural spirit, something "in the air" which strikes several persons simultaneously and thus creates meaning simply by common recognition. In this case, Stamp Act, Liberty, Providence, and Theater conjoin in a reference to Shakespeare; and though the Revolutionary generation would speak a common political language scooped out of their reading of Whig and selected Continental political philosophers, they would need something like what "Shakespeare" represents: an instantly recognized symbolic language, whose proper frame, the stage, confers an imaginative power to otherwise quotidian acts. In other words, even life in a mechanistic universe (as Isaac Newton recognized) may require intrusions and adjustments—surprises as one might find in a cleverly plotted stage drama. Adams responds to another's public use of *Henry VIII* as if it were a part of some other public phenomenon, not some private or especially personal recognition only.

In his diary entries for the Stamp Act crisis, Adams betrays an exuberance about the workings of Providence on the American stage that later changes to solemnity as he takes on more responsibility. Like one of Rousseau's republicans, Adams often records with approval the outdoor festivals of celebration that follow significant events. In an entry for January 15, 1766, he describes an evening spent with the Sons of Liberty as they discuss how to react to the news of repeal of the

Stamp Act: "I heard afterwards they are to have such Illuminations, Bonfires, Piramids, Obelisks, such grand Exhibitions, and such Fireworks as were never before seen in America!—I wish they mayn't be disappointed" (DA, 1:294). For political actions "upon the Stage," in a favorite Adams phrase (for example, DA, 1:316), the appropriate theatrical response is spectacle—and Adams lists the range of possibilities open to ritual celebrants. Illuminated transparencies (framed boxes of thin paper on which slogans or pictures were drawn and lit from inside) make frequent appearances throughout the pre-Revolutionary period, and "exhibitions," which could be hung portraits or something like tableaux vivants, would be used later to telling effect as part of the Boston Massacre observances. Though Adams wishes the Sons of Liberty success in mounting their displays, the plan itself has far more importance than the executed reality; such plans are a symbolic acknowledgment of America's importance in providential history, as Adams's later favorable remarks on the massacre commemorations and the Boston Tea Party suggest. And even if mockery is sometimes a part of ritual affirmation (carts carrying pantomimists dressed as the Devil and Lord Bute, for instance), there remains a good deal of solemnity and spectacle to give credit to a rising nation.

With the people gathering for mass demonstrations (or, periodically, for mob violence), Adam begins to brood on both his country and his own role in its history. Unlike the naive sentiments expressed by Freneau and Brackenridge in their famous commencement poem, Adams foresees a more difficult path to rising glory. By 1771 he anticipates a break with England, long before the idea has popular currency. Things will get worse, he writes to Isaac Smith, Jr.: "War and Desolation shall close the melancholy Prospect. Out of such Desolation, Glory and Power, and Wonders may arise, to carry on the Designs of Providence" (AFC, 1:82). Increasingly, those "Designs" include him. Two years later, about to stand for election for membership in the Massachusetts Council (a seat he won, but his election was "negatived" by Governor Hutchinson), Adams considers his future conduct: "If I should be called in the Course of Providence to take a Part in public Life, I shall Act a fearless, intrepid, undaunted Part, at all Hazards—tho it shall be my endeavour likewise to act a prudent, cautious and considerate Part" (DA, 2:82). Thus it seems that Adams has been preparing himself for years for this moment, not only by his active involvement in legal and political affairs but also by his rhetorical-philosophical stance. Having seen the world as a stage, and one directed by Providence at that, Adams, as a reader of Epictetus, would consider carefully the part he must play.

Whatever it is, however, the role will not be comic. Like her husband, Abigail Adams has her antennae in the air and reads those Baconian "secret, invisible Connections and communications" as well as anyone. In a letter to Mercy Warren praising the fierce patriotism of her play, *The Adulateur*, Abigail expresses her fear of civil war and bloodshed. Though she is premature, her response to the tensions excited by the presence of the tea ship *Dartmouth* in the days before the Tea Party suggests how seriously she and her circle take the theatrical imperative: "Such is the present Spirit that prevails that if once they are made desperate Many, very Many of our Heroes will spread their lives in the cause, with the Speech of Cato in their Mouths, 'What a pitty it is, that we can dye but once to save our Country'" (*AFC*, 1:88). That the quoted speech from Addison's play would be essentially the last words ascribed to the captured American spy, Nathan Hale, less than three years later bears out her point: the times call for tragic drama and a shared dramatic discourse.

Events that follow only confirm for the patriots their united assumptions about the linked discussions of Providence and stage. After receiving word that Boston harbor would be closed to trade, John Adams theorizes to Abigail about the consequences, using a language that reinforces her Catonic prophecy: "We live my dear soul, in an Age of Tryal. What will be the Consequence I know not. The Town of Boston, for ought I can see, must suffer Martyrdom: It must expire: And our principal Consolation is, that it dies in a noble Cause. The Cause of Truth, of Virtue, of Liberty and of Humanity: and that it will probably have a glorious Reformation, to greater Wealth, Splendor and Power than ever" (May 12, 1774, *AFC*, 1:107). Adams avoids the histrionics of Whig sentimentalists (though he notes with approval Hancock's speech on the fourth anniversary of the massacre) (*DA*, 2:91). Instead, he combines Romanized political rhetoric with a Matherian vision of wonderful works, enacted out of the stage of self and onto the theater of Providence. As the popular demonstrations against Parliament and the British cabinet show, the wickedness of devils ultimately exposes itself as buffoonery; and thus those committed to the sacred cause of liberty must take pains not only to act out of their integrity but also to avoid being seen on the same stage as those who would degrade the performance. If patriotic Americans conceive of their actions as on a theater of Providence, then it is necessary to expel the devils from it. When Thomas Hutchinson's history of Massachusetts first begins to appear, John Adams notes (with some surprise) the "Disposition" of "his Country men . . . to hiss it from the Stage" (Mar. 17, 1766, DA, 1:306). Thus governmental actions inimical to American interests play as "Farce" (see, for example, DA, 1:310).

Perhaps Mercy Warren's response later to yet another British insult, the Massachusetts Government Act (1774), with its provision for a Crown-appointed Council, summarizes best what John and Abigail have been feeling: no triumph can be achieved without first elevating both drama and discourse to the most exalted levels. As she tells Abigail, "I think the appointment of the new counsel is the last comic Scene we shall see Exhibite'd in the state Farce which has for several years been playing off. I fear the Tragic part of the Drama will hastely Ensue, and that Nothing but the Blood of the Virtuous Citizens Can repurchase the Rights of Nature, unjustly torn from us by the united arms of treachery and Violence" (Aug. 9, 1774, AFC, 1:138). The patriot rhetoric of New Englanders never strays far from the image of a city on a hill. Once conceived as tragedy, the political crises of the 1770s attach themselves to an enlarged sense of mission; John Adams, then, does not exaggerate when he writes to Abigail of his trust in Providence and the "Designs of Heaven" for making the dangers facing an occupied Boston not only a rallying point for all the colonies but also "a Cause which interests the whole Globe" (May 2, 1775, AFC, 1:192; see Shaw, John Adams, 90).

Though denied a seat on the old Massachusetts council, Adams finds the role he anticipated earlier—as a member of the Continental Congress. With some excitement, Adams records that "there is a new, and a grand Scene open before me—a Congress" and that this body "will be an assembly of the wisest Men upon the Continent" (June 20, 1774, DA, 2:96). Yet Adams does not enter the scene simply for himself; as Abigail almost poignantly writes to her husband, "I long impatiently to have you upon the Stage of action," meaning as well, perhaps, that she would love to be in the thick of it herself (Aug. 19, 1774, AFC, 1:143). Regardless, the stage language functions as a shared code: their most private desires emerge at this time as hopes for public performance. For Abigail, the figure in John's letter to her written en route to Philadelphia can be no idle one: "Tomorrow," he writes from Princeton, "we reach the Theatre of Action" (Aug. 28, 1774, AFC, 1:144).

By mid-1776 the debates in that theater had turned from the practical matters of governance and war to the issue of full independence from Britain. The army had met with some success in forcing the British from Boston, but politically the Congress was not resolved on the independency question. In writing to his cousin Zabdiel Adams, a minister who had urged his congressional relative to support independence, John betrays some frustrations with the work of Congress and his public role in it. Echoing Hamlet, he considers that the seeming leisure of the cleric "in investigating the Moral Causes of our Miseries, and in pointing out the Remedies is devoutly to be wished. . . . Those who tread the public Stage, in Characters the most extensively conspicuous, meet with so many Embarrassments, Perplexities, and Disappointments, that they have often reason to wish for the peaceful Retreats of the Clergy" (June 21, 1776, AFC, 1:21–22). But Adams has essentially traded that intimate theater, as Cotton Mather describes it, of the believer and his God for a theater exposed; and as he had reflected on years before, with his experience in the dramatic reading club, his particular style of oratory had carried him to the law. So now, having phrased his life so frequently in the theater of action, not that of retreat, there could be no lingering, no devout wishful thinking. He is well aware, as he wrote in his diary ten years before, that "the Time will not be long e're, many who are now upon the Stage will be in their Graves" (DA, 1:316). Out of that dutiful urgency, he decides to remain on the theater of action for yet awhile longer.

Like Joseph Warren, who seems by the force of his sentimentalist rhetoric to require martyrdom at Bunker Hill, Adams appears as impelled by the shape of his figural language as by his own devotion to principle. Having already declared the Boston Tea Party "an Epocha in History," Adams writes to Abigail that the signing of the Declaration of Independence on July 2, 1776, is to be another of those signal days. In this case, he develops the meaning of the event further, portraying the signing in terms of its Rousseauvian consequences, as matter for future republican celebrations, and its Matherian implications, as cause for a jeremiad:

> The Second day of July 1776, will be the most memorable Epocha, in the History of America.—I am apt to believe that it will be celebrated, by succeeding Generations, as the great anniversary Festival. It ought to be commemorated, as the Day of Deliverance by solemn Acts of Devotion to God Almighty. It ought to be solemnized with Pomp and Parade, with Shews, Games, Sports, Guns, Bells, Bonfires and Illuminations from one End of this Continent to the other from this Time forward forever more.
>
> You will think me transported with Enthusiasms but I am not.—I am well aware of the Toil and Blood and Treasure, that it will cost Us to maintain this Declaration, and support and defend these States.—Yet through all the Gloom I can see the Rays of ravishing Light and Glory. (July 3, 1776, AFC, 2:30–31)

The ludic impulses of a people must be channeled toward a solemn end; yet at the same time, they must be given vent in a full array of theatrical activities. To Zabdiel Adams, he suggests that before there can be retreat there must first be action; so now to Abigail he says that before there can be comic extravaganza (solemn, of course), tragedy must precede it. Though Adams could not anticipate that the day to be celebrated would be July 4, the day of the publication of the Declaration—and, as the date fifty years later of Adams's own death, a day that appears to have been providentially chosen—his picture once again proves prescient. So there is some irony, perhaps, in Adams's recollection of the day years later, when bitterness over what he saw as the neglect of his role in history would consume him: " 'The Declaration of Independence I always considered as a theatrical show,' he told Benjamin Rush. 'Jefferson ran away with all the stage effect . . . and all the glory of it' " (June 21, 1811, Shaw, *John Adams*, 100).

Adams, of course, is not alone in anticipating future glory; many writers of the period repeat the image of a glorious show or pageant succeeding one of darkness, though they are motivated by diverse ideological or rhetorical stances. Evangelicals like Timothy Hilliard insist that contrary to liberal theologians or to anyone adhering to what Catherine Albanese describes as the *deus otiosus*, the lazy, distant divinity (117), God still listens to, feels for, saves us as before; he is no "less disposed to deliver those that trust in him than he ever was" (Hilliard, 13). In other words the special providences still hold. Indeed, anyone with sense can see how this is so. After all, says Samuel Sherwood, "there is no part of this terraqueous globe better fitted and furnished in all the essential articles and advantages, to make a great and flourishing empire; no part of the earth, where learning, religion, and liberty have flourished more for the time. And as to the rapid increase of its inhabitants, and swift population, it cannot be paralleled in all history" (17). For some evangelicals, this prophesying of future glory takes on a millennialist coloring. In 1776 Ebenezer Baldwin, for instance, imagines America "shall be the principal Seat of that glorious Kingdom, which Christ shall erect upon Earth in the latter Days" and looks forward to the time in 1976 when "the American Empire will be in its Glory" (38, 39n). Likewise, for his Plymouth anniversary sermon of 1777, Samuel West sees in Isaiah 66 "a prophecy of the dispensations of divine providence towards his church and people in New England" that allows him to remain confident of victory and American independence: "This Country will become the seat of civil and religious liberty . . . so that our Zion shall become the delight and the praise of the whole earth" (6, 49; see P. Davidson, 249, 250). But even millenarian piety blends with the theatrical language of the time. In words that John Adams would no doubt second, David Humphreys remarks that his country "was probably discovered in the maturity of time, to become a theater for displaying the illustrious designs of Providence" (quoted in Bercovitch, *American Jeremiad*, 122); and when the president of the College of William and Mary, James Madison (cousin of the future United States president), uses nearly the same phrasing, he adds that rhetorical heightening so likely to stir a patriotic audience. Let us, he asks his fellow Virginians, "turn our eyes to the scene which now lies before us, a scene, which, whilst it exhibits as it were, living proofs of the subject, upon which we speak, cannot fail, at the same time, to revive within us that love for a country, favoured by Heaven itself, which nothing but death shall overcome.—For lo! America has become the theatre, whereon the providence of God is now manifested" (A *Sermon, preached in the County of Botetourt,* 11; see Ginsberg, 31). Still moved by ancient figures of the world as a stage upon which the divine displays its will, and coached by a providential prompter, John Adams and his fellow patriots could well afford to pledge "our Lives, our Fortunes and our sacred Honor" in the cause of liberty. Cast as they were as heroes of the tragedy then playing on the Theater of Action, they knew that another show, a pageant of glory, was yet to come.

IV

The Theater

of Glory,

1776–1789

CHAPTER ELEVEN

A Theater Just Erected:
America at War

*A*s Americans entered the era of independence, those committed to the patriot cause tied their hopes to Washington's army, the Continental Congress, and the designs of Providence; and for the easily discouraged, the beginning of the war would have required an especial faith in the latter. Nevertheless, with God conceived of as the Great Director, America as a Theater of Providence, and the war effort as the Stage of Action, Americans could marshal their energies toward fulfilling roles in a divinely appointed Tragedy, the completion of which would leave the stage open for a Spectacle of Glory, the end of one show and perhaps the beginning of another. Those on the side of Yankee Doodle and hasty pudding did not need ethnographers or sociologists to tell them that a dramaturgical model helps explain societal interactions; they knew already, and knew it dynamically, that America likened to a stage was not simply a rhetorical trick: it was an article of faith. Insofar as rhetoric reflects reality, the theatrical figures of speech and the playlike rituals of the Revolutionary period mirror a society in political upheaval. At the same time, the reverse also holds; and with the outbreak of war shaped as much by rhetoric as principle, the insistence during the previous decade—indeed, since the beginnings of English civilization in America—that the colonial situation is a special theater where the drama of history will be played, leads men and women of the time to need war, need catastrophe, in order to resolve the tensions created by the providential plot.

During the war, the actual theater remains a renegade institution; while the British set up as lively a theatrical culture as conditions would permit, first in Boston, briefly in Philadelphia, and for the duration of the war in New York, the Continental Congress passed a resolution in 1774 to "discountenance and discourage every species of extravagance and dissipation, especially all horse-racing, and all kinds of gaming, cockfighting, exhibitions of shows, plays, and other expensive diversions and entertainments" (*Journals of Congress*, 1:33, quoted in Albanese, 196). Plays did not disappear behind patriot lines; Washington staged *Cato* at Valley Forge in spring 1778 no doubt to inspire morale, and the army situated in Portsmouth, New Hampshire, witnessed a production of *Coriolanus* (Dunn, 120; Silverman, *Cultural History*, 350, 364–65). But when later that same year Lafayette asked the president of Congress, Henry Laurens of South Carolina, to see a play, the president politely refused. The Congress had just passed a second law, firmer this time, "for the suppression of theatrical amusements," and while it was not universally enforced, it made its point to patriots that a living theater was not consistent with a metaphoric one (Albanese, 197).

Still, political closet dramas continue to appear, and the best of those make use of theater metaphors as a way of justifying the form. In 1776, three plays of note are published. Hugh Henry Brackenridge's *The Battle of Bunkers-Hill: A Dramatic Piece of five acts, in heroic measures* is a series of declamations, designed by the then-schoolteacher as an "exercise in oratory" (Meserve, 82), but one which gives dignity (if not accuracy) to the events surrounding the first major battle of the war. Following Washington's retreat from Long Island, an anonymous Tory propagandist wrote *The Battle of Brooklyn. A farce of two acts. As it was performed on Long Island, on Tuesday the 27th day of August, 1776. By the representatives of the tyrants of America assembled at Philadelphia*, a scathing piece of satire clearly intended to reduce the American effort to the lowest and most laughable type of entertainment. These two plays represent the poles of Revolutionary rhetoric: patriotic heroic tragedy against British-Tory mocking farce, the one a strategy of elevation and encouragement, the other of deflation and discouraging humiliation.

The most interesting of the 1776 plays is one by the otherwise little-known John Leacock, *The Fall of British Tyranny; or, American Liberty Triumphant*. As with the others, the subtitle reveals much: *The First campaign. A tragic-comedy of five acts. As lately planned at the Royal Theatrum Pandemonium at St. James's. The principal place of action in America.* Written sometime after the appearance of *Common Sense* in January 1776 but before the British evacuation of Boston (Meserve, 78), Leacock's play is especially aware of itself as a play and makes much of the cross-references between itself and a world already figured as a stage. The action opens with the British ministers plotting their anti-American strategy; they are led by the sinister Lord Paramount (Bute) who works his Machiavellian designs against both America and the present British government. Some peers and commoners assert colonial rights, Lord Wisdom (Chatham) and Lord Patriot (Wilkes) among them; but the tone in the first acts is one marked by bad humor and comic villainy. Later, however, the drama shifts from British-Tory farce to patriot tragedy. Sufferings at Bunker Hill, Quebec, and Ticonderoga are all presented as the intense sacrifices a people in travail must bear. The play ends with Generals Washington and Putnam dedicating themselves to fight for liberty, no matter how bad the situation now.

Dedicated satirically by the homespun patriot hero Dick Rifle, the play opens with Rifle's address "To LORD BOSTON [General Thomas Gage], and the REMNANT of the ACTORS, MERRY ANDREWS, and strolling PLAYERS, in Boston, LORD KIDNAPPER [Lord Dunmore, the embattled Virginia royal governor], and the rest of the PIRATES and BUCCANEERS . . . in AMERICA" (iii). Rifle/Leacock pursues a middle course between comic deflation and heroic enhancement, throwing back at the British their own misbegotten mode of amusement but recognizing all the while where the real theater is:

> *My Lords and Gentlemen,*
> Understanding you are vastly fond of plays and farces, and frequently exhibit them for your own amusement, and the laudable purpose of ridiculing your masters (the *Yankees*, as you call 'em) it was expected you would have been polite enough to have favoured the world, or America at least, (at whose expense you act them) with some of your play-bills, or with a sample of your composition.   (iii)

Where the British turn all to farce, the American presenter forbears "to copy your churlishness"; after all, "as the most of you have already acted your particular parts of it, both comic and tragic, in reality at Lexington, Bunker's-hill, the Great-Bridge, &c. &c. &c. to the very great applause of yourselves, tho' not of the whole house, no doubt you will preserve the marks, or memory of it, as long as you live . . . on your posteriors" (iii). The play being dedicated to the British is a "re-acting [of] this Tragi-Comedy" that has already gone before, one they have not understood because they have expected to be entertained, not engaged. They have applauded themselves in the small world of their stage amusements but missed the fact that the larger world awaits for their successors to mount the macrocosmic boards. Therefore Rifle regrets he cannot join them because he realizes how threatening the shifting perspective he brings is to the British cause: "I have reason to think you would not of choice let me come within three hundred yards of your stage, lest I should rob you of your laurels, receive the clap of the whole house, and pass for a second Garrick among you, as you know I always act with applause, speak bold— point blank—off hand—and without a prompter" (iv).

Rifle signs off somewhat less subtly than he begins: "I am, *My Lords and Gentlemen Buffoons,* Your already ready and humble servant, DIC RIFLE"; but he can afford to be smug. Unlike his British counterparts, the American gets his applause with his natural speech, unrehearsed, unprompted, but riflelike, direct, "point blank—off hand." These are also the qualities of the stage Yankee, a figure that would be made popular by Royall Tyler's *The Contrast,* but Rifle's assessment of his speech also foreshadows the program of Walt Whitman; both Leacock's swaggering Yankee and Whitman's loafing "kosmos" require the open air to be heard. To act in the world, away from the artifice of the playhouse, changes the conditions of performance. Leacock seems to say that it is no use for a Burgoyne (Mr. Caper in the play) to emulate or, as Lord Rawdon has said, be "our Garrick." If that famous actor has come to represent the epitome of the natural style, then, appropriately, the natural American would better fit the title of "a second Garrick"—especially if, as Americans are told by poets and preachers alike, they are to be the ones who bring the triumphant arts to their greatest height.

But that last consideration during the armed crisis could only be a dream deferred, for in a sense, *The Fall of British Tyranny* as a play destroys itself by its own terms of composition. As Kenneth Silverman asks rhetorically of wartime America, "What need for plays, when, as Francis Hopkinson said, 'AMERICA is at this time a scene of desolation and distress; a theatre whereon is acted a real tragedy'" (Hopkinson, *Miscellaneous Essays* [1792], 1:103, quoted in Silverman, *Cultural History*, 297). This tension arises in the prologue as well; ostensibly delivered by one Peter Buckstail, the poem is offered only because it is the "fashion" to have one—for in fact, the play is a call to supraplayhouse action:

> Now ring the bell—come forth, ye actors, come,
> The Tragedy's begun, beat, beat the drum,
> Let's all advance, equipt like volunteers,
> Oppose the foe, and banish all our fears.
> We will be free—or bravely we will die,
> And leave to Tories tyrants legacy,
> And all our share of its dependency.   (vii)

Through the prologue and Dick Rifle's satiric contrast between real and metaphoric theater, Leacock prevents himself from saying anything more with drama; he and his fellow patriots must do all their acting on the theater of war.

Certainly, the laws against stage plays would have suited the evangelical ministers who were themselves mounting a spirited campaign against British oppression. Topical sermons express the conflict as a moral struggle or, fueled by what James Davidson calls the "logic of millennial thought," as the approach of a distinct moment in theological history when the long-delayed achievement of a virtuous nation now seems at hand. Nevertheless, the patriot clergy add their own component to the general theatrical conception of the times. When Peter Thacher preaches to Massachusetts militiamen on the perils of 1777, he finds parallels in the Roman as well as the Jewish past. To speculate on a future where the Revolution has failed, Thacher, like many of his colleagues, resorts to sentimentalist scene setting with both the boldness of a prophet and the delicacy of a man of feeling:

But why doth busy imagination hurry me to a scene still more distressing, why doth it transport me to the field of blood, the place of execution for the friends of american liberty! Who doth it there call me to view led to the scaffold, with the dignity of *Cato*, the firmness of a *Brutus* and the gentleness of a *Cicero* in his countenance? It is the gallant *Washington* deserted by his countrymen and sacrificed because he loved his Country and fought in its defense! Of whom consists yonder group of heroes! It is an *Hancock*, an *Adams*, a *Franklin*, a *Lee*, an *Harrison* who—but I drop the curtain, I repress the bursting torment, my soul is bowed with unutterable grief!   ("Sermon on 2 Samuel 10.12, preached after Independence, 1777," in Sermons Collection, Box 2, Folder 37, American Antiquarian Society, quoted in Stout, 306)

What may strike us now—and most surely did strike loyalist ministers then—as a shameless appeal to emotions is an extension of Great Awakening enthusiasm to a new context, where the sacred cause is liberty and the showmanship carefully modulated to appeal to the broadest spectrum of listeners. With war on their soil and the threats to their safety material as well as spiritual, preachers like Thacher do not need to make themselves spectacles before the masses, as did the histrionic Whitefield a scant generation earlier. Though the great itinerants wept and gestured on their platform stages in front of thousands, the stages they meant to affect were the individual, internal stages of psychomachic contention. A Peter Thacher, on the other hand, asks the militiamen to look outside themselves, to turn their tears into external action on a larger theater—before the curtain is untimely dropped.

While histrionic rhetoric serves the patriot-evangelical cause, it is ultimately tangential to the matter of theater and its figures. For the British forces and their supporters, participation in theatricals becomes, in essence, a test of loyalty. A Hessian soldier, Johan Ewald, compares the baggage of American patriots and the British: in the one, he says, are books of political theory; in the "portmanteux" of the British, on the other hand, are "bags of hair powder, boxes of sweet-smelling pomatum, cards (instead of maps), and then often, on top of all, novels or stage plays" (Wright, 120). Indeed, wherever the main force of the British army establishes itself, the amusements of the stage come too. Following the truncated Boston season, a new one opens in occupied Philadelphia. Here the officers could show their talents as thespians and wooers, restoring an old theater with new scenery, fresh ladies in the boxes, and a well-worn motto, *"Totus mundus agit histrionem"* (Sargent, 170). Thus while Washington and his army lick their wounds at Valley Forge, the army of Howe could look forward to a splendid season on the boards.

For the first performance, a widow-and-orphan benefit staged on December 24, 1777, the multitalented officer John André penned a prologue that establishes how completely the British had given themselves over to a theatricalized vision of the war effort. André, who also served as a scene painter and a leading actor, sees fame on the field and bays on the stage as intimately connected:

> Once more, ambitious of theatric glory,
> Howe's strolling company appears before ye.
> O'er hills and dales and bogs, thro' wind and weather
> And many hair-breadth 'scape, we've scrambled hither.
> For we, true vagrants of the Thespian race,
> Whilst summer lasts ne'er know a settled place.
> Anxious to prove the merit of our band,
> A chosen squadron wanders thro' the land.
> How beats each Yankie bosom at our drum—
> —"Hark, Jonathan! zaunds, here's the strollers come!"
> (Sargent, 173)

In André's vision, the benighted Americans are overwhelmed by the soldierly performance of the British; the stroll from theater of war to stage of entertainment is without interruption, leaving the Yankees to marvel at British playing. With Washington encamped for the winter, no one fears a repeat of the *Blockade of Boston* episode, where rival theaters collided to the discomfiture of the British. For André and his fellow officers, exercise on the battlefield is simply the price of admission to the real shows on stage.

Of all the events during the war that distinguish British and American interests, few could rival the mounting of an extravaganza called *The Mischianza*. Based on various fetes held a few years before in England, *The Mischianza* was a monumental celebration of British luxury and power. In a lengthy letter, André, a chief designer of the pageant, details the elaborate ceremonies with rows of knights and squires, a regatta, ladies in Turkish dress, a cornucopia, and the like (Sargent, 186–97). Though for the brothers Howe nothing could show their contempt for the enemy as well as this, the sumptuousness of the affair proved to be much more ominous a sign than the self-congratulatory nature of *The Mischianza* was intended to display. For the Tory Israel Mauduit, the show could hardly be accepted as a pageant of triumph when its sponsoring general had yet to be victorious on the battlefield (17). Judge Thomas Jones of New York also recounts his objections to the squandering of time and resources on entertainments. Just as the Sons of Liberty hoped in 1766 to create an unexampled celebration, so the amusements planned by General Howe and Admiral Howe—games of faro, cockfights, plays, exhibitions of Oriental splendor—were "something before unknown to the New World, perhaps to the old" (*History of New York during the Civil War*, 1:237–61, quoted in Edelberg, 77).

Not surprisingly, then, when loyalist writers refer to a metaphoric stage, they do so in the tradition of a culture for whom theater remains an essentially unquestioned institution. An anonymous poem entitled, "The Epilogue" (1778), uses the endplay formula to urge peace between the two sides: "Our farce is now finish'd," the poem begins, trotting out the usual Tory figure for the war—an appropriate one in the context as the concluding show of the evening. The writer presses in deliberate doggerel the stage-world connection in terms familiar to a theatergoing public:

> Old Shakespeare, a poet, who should not be spit on,
> Altho' he was born in the island called Britain,
> Hath said that mankind are all players at best,
> A truth we'll admit of, for sake of the jest.
> (Pickering, 254)

The stage the writer has in mind is "puny"; and while the poet turns attention to hopes for peace between the Georges, he or she necessarily deflates the seriousness of the rift by keeping the reader aware of a world made small.

Other Tory poets, however, take a less charitable view of the proceedings, hoping to deflate through ridicule the patriot effort. One of the most notorious, the Anglican cleric Jonathan Odell, uses a dramatic trope to insist both on a reductive analogy to low amusement and on the ruthless antidemocratic bias of a society for whom theater equals culture. In "The Congratulation" (1779), for instance, Odell taunts his countrymen for their apparent failure to conclude a success-ful Franco-American alliance:

> Joy to great Congress, joy a hundred fold:
> The grand cajolers are themselves cajol'd!
> The farce of empire will be finish'd soon,
> And each mock-monarch dwindle to a loon.
> (Pickering, 222)

Odell reveals a host of Tory attitudes in this one stanza. Besides its tone of bitter mockery, the poem exposes the long-touted course of empire, the translatio imperii, as nothing more than a farce and the American rude mechanicals (or as Tory John Bullman calls them, "every silly clown and illiterate mechanic") who take on the roles of state and fancy themselves (player) kings as each but a "loon" (quoted in P. Davidson, 293). Odell would no doubt agree with fellow Tory poet Myles Cooper, who in *The Patriots of North America* (1775) decries what happens when the vulgar exceed their station; these patriots, "half Knaves, half Fools / . . . from their own dear Puppet-Show, / The World's great Stage, [only] pretend to know" (quoted in P. Davidson, 294).

Yet even a virulent antipatriot like Odell could turn theatrical tropes against his own side. A friend of John André, Odell tried his own hand at theatrical prologues. With British forces safely en-sconced in New York and Sir Henry Clinton, the new commander-in-chief, supportive of the theater, Odell wrote a prologue entitled, "The World's a Stage and All the Men and Women Merely Players" (1778). As his most recent literary biographer, Cynthia Dubin Edel-berg, describes it, the prologue is a "sermon in verse," a gentle tweak-ing of British-loyalist mores. Like his patriot opposites, Odell imag-ines a celestial casting director but one who has had relatively little success:

> Yes—from the days of Mother Eve till now,
> We've been playing, and—the Lord knows how!
> The Stage of Life presents, at every view,
> A thousand shifting Scenes; and yet how few,
> Among the busy millions do we find
> Content to play the part by Heaven assign'd!
> (Edelberg, 82)

As the title of the prologue implies, Odell's theatrum mundi holds forth to sight a Shakespearean comedy, not a providential tragedy. Drama serves as a commentary on social life, stripped of all but the vaguest historical assumptions; not surprisingly, Erasmus's *Praise of Folly* casts its shadow on Odell's text. By evoking "Heaven," the poet ascribes the universal significance to his observations, but unlike the patriots who use theatrical rhetoric, he stops short of any progressive vision. Things in this world, as for Shakespeare, are essentially the same, and people are subject to the standard acquisitive vices:

> In love, in politics, in peace or war,
> One day they covet, and the next abhor.
> In this alone they seem to act by rule;
> In every shifting scene to play the fool.   (82–83)

Thus one justifies stage drama for its reminder to human beings of their foolishness:

> Then let the mimic Scene, to candid eyes,
> Exhibit Vice and Folly as they rise.
> The Muse holds up her Glass, and if it show
> Our image there reflected—I suppose
> The wiser way would be, instead of railing
> To take the hint, and rectify the failing.   (83)

Applied to the patriots, Tory theatrical language aims to reduce high sentence to the farcical babbling of fools; applied to themselves, figures from the stage function as a conservative corrective for a theatrically self-referring culture. The scenes may be shifting, but the message remains the same: watch the play, see yourselves, "rectify the failing." Apparently, however, Clinton and his coterie did not want to "take the hint" from this poem; Odell's future prologues make no further mention of British "Vice and Folly" (Edelberg, 83).

Odell's social-aesthetic mimickry of Shakespeare reveals the limitations, finally, of the loyalist perspective. When theater only serves as criticism, it remains an ahistorical, antiprogressive trope, phrased either as denigrating spoof or self-serving reproof. What Catherine Albanese has to say about the Tories' inability to match the appeal of patriot "civil religion" applies to the use of theater as well: "The Loyalists failed, in the final analysis, not because they were poorer, less astute politically, less well educated, less shrewd, less situated in positions of communal responsibility, but because they had no story to match in cogency and inner truth the sacred story which the patriot leaders were noising abroad among the masses" (14). Not only did they lack a story—the vehicle by which the loyalists attempted to critique the war, theater *as it is*, could not match the rhetorical power of the more dynamic figure, theater *as it should be*. So perhaps it is that in any class revolution, as the American to some extent is, bourgeois theater must give way to providential drama, and amusement of the few must be overturned by the rituals and festivals of the many.

To be sure, nothing in a performance of *The Beaux' Stratagem*, to name one often-mounted play among the elite, could possibly match the force of ritualized mass demonstration on the popular imagination. Among the various effigy-burnings (of Hutchinson and Oliver, for instance) and cart shows (the Devil and Lord Bute or by 1780 Beelzebub and Benedict Arnold), one of the most curious and compelling character-rituals is that of Joyce Junior. The origins of this folk figure are obscure, but both before and during the war, this costumed horseman would lead processions gathered for summary judgment of those who represented oppressive power (Shaw, *American Patriots*, 189–91). Writing to her husband on April 10, 1777, Abigail Adams describes one such ritual. Five men identified as Tories "were carted out of Boston under the direction of Joice junr. who was mounted on Horse back with a Red coat, a white Wig and a drawn Sword, with Drum and fife following; a Concourse of people to the amount of 500 followed. They proceeded as far as Roxbury when he ordered the cart to be timped up, then told them if they were ever catchd in Town again it should be at the expence of their lives" (*AFC*, 2:218). With patriot life reenergized by theatricalized acts of genuine consequence, anything more remote from the perceived drama of war and revolutionary politics could not have the same impact. In a letter to Abigail written a month later from Philadelphia, John Adams tells his wife of an exhibition of wax sculpture by Patience Lovell Wright, America's first such artist. She includes all the right Whig heroes with appropriate allegorical scenes, and, charitably, Adams remarks that "there is Genius, as well as Taste and Art, discovered in the Exhibition." However, none of those qualities can overcome his chief objection: "The Imitation of

Life was too faint, and I seemed to be walking among a Group of Corps's, standing, sitting, and walking, laughing, singing, crying, and weeping. This Art I think will make but little Progress in the World" (May 10, 1777, AFC, 2:235). Though admittedly it is a leap from waxwork tableaux to living theater, the generalization still holds: no theater smaller or less dynamic than the streets, battlefields, and political halls of America can impel or compel the people to action, especially in a society with little taste for bourgeois amusements, as strongly as that theater figured for Providence.

And how the Adams family itched to be on that theater! By the war, Abigail's wish for John to be on the stage had already been fulfilled, but to her friend Mercy Warren she betrays some dissatisfaction with her own role, as a woman having to watch, presumably, the horrors of war: "O my dear Friend when I bring Home to my own Dwelling these tragical Scenes which are every week presented in the Publick papers to us, and only in Idea realize them, my whole Soul is distress'd. Were I a man I must be in the Field. I could not live to endure the Thought of my Habitation desolated, my children Butcherd, and I an inactive Spectator" (Aug. 14, 1777, AFC, 2:314). Abigail's uneasiness with her role contrasts with the Odellian vision of everyone remaining in an "assign'd" part. In another letter, she defends her sex against the notion that a renowned woman like Catharine Macaulay should be considered an exception to the gender, not the rule. After all, "the Females . . . have a part to act upon the great Theater, and a part not less important to Society" than that of men (to John Thaxter, Feb. 15, 1778, AFC, 2:391). Her own conception of that part may be domestic, but the fact that she speaks of an essential equality between the sexes in terms of responsibility in the great Theater suggests how the metaphor encodes a process of social upheaval.

Both John and Abigail realize, however, that they do not enter the stage only for themselves. In one of the most ringing appeals of *The Crisis*, number 1, Thomas Paine attacks those who would prefer peace in their time to making the world better for their children through sacrifice now. So it is, too, that the Adamses prepare their son, John Quincy, for the future to which they devote their actions. Study only the best authors, John tells his son, those "who will afford you the most solid Instruction and Improvement for the Part which may be allotted you to act on the Stage of Life" (Aug. 11, 1777, AFC, 2:307). In fact, for the son, that future would become present while war still persisted. Though only eleven, he goes with his father to France in 1778, enduring the dangers of wartime transatlantic travel, for the opportunity to reach the continent that John describes as "thou great Theatre of Arts, Sciences, Commerce, War" (DA, 2:292). That theater has its hazards, of course. As mother Abigail tells her child in a letter full of advice, "You have entrd early in life upon the great Theater of the world which is full of temptations and vice of every kind" (June [10?], 1778, AFC, 3:38). But significantly she urges him to return to history, not the stage, for instruction. For those in the theater of Providence, holding the mirror up to nature is never lesson enough.

Possibly because the stage-minded patriots anticipated a tragic struggle at the beginning, the length of war must have worked to their advantage; that it was not over quickly gave hope even in defeat that something better was to come. Expressing that confidence that Providence would turn the war fully in their favor, Mercy Warren returns to the theatrical figure in order to look past the expected defeat of the British: "America is a theatre just erected—the drama is here but begun, while the actors of the old world have run through every species of pride, luxury, venality, and vice—their characters will become less interesting, and the western wilds which for ages have been little known, may exhibit those striking traits of wisdom, and grandeur and magnificance, which the Divine oeconomist may have reserved to crown the closing scene" (to Abigail Adams, Mar. 15, 1779, AFC, 3:191). She varies the trope from the prewar usage to show that America is no longer a stage on the (old) world theater but is now its own house, as if to say that once having fulfilled the prophecies of transplantation, America ceases to need any other theater than itself. Nevertheless, she still retains the image of the "closing scene," the end in the beginning, the fulfillment of history in the birth of a nation, in a metaphor that ultimately represents a deflected Christography. In this sense, the new America is the New Testament, even the newborn Christ, the patriots so many martyrs, and the future glory of America a virtuous type of the theocratic millennium promised in Revelation. Phrased as *theater*, the focus remains resolutely public; salvation is imaged as the restoration of beauty and spectacle following the carnage on the theater of blood. The struggles of the individual resolve themselves in universal participation, and the safety of one's soul connects with the security of the nation. For many Americans, the Revolution was one of those signal moments in history, comparable to the birth of Christ in significance (Albanese, 107); in Mercy Warren's theater, progressive history is conflated, fast-forwarded to the show for which so many have been waiting.

If theater, a far less threatening image than the Day of Judgment, absorbs within its metaphoric boundaries the millennialist strivings of a nation at war, its ambiguities as a figure still persist. Having described in her letter to Abigail Adams a newly erected theater, Mercy Warren the following year seems nearly to raze it. Writing to Abigail, she expresses her weariness with the war: "*Curiosity* burns not so high in my Bosom as it has done in Former Days. I feel more Indifferent to the transactions on a Theatre which will soon be taken down, or the actors Removed to more permanent scenes" (Mar. 10, 1780. *AFC*, 3:296). To be sure, she is speaking of two different theaters—the one specifically connected with the war, and so of limited duration; and the other tied to the long-range life of the country, the place of display for risen glory. But the application of the metaphor to both situations leads potentially to future ambiguity. Patriots have engaged in an extraordinary rebellion of colony against mother country, risking parental disapproval and terrible punishment, yet they have urged themselves forward in a rhetoric of divine affirmation, figured in theatrical terms. How does one continue to refer to America in the language of the universal stage once the wartime show is over?

One episode near the end of the war highlights the tension between rival concepts or figures of stage. In September 1780, on his return from West Point where he has just schemed with Benedict Arnold, Major John André is captured by American militiamen and eventually brought to trial as a spy. For the popular British officer, by now Sir Henry Clinton's aide-de-camp, the arrest and charge must have come as a rude shock; he seems not to have understood, until late in the proceedings, which stage he played upon. For Washington, angry at Arnold's treason, mindful of the hanging of Nathan Hale, and needing to make clear to the British the seriousness of rebel resolve, there is no ambiguity. During his detainment, André claims to have been dressed as he is, a British officer; but at the trial, he is formally charged with wearing the clothes of deceit: *"That he changed his dress within our lines, and under a feigned name, and in a disguised habit"* (*Proceedings*, 13). Such a charge in wartime could bring only one punishment: "He ought to suffer death" (13). André's subsequent execution, at which the accused spy cut a noble, even tragic, figure in the eyes of observers, draws outraged cries from all fronts, including some patriots (see, for example, the eyewitness account included in *Major André's Journal*, 108–9). One loyalist speaks for many when he asks, "Why was that farce acted?" but he soon changes metaphor, calling Washington the "MURDERER of Major André" and "the principal actor in the tragedy, and the most guilty in this dark business" (Inglis, 20, 22). Washington, by allowing André's hanging to be carried out, at once deprives the New York stage of one of its leading players and bequeaths to future American theater history (through William Dunlap's 1798 play, *André*) a symbol of American ambivalence toward England (Amer). More importantly, though, he leaves no confusion about his own loyalties to the stage of history in the theater of the world (Scheer and Rankin, 381–88; Fliegelman, 215–19; Silverman, *Cultural History*, 377–82). Through the figure of the theatrum mundi, patriot rhetoric had given to Washington a tactical advantage that the British, trapped in a rhetoric of social performance, could not overcome.

For the Americans fighting the war as a providential drama, the satisfactions of triumph inspire a language of completion. Two days before the surrender at Yorktown, Philip Freneau published a poem in the *Freeman's Journal* that purports to be a letter from the despairing Cornwallis to his commander-in-chief, Sir Henry Clinton. In it, Freneau imagines the Americans' adversary as weary of the theater on which he has struggled:

> Tired with long acting on the bloody stage,
> Sick of the follies of a wrangling age,
> Come with your fleet, and help me retire
> To Britain's coast, the land of my desire.
> (*Poems*, 2:90)

For his own side, however, war's end gives another shape to the metaphor that Freneau assigns to Cornwallis.

Washington's great victory inspires his aide-de-camp to utter the winner's response to the conclusion of a theatrically framed conflict. "The play is over," the Marquis de Lafayette writes to the Comte de Maurepas, "the fifth act has just ended. I was a bit uneasy during the first acts, but my heart keenly enjoyed the last one" (Oct. 20, 1781, *Letters*, 422). For Lafayette, there would be time again to play on other stages. For his general, however, the end of the drama means more than simply a chance to celebrate. Stoic to the last, Washington speaks to his army before its disbandment in terms now thoroughly familiar to the troops: "Nothing now remains but for the actors of this mighty scene to preserve a perfect unvarying consistency of character through the very last act, to close the drama with applause; and to retire from the military theatre with the same approbation of angels and men which have crowned all their former actions" (Apr. 18, 1783, quoted in Albanese, 105–6). Washington is not yet finished, however; less eager than John Adams to mount the stage of action, no one more assiduously desires to get off it and out of the public eye than the commander-in-chief. Having been watched as a figure on a military stage for so long, and having fought the war with the play of *Cato* as his guide, he cannot help but frame his thoughts in the figure of theater. In his *Circular Letter* (1783), Washington explains to state governors his ideas about his country as he prepares to leave the public scene and congratulates his fellow citizens on what they have achieved. In doing so, he unites all the pieces of the nationalist theatrical formula in one succinct package. As Americans are now "acknowledged to be possessed of absolute freedom and independency, they are from this period to be considered as actors on a most conspicuous theatre, which seems to be peculiarly designed by Providence for the display of human greatness and felicity" (8). The beauty of the passage is hardly its originality; rather, it is the compactness with which Washington renders a sustaining rhetorical convention. For the literally retiring general, the "conspicuous theatre" of Providence has been the space on which he has defined for Americans the ideal public life. Therefore, as he prepares to resign his commission before Congress in Annapolis, December 23, 1783, he returns once more to the trope by which he has measured his actions: "Having now finished the work assigned me, I retire from the great theatre of Action, and bidding an Affectionate farewell to this August body under whose order I have so long acted, I here offer my Commission, and take my leave of all the employments of public life" (quoted in Middlekauff, 584).

In the noble wartime theater of a Washington, as in the prewar arena of John Adams, the actor accepts applause with reluctance; the applause confirms that the act was carried off, but it means nothing else. Satisfaction comes not from praise but from right performance and achievement. Washington seeks retreat at Mount Vernon because it represents a return, a reconnection to an older way of being; and thus, ironically, the metaphor that has given the participants in the war a dynamic code for change proves, at one level at least, to account also for stopping change. The political landscape and regnant ideology have been substantially altered by war and the rhetoric of war. When one then lets down the curtain, steps off the stage, and sends the spectators home, the prevision of continuous spectacle has no meaning without restoration of the theatrical figure.

At Yorktown, the British band played an old tune whose theme was familiar more than a century before to English radicals, "The World Turned Upside Down" (Hill, 308). For the foot soldier–mechanic–farmer class, the metaphoric drama has only been *like* a tragedy. In a true class revolution, the dramatic analogy more closely resembles a Plautine comedy of reversal but one in which the end is cut short. Once the senex is routed (the king defeated), keep the old man from coming back; once the servants (the people) seize power, retain it at all costs. The prewar crises unleashed popular ludic energies that could be turned by theorists and orators into mass political action. With war's end, and for many, with the world overturned, those play impulses need further outlets. To ask those citizens leaving the stage of war to return to a theatrically barren world, where the stage remains suppressed and the figure grows static, could possibly lead to unrest.

Two possibilities await an independent America: either the metaphor of an idealized theater can be subordinated, and, to celebrate a new freedom in the arts, the theaters opened to the full range of dramatic entertainments; or the metaphor can be continued, but the theaters limited to propaganda vehicles only. In the first case, a free theater risks the introduction of Old World vice into a young nation sensitive about its virtue. In the second, a metaphor needs revitalizing if it is to have any ideological value once the political-historical purpose to which it has been linked has been achieved. Undaunted, Americans try to do both: introduce an uncorrupt native theater *and* create the dynamic civil equivalent to the Theater of Action. In the new Republic, proponents of each of these theaters, long rivals on the American strand, make the dual effort to turn recent national history into new dramas that will be enacted on separate but sometimes overlapping stages.

~

CHAPTER TWELVE

Play and Earnest on the
Postwar Stage

*W*hereas hypocrisy is the bugbear of seventeenth-century moralists, luxury becomes the byword for those during and after the
Revolution. Outwardly focused, Americans denounce tyranny and
play for a world audience the roles of an enshackled people rising up in
righteous anger against their oppressors. Inwardly focused, however,
Americans take the evangelical line by denouncing an emerging
culture based on hypocrisy, greed, and prurience, those ills that irre-
vocably undermine and destroy the moral structure of a free society.
The worry over luxury appears in sermons, of course, but also in
political speeches and even in scientific talks. The astronomer David
Rittenhouse, for instance, while surveying for his Philadelphia audience current knowledge about the planets, pauses to discourse about
not only the British tyranny of 1775 but also the more pernicious entry
of luxury into the continent. Would that travel between Old World
and New, he wishes, were as impossible as a trip to the moon: "Let our
harbours, our doors, our hearts, be shut against luxury" (157).

For Americans in occupied cities, such feared luxury takes on a
decidedly British aspect, and it is not surprising that theater, which
becomes identified with British frivolity and corruption, should be
proscribed before and during the war. More threatening, however,
than the British imposition of their own corrupt urban ethos is the
willing adoption of vice by Americans themselves. In other words, as
the war progresses and success becomes a greater possibility, American
prophets find new fears to cast before the people, ones more insidious

because less obvious than redcoated regimentals. "States just emerging from oppression," worries James Dana in an election sermon from 1779, are especially susceptible to corruption: "Nothing hath a darker aspect on rising states than effeminate manners." And as American ministers have warned since the first backsliding sermon, the greatness of American civilization threatens to be compromised by a new degeneracy: "Methinks I see profusion and luxury coming in like a flood— corruption and bribery invading all ranks. . . . The LORD'S day devoted to amusements," as if to say that what defines the American role in the war is less liberty than the stance of virtue (26, 27, 31; see J. Davidson, 253). By war's end, amid the glow of victory and the sound of panegyrics to American greatness, ministers and others, as Nathan O. Hatch points out, retrench and grasp at the jeremiad to prevent premature celebration. In *An Oration, Delivered at Ipswich* (Boston, 1783), Levi Frisbie exclaims joyously over the new peace between Great Britain and America, shouting, "America is free!" and proclaiming his inadequacy to "pay a particular attention to the numerous characters which have shone with a distinguished lustre upon the American stage"; but he also speaks to the frequently expressed need not to let military triumph obscure the real enemy in our midst: "If we sink into carelessness and indolence, pride and luxury, folly and dissipation; if envy, selfishness, avarice and ambition; if any or all of this brood of execrable vices gain an predominant influence over us, they will misguide our councils, corrupt our governments, enervate our strength, destroy our order and security, *dissolve our union*, blast all our glory and happiness, and plunge us into a tremendous gulf of infamy and wretchedness, from which we may never be able to emerge" (11, 20, 22–23; see Hatch, 161).

To act on this fear in light of postwar cultural realities—the people were, after all, tired of privation—poses a number of problems for those concerned with the arts and expression. The theater in New York, far from being shut down by the conquering Americans, continues to attract new patrons, including the future first president of the United States. Indeed, other cities become more theatrically active as well. In Boston, the most ruthlessly proscriptive of major cities against the theater, the postwar period shows how important the issue has become to a people used to the metaphor but not to the real thing. In *New Travels through North-America*, a book alleged to have been

written in 1781 by a French army chaplain and first published in
Philip Freneau's translation two years later, the Abbé Claude C. Robin
(after quoting Berkeley's poem "On the Prospect") describes in letter 1
the severe culture of the Bostonian on Sunday: "The pomp of ceremony is here wanting to shadow out the greatness of the *being* he goes
to worship" (14). Nevertheless, the theatrical impulse is not without its
energy, as one can see by observing the churchgoing behavior of New
England women. Robin writes an amused account of "the American
Ladies" that suggests what ministers and political orators have been
saying more seriously about their country for years: "Deprived of all
shows and public diversions whatever, the church is the grand theatre
where they attend, to display their extravagance and finery" (14).

Eventually, the church cannot hold the histrionic needs of a people
at peace. In the middle of the decade, the fashionable set propose a
Tea Assembly for dancing and other performing arts; but old patriots
oppose it for being precisely that invitation to vice they had feared
under British domination. Samuel Adams, writing in the *Massachusetts Centinel* as "The Observer," takes the well-worn antidissipation
line, criticizing the formation of a society that would include dancing
and gaming. About the proponents' desire to mount theatrical productions, however, he betrays some ambivalence rather than open condemnation: "The stage, which is not permitted among us, might
under proper regulations, be a school of morality" (Jan. 15, 1785,
reprinted in Wood, *Rising Glory*, 138). Adams is mocked in a rejoinder by Harrison Gray Otis ("Sans Souci"), who notes that even the
great Addison could not create a moral stage—so why should the
Observer bother to play Cato the Censor (*Massachusetts Centinel*,
Jan. 22, 1785, reprinted in Wood, *Rising Glory*, 142)? But whereas
Adams represents during the prewar era the radical edge of Revolutionary politics, he now speaks a more mainstream position. The
theater itself is not bad—but it ought to be used to teach morality and
not, as it is practiced in England, to undermine it.

The Boston debate eventually gets its comeuppance in an anonymous poem *Theatre* (1792?). The writer imagines the citizens of
Boston gathered in Faneuil Hall to hear speakers for and against the
opening of a theater. Resonus, the voice of the opposition, depicts a
corrupted world, where workers will drop their tools in their madness
to attend the stage and where "ev'ry ass . . . Must try to make himself a

poet" (4). Musacus, in support of the stage, argues that not only would virtues be spread but "Shaksperean geniuses, arising / Would soon, this world here, be surprising. / And native sparks around be toss'd on / The Theatre of this our Boston" (5). Before the debate can be settled, however, Jove enters with his scales: *"Non-theatrists, this dreadful day / With Theatrists, I now shall weigh"*—but the result is a blank, as if for the poet the debate itself is an absurdity (7).

For many Americans, the debate over theater reflects their identity as citizens of an emerging nation. Like others who follow prophecy of the new empire, the young Philip Freneau sees the country in the terms of a providential metaphor:

> Hail, happy land,
> The seat of empire, the abode of kings,
> The final stage where time shall introduce
> Renowned characters, and glorious works
> Of high invention and of wond'rous art.
> ("The Rising Glory of America" [1771], reprinted in *Poems*, 1:82–83)

Once the war is over, however, Freneau expresses a longing for the playhouse stage. In a prologue to a Philadelphia production of Beaumarchais's *Eugenie* and a farce, *The Lying Varlet*, Freneau gives voice to the suppressed need for theatrical entertainments in a land where the stage has been largely figural:

> Wars, cruel wars, and hostile Britain's rage
> Have banished long the pleasures of the stage;
> From the gay painted scene compelled to part,
> (Forget the melting language of the heart)
> Constrained to shun the bold theatric show,
> To act long tragedies of real woe,
> Heroes, once more attend the comic muse;
> Forget our failings, and our faults excuse.
> (*Freeman's Journal*, Jan. 9, 1782, reprinted in *Poems*, 2:108)

Whatever value these foreign plays may have in inaugurating a new period in American cultural history, they must be framed in the right patriotic spirit. As Freneau's *Freeman's Journal* describes the production, the plays were "succeeded" by dances and illuminations that celebrate Washington (in attendance), other worthies, and the thirteen states; in short, imported drama and farce are viewed in the context of a domestic "spectacle" (*Poems*, 2:108n).

A week later, Freneau, writing in the *Freeman's Journal* as "The Pilgrim," responds to a supposed letter from one Maria Flutter, who has seen *Eugenie*, liked it, but is not sure of the rightness of attending the drama. He rebukes his correspondent for not understanding the point of the play; "and he hereby prohibits her from ever attending plays 'till she is able to collect a number of useful morals and rational sentiments from what she sees and hears" (Jan. 16, 1782, reprinted in *Prose*, 53). Having just affirmed the theater in the previous issue of his journal, Freneau now denies to theater an unlimited franchise. The stage has its place

> yet by no means do I consent that regular theatrical entertainments shall immediately come into fashion. The diversions of the stage are doubtless (under proper restrictions) noble, manly and rational; but at present I judge them to be rather unseasonable, at least if generally permitted . . . . You languish for public shows. Have patience, madam, 'till the war is successfully finished—reflect how many of your countrymen are at this moment perishing in sickly prisons; dying with painful wounds, hunger and nakedness; facing death in the field of battle, of suffering all the vengeance that a cruel and exasperated enemy can inflict. Think on these things, madam, and be merry if you can.   (*Prose*, 54)

As a director of the new American culture, Freneau finds himself playing both supporter and critic of the rising stage as he, like the rest of his countrymen, struggles to find the right idiom for entertainments in a new republic. On the one hand, as he remarks in a poem, "The Distrest Theatre," "A State betrays a homely taste, / By which the stage is thus disgraced"; it might, by allowing theater, give itself another place "Where, drest in all the flowers of speech, / Dame virtue might her precepts teach." On the other hand, there are limits to American forbearance:

> Let but a dancing bear arrive,
> A pig, that counts you four, or five—
> And Cato, with his moral strain
> May strive to mend the world in vain.
> (*National Gazette* [Charleston], Nov. 21, 1791, reprinted
> in *Poems*, 2:404–5; on variants, see Leary, 164,
> and Hiltner, 357–60)

For Freneau, the actual stage takes its cue from the metaphor; make it come alive, he urges cities whose theaters are closed, but never let it stray from the ideologically correct position of ennoblement through virtue. That means, then, that the subjects of plays must match the needs of the audience. As he argues in an essay, "Royal Dangers in the American Stage," the theater must not be used, as it is in a monarchy, to numb the people to genuine problems. No "pouting queens" or "rakish princes" allowed; instead, only such entertainments "as inculcate an observance of the moral and social duties, or in some shape tend to better the heart, without vitiating the understanding by an overstrained address to the fancy" can be admitted (*National Gazette* [Charleston], Mar. 6, 1793, reprinted in *Prose*, 295; see Elliott, 135).

Thus, the fate of the stage and the place of the metaphor become intertwined during the postwar period. If, as we will see in the succeeding chapter, theatrical tropes still have some utility in expressing nationalist ideals, then one must be careful not to deflate the figural stage with too much buffoonery or "luxury" on an increasingly visible literal stage. That is, having once phrased the American mission in terms of its place on the great Theater of the World, patriot rhetoricians cannot adopt theatrical culture and its aestheticized trope—life as performance only—without reshaping it to serve revolutionary ends.

Consequently, as drama and theater become more widely accepted in postwar America, they make convenient vehicles for nationalist themes. The topical dramas of the early war years as well as others end up as staples for collegiate acting clubs. Claude C. Robin describes Harvard students putting on such nationalist favorites as "the battle of Bunkers Hill, the burning of Charlestown, the Death of General Montgomery, the capture of Burgoyne, the treason of Arnold, and the Fall of British Tyranny" (18; see Philbrick, 16, and Meserve, 128, 313n). As William W. Clapp, Jr., remarks in his *Record of the Boston Stage* (1853), "In the early days of the theatre, every public event of sufficient importance was immediately dramatized" (134); and in Robin's eyes this desire to find a homegrown drama, while it has its limitations (primarily in unsophisticated productions), has this advantage: "The drama is here reduced to its true and ancient origins" (18). This observation suggests that a new native drama maintains its purity in its originality; that is, in the way that prewar theatrical energies could be directed toward political ends, those same primitive energies can now be reshaped into nationalist shows that are staged without the actors' being concerned over quality of performance. As Rousseau implies, the only theater appropriate in an uncorrupted republic is a naive one.

In addition to dramas, and perhaps more important for a popular audience, are the grand spectacles of revolutionary affirmation. Washington is often the subject of part or all of many of these productions, as he is in John Parke's *Virginia: A Pastoral Drama on the Birthday of an Illustrious Personage and the Return of Peace, February 11, 1784* (see Meserve, 129, and Albanese, 149). But other heroes are celebrated as well, often in hybrid combinations of "pantomime, music, dancing, speeches, and odes" as in *The Apotheosis of Franklin; or, His Reception in the Elysian Fields* mounted in Charleston, 1796. One of the more curious shows is "The Soldier's Festival," which featured the extraordinary Deborah Sampson Gannett, a woman who served as a foot soldier during the war without her gender being discovered. In theaters, she would deliver an address about her experience (though apparently not really an account) and "equipd in complete uniform . . . go through the manual exercise" (quoted in Laska, 77). Thus on the same stage where such divertisements as "The Will—or, a School for Daughters" were played (Boston's Federal-Street Theatre, Mar. 22, 1802), Americans could see a woman dressed as a soldier speak lines written for her by a man (Herman Mann) about her own experiences as a woman disguised as a man in the Revolutionary War (see Laska, 76–78). If the situation recalls Shakespearean gender layering on the male-only Elizabethan stage, the joke may not have been apparent to the early national audience. The whole point of putting Deborah Gannett on the program in the first place was probably to lend solidity to an otherwise lightweight bill; that is, to bring on the stage of the Federal-Street Theatre an actor from the greater theater, the "blood-stained theater of action," and thus legitimize mere entertainment with a nationalist moral spectacle. But the presence of Gannett or any other old soldier on a stage fast moving toward melodrama and already home to farce also marks the tension between the seriousness of national mission and its exploited version on a bourgeois stage. Just as the Puritans feared the theater would draw attention from the pulpit, so committed revolutionaries feared the stage would diminish, even subvert, the providential glory of their actions. Nevertheless, by the time of the Constitutional Convention in 1787, theater in America was here to stay.

If the stage had not yet established itself as a "school of morality," it was busy entertaining Americans with Richard Sheridan's *School for Scandal*, a play that no doubt sparked one New York spectator, Royall Tyler, to write his own comedy of manners, *The Contrast* (1790). Tyler's field was the law, but as a youthful poet he had proposed marriage to the daughter of John and Abigail Adams—only to be banished (she was eventually taken to Europe) by young Nabby's father. This contrast, in Adams's eyes, between a lawyer whose business is law and nation and whose playfulness leads to the pretty and therefore frivolous amusement of penning verse lies behind the other contrasts in Tyler's play. The nationalist themes in *The Contrast* are expressed as a version of play versus earnest, as Johan Huizinga might phrase it, or of luxury versus sacrifice, each of which in the end amounts to a contrast between rival theaters of being.

As G. Thomas Tanselle notes in his study of Tyler's literary career, the American play, like its Restoration comedic forebears, uses the motif of theater self-consciously "for illustrating a distortion of values and for comparing the acting on-stage with the acting off-stage" (63). In fact, much of the humor in *The Contrast* comes from Charlotte's descriptions of audience behavior in the sidebox and, most famously, from the Yankee Jonathan's naive accounts of seeing *School for Scandal* and John O'Keeffe's comic opera *The Poor Soldier* as real life. But all the various contrasts that Tyler exploits—"affectation and plainness . . . city and country, hypocrisy and sincerity," Old World versus New—can be seen also as varieties of theatrical behavior: life as an ahistorical social performance versus life as an antihistrionic acting in history (Tanselle, 73). In *The Contrast*, the former represents debased, imported luxury, and the latter, ennobling native virtue; but Tyler himself finally stands somewhere between the two.

The villain of the play is the effete roué, Billy Dimple, a character described by the virginal Maria as "a depraved wretch, whose only virtue is a polished exterior" (1.2.14). Dimple has completely remade himself by the rules of Chesterfield: morality is outré, fashion de rigueur, and foreign manners and language the accoutrements of a gentleman. Tyler mocks this obsession with gentlemanliness to some extent by having Dimple's man, Jessamy, ape his master's sophistication, especially at the expense of the country rube, Jonathan; but for most of the play, Dimple and Jessamy are controlling figures, characters whose verbal dexterity allows them to act as standards in a society that willingly throws itself into a culture of performance.

Ironically, the most "natural" character in the play is Charlotte, an active participant in the theatricalized society of New York and sister to the stiff Yankee protagonist, Colonel Manly. Her giddiness and delighted gossip carry the play for its first two acts, but the humor she generates does not lead to mockery of her flitting about; instead, through her Tyler shows his own familiarity with the world she inhabits, one which, as Tanselle remarks, "took the theater for granted" (63). What David Humphreys contends in 1786, that American women do not "place their happiness, like Europe's dames, / In balls and masquerades, in plays and games" (22), no longer applies on the New York stage of 1787. In fact, because we first hear of Manly through Charlotte, we are predisposed to think him a bore. Charlotte describes for her friend Letitia how he has acted toward her during a stay at her father's home in the country: "He read me such lectures, out of pure brotherly affection, against the extremes of fashion, dress, flirting, and coquetry, and all the other dear things which he knows I dote upon, his conversation made me as melancholy as if I had been at church" (2.1, 18). The irony in Charlotte's treatment of her brother is that his contrast to fashion makes him appear a theatrical figure in sophisticated New York. Were I to introduce you "to the polite circles in the city," she tells him when he first appears on stage, "the belles would think you were a player run mad, with your head filled with old scraps of tragedy" (2.1, 21).

Thus Manly, the earnest patriot, steeped in Revolutionary Stoicism, can never appear on the stage of society without seeming to be an actor; since everyone *acts*, the sincere character shows himself to be lunatic or histrionic but, in either case, incredible, not to be believed for what he claims to be. The stage itself mocks sincerity by its very being; no one can appear in a theater as him or herself when everyone else either acts or expects acting. Both Captain John Smith and Cotton Mather feel violated when their "tragedies" are deflated on stage; the earnest historical figures are made straight men to the antic needs of plays. Even when Deborah Sampson Gannett appeared in shows, she had to come costumed and to deliver lines written for her by someone else; the reality of her life could not in itself be made to fit the entertainment demands of her time. In *The Contrast* the character Manly enters the play space of Dimple and his circle, where the appearance of sincerity is applauded because it is fake, and initially Dimple fools Manly into thinking that he affirms patriot values. The audience, recognizing themselves in the characters on stage, see Dimple's act for what it is; but to keep the play from toppling, the actor who plays Manly must make a good show of sincerity as well, since Tyler's comedy must attempt to redefine the proportion of play and seriousness allowable in the new Republic.

For a time, though, it appears that the frivolousness indulged in by the normative characters will be exalted, as if it were the Puritans' worst nightmare suddenly come to life. As was noted earlier, some Puritans did not question the legitimacy of the theater as an idea, particularly when it was linked to the life of faith as an institution for moral instruction; or if theater was condemned, then perhaps the drama would be affirmed as an ennobling literature. What most Puritans feared, however, was the proliferation of play and its permanent enfranchisement against the earnest needs of church, colony, and society. By the time of the war, hypocrisy as a standard of behavior is assigned to the British and their Tory sympathizers; thus what Charlotte describes as a typical evening at the theater, while delivered as light comedy, shows itself in the context of the play to be rank imitation of degenerate British mores:

> Everything is conducted with such decorum,—first we bow round to the company in general, then to each one in particular, then we have so many inquiries after each other's health, and we are so happy to meet each other, and it is so many ages since we last had that pleasure, and if a married lady is in company, we have such a sweet dissertation upon her son Bobby's chin-cough; then the curtain rises, then our sensibility is all awake, and then by the mere force of apprehension, we torture some harmless expression into a double meaning, which the poor author never

dreamt of, and then we have recourse to our fans, and then we blush, and then the gentlemen jog one another, peep under the fan, and make the prettiest remarks; and then we giggle and they simper, and they giggle and we simper, and then the curtain drops, and then for nuts and oranges, and then we bow, and it's pray, Ma'am take it, and pray Sir keep it, and, oh! not for the world Sir; and then the curtain rises again, and then we blush, and giggle, and simper, and bow, all over again. Oh! the sentimental charms of a side-box conversation!   (2.1, 22–23).

Interestingly, Manly joins the others in laughter at Charlotte's remarks. He recognizes—or thinks he does—in his sister's diverting account a legitimate moral exercise, in the tradition, possibly, of Erasmus: "Well, sister, I join heartily with you in the laugh; for, in my opinion, it is as justifiable to laugh at folly as it is reprehensible to ridicule misfortune" (2.1, 23). Like those other sincere actors on the figural American stage, Manly naturally fears his efforts will be ridiculed in the low theater of British luxury; and with Charlotte's description, he gives voice to the playwright's plea for serious attention to the efforts of playwrights, at least those who follow in the moralist tradition.

Unfortunately, Tyler does not develop this cue from Manly. Charlotte shifts the discussion to Manly's clothes and, in particular, the old regimental coat that, long after the war, is out of fashion. We see in Charlotte's diversion that what constitutes folly cannot be readily identified; when theatricality is the norm, all reality becomes tied to illusion. Manly rushes to defend his old coat rather than explain his remarks on theater; this action gives him high-flown sentiments to speak on Stoic adherence to patriotic beliefs but prevents his development as a more complex character. This happens again later, in the fourth act, when Dimple, Manly, Letitia, and Charlotte talk of the theater again. Manly asks Dimple, "Do you never attend the theatre, Sir?" (4.1, 58), as if to suggest that attention at the theater, from Manly's point of view, can be a wholesome activity. Dimple, however, uses that question as an opportunity to ridicule American productions and to engage Manly in a comparison/contrast between superior European culture and inferior native talent. Manly ends up defending his country, not the theater; but Tyler implies that Manly's sentiments, which affirm the moral rightness of laughter at folly and the primacy for patriots of American culture, could be made consonant with a native stage tradition.

Even so, Tyler leaves that question unresolved; after all, he has imitated a British form, the Restoration comedy, in order to make his point that the American theater can be favorably compared to its overseas cousin. The theater that a Manly would affirm might, in fact, be too constricting for a Tyler to write for. Manly's chief role in the play is to denounce luxury, which he does in the long, tendentious soliloquy in act 3, scene 2. That speech, delivered at "The Mall," the meeting place of the beau monde, takes the form of a Senecan declamation, basically in character for Manly (and familiar to college graduates in the audience) but out of step with the sprightliness of the rest of the play. As a piece of theater, the speech is a near disaster, but as a statement of theme, it carries the burden of the whole drama. Using language from sermons and orations on the subject, Manly addresses what by 1787 is a well-known litany of ills brought in by "luxury": "Luxury is surely the bane of a nation. . . . Luxury! which renders a people weak at home, and accessible to bribery, corruption, and force from abroad" (3.2, 48). By implication from the previous scenes, Manly includes in his category of luxury the simpering, mincing sidebox conversations of an aestheticized, theatricalized culture; what he cannot countenance is the unmanning of patriotic commitment to the evangelical virtues that motivated Revolutionary idealism.

As an actor himself on the world stage, Manly knows history, and he speaks a language of empire and decay that comes directly from the warning sermons preached at war's end. What he fears he sees in his own country can be found in ancient Greece; that great civilization was later undermined by luxury, but it once gave to the world the model of a state: "The kings of Greece devoted their lives to the service of their country, and her senators knew no other superiority over their fellow-citizens than a glorious pre-eminence in danger and virtue. They exhibited to the world a noble spectacle—a number of independent states united by a similarity of language, sentiment, manners, common interest, and common consent in one grand mutual league of protection" (3.2, 48). The ideal nation is a "noble spectacle"; as Plato suggests in the *Laws*, it adopts the form of a tragedy. Thus nobility of sentiment in *The Contrast* is spoken by a character whom

Charlotte teases as a "player run mad, with your head filled with old scraps of tragedy." Manly, however, concerns himself with a more universal audience than the belles of the city. Patriotism displays itself in history as spectacle, expressed as "the common good" against the pernicious "pursuit of private interest." Individual actors in the spectacle take those parts appointed by a wise, overseeing Providence; they cannot, at risk of the nation, re-create themselves in self-chosen roles that serve private rather than corporate ends. Ultimately, the nation as a whole is an actor in the providential theater, fulfilling its obligation to history to be an example to others, "the safe asylum of liberty" (3.2, 48).

When Manly exposes Dimple as the self-serving reprobate he is, triumphs over him, and engages the virtuous Maria to be married, he earns the right to speak the moral of the play—oddly enough, in his most theatrically self-aware lines: "And I have learned, that probity, virtue, honour, though they should not have received the polish of Europe, will secure to an honest American the good graces of his fair countrywomen, and, I hope, the applause of THE PUBLIC" (5.2, 79). For his nationalist moral and for the type of American he represents, Manly requests applause from "THE PUBLIC," the citizenry. In essence, the antihistrionic Manly has seized the bourgeois stage of society, expelled its chief corrupter, Dimple (who, because he does not even watch the plays he attends, misses the point of theater as surely as the benighted Jonathan), and converted it into a literal representation of the metaphoric stage that Americans have imagined themselves inhabiting for nearly two centuries. Macrocosm and microcosm, world stage and local theater, world history and American history come together in Manly's patriotic appeal to his nation—and the actor's request to his audience—for applause for a show well performed.

Though Manly repudiates social theatricality, he shows some understanding of and sympathy for the theater itself (after all, one of the major subscribers to Tyler's play was Washington, the model for Manly's heroic sentiments). Manly's "waiter," however, the comic Yankee Jonathan, cannot comprehend theater at all; in the theatrically self-conscious society of the play, Jonathan is the butt of most of the low humor. The idea of the naive spectator is not new to Tyler. Ben

Jonson's Bartholomew Cokes in *Bartholomew Fair* and the Citizen and his wife, Nell, in Francis Beaumont's *The Knight of the Burning Pestle* are Jacobean antecedents (see Righter, 83). A more immediate source, however, might be Baron de Montesquieu's *Persian Letters*, published in English translation in 1722. A frequently read author among Whig intellectuals, Montesquieu here uses the motif of letters from traveling Persians to comment on European society—and to expose the dangers of luxury, as they appear through accounts of life in the Persian seraglio. In letter 26 from the Persian Rica to an unknown recipient, the writer describes in detail the habits of those who attend the Parisian theater. To some degree, the letter combines elements of naïveté with descriptions of theatrical behavior in the audience similar to those provided by Charlotte and Billy Dimple:

> I Yesterday saw a very odd thing, tho' it is done everyday at *Paris*. About Evening all the People get together to go and act a kind of Mimickry, which I heard call a Play: the chief part of the performance is upon a scaffold, which they call the Stage: on both sides of it are little Nests which they call Boxes, where men and women act silent Scenes together almost like those which we have in *Persia*.
>
> Sometimes you see an amorous Lady that looks languishing upon account of her neglected passion: then another with sparkling eyes and a passionate look perfectly devours her lover with her regards, which he returns as ardently: all the passions are painted in their faces, and expressed with an eloquence which is the more lively for being dumb. There the Actors shew but half their bodies, and generally wear a muff out of modesty to conceal their Arms. Underneath is a great company of people standing, who laugh at those who are aloft upon the Stage, and these latter laugh at those below in their turn.   (1:95–96)

Though Rica may be somewhat uncomprehending, he is no fool; his naïveté is a vehicle for the author's satire on *"French* Plays, Playhouses, Fops and Actresses," as the eighteenth-century translator, John Ozell, lists the contents of letter 26. By contrast, Jonathan's simpleminded account in *The Contrast* of watching the action in a place where "they lifted a great green cloth and let us look right into the next neighbor's house" (3.1, 41) ends up satirizing rural Calvinist strictures on the theater rather than the stage itself. When told that he was at a playhouse, Jonathan exclaims to Jessamy and Jenny, "Mercy on my soul! did I see the wicked players?" (3.1, 43).

Thus, while, through Manly, Tyler warns his fellow Americans not to become absorbed in the limiting fixation with social performance, he tries through Jonathan to have fun with the figure of the likable American oaf, the "true blue son of liberty" but hopelessly naive spectator and interpreter of (urban) life. As Freneau says in a preindependence poem, "Not Catos, or Platos engross every play, / For clowns and clod-hoppers must, too, have their day" (*Poems*, 1:132). In other words, by making fun of Jonathan, Tyler affirms the theater, and by including Jonathan, Tyler hopes to find an American idiom in which that theater might be expressed (against Dimple's preference for the foreign stage). It is ironic, certainly, that the most famous American play for many years should feature at its comic center a character who, though he has heard about theater often enough from his hometown preacher, cannot comprehend the conventions of the stage.

Tyler's play marks a curious counterturn from the vision of America as an idealized stage. Using a foreign vehicle though mocking foreign manners, and appealing to an audience with worldly tastes while celebrating homespun localism, the playwright features antitheatrical native heroes in a form—the staged comedy of manners—that exposes them to deflation. The result is a propaganda drama that entertains—or is it entertainment with a dose of patriotism tossed in? In the hands of a producer who values the box office potential of a stage buffoon more than the civic duty to promulgate ennobling principles, this one play shows that the ability of the playhouse to do for the country what the metaphor has just done seems significantly compromised. As a play about social performance, *The Contrast* already points toward theatrical metaphors other than that of the providential stage. For staunch patriots, however, the extratheatrical theatrum mundi, distinct from its microcosmic, intratheatrical version, still holds its importance as a figure in which to express the national mission. The growth of stage drama notwithstanding, American writers in the postwar era look for fresh ways to enliven an old trope.

CHAPTER THIRTEEN

Stage Metaphor and the New Republic

A problem faced by those who foment revolution is what one does with the rhetoric that got them to turn the world upside down in the first place. In a world where people act out of a sense of becoming, nothing threatens the continued appeal to act toward an end as much as arrival. For millennialists, of course, there can be nothing else to say once the millennium comes; and for jeremiadical Americans, there is the threat that with the achievement of promised glory, prophets must lapse into silence. In the case of the American Revolution, speakers and writers face several choices: they can drop the old rhetoric and find a new one; they can try to continue the old rhetoric in hopes that it still has life left; or they can recalculate the old rhetoric by declaring that the promised event has not really been achieved after all—and therefore start over on a fresh cycle of becoming.

This is not to say, with intentional fallacy, that any American writer sat and pondered what he or she would do with theatrical figures once the war was over; but the persistence of any metaphor whose premise is that the achievement of American independence is the fifth act of a long drama cannot continue without change. Lafayette no doubt spoke for war-weary citizens, patriot or not, when he said that the surrender at Yorktown marked the drama's end. But in the subsequent struggle for a mode of governance that matched the republican ideals of the Revolution, and in the search for an appropriate iconography to reflect the new politics, writers do not seem willing to purge dramatic or theatrical tropes from their repertoire. One only has to look at the remark by Benjamin Rush in 1787 to see the necessity of clinging to one of the most popular and potent metaphors of the age. Like Lafayette, Rush declares the war finished; but in contrast, the Philadelphian distinguishes between the battles and the principles behind them: "The war is over: but this is far from being the case with the American revolution. On the contrary, nothing but the first act of the great drama is closed. It remains yet to establish and perfect our new forms of government; and to prepare the principles, morals, and manners of our citizens, for these forms of government, after they are established and brought to perfection" ("An Address to the People of the United States," *American Museum*, Jan. 1787, quoted in Bailyn, *Origins*, 230). By Rush's refiguration, the drama has not ended after all; there are still four acts left.

This strategic use of drama has a distinct advantage of keeping before the public a familiar image for progress and thus of continuing to appeal to Americans' sense of becoming. At the same time, it restarts the clock of expectations; as liberal theologians noted earlier in the century, the more immediate the promise of fulfillment, the more demanding are the people to achieve it. Better to flatten and lengthen the upward slope to one of evolutionary change than leave it short and steep, or worse, have it become circular and revolving and thus overturn all that has been accomplished. Ironically, the stage serves both to propel action toward a definite and, if tragic, cathartic end, figurally aiding the cause of rebellion against changeless tyranny, and to comfort those who, once the ends of rebellion have been accomplished, look for a familiar and fixed point of reference. The drama is over, or the drama is only begun; but the stage that was there before is there still.

Another strategy emerges out of the nature of American entertainments themselves. The period after the war witnesses not only the great debate on the Constitution but also the renewed arguments about the place of theater in the new Republic. The end of the war and other patriotic events are celebrated by spectacles and processions, as if Rousseau's prescription for republican theater were come alive; and consequently, some versions of theatrical metaphor reflect this broadened, amphitheatrical or arenalike mode of perception. The very

achievement of independence, with all its republican rituals of mutual consultation and "perfect equality," displays itself to the world as a
"glorious spectacle" (Madison, *A Sermon Preached before the Conven-*
tion, 5). In the rising glory *Poem on the Happiness of America* (1786),
David Humphreys speaks the popular postwar patriot message of
gratitude—to Providence, usually—for those who served their country so nobly: "Ye happy mortals, whom propitious fate / Reserv'd for
actors on a stage so great!" (5). Against the limitations of the closed
stage, which Rousseau identifies with privilege and antirepublicanism, Humphreys posits a larger platform, once coincident with the
land, open and vast. In his conclusion, as Mason Lowance notes,
Humphreys gives the whole vision a millennialist tone, but it is one
where drama has been supplanted by the spectacle of the achieved new
empire. Instead of the bloodbaths that end decrepit Old World civili-
zations, a new image appears:

> Why turns the horizon red? the dawn is near—
> Infants of light, ye harbingers appear!
> With ten-fold brightness gild the happier age,
> And light the actors o'er a broader stage!
> This drama closing—ere th' approaching end,
> See Heav'ns perennial year to earth descend!
> Then wake, Columbians! fav'rites of the skies
> Awake to glory and to rapture rise.
> (50–51; Lowance, 219)

The postwar rhetoric of Humphreys curiously parallels that of post-
World War II China; and in the Communist pageants, such as *The*
East Is Red, one finds a similar attempt to reconceive theater for the
purpose of expressing the popular values of a mass revolution. Without stretching the analogy too far, we can see the implications: to exalt
the work of the people as actors, stage must not be confused with the
enclosed space of bourgeois theater. At the same time, popular political culture becomes saturated with performative values; but, whereas
in China, the constant sense of being watched turns inward and
becomes the savage social paranoia of the Cultural Revolution, in
America it turns outward. Citizens there are actors watched and
applauded *from without* on the enormous theatrum mundi.

For the patriot clergy, the postwar era presents a number of dilemmas. On the one hand, the war has been a success; the *cause* of America's ills, its unnatural attachment to wicked Britain, has been removed, and with its elimination, one could hope, by the logic of evangelical rhetoric, to enter an era of purity unmatched since those paragons, the fathers, stalked and wrestled with the evils of a new land. Like the poets, then, ministers give vent to rising glory impulses—or perhaps it is better to say risen glory. For his Election Day sermon of 1783, the president of Yale, Ezra Stiles, announces to his Hartford audience, "Already does the new constellation of the United States begin to realize this glory. It has already risen to an acknowledged sovereignty among the republics and kingdoms of the world" (*United States*, 438). On the other hand, if glory is come, then those ills that remain will stand out even more as last blockages to the long-delayed realization "of the *Magnalia Dei*—the great events in God's moral government designed for eternal ages to be displayed in these ends of the earth" (447). As James Davidson explains, this attempt to "hasten that day" of the millennium produces among some preachers a rabid antivice rhetoric, aimed primarily, as explained above, at eliminating "corruption" (255–97) but having the effect ultimately of making millennialist preaching obsolete.

The loss of ministerial authority may also have something to do with the preachers' own eloquence. Having for so many years functioned as a substitute theater in the life of the colonies, these men could no longer hold their own in a more theatricalized age. A New Haven clergyman complains that after the war, "many people expected every minister to be an accomplished essayist and the pulpit to be a theater for oratorical display"—but few pastors wish to make themselves the objects of secular adoration (Moses Welch, "The Relations of Pastor and People," quoted in Elliott, 41). As Harry Stout and Donald Weber show, the patriot ministers succeed in forging a dynamic rhetoric of traditional Puritan themes with contemporary political language in order to express their forthright support of the war effort; but while much of the rhetoric remains, the perhaps unexpected achievement of near-paradise—at least in expression—forces the clergy out of the limelight or, as Weber says, to wish "to get out of history" altogether (Weber, 149; see Stout, 316).

For someone like Stiles, postwar politics must be shaped by the same priorities as have always motivated evangelicals; thus the risen glory already achieved "will be swallowed up and lost in the glories of immortality." The metaphorical stage seems little different from that of sixteenth-century nonconformists: the message is still that of John Foxe's play *Christus Triumphans*. Our acting has one end, says Stiles: "Be it our great ambition, or incessant endeavor, to act our parts worthily on the stage of life, as looking for and hastening to the coming of our Lord Jesus Christ" (519). But this deliberate archaism cannot be made to mesh fully with the new realities of the republican order, whose perpetuation of itself as a glorious achievement requires a different logic, an altered rhetoric, from that of evangelical millennialism. There is, after all, a new set of fathers, living still or of immediate and sacred memory. Indeed, with the deaths of the leading patriots commemorated in spectacular entertainments (the apotheosis of Franklin being but one example), there hardly seems room for Christ to set foot on the stage at all. Thus the switch from Election Day sermon to Fourth of July oration marks more than simply a shift from an essentially sacred to an essentially secular mode of address. After all, as Sacvan Bercovitch suggests, the speeches on Independence Day still ring with the tones of the jeremiad. The theater of war has been in the words of many a theater of action, the memory of which fills the sacred needs of a holy day. Simeon Baldwin in his July 4, 1788, *Oration Pronounced before the Citizens of New-Haven* reminds his listeners of the greatness of the war effort: "Most of us have been anxious spectators—many in this assembly peculiar sufferers and some distinguished actors in those interesting scenes" (7). At the same time, Baldwin uses the standard hyperbole of the time to announce that it is "impossible to do justice to the merits of those patriots who performed conspicuous parts on the theatre of those actions we this day commemorate" (8; see Albanese, 105).

Daniel Foster, preaching the Massachusetts election sermon for 1790, turns to theatrical figures several times to enforce the link between America's Christian foundations and its new status as a politically free nation. As a rhetoric of enhancement, theater matches the grandness of his theme: "That days of greater peace and happiness, then have ever dawn'd upon the church and world, are before us in

America" (22). Foster seizes upon the progressive view of history in order to keep the eyes of Americans on the millennialist future. We can date our history, he suggests, from the time of Christ: "Since he appeared on the theatre of life, the church and world have pressed on for ages, thro' the fire of persecution . . . 'Till the Angel of the Lord pointed our forefathers to this Western world" (22–23). Consequently, all present secular happiness that has resulted from the Revolution is tied inextricably to that dramatized past and to the religious spectacle ahead, figured in terms of the stage: "From the rise and present exaltation of America, we conclude she is to be the theatre, where the latter day glory shall be displayed; and the medium through which religion, liberty and learning, shall be handed round creation" (35; see Bercovitch, *American Jeremiad*, 141). Thus, while Foster's peroration holds political and religious consecration in balance, by 1802, if not well before, a speaker like Noah Webster, Jr., can reenvision that stage for new generations who need to be told what to worship:

> Let the youth of our country, who were not spectators of the distresses of the war; but who have entered upon the stage of life in time to see the silver locks of the revolutionary patriots, and to witness the scars and the poverty of the war-worn soldier. . . .
>
> Let us, with a solemn pleasure, visit [Washington's] tomb; there to drop a tear of affection, and heave a fervent sigh, over departed greatness. . . . There let us pluck a sprig of the willow and the laurel that shade the ashes of a WASHINGTON, and bear it on our bosoms, to remind us of his amiable virtues, his distinguished atchievements [*sic*], and our irreparable loss! (28, 30)

That the American stage was a special one—the "theater of new scenery" as Josiah Bent, Jr., calls it in 1826—few citizens of patriotic sympathies would doubt. Indeed, much postwar rhetoric seems to enshrine the theatrical metaphor and fix it as a figure for glorious triumph. Not everyone appears willing to take up Benjamin Rush's tactic and declare the play only just begun. One can understand readily the desires of some revolutionaries to want to savor their achievement rather than look further for new stages or new dramas. The poems of Joel Barlow, for instance, often adopt a visionary stance that relies on theatrum mundi for its full effect. In his 1781 commencement poem at Yale, Barlow pictures for his classmates the world that awaits them: "Fate calls us hence the world's broad stage to tread, / Act a short part, and mingle with the dead" (*Works*, 2:29); but that image seems far bleaker than the overall message of the poem. The war is nearly over; a whole country, a new empire, waits to be built: "On this broad theatre, unbounded spread, / In different scenes, what countless throngs must tread" (2:33). And while the war itself has been a stage of display for American heroes, the postwar era offers new opportunities for a rising democracy, "a theatre of action for every citizen of a great country" (*Oration*, 18–19).

Barlow's most ambitious treatment of the worldly theater occurs in his epic, *The Vision of Columbus* (1787). To a dejected and imprisoned Columbus, a seraph appears who takes the discoverer to the Mount of Vision and displays before him scenes of the South and North America to come. Each exercise at epical scene making creates for Columbus a "broad theatre" on which to view extraordinary events (*Works*, 2:165). The founding of the United States the angel depicts as a signal event in the progress of history: the creation of a democratic, unified state, swelling with creative genius, that provides a model for a unified government of the entire world. As Columbus looks down upon the last vision provided for him, the angel limns a "rational" millennium, as Barlow calls it, where world leaders, following the American example, get together in a concord of nations:

> Now, far beneath his view, the important age
> Leads the bold actors on a broader stage;
> When, clothed majestic in the robes of state,
> Moved by one voice, in general council meet
> The fathers of all empires: 'twas the place,
> Near the first footsteps of the human race;
>
> . . . .
>
> A spacious structure rose, sublimely great,
> The last resort, the unchanging scene of State.
> (2:355–56)

For Barlow and others, the world theater opens on a fixed panorama and spectacle of union, a "scene of State" that plays itself out with all the immutability of a show in the heavenly amphitheater.

Barlow's broad theaters must, however, coexist with other figural stages in the 1780s. As the British have for a long time, American observers are beginning to see life as a set of performances to be amused by, outside of providential history. Francis Hopkinson, for instance, writing in the *Pennsylvania Packet* of March 1, 1785, finds quotidian events to be so many "common" entertainments: "My present fancy is to suppose the public news papers as so many real theatres, on which some play or farce is daily exhibited for my amuse-ment" (158). On the other side is the theater of duplicity and revenge, called up early in the war by wounded Tories exposing the hypocrisy of their patriot countrymen; now, however, it is those opposed to the constitutional authority of a new federal government who adopt the trope. In the constitutional debates after the 1787 convention, the Antifederalist rhetoric often reaches a fever pitch, punctuated by cries of deceit and disguise. "Centinel," writing in the *Independent Ga-zetteer*, urges the people of Pennsylvania to "discover the masqued aristocracy" that the Federalists "are attempting to smuggle upon you under the suspicious garb of republicanism" (Nov. 8, 1787, quoted in Kenyon, 17). Luther Martin, an Antifederalist responding in the *Maryland Journal* to attacks that he has been two-faced, asserts that he "acted no 'contradictory parts on the great political stage'" (Jan.–Mar. 1788, quoted in Kenyon, 175). As old alliances begin to break down and new factions develop, the business of settling on a constitution, or simply the business of making institutions work at all, might seem anticlimactic to a generation who have been told for over twenty years that their political-military victory would complete the entire history of civilization.

Mercy Otis Warren, who near the end of the war had expressed her own diminished enthusiasm, devoted much of her energy imme-diately after the conflict to writing her three-volume *History of the Rise, Progress, and Termination of the American Revolution* (1805). It is a peculiar book, full of both sententious moralizing and well-wrought passages of dignifying prose. She renders battles frequently as domestic tragedies, reminding us, as Robert Middlekauff has ob-served, that "the eighteenth-century battlefield was, compared with the twentieth, an intimate theater" (500); and appropriately, she uses theater as her basic trope for the events of the war. Yet as with her wartime writings, maybe even to a greater degree, Mercy Warren's theater is often grand and abstract and, like her history, overall (she often, but not always, demurs on sordid scenes) removed from the deflating events of ordinary life. This is not to say that she ignores viciousness; on the contrary, she often makes use of British—or American—excesses to drive home a moral point. But for her the American conflict only makes sense when it is projected upon an inclusive, Stoic theater of the world.

When historian Warren surveys the scene from her perch in Plymouth, she sees the whole of "the theatre of human action" (1:2) and declares it her duty not to "pronounce decidedly on the characters of the politician or the statesman till the winding up of the drama" (1:3). Despite her lofty remarks—and fortunately for her text—she envisions a theater of personalities, writ large. Her brother James Otis, she says, will be listed "among the most distinguished patriots who have expired on the 'blood-stained theatre of human action' " (1:85). When William Howe resigns his commission, he does not just return to England; rather, "we see him no more on the American theatre" (2:106). And George Washington, whose reputation grows during the war at the expense of Howe, displays his "rising fame" in competition "for the crown of victory, on a theatre that soon excited the curiosity, and awakened the ambition of the heroes and princes of Europe" (1:355).

Of all her theaters, the one alluded to in the last passage seems to engage her most, for it is that theater observed by others that best defines what America represents. Mercy Warren's rhetorical reconstruction of events serves largely to magnify them, but she does no more than what others were doing contemporaneously with the episodes she describes. If we recall John Adams's excitement in 1774 upon entering the new theater of the Continental Congress, then we can understand the historian's rendition of the beginnings of Congress as something other than idle metaphoric puffery. When Congress is summoned, no one knows much about the country or its people, "but she soon became the object of attention among the potentates of Europe, the admiration of both the philosophic and the brave, her fields the theatre of fame throughout the civilized world" (1:140). Though at this point in her narration, more action will follow, she already points toward the fate of the metaphor. Whatever dynamics may be suggested by a theater of action, a theater of fame seems not too removed from a hall of fame, a place where the great actors are exhibited for a reverential public and stared at in their fixed greatness. When Patience Lovell Wright mounts a real exhibition of waxen heroes in Philadelphia and others display busts, transparencies, and the like elsewhere, they are expressing in physical space what Mercy Warren renders metaphorically: the conclusion, in spectacle form, of a completed process.

That conclusion is, of course, providentially forged. While not everyone agrees that America is marked out for a special treatment in history, those who do not, like postwar John Adams, become, as Gordon Wood explains, increasingly "irrelevant" to a public who take for granted the providential basis for republican ideology (*Creation*, 567–92). Mercy Warren does not simply trumpet American greatness; in fact, in several places in her history she castigates American policy and practice when it veers into gratuitous violence and savagery. But like Philip Freneau in his postwar poem "On the Emigration to America and Peopling the Western Country" (1785), she sees beyond American depredations toward the Indians, for instance, to another view: "It is a pleasing anticipation, that the American revolution may be a means in the hands of Providence, of diffusing universal knowledge over a quarter of the globe, that for ages had been enveloped in darkness, ignorance, and barbarism" (2:127). This vision, however, is finally a static one, reflecting, perhaps, a greater wish to worship what has been done than to engage in any new prospects. In her final paragraph she returns to the theme of westward expansion in the post-Revolutionary era, foreseeing a time when the "western wilds" may reach that point "of improvement and perfection, beyond which the limits of human genius cannot reach; and this last civilized quarter of the globe may exhibit those striking traits of grandeur and magnificence, which the Divine OEconomist may have reserved to crown the closing scene, when the angel of his presence will stand upon the sea and upon the earth, lift up his hand to heaven, and swear by Him that liveth for ever and ever, that there shall be time no longer" (3:435–36). Though she speaks of "improvement," the picture she presents is one of current glory extended; the great drama is over, and what remain ahead are spectacles of affirmation.

Linked inextricably to the Revolutionary legacy is the exhibition of

events on a theater of universal significance. While theater as metaphor—and as developing institution—would continue to inform
American rhetoric in new and diverse ways, its connection to the
struggle for independence, the sacred cause of liberty, becomes encoded as a popular and vastly entertaining shrine in whose presence
future generations would be inspired to emulate the fathers. Like the
fourth theater of Captain Smith's quadrated world, Mercy Warren's
American theater is the last and best that history has to offer; but in her
very celebration of achievement, she leaves no formula for the revival
of the theater of fame in succeeding ages. That will come, but in more
immediate and stage-bound forms than the Stoic Warren might have
wished.

There is a footnote to Mercy Warren's *History* we might append
here. In discussing the appointment of Thomas Gage as new governor
in 1774 and his disallowing several new Massachusetts council members to sit, she says of her longtime friend John Adams that "his
appearance on the theatre of politics commenced at this period"
(1:132). To the retired and bitter President Adams, that line, as well as
her subsequent treatment of his career, had the effect of waving a red
coat before an old, but for his age no less angry, patriot bull. As Adams
read through the *History* in 1807, he must have been aghast at what he
saw as vicious treatment from a personal ally—and he did not wait to
finish the book before penning to her a series of vitriolic and outraged
letters that, with her own barbed rejoinders, led to a six-year break in
their relationship. How could she say he only entered "the theatre of
politics" in 1774?

> Does Mrs. Warren consider the House of Representatives as the only
> theatre of politics? Were not the courts of justice at that time, both
> superior and inferior, theatres of politics? Were not the Courts of Admi-
> ralty, general and special, theatres of politics? Were not the towns and
> their meetings theatres of politics? Were not the presses theatres of
> politics? Was not the Council Chamber, with the Governor and Council
> sitting in it, a theatre of politics? Was not every fireside, indeed, a theatre
> of politics?   (C. Adams, *Correspondence*, 354–55)

Adams's rhetorical questions isolate precisely those spaces and the
rituals enacted in them that show how powerfully the social conditions

of the prewar and wartime colonies shape themselves in the minds of observers into a theatrical view of American life. One might argue with performance theorists that courts and meetings are always theater; but certainly, ethnographers such as Victor Turner, Clifford Geertz, and Rhys Isaac would support the notion that the peculiar sociopolitical circumstances of late colonial life make theater the most dynamic metaphor for describing the American eighteenth century. In Adams's outburst at Warren, we can see something else: that for the participants in the events of the Revolutionary period, theater is a conscious, common, and often deliberately developed figure. Both Adams and Warren come to maturity when theatrum mundi becomes bonded to Whig ideology; both proclaim their allegiance to America in terms of theater and Providence. Now, in their seniority, these two practitioners of a rhetoric of theater enter anew into a theater of rhetoric to fight the war over again. Adams wants his place on the theater of fame to be assured, and no act on the theater of action to be ignored. Warren, unhappy over Adams's postwar drift to the right and his peculiar antirepublicanism, is not moved to rewrite the drama. The visits and letters between Quincy and Plymouth come to a virtual end (see Tichi, "Worried Celebrants," 286–90).

Through the mediating efforts of their mutual friend Elbridge Gerry, Adams and Warren eventually reconciled. Because there was a new war to engage their attention, the old one was left as history. In what amounts to a benediction, Adams writes to his friend and antagonist and wonders what those giants of the past, like Warren's brother James Otis, would have thought of "these times." For the survivors, however, history is about to pass them by. Adams closes his letter of reconciliation with what amounts to words of their mutual faith: "We have acted our parts. The curtain will soon be drawn upon us. We must leave the future to that Providence which has protected the past" (Nov. 24, 1813, Correspondence, 505).

❧

Instant Theater

$\mathcal{W}$hile theater as a metaphor for republican glory becomes enshrined in the celebratory rhetoric of a Fourth of July address or in the correspondence of an aging generation of retired revolutionaries, new forces are at work that revive and alter histrionic tropes for use in other areas of American life. With the success of *The Contrast* and the proliferation of American comic types, notably the stage Yankee, and with the growing popularity in the early national period of other plays and of playgoing, theatrical figures of speech become absorbed in new ways into American belles lettres, especially fiction. Cooper, Hawthorne, Melville, Twain, Howells, and James are only a few of the writers for whom theater becomes either an organizing principle of their prose or a source for analogies—or a means by which they can attack the falseness of their overly confident and commercial countrymen.

Yet as Americans work to find a rhetoric suitable for republican ideals, they discover that theater persists as more than a cliché. Republican institutions, including the theater, take on a new performative dimension; whereas ministers once took a play's length of time to deliver sermons, now lawyers at trial draw attention to themselves by taking hours for their deliveries (Ferguson, 69). With the circulation and eventual publication of Franklin's *Autobiography* (1818), Americans see that making up oneself has its rewards; and as star actors in nineteenth-century productions, laying claim to mass approval, seek to isolate their talents on stage and distinguish themselves from the rest of the cast, so Americans hell-bent for success imitate the formula of the socially observed individual, renowned for his appearance of humility (see Patterson, 3–33). Still, for many, the "Public theatre" of a retiring George Washington (*Writings*, 14:21) would be succeeded by the literal and figurative "spectacle" of a people who have achieved a comic reversal and turned the world upside down. In the new comic America, every citizen potentially becomes an actor in a pageant of affirmation.

Nevertheless, once theater is admitted as a mass entertainment, released from the libraries of ministers and lawyers, and staged in commercial theaters rather than on global platforms or in the shuttered rooms of collegiate debate clubs, it loses its Stoic-tragic edge and ceases to serve as a metaphor capable of arousing revolutionary fervor. My point has been all along that theater will out in one form or another and that the peculiar circumstances of American settlement produced a culture that was at once poor in playhouses but rich in figural stages. What must have seemed to urbanized Britons as colonial cultural deprivation was in fact a political advantage; but having used the trope of the providential theater successfully to achieve independence, Americans find no further utility in suppressing stage amusements.

This meant that grafted onto the old tradition—the providential drama of civilization enacted on the hill-stage of America in the theater of the world—was a new one in which American history could be converted quickly into theatrical performance. During the war, American writers used closet drama as a vehicle for the theatrical conversion of political events, but a drama that redirected its readers back to the real-world stage of the theatrum mundi; when the British used actual performances of plays in order to vamp the current political scene in America, they called attention to the stage actors instead, as in the *Blockade of Boston* episode, creating confusion and inciting from some supporters disgust. In postwar America, however, with high-minded theatrical metaphors still part of the popular rhetoric, the desires both to turn recent political events into staged ones and to keep Americans playing before the eyes of the world merge into a hybrid discourse where metaphor and institution remain in flux.

Such a mixed discourse has its ironies, of course. In the postwar

period, for example, not all ardor for independence could be recon-
verted into peaceful recreation. In 1786, a large number of poor
farmers in western Massachusetts initiated a series of protests, at first
vocal, then violent, against harsh commonwealth economic policies.
Among the rebels were former Revolutionary soldiers who, as one
contemporary historian put it, had "the applause of the world . . .
fresh on their minds, and . . . felt a title to retirement and repose";
when unfavorable politics and economic depression prevented them
from enjoying such applause, they banded together in the insurrection
known now as Shays' Rebellion (Minot, 16). Without articulate orators or well-educated leaders who could demand the attention of the
ruling patriot elite, the Shaysites were forced to frame their demands
as a "mob" protest but one unsanctified by the rhetoric of a providential stage. As a consequence, many firm patriots, once themselves
supportive of Boston street protests against the British, now lined up to
condemn the rebels. Samuel Adams, John Hancock, David Humphreys, Noah Webster, Abigail Adams, and Mercy Otis Warren (who
apparently urged her son Harry to enlist in the anti-Shays militia)—all
contributors to the metaphoric theater on which the Revolution was
fought—all spoke against the rebellion or directly participated in its
suppression (for an overview of the conflict and the roles played by
prominent patriots, see Szatmary). Having declared their drama on
the providential stage a triumph, the lettered patriots were unwilling to
see the world turned upside down again.

Accompanying the force sent to suppress the rebels was Major
Royall Tyler, an aide-de-camp to General Benjamin Lincoln. After
the battles in early 1787 that scattered the rebel bands, Tyler was sent
on February 13 or 14 to Vermont with the object of capturing Daniel
Shays himself and persuading the neighboring government to cooper-
ate with Massachusetts in ending the uprising. Though he failed to
catch Shays, Tyler through his eloquence apparently talked a church-
ful of unarmed insurgents into abandoning their cause and a meetinghouse full of Vermont legislators into coming to Massachusetts's assistance. By March he was in Boston, and by March 12 in New York,
seeking cooperation from that government. Within five weeks of his
arrival, on April 16, 1787, *The Contrast* was playing on the stage of
the John Street Theater. In less than three months, Tyler had gone

from being a key figure in suppressing rebellion to figuring himself in a letter as "the center" of government action ("How I wish you could look in upon me," he writes to friends) to employing theatrical figures of speech in a play about a Revolutionary patriot, Manly, who has just arrived in the city after fighting the Shays' rebels (Minot, 156–59; Szatmary, 108; Tanselle, 19– 23). For western Massachusetts farmers, the need to theatricalize their demands led to alienation, violence, defeat, and their desperate flight from home or surrender; for the eastern Massachusetts lawyer, who found himself at "center" stage in the government's cause, the need for theater led past his civic duties to urban civility—writing a play that justifies the need for an American drama—applause from a bourgeois audience in New York, and elevation among the fashionable to instant celebrity status.

Tyler's example illustrates what happens when theaters cannot be separated. For John Smith or Cotton Mather or John Adams, there was no question that the global theater on which they acted would be compromised by the presence of topical comic plays that reduced their principled strivings to mere entertainment. To represent the nation in oneself, one must not pander to a medium that contracts the worldwide importance of one's actions to the microcosm of the small stage. Yet for many Americans, the stage seems to have been precisely that medium where one's significance could be enhanced. For Tyler and his fellow citizens in a post-Revolutionary climate, the allure of theatrical applause was far more seductive than the approval of the "All-Seeing Eye of God." The theater of Providence was no longer theater enough.

Since Tyler's day and well beyond, new media have added new dimensions to performance tropes. But while television may have replaced the stage as the most readily imagined medium through which Americans metaphorically measure political events, theatrical figures of speech live on, even if they often must share the spotlight. In a recent newspaper column, for example, Ellen Goodman looks at current events—a sheriff's arrest of a pop singer for obscenity and a debate in Congress over an amendment to prohibit flag desecration— as indistinguishable from the media that publicize them. "It's the American way," Goodman says of the sheriff and the singer, both guests after the arrest on a popular television talk show: "One minute you're arresting a guy and the next minute you're in the green room with him." Once on camera, the two men then "played their parts like polished performers assigned the roles of enemies." In Congress, she continues, "the players are feeling the dramatic heat of flag burning," as congressmen and women are forced to take simpleminded positions on First Amendment problems "in the era of the 30-second spot." Her point is this: "These days it seems every issue becomes instant theater." By "theater" she means what Neil Postman does by "television": a medium whose form undermines the seriousness and complexity of political debate. And as Postman would add, the appearance in the same medium of singer and congressman, talk show host and news reporter, ultimately reduces everything to instant entertainment.

And yet, as I have tried to show, framing American experience as theater, even instant theater, is nothing new in itself. But the theater to which early Americans committed themselves and converted their events of great moment was of a different order altogether.

WORKS CITED

While I have made use of early imprints or microphotographed originals in doing research, I have, wherever it seemed suitable, cited more recently published facsimile or modern editions of texts. Because the latter are more generally available to scholars, it is hoped that the references will be of use to readers who lack immediate access to specialized collections.

All references to the Bible, unless contained within quotations, are to *The New Oxford Annotated Bible with the Apocrypha*, edited by Herbert G. May and Bruce M. Metzger (New York: Oxford University Press, 1977).

Abbreviations of frequently cited works are listed in the frontmatter.

Abel, Lionel. *Metatheatre: A New View of Dramatic Form*. New York: Hill and Wang, 1963.

Adams, Charles F. *Three Episodes of Massachusetts History*. 2 vols. 1892. Reprint. New York: Russell and Russell, 1965.

————, ed. *Correspondence between John Adams and Mercy Warren*. Boston, 1878. Reprint. New York: Arno, 1972.

————, ed. *Familiar Letters of John Adams and His Wife, Abigail Adams, During the Revolution*. Cambridge, Mass.: Riverside, 1876.

Adams, John. *Diary and Autobiography of John Adams*. Ed. L. H. Butterfield et al. 4 vols. Cambridge, Mass.: Belknap, 1961.

———— *The Works of John Adams*. Ed. Charles Francis Adams. 10 vols. Boston: Little, Brown, 1856.

Adams, John, et al. *Adams Family Correspondence*. Ed. L. H. Butterfield et al. 4 vols. Cambridge, Mass.: Belknap, 1963–73.

Addison, Joseph. *The Miscellaneous Works of Joseph Addison*. Ed. A. C. Guthkelch. Vol. 1, *Poems and Plays*. London: G. Bell, 1914.

Addison, Joseph, Richard Steele, et al. *The Spectator*. Ed. G. Gregory Smith. 4 vols. London: Dent, 1907.

Agnew, Jean-Christophe. *Worlds Apart: The Market and the Theater in*

Anglo-American Thought, 1550–1750. Cambridge: Cambridge University Press, 1986.

Albanese, Catherine L. *Sons of the Fathers: The Civil Religion of the American Revolution*. Philadelphia: Temple University Press, 1976.

Allman, Eileen Jorge. *Player-King and Adversary: Two Faces of Play in Shakespeare*. Baton Rouge: Louisiana State University Press, 1980.

André, John. *Major André's Journal*. Ed. William Abbatt. Tarrytown, 1930. Reprint. New York: Times/Arno, 1968.

Arner, Robert D. "The Death of Major André: Some Eighteenth-Century Views." *Early American Literature* 11 (1976): 52–67.

Augustine, Bishop of Hippo. *City of God*. Trans. Marcus Dods; intro. Thomas Merton. New York: Modern Library, 1950.

———. *Expositions on the Book of Psalms*. 6 vols. Oxford, 1848–57.

Aurelius, Marcus. *The Meditations*. Trans. G. M. A. Grube. Indianapolis: Bobbs-Merrill, 1963.

Bacon, Francis. *Selected Writings*. Ed. Hugh G. Dick. New York: Modern Library, 1955.

Bailyn, Bernard. *The Ideological Origins of the American Revolution*. Cambridge: Harvard University Press, 1967.

———, ed. *Pamphlets of the American Revolution, 1750–1776*. Vol. 1, 1750–65. Cambridge, Mass.: Belknap, 1965.

Baldwin, Ebenezer. *The Duty of Rejoicing under Calamities and Afflictions*. New York, 1776.

Baldwin, Simeon. *An Oration Pronounced before the Citizens of New-Haven, July 4th, 1788*. New Haven, 1788.

Bale, John. *A Comedy Concerning Three Laws of Nature, Moses, and Christ*. Ed. John S. Farmer. London: Tudor Facsimile Texts, 1908.

Barbour, Philip L. "Captain John Smith and the London Theatre." *Virginia Magazine of History and Biography* 83 (1975): 277–79.

———. *The Three Worlds of Captain John Smith*. Boston: Houghton Mifflin, 1964.

Barish, Jonas. *The Antitheatrical Prejudice*. Berkeley: University of California Press, 1981.

Barlow, Joel. *An Oration, Delivered at the North Church in Hartford at the Meeting of the Connecticut Society of the Cincinnati, July 4th, 1787*. Hartford, 1787.

———. *The Works of Joel Barlow*. Ed. William K. Bottorff and Arthur L. Ford. 2 vols. Gainesville, Fla.: Scholars' Facsimiles and Reprints, 1970.

Barnum, P. T. *Struggles and Triumphs; or, Forty Years' Recollections of P. T. Barnum Written by Himself*. Hartford: J. B. Burr, 1869. Abr. ed., ed. Carl Bode. New York: Penguin, 1981.

Barton, Andrew [Thomas Forrest?]. *The Disappointment*. Philadelphia, 1796.

Battis, Emery. *Saints and Sectaries: Anne Hutchinson and the Antinomian Controversy in the Massachusetts Bay Colony*. Chapel Hill: University of North Carolina Press, 1962.

The Battle of Brooklyn, A Farce of Two Acts. New York, 1776.

Beales, Ross W., Jr. "The Child in Seventeenth-Century America." In *American Childhood: A Research Guide and Historical Handbook*, ed. Joseph M. Hawes and N. Ray Hiner, 15–56. Westport, Conn.: Greenwood, 1985.

Beard, Thomas. *The Theatre of Gods Judgements*. 4th ed. London, 1648.

Bellamy, Joseph. *True Religion Delineated*. Boston, 1750.

Bercovitch, Sacvan. *The American Jeremiad*. Madison: University of Wisconsin Press, 1978.

———. *The Puritan Origins of the American Self*. New Haven: Yale University Press, 1975.

Binney, Barnabas. *An Oration on the Late Public Commencement at Rhode-Island College in Providence, September 1774*. Boston, 1774. Reprinted in *The Colonial Idiom*, ed. David Potter and Gordon L. Thomas, 51–74. Carbondale: Southern Illinois University Press, 1970.

Boucher, Jonathan. *A View of the Causes and Consequences of the American Revolution in Thirteen Discourses*. 1797. Reprint. New York: Russell and Russell, 1967.

Bouwsma, William J. *John Calvin: A Sixteenth-Century Portrait*. New York: Oxford University Press, 1988.

Bowdoin, James, Dr. Joseph Warren, and Samuel Pemberton. *A Short Narrative of the Horrid Massacre in Boston*. Boston, 1770. Reprinted in *Tracts of the American Revolution, 1763–1776*, ed. Merrill Jensen, 207–32. Indianapolis: Bobbs-Merrill, 1967.

Boyer, Paul, and Stephen Nissenbaum, eds. *The Salem Witchcraft Papers: Verbatim Transcripts of the Legal Documents of the Salem Witchcraft Outbreak of 1692*. 3 vols. New York: Da Capo, 1977.

Brackenridge, Hugh Henry. *The Battle of Bunkers-Hill, A Dramatic Piece*. Philadelphia, 1776.

Bradbrook, M. C. *The Rise of the Common Player: A Study of Actor and Society in Shakespeare's England*. London: Chatto and Windus, 1962.

Bradford, William. *Of Plymouth Plantation, 1620–1647*. Intro. Francis Murphy. New York: Modern Library, 1981.

Bradstreet, Anne. *The Complete Works of Anne Bradstreet*. Ed. Joseph R. McElrath, Jr., and Allan P. Robb. Boston: Twayne, 1981.

Breitwieser, Mitchell Robert. *Cotton Mather and Benjamin Franklin: The*

Price of Representative Personality. Cambridge: Cambridge University Press, 1984.

Brown, Alexander. *The Genesis of the United States . . . 1605–1616.* Vol. 1. Boston: Houghton Mifflin, 1891.

Brown, Alice. *Mercy Warren.* New York: Scribner's, 1896.

Browne, Thomas. *The Works of Sir Thomas Browne.* Ed. Geoffrey Keynes. Vol. 1. Chicago: University of Chicago Press, 1964.

Bulkeley, Gershom. *The People's Right to Election or Alteration of Government in Connecticut, Argued in a Letter.* Philadelphia, 1689.

Bulkeley, Peter. *The Gospel-Covenant; or The Covenant of Grace Opened.* 2d ed. London, 1651.

Bunyan, John. *The Complete Works.* Ed. Henry Stebbing. Vol. 2. New York: Johnson Reprint, 1970.

Burke, Kenneth. *A Grammar of Motives.* Englewood Cliffs, N.J.: Prentice-Hall, 1945.

———. *The Philosophy of Literary Form: Studies in Symbolic Action.* 3d ed. Berkeley: University of California Press, 1973.

Burns, Elizabeth. *Theatricality: A Study of Convention in the Theatre and in Social Life.* New York: Harper and Row, 1972.

Burr, George Lincoln, ed. *Narratives of the Witchcraft Cases, 1648–1706.* New York: Scribner's, 1914.

Burton, Robert. *The Anatomy of Melancholy.* Ed. Holbrook Jackson. New York: Vintage, 1977.

Bush, Sargent, Jr. "'Revising What We Have Done Amisse': John Cotton and John Wheelwright, 1640." *William and Mary Quarterly,* 3d ser., 45 (1988): 733–50.

———. *The Writings of Thomas Hooker: Spiritual Adventure in Two Worlds.* Madison: University of Wisconsin Press, 1980.

Byles, Mather. *The Flourish of the Annual Spring.* Boston, 1741.

———. *A Sermon, Delivered March 6th 1760.* New London, Conn., 1760.

Calderwood, James L. *Shakespearean Metadrama: The Argument of the Play in "Titus Andronicus," "Love's Labour's Lost," "Romeo and Juliet," "A Midsummer Night's Dream," and "Richard II."* Minneapolis: University of Minnesota Press, 1971.

Caldwell, Patricia. "The Antinomian Language Controversy." *Harvard Theological Review* 69 (1976): 345–67.

———. *The Puritan Conversion Narrative: The Beginnings of American Expression.* Cambridge: Cambridge University Press, 1983.

Calef, Robert. *More Wonders of the Invisible World.* London, 1700. Excerpt reprinted in *Narratives of the Witchcraft Cases, 1648–1706*, ed. George Lincoln Burr, 296–393. New York: Scribner's, 1914.

Calvin, John. *Commentaries on the First Book of Moses Called Genesis.* Trans. John King. Vols. 1–2, *Calvin's Commentaries*. Edinburgh: Calvin Translation Society, 1844–1856. Reprint. Grand Rapids, Mich.: Baker Book House, 1979.

Cannon, Charles K. "'As in a Theater': *Hamlet* in the Light of Calvin's Doctrine of Predestination." *Studies in English Literature, 1500–1900* 11 (1971): 203–22.

Capp, B. S. *The Fifth Monarchy Men: A Study in Seventeenth-Century English Millenarianism.* London: Faber and Faber, 1972.

Carson, Jane. *Colonial Virginians at Play.* Williamsburg: Colonial Williamsburg, 1965.

Cassirer, Ernst, Paul Oskar Kristeller, and John Herman Randall, Jr., eds. *The Renaissance Philosophy of Man.* Chicago: University of Chicago Press, 1948.

Chauncy, Charles. *Enthusiasm Described and Caution'd Against.* Boston, 1742. Reprinted in *The Great Awakening: Documents Illustrating the Crisis and Its Consequences*, ed. Alan Heimert and Perry Miller, 229–56. Indianapolis: Bobbs-Merrill, 1967.

———. *Seasonable Thoughts on the State of Religion in New-England.* Boston, 1743. Excerpt reprinted in *The Great Awakening: Documents Illustrating the Crisis and Its Consequences*, ed. Alan Heimert and Perry Miller, 293–322. Indianapolis: Bobbs-Merrill, 1967.

Chrysostom, Saint John. *Commentary on Saint John the Apostle and Evangelist.* Trans. Sister Thomas Aquinas Goggin. Vol. 1, *Homilies 1–47.* Washington, D.C.: Catholic University of America Press, 1957. Vol. 2, *Homilies 48–88.* New York: Fathers of the Church, 1960.

Cicero, Marcus Tullius. *Selected Works.* Trans. Michael Grant. Baltimore: Penguin, 1971.

Clapp, William W., Jr. *Record of the Boston Stage.* Boston: J. Munroe, 1853.

Colbourn, H. Trevor. *The Lamp of Experience: Whig History and the Intellectual Origins of the American Revolution.* Chapel Hill: University of North Carolina Press, 1965.

Colman, Benjamin. *The Piety and Duty of Rulers to Comfort and Encourage the Ministry of Christ.* Boston, 1708. Reprinted in *The Colonial Idiom*, ed. David Potter and Gordon L. Thomas, 412–29. Carbondale: Southern Illinois University Press, 1970.

———. *Practical Discourses on the Parable of the Ten Virgins.* 2d ed. Boston, 1747.

Curtius, Ernst Robert. *European Literature and the Latin Middle Ages*. Trans. Willard R. Trask. New York: Pantheon, 1953.

DaMatta, Roberto. "Carnival in Multiple Planes." In *Rite, Drama, Festival, Spectacle: Rehearsals toward a Theory of Cultural Performance*, ed. John J. MacAloon, 208–40. Philadelphia: Institute for the Study of Human Issues, 1984.

Dana, James. *A Sermon, Preached before the General Assembly*. Hartford, 1779.

Danforth, Samuel. *Errand into the Wilderness*. Cambridge, Mass., 1671. Reprinted in *The Wall and the Garden: Selected Massachusetts Election Sermons, 1670–1775*, ed. A. W. Plumstead, 54–77. Minneapolis: University of Minnesota Press, 1968.

Darling, Thomas. *Some Remarks on Mr. President Clap's History and Vindication of the Doctrines of the New-England Churches, & c*. New Haven, 1757. Excerpt reprinted in *The Great Awakening: Documents Illustrating the Crisis and Its Consequences*, ed. Alan Heimert and Perry Miller, 585–92. Indianapolis: Bobbs-Merrill, 1967.

Davidson, James West. *The Logic of Millennial Thought: Eighteenth-Century New England*. New Haven: Yale University Press, 1977.

Davidson, Philip. *Propaganda and the American Revolution, 1763–1787*. Chapel Hill: University of North Carolina Press, 1941.

Davies, Samuel. *Virginia's Danger and Remedy. Two Discourses*. Williamsburg, 1756. Facsimile reprint in *Sermons and Cannonballs: Eleven Sermons on Military Events of Historic Significance during the French and Indian Wars, 1689–1760*, ed. James A. Levernier and Douglas R. Wilnes, Delmar, N.Y.: Scholars' Facsimiles and Reprints, 1982.

Davis, Richard Beale. *A Colonial Southern Bookshelf*. Athens: University of Georgia Press, 1979.

Dickens, Charles. *American Notes for General Circulation*. London: Chapman and Hall, 1850.

Dickinson, John. *The Late Regulations respecting the British Colonies on the Continent of America Considered*. Philadelphia, 1765. Reprinted in *Pamphlets of the American Revolution, 1750–1776*. Vol. 1, 1750–65, ed. Bernard Bailyn, 669–91. Cambridge, Mass.: Belknap, 1965.

———. *A Letter from the Country, to a Gentleman in Philadelphia . . . November 27, 1773*. Philadelphia, 1773.

Donne, John. *Poetry and Prose*. Ed. Frank J. Warnke. New York: Modern Library, 1967.

———. *The Sermons of John Donne*. Ed. George R. Potter and Evelyn M. Simpson. 10 vols. Berkeley: University of California Press, 1953–62.

Downey, James. *The Eighteenth-Century Pulpit: A Study of the Sermons of Butler, Berkeley, Secker, Sterne, Whitefield, and Wesley.* Oxford: Oxford University Press, 1969.

Dunn, Esther Cloudman. *Shakespeare in America.* New York: Macmillan, 1939.

Edelberg, Cynthia Dubin. *Jonathan Odell, Loyalist Poet of the American Revolution.* Durham: Duke University Press, 1987.

Edwards, Jonathan. *Apocalyptic Writings.* Ed. Stephen J. Stein. Vol. 5, *The Works.* New Haven: Yale University Press, 1977.

———. *The Great Awakening.* Ed. C. C. Goen. Vol. 4, *The Works.* New Haven: Yale University Press, 1972.

———. *A History of the Work of Redemption.* 1777. Excerpt reprinted in *The Great Awakening: Documents Illustrating the Crisis and Its Consequences,* ed. Alan Heimert and Perry Miller, 21–34. Indianapolis: Bobbs-Merrill, 1967.

———. *Sinners in the Hands of an Angry God.* Boston, 1741.

Edwards, Richard. *Richard Edwards's "Damon and Pithias": A Critical Old-Spelling Edition.* Ed. D. Jerry White. New York: Garland, 1980.

Elliott, Emory. *Revolutionary Writers: Literature and Authority in the New Republic, 1725–1810.* New York: Oxford University Press, 1982.

Emerson, Everett. *Captain John Smith.* New York: Twayne, 1971.

———. "Captain John Smith as Editor: *The Generall Historie.*" *Virginia Magazine of History and Biography* 75 (1967): 143–56.

———, ed. *American Literature, 1764–1789: The Revolutionary Years.* Madison: University of Wisconsin Press, 1977.

Epictetus. *The Enchiridion.* 2d ed., trans. Thomas W. Higginson; intro. Albert Salomon. Indianapolis: Bobbs-Merrill, 1955.

Erasmus, Desiderius. *The Praise of Folly.* Trans. Leonard F. Dean. Chicago: Packard, 1946.

Erikson, Kai T. *Wayward Puritans: A Study in the Sociology of Deviance.* New York: Wiley, 1966.

Erskine-Hill, Howard. *The Augustan Idea in English Literature.* London: Edward Arnold, 1983.

"The Examination of Mrs. Anne Hutchinson at the Court at Newtown." In *The Antinomian Controversy, 1636–1638: A Documentary History,* ed. David D. Hall, 311–48. Middletown, Conn.: Wesleyan University Press, 1968; rev. ed., Durham, N.C.: Duke University Press, 1990.

Ferguson, Robert A. *Law and Letters in American Culture.* Cambridge: Harvard University Press, 1984.

Fergusson, Francis. *The Idea of a Theater: A Study of Ten Plays. The Art of*

Drama in Changing Perspective. Princeton: Princeton University Press, 1949.

Fielding, Henry. *The History of Tom Jones.* Ed. R. P. C. Mutter. New York: Penguin, 1966.

Firmin, Giles. *The Real Christian, or A Treatise of Effectual Calling.* London, 1670. Reprint. Boston, 1742.

Fisch, Harold. "Shakespeare and 'The Theatre of the World.'" In *The Morality of Art: Essays Presented to G. Wilson Knight by His Colleagues and Friends,* ed. D. W. Jefferson, 76–86. New York: Barnes and Noble, 1969.

Fliegelman, Jay. *Prodigals and Pilgrims: The American Revolutionaries against Patriarchal Authority, 1750–1800.* Cambridge: Cambridge University Press, 1982.

Ford, Paul Leicester. *Washington and the Theatre.* New York: Dunlap Society, 1899.

Forker, Charles R. "Shakespeare's Theatrical Symbolism and Its Function in *Hamlet.*" *Shakespeare Quarterly* 4 (1963): 215–29.

Foster, Daniel. *A Sermon Preached before His Excellency John Hancock, Esq. Governour.* Boston, 1790.

Foxe, John. *Two Latin Comedies by John Foxe the Martyrologist: "Titus et Gesippus"; "Christus Triumphans."* Ed. and trans. John Hazel Smith. Ithaca, N.Y.: Cornell University Press, 1973.

Franklin, Benjamin. *The Autobiography and Selections from His Other Writings.* Ed. Herbert W. Schneider. Indianapolis: Bobbs-Merrill, 1952.

Fraser, Russell. *The War against Poetry.* Princeton: Princeton University Press, 1970.

Freneau, Philip. *The Poems.* Ed. Fred Lewis Pattee. 3 vols. Princeton: Princeton University Library, 1903.

———. *The Prose.* Ed. Philip M. Marsh. New Brunswick, N.J.: Scarecrow, 1955.

Fried, Michael. *Absorption and Theatricality: Painting and Beholder in the Age of Diderot.* Berkeley: University of California Press, 1980.

Frisbie, Levi. *An Oration, Delivered at Ipswich.* Boston, 1783.

Fritz, Jean. *Cast for a Revolution: Some American Friends and Enemies, 1728–1814.* Boston: Houghton Mifflin, 1972.

Fussell, Paul, ed. *English Augustan Poetry.* Garden City, N.Y.: Anchor, 1972.

Galloway, Joseph. *A Candid Examination of the Mutual Claims of Great Britain and the Colonies.* New York, 1775. Reprinted in *Tracts of the American Revolution, 1763–1776,* ed. Merrill Jensen, 350–99. Indianapolis: Bobbs-Merrill, 1967.

Garden, Alexander. *Regeneration, and the Testimony of the Spirit.* Boston,

1741. Excerpt reprinted in *The Great Awakening: Documents Illustrating the Crisis and Its Consequences*, ed. Alan Heimert and Perry Miller, 47–61. Indianapolis: Bobbs-Merrill, 1967.

Gay, Carol. "The Fettered Tongue: A Study of the Speech Defect of Cotton Mather." *American Literature* 46 (1975): 451–64.

Gay, Frederick L., ed. "Note and Documents on Rev. Francis Marbury." *Massachusetts Historical Society Proceedings* 48 (1915): 280–91.

Geertz, Clifford. *The Interpretation of Cultures*. New York: Basic Books, 1973.

———. *Negara: The Theatre State in Nineteenth-Century Bali*. Princeton: Princeton University Press, 1980.

Ginsberg, Elaine K. "The Patriot Pamphleteers." In *American Literature, 1764–1789: The Revolutionary Years*, ed. Everett Emerson, 19–38. Madison: University of Wisconsin Press, 1977.

Godfrey, Thomas. *The Prince of Parthia: A Tragedy*. Ed. Archibald Henderson. Boston: Little, Brown, 1917.

Goffman, Erving. *The Presentation of Self in Everyday Life*. Garden City, N.Y.: Doubleday/Anchor, 1959.

Goodman, Ellen. "Nation Needs Bigger Wait-Just-a-Minute Club." Raleigh *News and Observer*, June 19, 1990, A9.

Gosson, Stephen. *Playes Confuted in Five Actions*. London, 1582. Facsimile reprint. New York: Garland, 1972.

Greenblatt, Stephen. *Renaissance Self-Fashioning: From More to Shakespeare*. Chicago: University of Chicago Press, 1980.

Greven, Philip. *The Protestant Temperament: Patterns of Child-Rearing, Religious Experience, and the Self in Early America*. New York: Knopf, 1977.

Griswold, Wesley S. *The Night the Revolution Began: The Boston Tea Party, 1773*. Brattleboro, Vt.: Stephen Greene, 1972.

Gura, Philip F. *A Glimpse of Sion's Glory: Puritan Radicalism in New England, 1620–1660*. Middletown, Conn.: Wesleyan University Press, 1984.

Hall, David D. *The Faithful Shepherd: A History of the New England Ministry in the Seventeenth Century*. Chapel Hill: University of North Carolina Press, 1972.

———. "A World of Wonders: The Mentality of the Supernatural in Seventeenth-Century New England." In *Seventeenth-Century New England*, ed. David D. Hall and David Grayson Allen, 239–74. Boston: Colonial Society of Massachusetts, 1984.

———, ed. *The Antinomian Controversy, 1636–1638: A Documentary History*. Middletown, Conn.: Wesleyan University Press, 1968; rev. ed., Durham, N.C.: Duke University Press, 1990.

Hall, Joseph. *Meditations and Vows, Divine and Moral.* Ed. Charles Sayle. New York: Dutton, 1901.

Hambrick-Stowe, Charles E. *The Practice of Piety: Puritan Devotional Discipline in Seventeenth-Century New England.* Chapel Hill: University of North Carolina Press, 1982.

Harris, Kenneth Marc. *Hypocrisy and Self-Deception in Hawthorne's Fiction.* Charlottesville: University Press of Virginia, 1988.

Hastings, George Everett. *The Life and Work of Francis Hopkinson.* Chicago: University of Chicago Press, 1926.

Hatch, Nathan O. *The Sacred Case of Liberty: Republican Thought and the Millennium in Revolutionary New England.* New Haven: Yale University Press, 1977.

Hawes, Joseph M., and N. Ray Hiner, eds. *American Childhood: A Research Guide and Historical Handbook.* Westport, Conn.: Greenwood, 1985.

Hawthorne, Nathaniel. *The Scarlet Letter.* 2d ed., ed. Sculley Bradley et al. New York: Norton, 1978.

Heimert, Alan. *Religion and the American Mind from the Great Awakening to the Revolution.* Cambridge: Harvard University Press, 1966.

Heimert, Alan, and Andrew Delbanco, eds. *The Puritans in America: A Narrative Anthology.* Cambridge: Harvard University Press, 1985.

Heimert, Alan, and Perry Miller, eds. *The Great Awakening: Documents Illustrating the Crisis and Its Consequences.* Indianapolis: Bobbs-Merrill, 1967.

Henry, Stuart C. *George Whitefield: Wayfaring Witness.* New York: Abingdon, 1957.

Herbert, George. *The Works.* Ed. F. E. Hutchinson. Oxford: Clarendon, 1941.

Heywood, Thomas. *An Apology for Actors.* London, 1612. Facsimile reprinted with *A Refutation of the Apology for Actors* by I. G. Ed. Richard H. Perkinson. New York: Scholars' Facsimiles and Reprints, 1941.

Hill, Christopher. *The World Turned Upside Down: Radical Ideas during the English Revolution.* London: Temple Smith, 1972.

Hilliard, Timothy. *The duty of a PEOPLE under the oppression of MAN, to seek deliverance from GOD.* Boston, 1774. Facsimile reprinted in *Revolutionary War Sermons,* ed. David R. Williams. Delmar, N.Y.: Scholars' Facsimiles and Reprints, 1984.

Hiltner, Judith R. *The Newspaper Verse of Philip Freneau: An Edition and Bibliographical Survey.* Troy, N.Y.: Whitston, 1986.

Holden, William P. *Anti-Puritan Satire, 1572–1642.* New Haven: Yale University Press, 1954.

Hollis, C. Carroll. *Language and Style in "Leaves of Grass."* Baton Rouge: Louisiana State University Press, 1983.

Hookcr, Thomas. *The Application of Redemption.* London, 1657. Facsimile reprint. New York: Arno, 1972.

———. *The Carnal Hypocrite.* London, 1638. Reprinted in *Thomas Hooker: Writings in England and Holland, 1626–1633,* ed. George H. Williams et al., 91–123. Cambridge: Harvard University Press, 1975.

———. *The Christians Two Chiefe Lessons, viz. Self-Deniall and Self-Tryall.* London, 1640. Facsimile reprint. New York: Arno, 1972.

———. *The Poore Doubting Christian Drawn Unto Christ.* 1629. Reprinted in *Thomas Hooker: Writings in England and Holland, 1626–1633,* ed. George H. Williams et al., 152–86. Cambridge: Harvard University Press, 1975.

———. *The Soules Exaltation.* London, 1638. Facsimile reprint. New York: AMS, 1982.

———. *The Soules Humiliation.* 3d ed. London, 1640. Facsimile reprint. New York: AMS, 1981.

———. *The Soules Implantation.* London, 1640. Facsimile reprint. New York: AMS, 1981.

———. *The Soules Preparation for Christ.* 4th ed. London, 1638. Facsimile reprint. New York: AMS, 1982.

Hopkinson, Francis. *Comical Spirit of Seventy-Six: The Humor of Francis Hopkinson.* Ed. Paul M. Zall. San Marino, Calif.: Huntington Library, 1976.

Horace and Persius. *The Satires.* Trans. Niall Rudd. Harmondsworth: Penguin, 1973.

Horst, Irvin Buckwalter. *The Radical Brethren: Anabaptism and the English Reformation to 1558.* Nieuwkoop: B. de Graaf, 1972.

Hudson, Anne. *The Premature Reformation: Wycliffite Texts and Lollard History.* Oxford: Clarendon, 1988.

———, ed. *Selections from English Wycliffite Writing.* Cambridge: Cambridge University Press, 1978.

Huizinga, Johan. *Homo Ludens: A Study of the Play Element in Culture.* Boston: Beacon, 1950.

Humphreys, David. *A Poem on the Happiness of America.* Hartford, 1786.

Hutchinson, Thomas. *The History of the Colony and Province of Massachusetts-Bay.* Ed. Lawrence Shaw Mayo. Vol. 1. Cambridge: Harvard University Press, 1936.

Hyneman, Charles Shang, and Donald S. Lutz, eds. *American Political Writing During the Founding Era, 1760–1805.* 2 vols. Indianapolis: Liberty Press, 1988.

Inglis, Charles. *The Case of Major John André.* New York, 1780.

Isaac, Rhys. "Dramatizing the Ideology of Revolution: Popular Mobilization in Virginia, 1774 to 1776." *William and Mary Quarterly,* 3d ser., 33 (1976): 357–85.

————. *The Transformation of Virginia, 1740–1790.* Chapel Hill: University of North Carolina Press, 1982.

Jensen, Merrill, ed. *Tracts of the American Revolution, 1763–1776.* Indianapolis: Bobbs-Merrill, 1967.

John of Salisbury. *Frivolities of Courtiers and Footprints of Philosophers: Being a Translation of the First, Second, and Third Books and Selections from the Seventh and Eighth Books of the Policraticus of John of Salisbury.* Trans. Joseph B. Pike. Minneapolis: University of Minnesota Press, 1938.

Johnson, Edward. *Johnson's Wonder-Working Providence, 1628–1651.* Ed. J. Franklin Jameson. New York: Scribner's, 1910.

Jonson, Ben. *Three Comedies: Volpone, The Alchemist, Bartholomew Fair.* Ed. Michael Jamieson. Harmondsworth: Penguin, 1966.

Kendall, Ritchie D. *The Drama of Dissent: The Radical Poetics of Nonconformity, 1380–1590.* Chapel Hill: University of North Carolina Press, 1986.

Kenyon, Cecilia M., ed. *The Antifederalists.* Indianapolis: Bobbs-Merrill, 1966.

Kernan, Alvin B. *The Playwright as Magician: Shakespeare's Image of the Poet in the English Public Theater.* New Haven: Yale University Press, 1979.

Kibbey, Ann. *The Interpretation of Material Shapes in Puritanism: A Study of Rhetoric, Prejudice, and Violence.* Cambridge: Cambridge University Press, 1986.

Labaree, Benjamin Woods. *The Boston Tea Party.* New York: Oxford University Press, 1964.

Lafayette, Marquis de. *Lafayette in the Age of the American Revolution: Selected Letters and Papers, 1776–1790.* Ed. Stanley J. Idzerda et al. Vol. 4, April 1, 1781–December 23, 1781. Ithaca, N.Y.: Cornell University Press, 1981.

Lakoff, George, and Mark Johnson. *Metaphors We Live By.* Chicago: University of Chicago Press, 1980.

Lamont, William M. *Marginal Prynne, 1600–1669.* London: Routledge, 1963.

Lang, Amy Schrager. "'A Flood of Errors': Chauncy and Edwards in the Great Awakening." In *Jonathan Edwards and the American Experience,* ed. Nathan O. Hatch and Harry S. Stout. New York: Oxford University Press, 1988.

———. *Prophetic Woman: Anne Hutchinson and the Problem of Dissent in the Literature of New England*. Berkeley: University of California Press, 1987.

Laska, Vera O. *"Remember the Ladies": Outstanding Women of the American Revolution*. Boston: Commonwealth of Massachusetts Bicentennial Commission, 1976.

Leacock, John. *The Fall of British Tyranny; or American Liberty Triumphant*. Philadelphia, 1776.

Leary, Lewis. *That Rascal Freneau: A Study in Literary Failure*. New Brunswick, N.J.: Rutgers University Press, 1941.

Lemay, J. A. Leo. "The Voice of Captain John Smith." Review of *The Complete Works of Captain John Smith*, ed. Philip L. Barbour. *Southern Literary Journal* 20 (1987): 113–31.

Leonard, Daniel, and John Adams. "Massachusettensis and Novanglus (1774–1775)." In *Tracts of the American Revolution, 1763–1776*, ed. Merrill Jensen, 277–349. Indianapolis: Bobbs-Merrill, 1967.

Leverenz, David. *The Language of Puritan Feeling: An Exploration in Literature, Psychology, and Social History*. New Brunswick, N.J.: Rutgers University Press, 1980.

Levernier, James A., and Douglas R. Wilnes, eds. *Sermons and Cannonballs: Eleven Sermons on Military Events of Historic Significance during the French and Indian Wars, 1689–1760*. Delmar, N.Y.: Scholars' Facsimiles and Reprints, 1982.

Levin, David, ed. *Jonathan Edwards: A Profile*. New York: Hill and Wang, 1969.

Levin, Samuel R. *Metaphoric Worlds: Conceptions of a Romantic Nature*. New Haven: Yale University Press, 1988.

Levy, Babette May. *Preaching in the First Half Century of New England History*. Hartford: American Society of Church History, 1945.

Litto, Fredric M. "Addison's *Cato* in the Colonies." *William and Mary Quarterly*, 3d ser., 23 (1966): 432–49.

Loftis, John. *The Politics of Drama in Augustan England*. Oxford: Clarendon, 1963.

Long, A. A. *Hellenistic Philosophy: Stoics, Epicureans, and Sceptics*. 2d ed. Berkeley: University of California Press, 1986.

Lovejoy, David S. *Religious Enthusiasm in the New World: Heresy to Revolution*. Cambridge: Harvard University Press, 1985.

———, ed. *Religious Enthusiasm and the Great Awakening*. Englewood Cliffs, N.J.: Prentice-Hall, 1969.

Lowance, Mason, I., Jr. *The Language of Canaan: Metaphor and Symbol in*

New England from the Puritans to the Transcendentalists. Cambridge: Harvard University Press, 1980.

MacAloon, John J., ed. *Rite, Drama, Festival, Spectacle: Rehearsals toward a Theory of Cultural Performance*. Philadelphia: Institute for the Study of Human Issues, 1984.

Mack, Maynard, Jr. *Killing the King: Three Studies in Shakespeare's Tragic Structure*. New Haven: Yale University Press, 1973.

McLuhan, Marshall. *Understanding Media: The Extensions of Man*. New York: McGraw-Hill, 1964.

Madison, James. *A Sermon Preached before the Convention of the Protestant Episcopal Church in the State of Virginia*. Richmond, 1786.

——. *A Sermon, preached in the County of Botetourt*. Richmond, 1781.

Marprelate, Martin [pseud.]. *The Marprelate Tracts, 1588, 1589*. Ed. William Pierce. London: Clarke, 1911.

Marshall, David. *The Figure of Theater: Shaftesbury, Defoe, Adam Smith, and George Eliot*. New York: Columbia University Press, 1986.

——. *The Surprising Effects of Sympathy: Marivaux, Diderot, Rousseau, and Mary Shelley*. Chicago: University of Chicago Press, 1988.

Marvell, Andrew. *Complete Poetry*. Ed. George DeF. Lord. New York: Modern Library, 1968.

Mather, Cotton. *Advice from Taberah*. Boston, 1711. Facsimile reprinted in Cotton Mather, *Days of Humiliation, Times of Affliction and Disaster: Nine Sermons for Restoring Favor with an Angry God*. Intro. George Harrison Orians. Gainesville, Fla.: Scholars' Facsimiles and Reprints, 1970.

——. *Bonifacius: An Essay upon the Good*. Ed. David Levin. Cambridge, Mass.: Belknap, 1966.

——. *Days of Humiliation, Times of Affliction and Disaster: Nine Sermons for Restoring Favor with an Angry God*. Intro. George Harrison Orians. Gainesville, Fla.: Scholars' Facsimiles and Reprints, 1970.

——. *Diary*. Ed. Worthington C. Ford. 2 vols. 1912. Reprint. New York: Ungar, n.d.

——. *An Elegy on The Much-to-be-deplored Death of . . . Mr. Nathaneal Collins*. Boston, 1685.

——. *Humiliations follow'd with Deliverances*. Boston, 1697. Facsimile reprinted in Cotton Mather, *Days of Humiliation, Times of Affliction and Disaster: Nine Sermons for Restoring Favor with an Angry God*. Intro. George Harrison Orians. Gainesville, Fla.: Scholars' Facsimiles and Reprints, 1970.

——. *Magnalia Christi Americana*. Ed. Thomas Robbins. 2 vols. 1852. Reprint. New York: Russell and Russell, 1967.

————. *Manuductio ad Ministerium: Directions for a Candidate of the Ministry.* Boston, 1726. Facsimile reprint. New York: Columbia University Press, 1938.

————. *Memorable Providences, Relating to Witchcrafts and Possessions.* Boston, 1689. Reprinted in *Narratives of the Witchcraft Cases, 1648–1706,* ed. George Lincoln Burr, 93–143. New York: Scribner's, 1914.

————. *Ratio Disciplinae Fratria Nov-Anglorum.* Boston, 1726. Facsimile reprint. New York: Arno, 1972.

————. *The Saviour with his Rainbow.* London, 1714. Facsimile reprinted in Cotton Mather, *Days of Humiliation, Times of Affliction and Disaster: Nine Sermons for Restoring Favor with an Angry God.* Intro. George Harrison Orians. Gainesville, Fla.: Scholars' Facsimiles and Reprints, 1970.

————. *Selected Letters of Cotton Mather.* Ed. Kenneth Silverman. Baton Rouge: Louisiana State University Press, 1971.

————. *Selections.* Ed. Kenneth Murdock. 1926. Reprint. New York: Hafner, 1973.

————. *The Short History of New England.* Boston, 1694.

————. *Thaumatographia Christiana.* Boston, 1701.

————. *The Wonders of the Invisible World.* Boston, 1693.

Mather, Increase. *An Arrow against Profane and Promiscuous Dancing.* Boston, [1686].

————. *A Call from Heaven to the Present and Succeeding Generations.* Boston, 1697. Facsimile reprinted in Increase Mather, *Jeremiads.* New York: AMS, 1984.

————. *David Serving His Generation.* Boston, 1698. Facsimile reprinted in Increase Mather, *Jeremiads.* New York: AMS, 1984.

————. *A Discourse Concerning Faith and Fervancy in Prayer.* Boston, 1710.

————. *A Discourse Concerning the Uncertainty of the Times of Men, and the Necessity of being Prepared for Sudden Changes & Death.* Boston, 1697. Reprinted in *The Colonial Idiom,* ed. David Potter and Gordon L. Thomas, 377–94. Carbondale: Southern Illinois University Press, 1970.

————. *Doctrine.* New York: AMS, 1985.

————. *The Doctrine of Divine Providence Opened and Applyed.* Boston, 1684. Facsimile reprinted in Increase Mather, *Doctrine.* New York: AMS, 1985.

————. *Jeremiads.* New York: AMS, 1984.

————. *Kometographia. Or A Discourse Concerning Comets.* Boston, 1683.

Mauduit, Israel. *Strictures on the Philadelphia Mischianza.* Philadelphia, 1780.

Mayhew, Jonathan. *A Discourse concerning Unlimited Submission and Non-resistance to the Higher Powers.* Boston, 1750. Reprinted in *Pamphlets of the American Revolution, 1750–1776.* Vol. 1, 1750–65, ed. Bernard Bailyn, 212–47. Cambridge, Mass.: Belknap, 1965.

————. *A Sermon.* Boston, 1754. Reprinted in *The Wall and the Garden: Selected Massachusetts Election Sermons, 1670–1775,* ed. A. W. Plumstead, 289–319. Minneapolis: University of Minnesota Press, 1968.

Meserole, Harrison T., ed. *Seventeenth-Century American Poetry.* Garden City, N.Y.: Anchor, 1968.

Meserve, Walter J. *An Emerging Entertainment: The Drama of the American People to 1828.* Bloomington: Indiana University Press, 1977.

Middlekauff, Robert. *The Glorious Cause: The American Revolution, 1763–1789.* New York: Oxford University Press, 1982.

Miller, Perry. *Errand into the Wilderness.* New York: Harper and Row, 1964.

————. *The New England Mind: From Colony to Province.* Cambridge, Mass.: Belknap, 1953.

————. *Orthodoxy in Massachusetts, 1630–1650.* Intro. David D. Hall. New York: Harper and Row, 1970.

Minot, George Richards. *The History of the Insurrections in Massachusetts in the Year Seventeen Hundred and Eighty Six.* 1788. 2d ed. 1810. Facsimile reprint. Freeport, N.Y.: Books for Libraries, 1970.

Mitchell, Jonathan. *A Discourse of the Glory To which GOD hath called Believers.* 2d ed. Boston, 1721.

Montesquieu, Baron de (Charles de Secondat). *Persian Letters.* Trans. John Ozell. 2 vols. London, 1722. Facsimile reprint. New York: Garland, 1972.

More, Thomas. *Utopia.* Ed. Edward Surtz. New Haven: Yale University Press, 1964.

Morgan, Edmund S., and Helen M. Morgan. *The Stamp Act Crisis: Prologue to Revolution.* Rev. ed. New York: Collier, 1967.

Murdock, Kenneth. *Literature and Theology in Colonial New England.* 1949. Reprint. Westport, Conn.: Greenwood, 1976.

Nelson, Robert J. *Play within a Play. The Dramatist's Conception of His Art: Shakespeare to Anouilh.* New Haven: Yale University Press, 1958.

Orgel, Stephen. *The Illusion of Power: Political Theater in the English Renaissance.* Berkeley: University of California Press, 1975.

Otis, James. *The Rights of the British Colonies Asserted and Proved.* Boston, 1764. Reprinted in *Pamphlets of the American Revolution, 1750–1776.* Vol. 1, 1750–65, ed. Bernard Bailyn, 418–82. Cambridge, Mass.: Belknap, 1965.

Paine, Thomas. *Common Sense*. Philadelphia, 1776. Reprinted in *Tracts of the American Revolution, 1763–1776*, ed. Merrill Jensen, 400–446. Indianapolis: Bobbs-Merrill, 1967.

Parsons, Jonathan. "Account of the Revival of Religion at Lyme." In *The Christian History . . . for the Year 1744*, ed. Thomas Prince. Boston, 1745. Excerpt reprinted in *The Great Awakening: Documents Illustrating the Crisis and Its Consequences*, ed. Alan Heimert and Perry Miller, 36–40, 188–91, 196–200. Indianapolis: Bobbs-Merrill, 1967.

Patterson, Mark R. *Authority, Autonomy, and Representation in American Literature, 1776–1865*. Princeton: Princeton University Press, 1988.

Pemberton, Ebenezer. *The Divine Original Dignity of Government Asserted*. Boston, 1710.

Petronius. *The Satyricon*. Rev. ed., trans. J. P. Sullivan. New York: Penguin, 1986.

Philbrick, Norman, ed. *Trumpets Sounding: Propaganda Plays of the American Revolution*. New York: Blom, 1972.

Pickering, James H., ed. *The World Turned Upside Down: Prose and Poetry of the Revolution*. Port Washington, N.Y.: Kennikat, 1975.

Pico della Mirandola, Giovanni. "Oration on the Dignity of Man." Trans. Elizabeth Livermore Forbes. In *The Renaissance Philosophy of Man*, ed. Ernst Cassirer, Paul Oskar Kristeller, and John Herman Randall, Jr., 223–54. Chicago: University of Chicago Press, 1948.

Pierce, William. *An Historical Introduction to the Marprelate Tracts*. London: Constable, 1908.

Piercy, Josephine K. *Anne Bradstreet*. New Haven: College and University Press, 1965.

Plato. *The Laws*. Trans. Thomas L. Pangle. New York: Basic Books, 1980.

———. *Philebus*. Trans. J. C. B. Gosling. Oxford: Clarendon, 1975.

———. *The Republic*. Trans. Francis MacDonald Cornford. New York: Oxford University Press, 1945.

Plautus. *The Pot of Gold and Other Plays*. Trans. E. F. Watling. Harmondsworth: Penguin, 1965.

Plumstead, A. W., ed. *The Wall and the Garden: Selected Massachusetts Election Sermons, 1670–1775*. Minneapolis: University of Minnesota Press, 1968.

Postman, Neil. *Amusing Ourselves to Death: Public Discourse in the Age of Show Business*. New York: Penguin, 1986.

Potter, David, and Gordon L. Thomas, eds. *The Colonial Idiom*. Carbondale: Southern Illinois University Press, 1970.

Prince, Thomas. *A Chronological History of New-England*. Boston, 1736.

Proceedings of a Board of General Officers . . . Respecting Major André . . .
    Sept. 19, 1780. Philadelphia, 1780.

Prynne, William. *Histrio-Mastix.* London, 1633. Facsimile reprint. New
    York: Garland, 1974.

Rankin, Hugh F. *The Theater in Colonial America.* Chapel Hill: University
    of North Carolina Press, 1965.

"A Report of the Trial of Mrs. Ann Hutchinson before the Church in Boston,
    March, 1638." In *The Antinomian Controversy, 1636–1638: A Docu-
    mentary History,* ed. David D. Hall, 350–88. Middletown, Conn.: Wes-
    leyan University Press, 1968; rev. ed., Durham, N.C.: Duke University
    Press, 1990.

Righter, Anne. *Shakespeare and the Idea of the Play.* London: Chatto and
    Windus, 1962.

Rist, John M. "The Stoic Concept of Detachment." In *The Stoics,* ed.
    John M. Rist, 259–72. Berkeley: University of California Press, 1978.

————, ed. *The Stoics.* Berkeley: University of California Press, 1978.

Rittenhouse, David. *An Oration, & c.* Philadelphia, 1775. Reprinted in *The
    Colonial Idiom,* ed. David Potter and Gordon L. Thomas, 142–63.
    Carbondale: Southern Illinois University Press, 1970.

Robin, Claude C. *New Travels through North-America: In a Series of Letters.*
    Philadelphia, 1783.

Rosenmeier, Jesper. "New England's Perfection: The Image of Adam and the
    Image of Christ in the Antinomian Crisis, 1634–1638." *William and
    Mary Quarterly,* 3d ser., 27 (1970): 435–59.

Rousseau, Jean-Jacques. *Politics and the Arts: Letter to M. D'Alembert on the
    Theatre.* Trans. Allan Bloom. Glencoe, Ill.: Free Press, 1960.

Rush, Benjamin. *The Autobiography of Benjamin Rush: His "Travels
    through Life" together with His Commonplace Book for 1789–1813.* Ed.
    George W. Corner. Princeton: Princeton University Press, 1948.

Sargent, Winthrop. *The Life and Career of Major John André.* Ed. William
    Abbatt. New York, 1902. Facsimile reprint. New York: Garrett, 1969.

Sasek, Lawrence A. *The Literary Temper of the Puritans.* Baton Rouge:
    Louisiana State University Press, 1961.

Scheer, George F., and Hugh Rankin. *Rebels and Redcoats.* New York:
    World, 1957.

Schleiner, Winfried. *The Imagery of John Donne's Sermons.* Providence:
    Brown University Press, 1970.

Schlochauer, Ernst J. "Shakespeare and America's Revolutionary Leaders."
    Shakespeare Quarterly 12 (1961): 158–60.

Schneider, Herbert Wallace. *The Puritan Mind.* New York, 1930. Reprint.
    Ann Arbor: University of Michigan Press, 1958.

Schweitzer, Ivy. "Anne Bradstreet Wrestles with the Renaissance." *Early American Literature* 23 (1988): 291–312.

Seelye, John. *Prophetic Waters: The River in Early American Life and Literature*. New York: Oxford University Press, 1977.

Seneca. *Ad Lucilium Epistulae Morales*. Trans. Richard M. Gummere. Vol. 2. New York: Putnam's, 1920.

———. *Four Tragedies and Octavia*. Trans. E. F. Watling. Baltimore: Penguin, 1966.

Sennett, Richard. *The Fall of Public Man: On the Social Psychology of Capitalism*. New York: Vintage, 1978.

Sewall, Samuel. *The Diary of Samuel Sewall, 1674–1729*. Ed. M. Halsey Thomas. 2 vols. New York: Farrar, Straus and Giroux, 1973.

———. *Letter-Book of Samuel Sewall*. 2 vols. *Massachusetts Historical Society Collections*, 6th ser., 1–2. Boston, 1886–88.

Shakespeare, William. *The Complete Plays and Poems*. Ed. William Allan Neilson and Charles Jarvis Hill. Boston: Houghton Mifflin, 1942.

Shaw, Peter. *American Patriots and the Rituals of Revolution*. Cambridge: Harvard University Press, 1981.

———. *The Character of John Adams*. Chapel Hill: University of North Carolina Press, 1976.

Shepard, Thomas. *Confessions*. Ed. George Selement and Bruce C. Woolley. Boston: Colonial Society of Massachusetts, 1981.

———. *God's Plot: The Paradoxes of Puritan Piety: Being the Autobiography and Journal of Thomas Shepard*. Ed. Michael McGiffert. Amherst: University of Massachusetts Press, 1972.

———. *The Works*. Ed. John Adams Albro. 3 vols. Boston, 1853. Facsimile reprint. Hildesheim, W.Ger.: Georg Olms, 1971.

Shepard, Thomas, [Jr.] *Eye-Salve or a Watch-Word for Our Lord Jesus Christ unto His Churches in New England*. Cambridge, Mass., 1673.

Sherwood, Samuel. *The Church's Flight into the Wilderness: An Address on the Times*. New York, 1776. Facsimile reprinted in *Revolutionary War Sermons*, ed. David R. Williams. Delmar N.Y.: Scholars' Facsimiles and Reprints, 1984.

Shuffelton, Frank. *Thomas Hooker, 1586–1647*. Princeton: Princeton University Press, 1977.

Shurtleff, Nathaniel B., ed. *Records of the Governor and Company of the Massachusetts Bay in New England*. Vol. 1, 1628–41. Boston, 1853. Facsimile reprint. New York: AMS, 1968.

Shurtleff, William. *A Letter to those of his brethren in the Ministry who refuse to admit the Rev. Mr. Whitefield into their Pulpits*. Boston, 1745. Excerpt reprinted in *The Great Awakening: Documents Illustrating the Crisis and Its Consequences*, ed. Alan Heimert and Perry Miller, 355–63. Indianapolis: Bobbs-Merrill, 1967.

Silverman, Kenneth. *A Cultural History of the American Revolution: Painting, Music, Literature, and the Theatre in the Colonies and the United States from the Treaty of Paris to the Inauguration of George Washington, 1763–1789.* New York: Crowell, 1976.

———. *The Life and Times of Cotton Mather.* New York: Harper and Row, 1984.

Silverman, Kenneth, ed. *Colonial American Poetry.* New York: Hafner, 1968.

Simms, William Gilmore. *The Life of Captain John Smith, the Founder of Virginia.* New York: Coolidge, 1846.

Smith, John. *The Complete Works of Captain John Smith.* Ed. Philip L. Barbour. 3 vols. Chapel Hill: University of North Carolina Press, 1986.

Smith, Page. *A New Age Now Begins.* 2 vols. New York: McGraw-Hill, 1976.

Solberg, Winton, V. *Redeem the Time: The Puritan Sabbath in Early America.* Cambridge: Harvard University Press, 1977.

Somkin, Fred. *Unquiet Eagle: Memory and Desire in the Idea of American Freedom, 1815–1860.* Ithaca, N.Y.: Cornell University Press, 1967.

Spengemann, William C. *A Mirror for Americanists: Reflections on the Idea of American Literature.* Hanover, N.H.: University Press of New England, 1989.

Stanford, Ann. *Anne Bradstreet: The Worldly Puritan.* New York: Twayne, 1965.

Stiles, Ezra. *A Discourse on the Christian Union.* Boston, 1761. Excerpt reprinted in *The Great Awakening: Documents Illustrating the Crisis and Its Consequences*, ed. Alan Heimert and Perry Miller, 594–608. Indianapolis: Bobbs-Merrill, 1967.

———. *The United States Elevated to Glory and Honor.* New Haven, 1783. Reprinted in *The Pulpit of the American Revolution: or, The Political Sermons of the Period of 1776*, ed. John Wingate Thornton, 397–520. Boston, 1860. Facsimile reprint. New York: Da Capo, 1970.

Stiles, Isaac. *A Looking-glass for Chang[e]lings.* New London, Conn., 1743. Excerpt reprinted in *The Great Awakening: Documents Illustrating the Crisis and Its Consequences*, ed. Alan Heimert and Perry Miller, 306–22. Indianapolis: Bobbs-Merrill, 1967.

Stoddard, Solomon. *The Defects of Preachers Reproved.* New London, Conn., 1724. Reprinted in *The Colonial Idiom*, ed. David Potter and Gordon L. Thomas, 430–42. Carbondale: Southern Illinois University Press, 1970.

Stoever, William K. B. *"A Faire and Easie Way to Heaven"*: *Covenant Theology and Antinomianism in Early Massachusetts*. Middletown, Conn.: Wesleyan University Press, 1978.

Stough, Charlotte. "Stoic Determinism and Moral Responsibility." In *The Stoics*, ed. John M. Rist, 203–31. Berkeley: University of California Press, 1978.

Stout, Harry S. *The New England Soul: Preaching and Religious Culture in Colonial New England*. New York: Oxford University Press, 1986.

Strong, Roy. *Splendor at Court: Renaissance Spectacle and the Theater of Power*. Boston: Houghton Mifflin, 1973.

Stroup, Thomas B. *Microcosmos: The Shape of the Elizabethan Play*. Lexington: University of Kentucky Press, 1965.

Stubbes, Philip. *The Anatomie of Abuses*. Ed. Frederick J. Furnivall. Parts I, 1, and I, 2. London: New Shakespeare Society, 1877–79.

Szatmary, David P. *Shays' Rebellion: The Making of an Agrarian Insurrection*. Amherst: University of Massachusetts Press, 1980.

Tanselle, G. Thomas. *Royall Tyler*. Cambridge: Harvard University Press, 1967.

Taylor, Edward. *The Poems of Edward Taylor*. Ed. Donald E. Stanford. New Haven: Yale University Press, 1960.

Tennent, Gilbert. *The Danger of an Unconverted Ministry*. 2d ed. Philadelphia, 1741. Reprinted in *The Great Awakening: Documents Illustrating the Crisis and Its Consequences*, ed. Alan Heimert and Perry Miller, 72–99. Indianapolis: Bobbs-Merrill, 1967.

———. *The Necessity of Holding Fast the Truth*. Boston, 1743. Excerpt reprinted in *The Great Awakening: Documents Illustrating the Crisis and Its Consequences*, ed. Alan Heimert and Perry Miller, 492–504. Indianapolis: Bobbs-Merrill, 1967.

———. "Preface." In *The Unsearchable Riches of Christ*. Boston, 1739. Reprinted in *The Great Awakening: Documents Illustrating the Crisis and Its Consequences*, ed. Alan Heimert and Perry Miller, 15–19. Indianapolis: Bobbs-Merrill, 1967.

Terence. *The Complete Comedies of Terence*. Trans. Palmer Bovie, Constance Carrier, and Douglass Parke; ed. Palmer Bovie. New Brunswick, N.J.: Rutgers University Press, 1974.

Tertullian. *The Writings of Tertullian*. Ed. Alexander Roberts and James Donaldson. Vol. 1. Edinburgh: Clark, 1869.

Theatre. [Boston, 1792].

Thornton, John Wingate, ed. *The Pulpit of the American Revolution: or, The Political Sermons of the Period of 1776*. Boston, 1860. Facsimile reprint. New York: Da Capo, 1970.

Thorpe, William. *Examinacions Thorpe and Oldcastle*. Antwerp, 1530. Facsimile reprint. Amsterdam: Theatrum Orbis Terrarum, 1975.

Tichi, Cecilia. "Thespis and the 'Carnal Hipocrite': A Puritan Motive for Aversion to Drama." *Early American Literature* 4 (1969): 86–103.

———. "Worried Celebrants of the American Revolution." In *American Literature, 1764–1789: The Revolutionary Years*, ed. Everett Emerson, 275–91. Madison: University of Wisconsin Press, 1977.

Toulouse, Teresa. *The Art of Prophesying: New England Sermons and the Shaping of Belief*. Athens: University of Georgia Press, 1987.

Trenchard, John, and Thomas Gordon. *Cato's Letters; or Essays on Liberty, Civil and Religious, and other important Subjects*. 3d ed. 4 vols. London, 1733. Facsimile reprinted in 2 vols. New York: Russell and Russell, 1969.

Trumbull, John. *The Satiric Poems of John Trumbull: "The Progress of Dulness," "M'Fingal."* Ed. Edwin T. Bowden. Austin: University of Texas Press, 1962.

Tuan, Yi-Fu. *Segmented Worlds and Self: Group Life and Individual Consciousness*. Minneapolis: University of Minnesota Press, 1982.

Turner, Victor. *Dramas, Fields, and Metaphors: Symbolic Action in Human Society*. Ithaca, N.Y.: Cornell University Press, 1974.

———. *From Ritual to Theatre: The Human Seriousness of Play*. New York: Performing Arts Journal Publications, 1982.

Tyler, Royall. *The Contrast, A Comedy in Five Acts*. Philadelphia, 1790.

van den Berg, Kent T. *Playhouse and Cosmos: Shakespearean Theatre as Metaphor*. Newark: University of Delaware Press, 1985.

Van Laan, Thomas F. *Role-playing in Shakespeare*. Toronto: University of Toronto Press, 1978.

Vaughan, Alden T., ed. *Chronicles of the American Revolution*. New York: Grosset and Dunlap, 1965.

Vives, Juan Luis. "A Fable about Man." Trans. Nancy Lenkeith. In *The Renaissance Philosophy of Man*, ed. Ernst Cassirer, Paul Oskar Kristeller, and John Herman Randall, Jr., 387–93. Chicago: University of Chicago Press, 1948.

Walzer, Michael. *The Revolution of the Saints: A Study in the Origins of Radical Politics*. Cambridge: Harvard University Press, 1965.

Ward, Nathaniel. *The Simple Cobler of Aggawam in America*. Ed. P. M. Zall. Lincoln: University of Nebraska Press, 1969.

Warnke, Frank J. *Versions of Baroque: European Literature in the Seventeenth Century*. New Haven: Yale University Press, 1972.

Warren, Mercy Otis. *The Blockheads: or, The Affrighted Officers. A Farce*. Boston, 1776. Reprinted in *Trumpets Sounding: Propaganda Plays of the*

American Revolution, ed. Norman Philbrick, 149–68. New York: Blom, 1972.

———. *History of the Rise, Progress, and Termination of the American Revolution*. 3 vols. Boston, 1805.

Washington, George. *A Circular Letter, from His Excellency George Washington, Commander in Chief of the Armies of the United States of America*. Philadelphia, 1783.

———. *The Writings*. Ed. Worthington Chauncey Ford. 14 vols. New York: Putnam's, 1889–93.

Weber, Donald. *Rhetoric and History in Revolutionary New England*. New York: Oxford University Press, 1988.

Webster, John. *The Duchess of Malfi*. Ed. Fred B. Millett. New York: Appleton-Century-Crofts, 1953.

Webster, Noah, Jr. *An Oration Pronounced before the Citizens of New Haven on the Anniversary of the Declaration of Independence; July, 1802*. New Haven: Morse, 1802.

Weinbrot, Howard D. *Augustus Caesar in "Augustan" England: The Decline of a Classical Norm*. Princeton: Princeton University Press, 1978.

Weisinger, Herbert. "Theatrum Mundi: Illusion as Reality." In *The Agony and the Triumph: Papers on the Use and Abuse of Myth*, 58–70. East Lansing: Michigan State University Press, 1964.

West, Samuel. *An Anniversary Sermon, Preached at Plymouth, December 22nd, 1777*. Boston, 1778.

Wetmore, Izrahiah. *A Sermon Preached before the Honorable General Assembly*. New London, Conn., 1773.

White, Elizabeth Wade. *Anne Bradstreet: "The Tenth Muse."* New York: Oxford University Press, 1971.

Whitefield, George. *George Whitefield's Journals (1737–1741)*. Ed. William Wale. 1905. Facsimile reprint, ed. William V. Davis. Gainesville, Fla.: Scholars' Facsimiles and Reprints, 1969.

Whitman, Walt. *Leaves of Grass*. Ed. Sculley Bradley and Harold W. Blodgett. New York: Norton, 1973.

Wigglesworth, Michael. *The Day of Doom, or a Poetical Description of the Great and Last Judgment, with other poems*. Ed. Kenneth B. Murdock. 1929. Reprint. New York: Russell and Russell, 1966.

———. *The Diary of Michael Wigglesworth, 1653–1657: The Consciousness of a Puritan*. Ed. Edmund S. Morgan. New York: Harper and Row, 1965.

———. "Prayse of Eloquence." Excerpted in *The Colonial Idiom*, ed. David Potter and Gordon L. Thomas, 8–12. Carbondale: Southern Illinois University Press, 1970.

Williams, David E. "'Behold a Tragick Scene Strangely Changed into a Theatre of Mercy': The Structure and Significance of Criminal Conversion Narratives in Early New England." *American Quarterly* 38 (1986): 827–47.

———. "Puritans and Pirates: A Confrontation between Cotton Mather and William Fly in 1726." *Early American Literature* 22 (1987): 233–51.

Williams, David R., ed. *Revolutionary War Sermons.* Delmar, N.Y.: Scholars' Facsimiles and Reprints, 1984.

Williams, George H., et al., eds. *Thomas Hooker: Writings in England and Holland, 1626–1633.* Cambridge: Harvard University Press, 1975.

Williams, Raymond. *Drama in a Dramatised Society.* Cambridge: Cambridge University Press, 1975.

Williams, Selma R. *The Divine Rebel: The Life of Anne Marbury Hutchinson.* New York: Holt, Rinehart and Winston, 1981.

Wills, Garry. *Cincinnatus: George Washington and the Enlightenment.* Garden City, N.Y.: Doubleday, 1984.

Wilshire, Bruce. *Role Playing and Identity: The Limits of Theatre as Metaphor.* Bloomington: Indiana University Press, 1982.

Wilson, Garff B. *Three Hundred Years of American Drama and Theatre: From "Ye Bear and Ye Cubb" to "Hair."* Englewood Cliffs, N.J.: Prentice-Hall, 1973.

Winslow, Ola. *Jonathan Edwards, 1703–1758: A Biography.* New York: Macmillan, 1940.

Winthrop, John [1588–1649]. *The History of New England from 1630 to 1649 [The Journal].* Ed. James Savage. 2 vols. Boston: Little, Brown, 1853.

———. *A Short Story of the Rise, reign, and ruine of the Antinomians, Familists, & Libertines.* 2d ed. London, 1644. Reprinted in *The Antinomian Controversy, 1636–1638: A Documentary History,* ed. David D. Hall, 201–310. Middletown, Conn.: Wesleyan University Press, 1968; rev. ed., Durham, N.C.: Duke University Press, 1990.

Winthrop, John, et al. *Winthrop Papers.* Vol. 2, 1623–30. Boston: Massachusetts Historical Society, 1931.

Winthrop, John [1681–1747]. "Correspondence of John Winthrop, F. R. S." *Massachusetts Historical Society Collections,* 6th ser., 5 (1892): 371–439.

Winton, Calhoun. "The Theatre and Drama." In *American Literature, 1764–1789: The Revolutionary Years,* ed. Everett Emerson, 87–104. Madison: University of Wisconsin Press, 1977.

Wirt, William. *The Life of Patrick Henry.* 4th rev. ed. New York: McElrath and Bangs, 1831.

Wood, Gordon S. *The Creation of the American Republic, 1776–1787.* Chapel Hill: University of North Carolina Press, 1969.

———. "Rhetoric and Reality in the American Revolution," *William and Mary Quarterly,* 3d ser., 23 (1966): 3–32.

———, ed. *The Rising Glory of America, 1760–1820.* New York: Braziller, 1971.

Wright, Esmond, ed. *The Fire of Liberty.* New York: St. Martin's, 1983.

Yates, Frances A. *Theatre of the World.* Chicago: University of Chicago Press, 1969.

Zimmer, Anne Y. *Jonathan Boucher: Loyalist in Exile.* Detroit: Wayne State University Press, 1978.

Zobel, Hiller B. *The Boston Massacre.* New York: Norton, 1970.

Zuckerman, Michael. "The Fabrication of Identity in Early America." *William and Mary Quarterly,* 3d ser., 34 (1977): 183–214.

INDEX

Actors, 168, 214. *See also* Citizen actors; Professional actors; True actors

Adams, Abigail (Nabby), 235, 272

Adams, Abigail Smith, 225, 230–44, 257, 258–59, 272, 295

Adams, Charles Francis, 230

Adams, John, xiv, 7, 10–11, 26, 49, 208–9, 219, 226, 230–44, 257–59, 262, 263, 272, 288, 289, 290–91, 296

Adams, John Quincy, 7, 235, 258–59

Adams, Samuel, 267, 295

Adams, Zabdiel, 241, 242

Addison, Joseph, 180, 182–84, 186, 210, 239, 267. See also *Cato*

Aeschylus, 20

Aestheticized view of culture, 181, 184, 185, 187, 198–200, 205, 276. *See also* British urban culture, Performance criticism; Social performance

Age of theatricality, 177–83. *See also* Theatricality

Agnew, Jean-Christophe, xv–xvi, 77, 102, 108

Agon, 62–63, 64, 101. *See also* Agonistic arena

Agonistic arena, 5, 7, 148, 172

Albanese, Catherine, 204, 243, 256–57

All-Seeing Eye. *See* Spectating

André, John, 253–54, 255, 260–61

Andros, Edmund, 155

Antifederalists, 287

Antinomian crisis, 127–46, 148, 164

Anti-Puritan prejudice, 81. *See also* Stage martyrdom

Antitheatrical prejudice, 77. *See also* Barish, Jonas

Apocalypse, 61, 65, 110–11. *See also* Foxe, John; Millennialism; Tertullian

Apotheosis of Franklin, The, 271, 284

Applause seeking, 22, 23, 36, 89, 170, 171–72, 277, 296. *See also* Mather, Cotton

Arena, Turner's use of, 129, 134

Aristophanes, 20, 119, 160

Aristotle, 19–20

Arnold, Benedict, 257, 260

Arrianus, Flavius, 26

Augustan Age in England, 15, 177–78. *See also* Addison, Joseph; Age of theatricality

325

Augustine, Bishop of Hippo, 29, 30–32
Aurelius, Marcus, 24, 26–29

Backus, Isaac, 197
Bacon, Francis, 53
Bailyn, Bernard, 182
Baldwin, Ebenezer, 243
Baldwin, Simeon, 284
Bale, John, 63–64
Barbour, Philip L., 86
Barish, Jonas, 77, 125–26, 207
Barker, James Nelson, 91
Barlow, Joel, 285–86
Barnum, P. T., 3
Barton, Andrew, 213
Battle of Brooklyn, The, 248
Baxter, Joseph, 125
Baxter, Richard, 78, 79
Beard, Thomas, 72–75, 81, 121, 134, 155
Beaumarchais, Pierre de, 268
Beaumont, Francis, 278
Beckett, Samuel, 66
Bellamy, Joseph, 202–3
Bent, Josiah, Jr., 7–8, 285
Bercovitch, Sacvan, 164, 168
Berkeley, George, 184–85, 186, 236, 267
Bicentennial, 1
Binney, Barnabas, 223
Blockade of Boston, The, 227–29, 253, 294
Boaistuau, Pierre, 42–43
Book as performance, 89, 180. *See also* Marprelate, Martin
Book-being, 48–49
Boston Massacre, 201, 213–17, 220, 233, 238
Boston Tea Party, 10, 220–24, 238, 241
Boucher, Jonathan, 218–19
Bowdoin, James, 214

Brackenridge, Hugh Henry, 217, 227, 238, 248
Braddock, Edward, 203
Bradford, William, 108, 131, 155
Bradstreet, Anne, 2, 116–18
Bradstreet, Simon, 154
Breach, Turner's use of, 131
Breitwieser, Mitchell Robert, 148, 149, 166, 170
British urban culture, 177–79, 181–82, 185, 191, 198, 222, 294. *See also* Aestheticized view of culture; Social performance
Brockwell, Charles, 198–200, 218
Browne, Thomas, 55–56
Bulkeley, Gershom, 103
Bulkeley, Peter, 103, 104, 105
Bullman, John, 255
Bunker Hill, Battle of, 217, 226–27, 248, 249
Bunyan, John, 103–4
Burgoyne, John, 224, 226–29, 250. See also *Blockade of Boston, The*
Burke, Kenneth, xv, 128–29, 138
Burton, Robert, 16–17, 45, 57–60, 85, 97
Bute, John Stuart, Earl of, 209, 257
Byles, Mather, 202, 204
Byrd, William, 179

Caldwell, Patricia, 137
Calef, Robert, 146–47, 158
Calvin, John, 24, 66–69, 101
Calvinism, 66, 75, 81. *See also* Calvin, John; Puritans; Theater of Providence
Carnival, 83
Catastrophe, 160, 164, 247
Catharsis, 193
Cato, Marcus Porcius (the Elder), 24, 150, 183, 267
Cato, Marcus Porcius (the Younger), 26, 29, 50, 150, 184. *See also* Ad-

dison, Joseph; *Cato*; Stoicism; Tren-
chard, John, and Thomas Gordon
Cato, 182–84, 210, 211, 224, 239,
248, 262. *See also* Addison, Joseph;
Cato, Marcus Porcius (the Younger)
Charles I, 59
Chauncy, Charles, 195–98, 208
Chesterfield, Philip Stanhope, fourth
earl of, 178, 273
China, 123, 282
Chrysostom, John, 30, 32–33, 121
Church, Benjamin, 156, 164
Church and theater, 32–33, 61–84,
101–73, 190, 267. *See also* Great
Awakening
Church fathers, 29–34. *See also* Au-
gustine, Bishop of Hippo;
Chrysostom, John; Tertullian
Cibber, Colley, 178
Cicero, 24–25, 28
Citizen actors, 149, 164, 282
Citizen Kane, 3–4
City on a hill, 11, 102–4, 137, 240.
See also Hill-stage
Clap, Thomas, 200
Clapp, William W., Jr., 270
Clarke, Richard, 221
Class reversal, 213. *See also* Plautus;
World turned upside down
Clinton, Henry, 255, 256, 260, 261
Cobbett, Thomas, 111–12
Coddington, William, 142
Collins, Nathanael, 165
Colman, Benjamin, 112, 202
Colonization and rhetoric, xi–xii. *See
also* New England; Virginia
Columbus, Christopher, 185, 286
Comic deflation, 161, 181, 191, 248,
274. *See also* Plautus; Tory political
rhetoric
Commonwealth (English), 82–84,
101, 106
Contemptus mundi, 54, 55
Cooper, Myles, 255

1 Corinthians 4.9, 11, 80, 104, 223
Cornwallis, Charles, 261. *See also*
Yorktown
Cotton, John, 104, 108, 127–28, 132–
33, 135, 143, 144, 167–68
Cotton, John (the Younger), 149
Crashaw, William, 11
Crisis, Turner's use of, 131. *See also*
Antinomian crisis
Cromwell, Oliver, 82, 83
Culture and rhetoric, xiv. *See also*
Theater metaphor; Theatrics of cul-
ture; Theatrum mundi

Dana, James, 266
Danforth, Samuel, 105
Darling, Thomas, 200
Davidson, James West, 251, 283
Davies, Samuel, 203
Declaration of Independence, 10, 242
Dell, William, 82
Democritus, 16, 57. *See also* Burton,
Robert
Dickens, Charles, 3
Dickinson, John, 15, 16, 19
Donne, John, 54–55
Douglass, David, 191, 209, 211, 213,
218
Downey, James, 187
Drama as metaphor, 221
Drama of mimesis, 126
Drama of salvation, 61, 64, 106, 110
Drowne, Samuel, 214
Dryden, John, 119
Dudley, Joseph, 161
Dudley, Thomas, 140, 142
Dumb show, 155
Dummer, William, 152
Dunlap, William, 261
Dyer, Mary, 140

Edelberg, Cynthia Dubin, 255
Edwards, Jonathan, 75, 108–9, 179–
80, 187–88, 192, 194–97

Edwards, Richard, 42, 43, 45
Edwards, Sarah Pierrepont, 188–89
Election Day sermons, 9–10, 123–24, 125, 192, 203, 283, 284, 285
Eliot, John, 151, 155
Eliot, T. S., 9, 58
Elizabeth I, 117–18
Enchantment, 158–59. See also Thaumaturgy
English Civil War. See Commonwealth (English)
Entertainment and political discourse. See Television
Epictetus, 24, 25–26, 28, 124, 226, 232, 233, 239
Erasmus, 40–41, 256, 275
Erikson, Kai, xiv, 101–2, 129, 142–43, 144
Euripides, 20, 119
Ewald, Johan, 252
"Examination of Mrs. Anne Hutchinson at the Court at Newtown," 140–43
Exceptionalism, xii, xiii
Execution sermons, 171, 173
Ex tempore preaching, 187, 205
Extratheatrical imagination, 90, 279. See also Intratheatrical imagination; Microcosm and macrocosm

Family of Love, 136
Farquhar, George, 210, 257
Fashion, 151
Fenner, Dudley, 76
Festival, 4, 207–8, 237–38. See also Rousseau, Jean-Jacques
Field, Turner's use of, 129, 130, 164
Fielding, Henry, 177–78
Fifth act, 185, 186, 262, 280. See also Berkeley, George; Lafayette, Marquis de
Fifth Monarchy, 82, 83, 189
Firmin, Giles, 78
Fleming, Abraham, 44

Foote, Samuel, 190
Ford, Cadwallader, 230
Foster, Daniel, 284–85
Fourth of July orations, 284, 285, 293. See also Bent, Josiah, Jr.; Bicentennial
Foxe, John, 64–66, 110, 123, 194, 284
Franklin, Benjamin, xvi (n. 1), 191, 207, 231, 293
Freher, Paulus, 165, 168–69
French and Indian War, 201, 204
Freneau, Philip, 238, 261, 267, 268–70, 279, 289
Frisbie, Levi, 266

Gage, Thomas, 290. See also Leacock, John
Galloway, Joseph, 219
Gannett, Deborah Sampson, 271, 274
Garden, Alexander, 189–90
Garrick, David, 178, 187, 224, 226, 235, 250
Gayton, Edmund, 84
Geertz, Clifford, xv, 129, 291
Generations, passage of, 121–22, 125–26
Gerry, Elbridge, 291
Glass as metaphor, 55, 153
Glorious Revolution, 154, 155
Godfrey, Thomas, Jr., 213
Goffman, Erving, xiv, xv, 129. See also Performance criticism
Goodman, Ellen, 296–97
Gordon, Thomas. See Trenchard, John, and Thomas Gordon
Gorton, Samuel, 136
Gosson, Stephen, 79. See also Puritans: attacks on theater by
Great Awakening, 186–200, 202, 205, 218. See also Chauncy, Charles; Edwards, Jonathan; Whitefield, George
Great Director, 72–73, 226, 229, 247
Greeks and theater, 15, 16–20, 201.

See also Aeschylus; Aristophanes;
Euripides; Sophocles
Greenblatt, Stephen, 149
Grent, William, 11, 96, 97
Greven, Philip, 149
Gridley, Jeremiah, 208
Griswold, Wesley S., 220–21
Gunnell, Richard, 97
Gura, Philip, 122, 136, 137

Hale, John, 147
Hale, Nathan, 239, 260
Hall, Joseph, 74–75
Hallam, Lewis, 191, 209
Hancock, John, 215–16, 295
Harvard College, 119, 231, 270
Hatch, Nathan O., 204, 266
Hawthorne, Nathaniel, 5–6, 162, 293
Heimert, Alan, 189, 191, 204
Henry, Patrick, 184, 224
Heywood, Thomas, 79–80
Hilliard, Timothy, 243
Hill-stage, 105, 126, 143, 172, 226,
229, 294. See also Bunyan, John;
City on a hill
Hollis, C. Carroll, 4–5
Homer, 163
Hooker, Thomas, 67, 104, 108, 112–
15, 124, 144, 151, 168, 170. See
also Hypocrisy
Hooten, Joseph, Jr., 214
Hopkinson, Francis, 211–12, 251, 287
Horace, 22, 25, 26
Howe, William, 253, 254, 288
Huizinga, Johan, 41, 272. See also
Ludic world; Play
Humphreys, David, 243, 273, 282,
295
Hunter, Martin, 228
Hutchinson, Anne, 101, 127–45, 146,
172
Hutchinson, Thomas, 208, 209, 219,
238, 240, 257

Hypocrisy, 111–15, 116, 123, 150–51,
193–94, 226, 265
Hypocrite-actor. See Hypocrisy

"I. H." (John Healey?), 89
Interregnum. See Commonwealth
(English)
Intratheatrical imagination, 90, 279.
See also Extratheatrical imagination;
Microcosm and macrocosm; Perfor-
mance criticism
Isaac, Rhys, xvii, 222, 291

James, John, 125
James, Richard, 97
Jefferson, Thomas, 7, 242
Jesus Christ and theater, 158, 193,
195, 259–60. See also Apocalypse;
Colman, Benjamin; Foxe, John;
Millennialism; Tertullian
John of Salisbury, 34–37, 40, 57, 151,
221. See also Totus mundus agit
histrionem
Johnson, Edward, 103, 112
Johnson, Mark, 9
Jones, Thomas, 254
Jonson, Ben, 58, 81, 97, 119, 159
Joyce Junior, 257
Jubilee of 1826, 7–8
Julius Caesar, 74, 96, 97. See also
Shakespeare, William: Julius Caesar

Kendall, Ritchie, 62, 64
King Philip's War, 156, 164–65

Labaree, Benjamin Woods, 223
Lafayette, Marquis de, 8, 248, 262,
280, 281
Lakoff, George, 9
Laurens, Henry, 248
Leacock, John, 249–51
Leonard, Daniel, 219
Leverenz, David, 108, 116
Levin, Samuel R., 9

Licensing Act of 1737, 178
Lillo, George, 210, 211
Lincoln, Benjamin, 295
Lollards, 62. *See also* Thorpe,
    William; *Tretise of Miraclys
    Pleyinge, A*
Lord Mayor's pageant, 84
Lovejoy, David, 136, 137
Lowance, Mason, 236, 282
Ludic world, 21. *See also* Plautus;
    Play; Theatrical impulse
Luxury, 265–77

Macaulay, Catharine, 258
McLuhan, Marshall, 2
Macrocosm. *See* Microcosm and
    macrocosm
Madison, James, 243–44, 282
Magic pen, 163, 166. *See also* Book as
    performance; Thaumaturgy
Mann, Herman, 271. *See also* Gan-
    nett, Deborah Sampson
Marbury, Francis, 134–35
Marlowe, Christopher, 73
Marprelate, Martin, 69–72, 161
Marshall, David, 180, 182
Martial, 183
Martin, Luther, 287
Marvell, Andrew, 59
Masks, 177, 179, 181
Masque, 58–59, 82, 93–94, 155
Masquerade of history, 163
Mass culture, 4
Massachusettensis and Novanglus, 219
Mather, Cotton, xiv, 48–49, 60, 88,
    126, 144, 146, 148–73, 179, 190,
    192, 196, 231, 241, 242, 274, 296;
    Bonifacius, 159–60; *The Christian
    Philosopher*, 156–57; *Elegy on . . .
    Nathanael Collins*, 165; *Magnalia
    Christi Americana*, 149, 150, 153–
    57, 161–70, 171, 172, 192; *Man-
    uductio ad Ministerium*, 168–69;
    Memorable Providences, 144–45;
    The Short History of New England,

158–59; *Thaumatographia Chris-
    tiana*, 158; *The Wonders of the Invis-
    ible World*, 157–58. *See also*
    National self; Puritans: rhetoric of;
    Stage martyrdom
Mather, Increase, 49, 119, 120–23,
    125
Mather, Nathaniel, 153–54
Mauduit, Israel, 254
Mayhew, Jonathan, 208
Metaphor (general), 9. *See also* The-
    ater metaphor; Theatrum mundi
Metatheater, xv, 43, 52
Microcosm and macrocosm, 81, 98,
    187, 188, 200, 226, 277, 296. *See
    also* Church and theater; Extra-
    theatrical imagination; Intratheatri-
    cal imagination; Tory political
    rhetoric; Whig political rhetoric
Millennialism, 83, 122, 169, 179–80,
    194–96, 202, 203, 208, 243, 251,
    259–60, 280, 282, 283, 285, 286.
    See also Apocalypse; Foxe, John;
    Tertullian
Miller, Arthur, 144
Miller, Perry, 106, 172
Milton, John, 94, 139
Mischianza, The, 253–54
Mitchell, Jonathan, 124, 125
Mock parricide rituals, xvii, 10, 208
Molière, 225, 234–35
Montesquieu, Baron de (Charles de
    Secondat), 278
More, Thomas, 39, 40
Morgan, James, 165
Münster, 138, 142, 164, 196

National self, xiv, 49, 94, 150, 169–
    73. *See also* Adams, John; Mather,
    Cotton; Smith, John; Whitman,
    Walt
Necromancy, 158, 162–63, 166, 168,
    173. *See also* Thaumaturgy
New Comedy, 21
New England, 11, 15. *See also* The-

atrum mundi: in early New England; in post-Revolutionary culture; in pre-Revolutionary culture; in Revolutionary War
Newton, Isaac, 237
Nonconformism: rhetoric of, 61–84, 101; theater of, 63–66. *See also* Calvinism; Puritans
Norton, John, 118
Noyes, Nicholas, 161–62

Odell, Jonathan, 226, 254–56
O'Keeffe, John, 272
Old Comedy, 28
Oliver, Peter, 208, 209, 219, 257
Opechancanough, 91
Orgel, Stephen, 58–59, 82
Otis, Harrison Gray, 267
Otis, James, Jr., 208, 288, 291
Otway, Thomas, 210
Ozell, John, 278

Paine, Thomas, 215, 217–18, 258
Paradigm, 129, 133
Parke, John, 271
Parsons, Jonathan, 192, 193
Paul, 29, 104, 122. *See also* 1 Corinthians 4.9
Pemberton, Ebenezer, 123–24
Pemberton, Samuel, 214
Pequot War, 127, 130–31
Performance criticism, 189, 199, 205, 291. *See also* Book as performance; Goffman, Erving; Social performance
Performative rhetoric, xviii. *See also* Marprelate, Martin; Mather, Cotton
Performative self, 148, 173, 179, 188
Perkins, William, 106
Peter, Hugh, 143
Petronius, 23, 35, 119
Philip. *See* King Philip's War
Phips, William, 166–67
Pico della Mirandola, Giovanni, 38–39, 58

Pilate, Pontius, 74
Plato, xiii, 16–20, 22, 26, 207, 225, 233, 276
Plautus, 20–23, 35, 88, 119, 120, 134, 159, 213, 263. *See also* World turned upside down
Play, xviii, 72, 108, 197, 206. *See also* Huizinga, Johan; Ludic world; Plautus
Pocahontas, 90, 97
Postman, Neil, 2, 181, 297
Powhatan, 92, 93, 94, 95
Prince, Thomas, 185–86, 197
Professional actors, 11, 160. *See also* Actors; Douglass, David; Hallam, Lewis; Luxury
Protest rituals, 197, 201, 208, 210, 212. *See also* Boston Massacre; Boston Tea Party; Mock parricide rituals; Ritual drama; Sons of Liberty; Stamp Act; Theater of the street
Providence, 236–37. *See also* Theater of Providence
Prynne, William, 30, 69, 76, 79, 80, 81, 104, 121, 155. *See also* Nonconformism; Puritans: attacks on theater by
Puppet, 17–19, 20, 25, 26–27, 157
Purchas, Samuel, 90
Puritans: attacks on theater by, 29–30, 75–81; rhetoric of, 69–84, 101–73. *See also* Calvinism; Mather, Cotton; Nonconformism
Pythagoras, 16

Quincy, Josiah, 235

Raleigh, Walter, 117
Rawdon, Francis, 226, 250
Redressive action, 131
Reintegration, 131
"Report of the Trial of Mrs. Anne Hutchinson before the Church in Boston, A," 140, 143

Representative personality, 148. *See also* National self
Republicanism and theater, 201–97
Restoration, 83–84. *See also* Farquhar, George; Lillo, George; Otway, Thomas
Revere, Paul, 214
Revolutionary War, xvii, xviii, 10–11, 203, 205, 241–64, 285
Rittenhouse, David, 265
Ritual drama, 101, 128, 129, 222. *See also* Mock parricide rituals; Protest rituals; Social drama
Robin, Claude C., 266–67, 270
Rogers, John, 123
Rogers, John, of Dedham, England, 78
Romans and theater, 20–24. *See also* Plautus; Stoicism
Rousseau, Jean-Jacques, 206–8, 237, 242, 271, 281, 282
Rush, Benjamin, 235, 242, 281, 285

Sabbath, 77–78. *See also* Church and theater
Salem witchcraft trials, 123, 138, 144, 145–47, 157. *See also* Witches
Salluste, Guillaume de, Seigneur du Bartas, 117
Saturnalia, 22, 210
Schweitzer, Ivy, 117–18
Seelye, John, 88, 98
Self-fashioning, 149
Seneca, 24, 25, 119, 159, 164
Sennett, Richard, xv, 177
Sewall, Samuel, 119–20, 133, 144, 145, 151, 155
Shaftesbury, third earl of (Anthony Ashley Cooper), 180, 182
Shakespeare, William, 42, 43–53, 54, 89, 90, 91, 96, 210, 224, 225, 231, 237, 256; *As You Like It*, xiii, 44–45, 117; *Coriolanus*, 248; *Hamlet*, xvi, 51–52, 53, 56, 58, 234, 241;

Henry VIII, 234, 236, 237; *Julius Caesar*, 49–50, 234; *King Lear*, 234; *Macbeth*, 45, 53, 164–65; *The Merchant of Venice*, 45, 211; *A Midsummer Night's Dream*, xviii, 200; *Othello*, 211, 234; *Richard II*, 47–48; *Richard III*, 46–47, 49, 50, 234; *The Taming of the Shrew*, 234; *The Tempest*, 49, 54, 90, 94, 98; *Timon of Athens*, 234; *Twelfth Night*, 46; *The Winter's Tale*, 54
Shaw, Peter, xvii, 208–9
Shays, Daniel. *See* Shays' Rebellion
Shays' Rebellion, 295–96
Shepard, Thomas, 103, 107, 111, 124, 126, 143, 153, 162
Shepard, Thomas, Jr., 125–26
Sheridan, Richard Brinsley, 272
Sherman, John, 123
Sherwood, Samuel, 243
Shurtleff, William, 191–92
Sibbes, Richard, 68–69
Silverman, Kenneth, xvii, 16, 150, 169, 212, 251
Simms, William Gilmore, 91
Smith, Isaac, Jr., 235, 238
Smith, John, xiii, xiv, 11, 48, 60, 85–98, 105, 159, 160, 161, 180, 190, 231, 274, 290, 296; *The Generall Historie*, 87, 88, 90, 91, 92, 93–94, 96, 98; *A Map of Virginia*, 92, 93, 96; *The Proceedings*, 91, 92, 94, 95; *A True Relation*, 89, 91, 92; *The True Travels*, 91, 96, 97
Social drama, xv, 130–31, 133, 135, 141, 144. *See also* Turner, Victor
Social performance, 24, 28, 85, 88, 98, 179, 222, 277, 279. *See also* Aestheticized view of culture; British urban culture; Performance criticism
Sola Scriptura, 130
Somkin, Fred, 8
Sons of Liberty, 210, 212, 220–21, 237–38, 254. *See also* Protest rituals
Sophocles, 19, 28, 119, 209

Spectacle, 4, 10, 61, 68, 154–56, 157, 162, 166, 223, 247, 276, 286, 289. *See also* Apocalypse; Bicentennial; Festival; Splendor; Tertullian; Theatrum mundi: in post-Revolutionary culture

Spectating, 122, 151–53, 199

Spengemann, William, xii

Splendor, 4, 68, 226. *See also* Masque; Spectacle

Stage martyrdom, 71, 97, 159–60, 190–91

Stamp Act, xvii (n. 2), 10, 201, 208, 209–10, 212, 214, 236, 237–38

Steele, Richard, 180

Stepney, Francis, 119

Stiles, Ezra, 200, 283, 284

Stiles, Isaac, 198

Stoddard, Solomon, 115

Stoicism, 21, 24–29, 37, 184, 273. *See also* Aurelius, Marcus; Cato, Marcus Porcius (the Younger); Cicero; Epictetus; Horace; Republicanism and theater; Seneca

Stone, Hugh, 165

Stout, Harry, 191, 203, 204, 283

Stubbes, Philip, 78, 79, 80, 81

Sufficient theater, 153, 161, 179

Swift, Jonathan, 161

Tableau, 202, 222, 229, 238, 257–58

Tanselle, G. Thomas, 272

Taylor, Edward, 109

Tea Act, 15. *See also* Boston Tea Party

Television, 1–3, 11, 181, 296–97

Tennent, Gilbert, 180, 192–95, 198

Terence, 159

Tertullian, 30, 33–34, 73, 120–21, 194

Thacher, Peter, 251–52

Thaumaturgy, 123, 156, 157–59, 162–63, 166, 192. *See also* Magic pen; Necromancy

Theater and society, xiv–xvi. *See also* Social drama; Social performance; Theater metaphor: as social trope

Theater as word, 180

Theater metaphor, xii, xvii, 205; as aesthetic trope, 205, 222 (*see also* Aestheticized view of culture); as cosmological trope, 8, 226 (*see also* Microcosm and macrocosm; Vives, Juan Luis); as epistemological trope, 8, 228 (*see also* Television); as geographical trope, 187, 196, 290 (*see also* Bent, Josiah, Jr.; Madison, James); as historical trope, xii–xiii, 161, 205 (*see also* Mather, Cotton; Warren, Mercy Otis); as ideological trope, xviii, 8 (*see also* Tory political rhetoric; Whig political rhetoric); as military trope, 87, 228, 287 (*see also* Blockade of Boston, The; Mischianza, The); as political trope, 167, 181, 290 (*see also* Adams, John; Plato; Tory political rhetoric; Warren, Mercy Otis; Whig political rhetoric); as psychological trope, 205 (*see also* Burton, Robert; Kendall, Ritchie); as social trope, 205 (*see also* Age of theatricality; Performance criticism; Social drama; Social performance). *See also* Shakespeare, William; Spectacle; Theatricality; Theatrum mundi

Theater of action, 236, 241, 247, 262

Theater of blood, 215–19, 227

Theater of God's Judgments, 72–75, 81, 167, 181, 216

Theater of Providence, xviii, 9–10, 66–69, 74, 75, 156, 163, 167, 200, 236, 239–40, 247, 258–59, 262–63, 291, 296. *See also* Adams, John; Providence; Puritans; Republicanism and theater; Theater of God's Judgments; Warren, Mercy Otis

Theater of the street, 200, 201–2, 220, 258. *See also* Protest rituals

Theatre, 267–68

Theatrical impulse, xviii, 212
Theatricality, xvii, 8, 35, 45, 85, 148,
  165, 190, 198, 213, 222, 275. *See
  also* Social performance
Theatrical persecution. *See* Stage martyrdom
Theatrical rhetoric, xi–xii. *See also*
  Theater metaphor
Theatrical urge. *See* Theatrical im-
  pulse
Theatrics of culture, xiv–xviii
Theatrou mestoi, 168
Theatrum mundi, xii, xiii, 10, 154,
  161, 177–78, 180, 186, 202, 203; in
  early New England, 101–73; in
  early Virginia, 85–98; in eighteenth
  century, 177–200; in post-
  Revolutionary culture, 265–96; in
  pre-Revolutionary culture, 201–41;
  in Revolutionary War, 241–64; in
  Western culture to 1630, 15–84. *See
  also* Microcosm and macrocosm;
  Theater metaphor
Thompson, Benjamin, 162, 163
Thorpe, William, 62–63, 64, 65, 134
Tory political rhetoric, 181–82, 219,
  226, 248, 254–57. *See also* Intra-
  theatrical imagination; Whig politi-
  cal rhetoric
Totus mundus agit histrionem, 57,
  151, 253
Tragedy of state, 19, 207, 247
Tragic elevation, 248. *See also* Comic
  deflation; Whig political rhetoric
Transcript. *See* Thorpe, William;
  Trials
Trenchard, John, and Thomas Gor-
  don, 182, 186
Tretise of Miraclys Pleyinge, A, 63
Trials, 127–47. *See also* Hutchinson,
  Anne; Salem witchcraft trials;
  Thorpe, William
True actors, 91–98, 224
Trumbull, John (painter), 217, 229
Trumbull, John (poet), 222

Tuan, Yi-Fu, xvi
Turner, Victor, xiv, 129–31, 133, 143,
  164, 291
Tyler, Royall, 217, 252, 272–79, 295–
  96

Vane, Henry, 83, 84, 132
Vennor, Thomas, 83
Vietnam War, 210
Virgil, 163
Virginia, 11, 15. *See also* Theatrum
  mundi: in early Virginia; in eigh-
  teenth century
Vives, Juan Luis, 39–40, 41, 42, 179

Walpole, Horace, 181
War against theater. *See* Puritans: at-
  tacks on theater by
Ward, Nathaniel, 118–19
Warren, Joseph, 214, 215, 216–17,
  241
Warren, Mercy Otis, 72–73, 224–26,
  230, 231, 234, 239, 240, 258–60,
  287–91, 295
Washington, George, 8, 182, 247,
  248, 253, 260, 261–63, 268, 277,
  285, 288, 294
Weber, Donald, 191, 204, 205, 283
Webster, John, 56
Webster, Noah, Jr., 285, 295
Welch, Moses, 283
Weld, Thomas, 140
West, Benjamin, 228–29
West, Samuel, 243
Wetmore, Izrahiah, 9–10
Wheelwright, John, 128, 132, 133
Whig political rhetoric, 181, 182–84,
  186, 204–5, 212, 215–18, 219,
  223, 226, 239–40, 252, 291. *See
  also* Extratheatrical imagination; Mi-
  crocosm and macrocosm; Tory polit-
  ical rhetoric
Whitefield, George, 180, 186–91,
  192, 207–8, 209

Whitman, Walt, 4–5, 6, 7, 49, 94,
    172–73, 250
Wigglesworth, Michael, 107, 109–11,
    160, 192
Wilkes, John, 210
Williams, David, 123
Williams, Raymond, 3
Williams, Roger, 130
Wilshire, Bruce, xiv, xv
Wilson, John, 128, 132, 136, 137, 143
Winslow, Ola, 187–88
Winter, Cornelius, 187
Winthrop, John, 11, 102, 104, 105,
    107, 111, 114, 127–44, 145–46,
    164. See also City on a hill

Winthrop, John (1681–1747), 161
Witches, 144–45, 163. See also Salem
    witchcraft trials; Thaumaturgy
Wonder-working. See Thaumaturgy
Woodward, James, 161
World stage. See Theatrum mundi
World turned upside down, 21, 82, 83,
    161, 173, 198, 213, 263, 280, 294,
    295. See also Plautus
Worseley, Edward, 96
Wright, Patience Lovell, 128–29, 257,
    289
Wyclif, John, 62

Yorktown, 8, 261, 263, 280

Jeffrey H. Richards teaches English at North Carolina State University. He is presently researching American novels from the period 1789–1800, is interested generally in the interrelation between American literature and culture, and plans a companion volume to *Theater Enough* that will examine theater metaphor and American culture from 1790–1865. He is a member of the Modern Language Association and the South Atlantic Modern Language Association.

Library of Congress Cataloging-in-Publication Data

Richards, Jeffrey H.
Theater enough : American culture and the metaphor of the world
      stage, 1607–1789 / by Jeffrey H. Richards.
                        p.   cm.
                  Includes index.
            ISBN 0-8223-1107-0
1. American literature—Colonial period, ca. 1600–1775—History
and criticism.   2. American literature—Revolutionary period,
1775–1783—History and criticism.   3. English literature—Early
   modern, 1500–1700—History and criticism.   4. English
   literature—18th century—History and criticism.   5. National
   characteristics, American, in literature.   6. United States—
Civilization—To 1783.   7. Colonies in literature.   8. America in
   literature.   9. Theater in literature.   10. Metaphor.   I. Title.
            PS186.R53   1991   810.9'001—dc20
                  90-47943   CIP